# Behavior Therapy
# for Depression
PRESENT STATUS AND FUTURE DIRECTIONS

# Behavior Therapy for Depression

## PRESENT STATUS AND FUTURE DIRECTIONS

Edited by

**LYNN P. REHM**

DEPARTMENT OF PSYCHOLOGY
UNIVERSITY OF HOUSTON
HOUSTON, TEXAS

*With a Foreword by Irene Elkin Waskow*

**ACADEMIC PRESS   1981**

*A Subsidiary of Harcourt Brace Jovanovich, Publishers*

New York   London   Toronto   Sydney   San Francisco

ACADEMIC PRESS, INC.
111 Fifth Avenue, New York, New York 10003

*United Kingdom Edition published by*
ACADEMIC PRESS, INC. (LONDON) LTD.
24/28 Oval Road, London NW1   7DX

**Library of Congress Cataloging in Publication Data**
Main entry under title:

Behavior therapy for depression.

   Includes bibliographies and index.
   1.  Depression, Mental—Addresses, essays, lectures.
2.  Behavior therapy—Addresses, essays, lectures.
I.  Rehm, Lynn P.  [DNLM: 1.  Depression—Therapy.
2.  Depression—Diagnosis. 3.  Behavior therapy.
WM 171 B419]
RC537.B44     616.85'2706      80–1104
ISBN 0–12–585880–9

PRINTED IN THE UNITED STATES OF AMERICA

81 82 83 84     9 8 7 6 5 4 3 2 1

TO SUE, ELIZABETH, AND SARAH

# Contents

# 3

## Issues Resulting from Treatment Studies 73
W. EDWARD CRAIGHEAD

# 4

## Toward a Second-Generation Model: A Problem-Specific Approach 97
ANTHONY BIGLAN AND MICHAEL G. DOW

# 5

## A Learned Helplessness Point of View 123
MARTIN E. P. SELIGMAN

# 6

## The Role of Self-Regulation 143
FREDERICK H. KANFER AND SUE HAGERMAN

# 7

## A Functional Analysis of Behavior Therapy    181
CHARLES B. FERSTER

# 8

## Matching Treatment to Patient Characteristics in an Outpatient Setting    197
PETER D. McLEAN

# 9

## Matching Treatment to Patient Characteristics in an Inpatient Setting    209
BRIAN F. SHAW

# 10

## A Model for Individualizing Treatment    231
ROBERT PAUL LIBERMAN

# 11

## Assessment: A Clinical and Cognitive Emphasis     255

CONSTANCE L. HAMMEN

# 12

## The Assessment of Overt Behavior     279

NEIL S. JACOBSON

# 13

## The Assessment of Deficits and Outcomes     301

MICHEL HERSEN

# 14

## Outcome Evaluation Strategies     317

ALAN E. KAZDIN

# 15

## Ritual and Reality: Some Clinical Implications of Experimental Designs 337

MARJORIE H. KLEIN AND ALAN S. GURMAN

# 16

## Future Directions 365

LYNN P. REHM

# List of Contributors

Numbers in parentheses indicate the pages on which the authors' contributions begin.

ANTHONY BIGLAN (97), *Oregon Research Institute, Eugene, Oregon 97403*

PAUL H. BLANEY (1), *Department of Psychology, University of Miami, Coral Gables, Florida 33124*

W. EDWARD CRAIGHEAD (73), *Department of Psychology, The Pennsylvania State University, University Park, Pennsylvania 16802*

MICHAEL G. DOW (97), *Department of Psychology, The Pennsylvania State University, University Park, Pennsylvania 16802*

CHARLES B. FERSTER (181), *Department of Psychology, The American University, Washington, D.C. 20016*

ALAN S. GURMAN (337), *Department of Psychiatry, University of Wisconsin— Madison, Madison, Wisconsin 53706*

SUE HAGERMAN (143), *Department of Psychology, University of Illinois, Champaign, Illinois 61802*

CONSTANCE L. HAMMEN (255), *Department of Psychology, University of California, Los Angeles, Los Angeles, California 90024*

MICHEL HERSEN (301), *Department of Psychiatry, Western Psychiatric Institute and Clinics, University of Pittsburgh School of Medicine, Pittsburgh, Pennsylvania 15261*

STEVEN D. HOLLON (33), *Department of Psychology, University of Minnesota, Minneapolis, Minnesota 55455*

NEIL S. JACOBSON (279), *Department of Psychology, University of Washington, Seattle, Washington 98105*

FREDERICK H. KANFER (143), *Department of Psychology, University of Illinois, Champaign, Illinois 61802*

ALAN E. KAZDIN (317), *Department of Psychiatry, Western Psychiatric Institute and Clinics, University of Pittsburgh School of Medicine, Pittsburgh, Pennsylvania 15261*

MARJORIE H. KLEIN (337), *Department of Psychiatry, University of Wisconsin—Madison, Madison, Wisconsin 53706*

ROBERT PAUL LIBERMAN (231), *Department of Psychiatry, UCLA School of Medicine, Camarillo State Hospital, Camarillo, California 93010*

PETER D. McLEAN (197), *Department of Psychiatry, University of British Columbia, Vancouver, British Columbia V6T 2A1, Canada*

LYNN P. REHM (365), *Department of Psychology, University of Houston, Houston, Texas 77004*

MARTIN E. P. SELIGMAN (123), *Department of Psychology, University of Pennsylvania, Philadelphia, Pennsylvania 19104*

BRIAN F. SHAW (209), *Department of Psychiatry, The University of Western Ontario, London, Ontario N6A 5A5, Canada*

# Foreword

The last 20 years have seen a great increase in the quality and quantity of research on depression. This research has dealt with the etiology, diagnosis, and treatment of depression. Most of it, including the treatment research, has been biologically oriented. The Clinical Research Branch of the National Institute of Mental Health has, during the last 10 years, focused a good bit of its energy on depression research, both as a reflection of and a further stimulation to work being done by independent researchers. A major reason for this focus is the significance of depression for public health. Although the true prevalence of depression is not known with precision, the President's Commission on Mental Health estimates that about one out of five Americans will have an affective disorder in his or her lifetime. The need for research on the depressive disorders and for the development and evaluation of promising treatment approaches is obvious. Most of the earlier efforts of the Clinical Research Branch in this area had been focused on the etiology, classification, and understanding of the psychobiology of depression. More recently, attention has turned to the stimulation of treatment research.

During the past 5 to 10 years, promising new approaches have been developed for the psychological treatment of depression. Studies have reported the effectiveness of some of these approaches with clinical and nonclinical depressed populations. Some of the most exciting work in this area has been done within a behavioral and a cognitive–behavioral framework. A variety of behaviorally oriented techniques and approaches has been described, including reinforcement of pleasant activities, self-control therapy techniques, social skills training, cognitive–behavioral approaches, and behavior treatment packages. A number of studies suggest the efficacy of these approaches (especially as compared to less structured therapy and other control conditions and, less frequently, to drugs) in reducing depressive symptoms and improving social functioning.

Although there is, then, a considerable amount of literature on the behavioral treatment of depression, it has been difficult to summarize the work in this area. The variety of patient and nonpatient populations used in these studies, the different means of assessing change, and other nonstandard aspects of the different studies make it difficult to draw conclusions from the literature. In addition, many of the approaches overlap both in theory and in the particular techniques being used, but it is often not clear what the commonalities and differences are, and what approaches or components of approaches may be helpful for particular types of depressed patients. There was clearly, then, a need for a review and integration of the work in this area.

It was in this context that the Psychotherapy and Behavioral Intervention Section of the Clinical Research Branch initiated the contract that culminated in the papers and the conference from which this volume is derived. The purpose of the project was not only to assess the "state of the art" but also to develop recommendations for research that would move the field forward. The recommendations were to encompass a general framework for future research, as well as suggestions for specific research initiatives that might lead to the identification of effective behavioral techniques (or combinations of techniques) with specific groups of depressed patients.

This project, under Dr. Rehm's competent direction, has more than accomplished the goals outlined. The contributors reviewed the current state of the field, pinpointed many important problems in the research to date, suggested ways to correct the current deficits, and outlined important directions for future research on the behavioral treatment of depression. In addition, they presented important theoretical formulations and analyses of research issues that have implications for treatment research more generally and also for research on the etiology, prevention, and understanding of depressive disorders. The results of this project should thus be of value not only to NIMH and to researchers in the behavioral treatment of depression but also to other researchers interested in depression and to psychotherapy researchers in general.

Of special interest to me in the discussion at the conference was the gradually increasing emphasis on the importance of interdisciplinary "cross-fertilization" in the area of depression. The behaviorally oriented researchers involved in this project were well aware of the contributions that can be made to their own work by researchers involved in more "traditional" psychiatric research on depression, by those working within a biological perspective, and from related research in sociology and epidemiology. In turn, it is very clear to me how much other researchers in the area of depression may gain from the systematic behaviorally oriented approach that is represented in this book.

**Irene Elkin Waskow**
CLINICAL RESEARCH BRANCH
NATIONAL INSTITUTE OF MENTAL HEALTH

# Preface

In a 1928 article in the *Journal of Nervous and Mental Diseases,* A. G. Ivanov-Smolensky, a physician working in Pavlov's laboratories, reported his observations of the behavior of a dog who was unable to make a complex discrimination in a classical conditioning experiment. The dog's behavior deteriorated on the conditioned response, on other conditioned responses, and on certain unconditioned responses. Ivanov-Smolensky speculated on the parallel between this animal's behavior and the symptoms and etiology of depression in humans. He offered a Pavlovian model of depression stated in terms of a disequilibrium between cortical and subcortical inhibition. This early interest in developing a conditioning model of depression was a promising start but one that did not have a significant influence on other researchers. There was almost a 40-year hiatus before behavioral models were again applied to depression.

In its early development, modern behavior therapy paid little attention to the phenomena of depression. The focus in the behavior therapy research of the 1950s and early 1960s was on anxiety and on the social behavior of institutionalized individuals. Only occasional references were made to depression, and these were often instances where a diagnosis of depression was interpreted in terms of anxiety or skill deficits. Two or three case studies describing desensitization in cases of mixed anxiety and depression were published during the early to mid-1960s.

The first systematic approach to depression from a behavioral perspective began in the late 1960s with the work of Peter Lewinsohn and his colleagues. Beginning in 1968, they published a series of case studies describing innovative procedures with depressed clients. It was not until 1973, however, that the first behavioral group design studies were published. In that year, Robinson and Lewinsohn reported an analog study comparing contingencies for controlling depressed talk within interviews. Shipley and Fazio reported two studies with college students involving the teaching of problem-solving skills, and McLean, Ogston, and Grauer reported on a complex behavioral program with depressed individuals and their spouses.

Since the mid-1970s, interest in behavioral approaches to depression has increased geometrically. A steady flow of case studies has described new treatment programs and techniques for depression. Group design studies have validated treatment programs and compared programs to one another, and a proliferation of behavioral models has helped to coordinate and direct research. Basic psychopathology research with a behavioral perspective has contributed new ideas to the therapy literature. In recent years, the trend toward integrating cognitive models into behavioral theories has strongly influenced the field of therapy for depression.

The result of this rapid growth of activity is a burgeoning literature of therapy techniques and packages, rationales and models that have developed in relative isolation from one another and from other research on depression. The time was ripe to step back and view the field in perspective. The impetus for just such a project came from the Clinical Research Branch of the National Institute of Mental Health. NIMH was interested in sponsoring a conference to make recommendations with regard to future funding of research on behavior therapy for depression. This conference was held in April 1979 at Western Psychiatric Institute and Clinics at the University of Pittsburgh, under the auspices of the Department of Psychiatry.

The chapters in this book are the outgrowth of papers originally presented at the conference. Contributors were chosen to represent a variety of perspectives on the topic of behavior therapy for depression. Major contributors to the literature on behavior therapy for depression, professionals associated with other aspects of depression research, and experts in behavior therapy and psychotherapy were invited to participate. The hope was to bring a broad range of expertise to the topic. The first three chapters by Blaney, Hollon, and Craighead survey different aspects of the field as it exists today. The next four chapters by Biglan and Dow, Seligman, Kanfer and Hagerman, and Ferster present theoretical analyses of depressive behavior in light of current knowledge. The three chapters that follow by McLean, Shaw, and Liberman discuss the problems of tailoring treatment to the individual client. The chapters by Hammen, Jacobson, and Hersen discuss various aspects of the assessment of depression where numerous problems have hampered behavior therapy research, and the chapters by Kazdin and by Klein and Gurman address design problems in depression therapy research. My final chapter attempts to pull together a variety of recommendations, explicit or implied, set forth in the preceding chapters.

The intent of this book is to offer to the field an analysis and some recommendations that will be helpful not only to researchers in the specific field of behavior therapy for depression but also to those interested in depression and behavior therapy research in general and to the knowledgeable clinician attempting to assess the variety of promising new therapies that have recently been described.

I would like to acknowledge the support of NIMH in the form of contract No. 278–78–0062 (ER) that funded the conference. It should be noted that the contents of this publication do not necessarily reflect the views or policies of the Department of Health, Education, and Welfare nor does anything in this publication imply endorsement by the U.S. government. Particular thanks are due to Irene Elkin Waskow for her support and advice from the perspective of NIMH. I would also like to acknowledge the support of the Department of Psychiatry of the University of Pittsburgh for their help in hosting the conference. Particular thanks are due to Drs. Thomas Detre and David Kupfer for their support, to Marcia Watson and Diane Vaksman for their hard work in making the conference run smoothly, and to Carol Kaufman for handling the financial aspects of the contract.

# Behavior Therapy
# for Depression
## PRESENT STATUS AND FUTURE DIRECTIONS

# 1

# The Effectiveness of Cognitive and Behavioral Therapies

The purpose of this chapter is rather simple: to present a comprehensive review of the empirical studies regarding the efficacy of cognitive and behavioral treatments of depression. The cognitive studies are reviewed first, then the behavioral ones. Studies are generally grouped on the basis of the intervention used rather than on the theoretical orientation that served as the researcher's inspiration; the one can often, but not always, be predicted from the other. In cases in which a single study reports data on several interventions, each relevant to a different section of the present chapter, the study is mentioned in each section.

Only controlled studies are reviewed. Unless otherwise noted, the description of unpublished dissertation studies is based on a reading of the dissertation itself, not of an abstract. It is presumed that the reader has some familiarity with the relevant clinical literature. Case studies that provided the inspiration for the controlled studies are not reviewed, nor are laboratory induction studies, even those whose goal was the reduction of dysphoric affect.

## Cognitive Therapy

For purposes of review, studies of cognitive therapy are divided into three groups. First are those involving essentially didactic or exposure sessions, with relatively little interaction between therapist and client. Next are individual treatment studies, then group treatment. In the didactic and exposure studies, it probably makes little difference if the context is individual or group. In the studies presented in the latter two sections, however, there is considerably more

1

BEHAVIOR THERAPY FOR DEPRESSION

Copyright © 1981 by Academic Press, Inc.
All rights of reproduction in any form reserved.
ISBN 0-12-585880-9

therapist–client interaction and the nature of the context is probably of consequence.

## Didactic and Exposure Interventions

Included here are studies in which the subject was evidently exposed rather passively to some kind of experience designed to reform his cognitions. The few studies of this sort are all unpublished dissertations.

Cooke (1974) reported a study in which the rationale (the inspiration for the study and the explanation given to the experimental subjects) was that one could use coverant conditioning techniques to counter the cognitive underpinning of depression. Specifically, he posited that, by encouraging coverants incompatible with the components of Beck's depressive triad, one could alleviate depression. Subjects were 23 undergraduates, obtained through counseling center contacts and through the media. Both experimental and control subjects were seen for four 1-hour sessions over 3 or 4 weeks. All subjects were taught to identify, monitor, and log their own depressive thoughts and were instructed to do this on a daily basis during treatment; this, they were told, would in itself help them deal with depression. Experimental subjects were, in addition, helped to develop a list of their own accomplishments, to serve as positive coverants, and were told to dwell on one of them before engaging in a high-probability behavior (pursuant to the Premack Principle). Dependent variables were the frequency of depressive thoughts (obtained from logs) and several measures of depressive affect and symptoms. Subjects in the experimental group did report a somewhat greater reduction in depressive thoughts, but there were no post-treatment differences in noncognitive indicants of depression.

Gioe (1975) reported a study designed to compare (a) a cognitive modification experience with (b) a positive group experience and with (c) a combination of the two; a no-treatment control was also considered. Subjects were 40 undergraduates with Beck Depression Inventory (BDI) scores of 9 or above and no report of recent death of a loved one or of recent illness; BDI means were in the 12–15 range. Cognitive modification subjects met in small groups five times for 30 minutes each. Each session involved relaxation training, presentation of positive statements (regarding the self, the world, and the future), each set of which was followed by the presentation of a pleasant scene. The positive group experience appears to have been a sensitivity group in which the focus was upon what is good in people. Subjects assigned to receive both experiences did so in the order: cognitive modification, then group experience. Dependent variables included the BDI, the Tennessee Self Concept Scale (TSCS), and ratings of verbal behavior in structured and unstructured contexts. On the BDI, the only significant difference was between the group receiving both experiences and the no-treatment control; that is, it could not be stated that the cognitive modification was better than no treatment or that it was of less value than both experiences. Other variables gave scattered evidence of the superiority of both experiences over either component alone, particularly over the positive group experience.

Nystedt (1976) reported a study in which the focus was on the usefulness of self-monitoring compared with additional self-administration of positive self-statements. Subjects were 43 undergraduate psychology students who were in the upper quartile of the local BDI distribution (their $M = 16.2$) and in the lower quartile of the TSCS distribution. One group was merely instructed to monitor and log their positive and negative self-statements during a 30-day period. A second group was instructed to monitor and log their self-statements regarding studying during this period. A third group was similar to the first but, following a 6-day monitoring-only baseline period, was asked to generate a list of 10 positive self-statements and to read one of them every time they entered or left a building during the subsequent 24 days. Dependent variables included the BDI, the TSCS, anagrams performance, and frequency counts taken from the logs. The log reports indicated that the third group did, as expected, increase positive self-statements during treatment, but no associated differential effect was shown on the BDI or on the anagrams. On the TSCS, this group was better off that the two controls at posttest, but this difference was negligible at subsequent follow-up.

Kirkpatrick (1977) compared four conditions: a cognitive–behavior modification condition, relaxation training, attention placebo, and no treatment. Subjects were 44 undergraduates identified on the basis of elevated Costello–Comrey Depression Scale (CCDS) scores obtained from mass class testing. Dependent variables included the CCDS, the BDI (pretreatment means were in the 11–15 range), a number of more indirect measures of depression, and measures of anxiety and irrational beliefs. Each of the three treatment conditions involved four small group meetings lasting 50–70 minutes over a 2-week period. All conditions received a rationale, homework assignments, practice or exercise related to the treatment, and discussion of the homework since the previous session. The cognitive modification condition was directed toward teaching the subjects to recognize their negative self-statements and replace them with positive alternatives. The attention placebo condition focused subjects' attention on past experiences that might be related to their current depressed state; no specific coping skill was suggested. The results indicated a general amelioration in all groups, but not differentially as a function of treatment. If anything, the cognitive modification group showed the least effectiveness of the treatments; Kirkpatrick suggested that such an inferiority of this method might be reflective of the fact that only in this group were subjects confronted with accepting responsibility for their feelings of dysphoria.

Weinberg (1977) compared four conditions: (a) a cognitive group therapy, in which the strategy was to ferret out irrational beliefs (such as the need to be loved) presumed to underlie symptoms, challenge them, and encourage the practice of rational self-statements; (b) a behavioral treatment involving encouragement to increase positive activities, problem solving, and social skills training; (c) sensitivity training, with a focus on emotional awareness; and (d) a waiting-list control group of subjects who, like treatment subjects, monitored their mood and activity level on a daily basis. There was a total of 39 subjects; treatment occurred in groups of about five (two groups per condition). Subjects were introductory psychology students who were not necessarily seeking treatment but who received prescreening and pretreatment scores on the BDI short form of 8 or above, with means around 13. Treatment groups met for 1 hour weekly over 4 weeks; in addition, there were structured homework assignments. A large number of assessment instruments were used pre- and posttreatment, with the crucial instruments given at 60-day follow-up as well. Results are complex and difficult to summarize, but their essence is perhaps captured by the following observations: There was no differential BDI improvement among groups and no evidence that the treatments had any specific impact upon variables related to their respective rationales (e.g., cognitive group therapy made no more difference on a measure of rational beliefs than did other treatments).

A summary of these five studies would have to indicate that, though it may be possible to get subjects to entertain more positive thoughts, there is no indication that this will have any enduring effect upon a depressive condition. On the other hand, there is little reason to believe that the interventions were effective in restructuring the subjects' belief systems; in fact, there was evidence in the Kirkpatrick and Weinberg studies that they were not. Accordingly, the failures of these studies need not be taken as particularly devastating to the cognitive therapy position.

## Individual Cognitive Therapy

In the studies that follow, subjects were more depressed and the treatment appears to have been more intensive than those discussed in the preceding section.

Schmickley (1976) reported a study that, though there was no control group as such, deserves inclusion in this review. Specifically, daily BDI data were obtained for periods before, during, and after treatment, and the slopes for the various periods were compared on a within-subject basis. Subjects were 11 women, new clients at a community mental health center, carefully screened for neurotic depression. All had pretreatment BDI scores of at least 17. The focus in treatment, which lasted for four sessions, was on helping subjects to identify their automatic, maladaptive depressive cognitions and to develop self-statements that challenged those cognitions. In addition, subjects developed a list of positive statements; as a homework assignment, they were told to read these statements before engaging in a high-probability behavior. Dependent variables included the Minnesota Multiphasic Personality Inventory (MMPI) and ratings provided by a relative or friend, in addition to the BDI. All significance tests were within subject, and the typical finding for the many that were done was that about a third of the subjects showed significant improvement as a function of treatment; some backsliding subsequently was also shown, though not to pretreatment levels. Though these findings are generally supportive of the effectiveness of this therapy, Schmickley failed to provide adequate discussion of how many individual subjects must show significant improvement for a general conclusion of effectiveness to be warranted. In addition, it should be noted that five of the subjects were concurrently taking antidepressant medications, though Schmickley observed that these subjects "did not contribute more than their share of changes in performance in the hypothesized direction [p. 136]."

Muñoz (1977) reported a study in which subjects were provided with 12 1-hour sessions of therapy. (It would appear that this study also comprises a portion of a larger study reported by Zeiss, Lewinsohn, and Muñoz [1979], in which the cognitive therapy described by Muñoz was compared with social skills training and an increase-pleasant-activities treatment, both of which will be discussed in greater detail later in this chapter. Though I cannot be sure that the studies described by Muñoz and by Zeiss *et al.* are one and the same, I will proceed on the assumption that they are.) Subjects were recruited through the media and met the following requirements: MMPI-D > 80 or D between 70 and 80 and D (depression) the highest scale; ratings based on the Grinker interview for factor 1 > 1.0 and the mean of the remaining factors > .70; depression the major presenting problem. Subjects ($N$ = approximately 10 –15 per condition) were assigned to immediate and delayed treatment conditions, such that, at the point at which the immediate group completed treatment, the delayed subjects were effectively a waiting-list control. The group means on the MMPI-D scale were in the 85–89 range. Therapy involved the following techniques: self-monitoring and logging positive and negative thoughts; increasing positive thoughts by self-instructions; rewarding oneself for accomplishments; thought stopping; obsessive time; and labeling thoughts as unnecessary, maladaptive, etc. Dependent variables included instruments specially developed for this study to assess negative outlook and negative self-statements. Briefly, all variables showed improvement during the period in which the immediate treatment group was treated, but none to a greater degree for the treated than for the yet untreated subjects. Zeiss *et al.* (1979) indicated that the combined treatment groups (cognitive, skills, and pleasant events) improved more than waiting-list controls, with no treatment superior to another.

Taylor and Marshall (1977) reported a study in which subjects were assigned to one of three treatment conditions—cognitive, behavioral, or cognitive–behavioral—or to a waiting-list condition. Forty-five subjects were recruited by media advertisement and were selected according to the following criteria: self-reported depression of at least 2 weeks duration, BDI score of at least 13 (actual group mean of 21.2), Dempsey D-30 score of at least 70, and not currently in treatment elsewhere. Subjects in each treatment condition had six 40-minute sessions; in each treatment, focus was on the context in which depression was most severe or most frequent and upon the cognitive and/or behavioral events surrounding that context. Subjects in the cognitive treatment condition were told that depressed mood was rooted in self-evaluations and were assisted in becoming aware of the thoughts that they had between an occurrence or action and depressed affect and in developing alternative self-statements. Subjects were encouraged to think of the use of alternative self-statements as a coping technique. Subjects were also required to construct a list of positive self-statements to read prior to engaging in high-probability behaviors. Subjects in the behavioral condition were told that depression results from insufficient positive reinforcement. The therapist aided the subjects in identifying the situations that elicited depression and in constructing alternative behavioral patterns in those situations. Modeling and role playing in therapy and rehearsal at home were used to instill these new behaviors; it was noted that often the focus was on the development of more assertive behaviors. In addition, treatment focused on helping subjects restructure their lives to increase the frequency of pleasant activities. Subjects receiving the combined cognitive–behavioral treatment were exposed to components of each, though of necessity not as much time could be spent on either of the two in this group. Results on measures of depression and of self-esteem indicated that the combined treatment was more effective than the average of the two component treatments, with no difference between the latter two. Although appropriate statistical comparisons are not reported, it appears that both the behavioral and the cognitive modules taken alone were considerably superior to the waiting-list condition.

Rush, Beck, Kovacs, and Hollon (1977) reported a study that compared cognitive therapy and antidepressant medication (imipramine). The cognitive therapy was largely as detailed more recently by Beck, Rush, Shaw, and Emery (1979). Subjects ($N = 41$) were applicants for treatment at an outpatient clinic who had scores of at least 17 on the BDI ($M = 30.1$) and 14 on the Hamilton Rating Scale for Depression (HRS-D) and who had a clear and unmixed depressive diagnosis; in addition, subjects who had a prior history of poor response to a tricyclic antidepressant were excluded. Cognitive therapy patients averaged about 15 50-minute sessions over a period of about 11 weeks. Treatment with the antidepressant lasted about as long but involved weekly supportive therapy visits of about 20 minutes. The results are easily summarized: Both groups showed improvement, but the cognitive therapy group showed considerably more. Moreover, a greater proportion of the antidepressant group discontinued their involvement in therapy prior to completion. Finally, the superiority of the cognitive therapy appears to have persisted well after treatment ceased; at 3-month follow-up, subjects continued to differ significantly, and a trend was still evident at 6 months.

Becker and Schuckit (1978) and Rush, Hollon, Beck, and Kovacs (1978) have exchanged comments regarding this study, the details of which will not be recounted here; in short, Becker and Schuckit have urged caution in the interpretation of the Rush et al. (1977) findings, and Rush et al. (1978), while agreeing that caution is needed, have taken issue with specific concerns raised by Becker and Schuckit. Of special interest are the results of a new analysis presented by Rush et al. (1978) indicating that the superiority of the cognitive treatment was manifest when acute and chronic subgroups of depressed patients were considered separately.

These studies are not easily summarized. On the one hand is a study (Muñoz, 1977) in which cognitive therapy failed to exceed even a waiting-list control, on the other is a study (Rush et al., 1977) in which such therapy was shown to be more effective than a standard, proven treatment. While there are many differences that may account for the discrepancy, the findings of the Taylor and Marshall (1977) study may offer an important clue. In that study, it appeared that a cognitive therapy was not as effective alone as with a behavioral component added. In fact, Beck et al.'s (1979) approach (used by Rush et al. [1977]) does have a substantial behavioral component, something apparently lacking in the treatment used by Muñoz (1977); this possibly accounts for the relative strength of the former.

## Cognitive Group Therapy

Morris (1975) compared a cognitively oriented group program with insight-oriented group therapy and a waiting-list control. Subjects were 51 depressed women, aged 18–67 (M = 35), whose BDI means were in the 21–28 range. They were recruited through mental health clinic files and referrals and through physician referrals; many received individual therapy and/or psychotropic medication concurrently. The groups were rather large, apparently in the 12–17 person range. The cognitive treatment included orientation to the cognitive model of affect and focus on the subjects' negative self-statements, irrational beliefs, and selective perception. Also included was a somewhat noncognitive component: helping subjects identify their own depressive behaviors that have a negative impact on others and exploring more positive alternatives (via rehearsal, etc.). Both the cognitive and insight groups met for six 90-minute sessions over 3 weeks. Results both at posttreatment and at 6-week follow-up indicated that the cognitive group was more effective at reducing depression than either the insight group or the waiting-list control.

LaPointe (1976) compared cognitive therapy with assertion training and insight therapy. Subjects were 33 women, aged 21–63, recruited through newspaper advertisements. Their BDI scores ranged from 15 to 31, with means in the mid- and low twenties. All treatment was provided in groups of five or six subjects, with two groups in each condition. Each group met 2 hours a week for 6 weeks. The focus in the cognitive group was on Beck's depressogenic errors. Results, obtained on measures of depression, assertiveness, and irrational beliefs at completion of treatment and 2 months thereafter, indicated improvement in all groups, with very little in the way of differential effects.

Shaw (1977) compared four conditions: cognitive therapy, behavioral therapy, nondirective therapy, and a waiting-list control. Subjects were 32 young adults referred from a student health service or self-referred who reported depression of at least 3 weeks duration. A number of screening criteria were used to ensure that subjects were substantially depressed and that this condition was relatively uncomplicated by other psychiatric problems. The BDI cutoff, for instance, was 18, with pretreatment means in the 25–30 range. Group therapy sessions met over a 4-week period, one 2-hour session per week. The descriptions of the groups as provided by Shaw give little information not obvious from the names of the conditions. The cognitive group recorded cognitions, identified distortions, and discussed the validity of beliefs that are related to depression. The behavioral group followed a protocol adapted from suggestions published by Lewinsohn and associates, including activity schedules, verbal contracts, and behavioral rehearsal. The nondirective group involved reflection of feelings and was specifically intended as a control for the effects of attention and assessment. Posttreatment evaluation on the BDI indicated that the cognitive group improved more than each other group and that the behavioral and nondirective groups were superior to the waiting-list group but not different from each other. One-month follow-up of the cognitive and behavioral group subjects showed that the difference between them was no longer significant.

Rush and Watkins (1979) have reported a study in which subjects were assigned to 20 sessions of cognitive group therapy ($N = 28$), individual cognitive therapy ($N = 9$), or individual cognitive therapy plus antidepressant medication ($N = 7$). Subjects were selected much as in the Rush et al. (1977) study, though with the BDI minimum raised to 20 (mean about 30). Though all therapy was carried out as prescribed by Beck and associates, the authors noted that the group context facilitated some unique components: the use of group members as role models for one another and the development of norms for compliance with treatment assignments (e.g., homework). Whereas in the Rush et al. study the medication was uniform and determined by research protocol, in this case the selection and dose of medication was left to the judgment of the treating physician. Group sessions lasted 75–90 minutes, while individual sessions lasted 50 minutes. BDI results indicated no significant difference between the two individual therapy conditions (though trends in the data suggest an added advantage of medication); both individual conditions were superior to the group treatment condition.

McDonald (1978) reported a study in which a cognitive–behavioral treatment was used as an adjunct to an existing day hospital program. Most of the subjects were concurrently on psychoactive medications, and many had had previous psychiatric hospitalizations. Since criteria for inclusion consisted of MMPI and BDI specifications only (MMPI-D at least 70, BDI at least 16), it seems likely that some of the subjects were schizophrenic or had other conditions. The 15 experimental and 13 control subjects had a BDI mean in the mid-20s. The controls had their usual day hospital treatment regime. The experimental treatment, which was integrated into the schedules of the experimental subjects, was guided by Beck's prescriptions, including the use of activity schedules and the identification of cognitive distortion patterns; other treatment components, such as group process and feedback, were also used. Groups met three times a week for 4 weeks. Results indicated that both groups improved on the dependent variables, the experimental subjects not significantly more so than the controls.

Besyner (1978) compared cognitive group therapy with a behavioral group condition, a nonspecific (quasi-Rogerian) group condition, and a waiting-list control. Subjects were persons recruited via a newspaper advertisement who were not presently in treatment elsewhere, had no history of psychosis or suicide attempts, and had BDI scores of 13 or above (mean BDI about 25). Of the 40 subjects who completed the study, 71% were female; the age range was 18–60. Therapy sessions lasted 2 hours—one session per week for 4 weeks. The cognitive group followed the writings of Beck and Meichenbaum and included didactic presentation of the cognitive model; a focus on self-statements, modeling, rehearsal, and coaching of verbalized cognitions; and related homework assignments. Dependent variables, which included the BDI, a self-statement inventory, and the Pleasant Events Schedule, were obtained posttreatment and 4 weeks thereafter (treatment groups only). The pattern of results on the BDI is as follows: At posttest the only significant difference was that the three treatment groups were better off than the waiting-list control, and at follow-up the cognitive and behavioral groups were better off than the nonspecific group, with the behavioral group superior to the cognitive. Though not as clear cut, results on other measures were similar. The import of this lies in the fact that the data suggest that the behavioral treatment may have been more effective in inducing both behavioral and cognitive change than was the cognitive treatment, in which case one could argue that the cognitive therapy had simply been inadequately implemented.

Finally, Head (1978) reported a study in which 13 subjects participating in a cognitive therapy group were compared with 9 assessment controls. Subjects were undergraduate psychology students whose BDI scores were at least 16 (means about 19) and who were participating in return for credit toward a course requirement that they take part in an experiment; note that they had not sought treatment. Therapy sessions were 90 minutes long, once weekly for 11 weeks. Controls took all assessment devices given to therapy subjects, including pre- and post-BDIs and weekly Profiles of Mood States (POMS). In short, while there was a general and significant pattern of decline of depression over the treatment period, there was no evidence that the decline was any greater for the treated than for the untreated group.

The seven available studies provide no basis for a coherent conclusion. In Morris (1975), Shaw (1977), and perhaps Besyner (1978), cognitive group therapy was superior to other conditions; in three other studies (Head, 1978; LaPointe, 1976; McDonald, 1978), it failed to add any treatment effectiveness. While the Rush and Watkins (1979) study did suggest that group cognitive

self-report and staff-rated data at the end of treatment and at 6-month follow-up, were reported on a detailed subject-by-subject fashion. They are about as supportive as such a small-sample (5 per group) study could be in indicating the effectiveness of assertion training (at least in combination with relaxation training). For instance, whereas the MMPI-D scale median of the assertion group fell to 59 at posttreatment and 58 at follow-up, the relaxation group showed no consistent pattern of improvement at either posttreatment or follow-up, and the contact control showed some improvement at posttreatment (MMPI-D median of 63) but not at follow-up (median = 92). Data obtained on the subjects' need for treatment during the follow-up period are consistent with this: Whereas all five assertion subjects needed no subsequent treatment, among the remaining 10 subjects, this was true for only two (one in each group).

A study by LaPointe (1976) in which group assertion training was compared with cognitive and insight therapies was described earlier. In that study, the assertion condition focused on expressing feelings, refusing unreasonable requests, making requests, and handling situations in which assertiveness was not accepted. Treatment had both didactic and role-playing components. As noted earlier, the three treatments being compared were not shown to be different in effectiveness from one another.

Hayman (1977) studied 26 women, mainly undergraduates, obtained through class announcements and media advertisements; all had BDI scores of at least 13 (mean around 18) and low scores on the College Self-Expression Scale (CSES), a measure of assertiveness. A number of subjects were concurrently in treatment elsewhere. The assertion training, which consisted of eight 2-hour sessions over a 4-week period, included modeling, cognitive restructuring, behavioral rehearsal, coaching, goal setting, and individual logs. Controls were awaiting delayed treatment and were thus waiting-list controls at the completion of the experimental subjects' training. Subjects showed reduced BDI scores during the treatment period, but this appeared unrelated to the condition to which the subject was assigned. There was some evidence that the experimental subjects improved on the CSES, without a comparable reduction being shown by the controls. This might be taken as indicating that assertiveness can improve without improvement in level of depression. On the other hand, the correlation between BDI change scores and CSES change was − .42, suggesting that improvements in the two variables do tend to co-occur.

Sanchez (1978) assessed the effectiveness of assertion training in a group context, in comparison with traditional insight-oriented group therapy. Subjects were 21 females and 11 males who had sought treatment at an outpatient psychiatric clinic. They were screened according to criteria similar to those used by Muñoz (1977), with an added requirement of an elevated score on an assertiveness inventory. The age range was 18–55, and BDI means were around 30. Groups consisted of eight subjects (two groups per condition). There were 10 90-minute sessions over a 5-week period. The assertion groups involved (a) didactic presentations; (b) discussion of relevant real-life encounters and reactions since the last session; (c) modeling; (d) rehearsal, involving coaching and feedback and reinforcement from other group members; and (e) homework (apparently including relaxation practice). Ten of the 16 control subjects received some kind of psychotropic medication, as prescribed independent of the study; none of the assertion subjects did. Results on measures of assertion and depression obtained at posttreatment indicated no difference between groups; however, at 1-month follow-up, the assertion groups were significantly better off on both kinds of measures than were the controls. Generally, what appears to have occurred is that subjects in both conditions improved during treatment; following treatment, improvement continued for the assertion subjects, while the control subjects showed some loss of ground. (To a limited extent, this pattern of results may have been due to the elimination of one assertion subject in the follow-up analysis—quite possibly the assertion subject who was worst off at posttreatment.) Strictly speaking, conclusions from this study (also from Hayman's [1977] study) must be limited by the fact that subjects were persons whose pretreatment test scores indicated not only depression but also a lack of assertiveness; however, this is not as major a limitation as it might at first appear to be, since, for instance, under the criteria that were used in the Sanchez study, 70% of the eligible depressed subjects were also eligible on the assertiveness criterion. Finally, Sanchez presented some additional data addressing the crucial question of whether or not changes in assertiveness really play a role in mood changes. Daily Depression Adjective Check List (DACL) and assertive behavior records were obtained such that it was possible to obtain within-subject simultaneous and lagged correlations. These data indicated that assertiveness on one day predicted mood level on the subsequent day appreciably better than mood level on one day predicted assertiveness on the next. This is, of course, consistent with the view that assertiveness is a worthy target variable in the treatment of depression.

Rehm, Fuchs, Roth, Kornblith, and Romano (1979) reported a study in which a group assertion program was compared with a "self-control" therapy module. This study is described in greater detail later in this chapter, but its findings regarding the assertion group can be summarized here. This treatment did have apparent effects upon behavioral assertiveness, but it was less clear whether depression was reduced as a result of the assertion training. One measure (the BDI) showed significant improvement pre- to posttherapy, another (MMPI-D) did not; in any case, the study lacked a no-treatment condition against which to compare such improvement.

Fagan (1979) compared assertion group therapy with traditional group therapy and with no treatment in a sample of young female Job Corps trainees, selected on the basis of their counselors' judgment that they were depressed. The mean BDI was about 21. Groups met for six sessions, each lasting 60–90 minutes. The two treatment groups showed very similar improvement on the BDI, and this improvement was not significantly greater than that for the no-treatment group. The nonsignificance must be viewed in the light of very great BDI heterogeneity and small sample sizes (only 19 completers across all three conditions).

As is the case for other section summaries in this chapter, one can hardly do more than express amazement at the diversity of outcomes. Taking for instance the seven assertion training studies, three (Lomont et al. 1969; Maish, 1972; Sanchez, 1978) are rather encouraging and four (Fagan, 1979; Hayman, 1977; LaPointe, 1976; Rehm et al., 1979) tend to be discouraging; moreover, the competing findings cannot be reconciled by considering the methodological strengths and weaknesses of the studies. It may, however, be of some consequence that, with the possible exception of the Rehm et al. research, those showing assertion training to be ineffective (or not remarkably effective) studied samples of subjects who were apparently less disturbed than those studied in the more encouraging studies.

One final comment about assertion training: Although it is, for important historical reasons, classed as a behavioral intervention, assertion training usually involves a strong cognitive component (addressing the subjects' beliefs about, for example, whether or not it is right for them to demand that others treat them decently). Such programs should thus be viewed as mixed cognitive–behavioral, albeit with a focus on a somewhat restricted sample of the various beliefs and behaviors that may be depression related.

## Pleasant Activities

Attempts to increase clients' frequency of involvement in rewarding activities are typically a part of almost any broad-based behavioral or cognitive approach. Studies reviewed in this section involved a condition in which such attempts appear to have constituted the dominant or sole focus of the treatment.

Padfield (1976) reported a study in which treatment based on Lewinsohn's clinical writings, apparently addressed primarily to the monitoring and increasing of pleasant activities, was compared with nondirective counseling. Subjects were 24 rural women of low socioeconomic status (SES), most having several children. Therapy took the form of 12 weekly individual sessions. Results were not clearly supportive of the superiority of either technique, though on one variable (Grinker interview rating of depression), the behavioral group showed greater improvement. However, a dependent variable indicating change in frequency of participant in pleasant events showed no difference between groups. Thus, even if one assumed that the behavioral group did show more improvement, it would be difficult to attribute that differential improvement to a difference in participation in pleasant activities.

Pace (1977, abstract only) reported a study in which 80 university students were randomly assigned to pleasant-activity monitoring or no-monitoring groups and to activity-related instructions or no-instruction groups. Further description of the sample or the treatments is not available, nor are detailed results presented. Pace did conclude, however, that "if increasing pleasant activity levels is of benefit in the treatment of depression, it is not so simply due to the effects of monitoring of instructions [p. 992]."

Hammen and Glass (1975) reported two studies in which undergraduates, preselected on the basis of high scores on a number of depression measures, were instructed to increase their pleasant-activities level for a 1-week period; subjects were told that it was a research study, not that it was a treatment of depression. Control conditions included a self-monitoring condition and an increase protein intake group. Although experimental subjects did show the requested increase, they showed no lessening of depression; in fact, they appeared to be more depressed at the end of the week than controls.

Barrera (1977, 1979) assessed the effectiveness of a group treatment focused on increasing the frequency of pleasant activities through self-monitoring, goal setting, planning of activities, and evaluating progress. Two control groups were included, a delayed-treatment group that only self-monitored mood and activity participation and enjoyment, and a waiting-list control. The 31 subjects were solicited through media advertisements and were screened as in the Muñoz (1977) study; pretreatment BDI means were in the mid-20s. Therapy consisted of four 2-hour sessions; written instructional materials were also provided. Though improvement was noted, at the end of the initial 4 weeks of therapy, the treated group had not improved significantly more than either control. However, the group that had self-monitored only was subsequently given the treatment, following which they showed more BDI improvement than the initially treated group (which self-monitored during this 4-week segment); there was even some evidence at 7-month follow-up that the 8-week package of self-monitoring followed by activities-increase training was superior. The superiority of this condition may have been due to any of a number of factors: Perhaps this group did not need to waste any treatment time learning to self-monitor; the therapists may have been more skilled, having just completed a similar group; or the 4 weeks may have sensitized subjects to the realtionship across time between activity participation and mood. An examination of the actual activity participation data, however, lent little support to the claim that the reason for the differential effect of this treatment sequence was related to a higher activity level in these subjects, though the author noted that it seemed that these subjects had been successfully induced to engage in activities that were more important and complex than otherwise prevailed in this population.

Craker (n.d.) studied seven subjects recruited by advertisement or by agency referral who showed both elevated levels of depression (e.g., BDI $M = 30.1$) and low levels of participation in pleasant events. Baseline data were obtained, and subjects served as their own controls. Though subjects did meet with the therapist over the 10-week treatment period, the treatment was primarily by a self-instructional manual given to the subjects. This manual instructed subjects, for instance, to select enjoyable activities and engage in them prior to engaging in a high-probability behavior. None of the subjects' logs indicated an increase of activities during the baseline period, but all five who used the procedures correctly showed clear increases with the onset of the treatment phase. However, while there were instances of abatement of depression, there was little evidence that these instances were tied temporally to induced increases in activity level.

Turner, Ward, and Turner (1979) compared an activities-increase treatment group with a group given a program of fitness exercises, a self-monitoring group that recorded daily activities and mood, and a client-centered group. Subjects were 56 university students and staff recruited through media advertisements whose DACL *T*-score was at least 70 (DACL raw score means about 20), who reported depression as their primary concern, and who were not in treatment elsewhere. Intervention consisted of five 50-minute interviews over a 30-day period. All subjects were led to expect that what they were doing would help lessen their depression. The results are supportive of the activities-increase treatment in two major respects: a greater increase in activity participation (especially in the last 2 weeks) and a greater reduction of depression as measured by the DACL.

One thing that may have distinguished Turner *et al.*'s (1979) study from those described previously is that an attempt was made to increase subjects' involvement in activities that would be pleasant for the particular individual, a feature that Lewinsohn (1975) has suggested may be crucial. The focus of treatment efforts on an optimal subset of pleasant events also characterizes the following studies.

Graf (1977) addressed the specific question of whether participation in specifically mood-related activities would alleviate depression. Subjects were 70 psychology students having BDI scores of 12 or more ($M = 15.6$); the study was structured not as a treatment but as a 2-week study on the relationship between mood and activities. One group was asked to increase their involvement in the items on a list of 47 activities found in prior research to be normatively mood related. A second group was asked to do likewise vis-à-vis a list of non-mood-related activities. A third group was asked to monitor, but not change, their rate of engaging in the activities on the mood-related list (the first two groups also monitored their participation in their listed activities). This instructional manipulation, in short, did not have the intended effects on activities, as reported in subjects' daily logs, nor did groups differ in daily mood ratings. However, the mood-related activities group did show more pre to post BDI improvement than did the other two groups pooled. Graf noted that, given that the activity variables were not successfully manipulated, it is not clear what this difference is to be attributed to. He raised the possibility of experimental demand, then dismissed it, saying that the non-mood-related activities subjects were under the same demand. One must take issue with this argument, however, on the basis of an examination of the list of activities these subjects were asked to increase; specifically, it is hard to believe that a subject, asked to do such things as go naked, sew, and dream at night (to list a few of the non-mood-related activities), would feel under any compulsion to show a resultant improvement, no matter what the experimenter said.

It was noted earlier that Zeiss *et al.* (1979) compared a cognitive treatment, a social skills treatment, and a pleasant-activities treatment; the last of the three will now be described. The subjects and design information are similar to that found in the description of the Muñoz (1977) report. A concerted attempt was made to identify specific activities that were mood related for each subject in the present treatment. Specifically, in the early days of the treatment, subjects monitored both their participation in a large number of pleasant activities and their mood on a daily basis. Therapists then reviewed the records with the patient, to target specific activities that appeared to covary across time with mood; special emphasis was placed on the increase of participation in these activities as well as in activities in general. Subjects were also trained in muscle relaxation and were given reading material on organizing one's time. There is no report of the effectiveness of this treatment taken alone, just that all three treatments were more effective than no treatment, none of the three more so than another. (It will be recalled that, taken alone, neither of the other treatments [Muñoz, 1977; Zeiss, 1977] was demonstrably effective.) This study included a multitude of dependent variables related to the various psychological processes usually posited as underlying the effectiveness of the three treatments. In no case did a particular treatment condition show a differential impact upon a predicted variable; for instance, there was no evidence at the end of treatment that activities-increase treatment subjects were experiencing more pleasant events than subjects in the other two treatments or, for that matter, than the no-treatment controls.

Hammen, Rook, and Harris (1979) have addressed one aspect of increase-activities treatment regimes that is ignored by its advocates but that may interfere with its therapeutic effectiveness: the possibility that subjects may attribute their participation in pleasurable activities to the experimenter's or therapist's requirements rather than to internal causal factors. This may account for the tendency in the Hammen and Glass (1975) studies described earlier for activities-increase subjects to report greater dysphoria than controls; in the words of Hammen *et al.* (1979), "increases in activity level which are not self-attributed may contribute little to improved mood [p. 4]." To explore this question, Hammen *et al.* carried out two studies in which an attempt was made to vary subjects' perceptions of the reasons they engaged in pleasant activities.

In Hammen *et al.*'s first study, 38 undergraduate psychology students were selected on the basis of scores on the BDI and the D-30 (raw score means of 13.8 and 13.2, respectively). Subjects were first given the Pleasant Events Schedule, and events that would be pleasant for the particular subject were identified. Subjects were then assigned to one of three groups: one in which they were asked to participate in 10 personally pleasurable activities, all specified by the experimenter; one in which they were asked to participate in 10 of 30 specified pleasant activities, with the subject deciding which 10; and a self-monitoring control. All subjects logged activities and mood on a daily basis for the 2 weeks following. The results indicated that, while the groups did not differ in the number of activities performed, they did differ in subsequent depressive state. The most depression was shown by the group that had no choice over which activities they increased, less depression was shown by the group having some choice, and the least depression by the self-monitoring group.

In the second study, 41 subjects similar to those used in the first study (BDI $M = 16.8$) were asked either to do as many of 100 personally pleasurable activities as they could or to self-monitor during a 2-week period. In addition, half in each condition were promised and paid 5 dollars for their participation upon completion. That is, external coercion—and perhaps attribution—was varied in two ways: in terms of instructions to engage in activities and in terms of monetary reward. Though groups did not differ on BDI at posttest, daily mood ratings indicated that paid subjects were more depressed than unpaid subjects; paid subjects also reported lower enjoyment of activities.

These studies suggest, at the very least, that therapist coercion to participate in more activities may have a side effect that undercuts any beneficial effect that the participation in those activities might provide. This might account for the very mixed results shown for the strategy. It would be gratuitous to speculate about the extent to which subjects actually felt externally coerced by their therapists in the various activities-increase treatment studies discussed. These findings do suggest, however, that therapists wishing to use these techniques would be wise to do their best to have clients see the origin of the new behavior as internal.

There is one last issue that merits discussion in this section: the use of the Premack Principle as a means of increasing activity. The procedure of having subjects engage in target behaviors prior to engaging in high-probability behaviors is very common. The popularity of this technique presumably stems from the fact that it may be not only a technique for getting target behaviors to be emitted, but also a way of seeing to it that they are rewarded. Nonetheless, it is an empirical question whether or not the technique makes any difference, a question that has until recently had no empirical attention except for one study by Robinson and Lewinsohn (1973), a study whose relevance is undercut by the fact that targeted activities were not particularly mood related and no depression-related dependent variable was monitored. There is now one very relevant study, and it will be reviewed next.

Haeger (1977) reported a study in which subjects responded to a media call for depressed persons (BDI median $= 26$). For persons to be included, they needed to be able to report three high-frequency behaviors and three low-frequency behaviors (which had fallen at least 50% in frequency during the current depressive episode). The use of the Premack Principle and, in addition, the use of experimenter verbal reinforcement for reports of performance of target behaviors were varied among the various experimental conditions. There were five conditions ($N$ = about 8 each): (a) Premack Principle plus verbal reinforcement; (b) Premack Principle instructions only; (c) non-Premack instructions to increase target behaviors plus verbal reinforcement; (d) an attention placebo focused on dietary behavior and on behavior monitoring; and (e) no treatment. Each treatment group had eight sessions, and groups (a), (b), and (c) in addition received other behavioral strategies (e.g., modeling and rehearsal). The results indicated improvement, but again not as a function of group. Generally, there appeared to be no association between increasing the frequency of targeted behaviors and improvement of depressive condition. The author did note that the Premack application did involve some logistic problems in cases in which a specified high-frequency behavior did not naturally follow a targeted behavior. This raises the possibility that "the frustration in arranging the pairing sometimes offset potential positive reinforcement effects [p. 152]."

By way of summarizing the findings, it should be obvious that the pleasant-activities prescription for depression—client to increase pleasant activities, client does so, client is rewarded, client's depression lifts—is not at all the normative finding in these studies. Indeed, one would be tempted to announce its funeral were it not for the fact that it was supported in one major study (Turner et al., 1979) and that, for unexplained reasons, activities-increase seemed in some studies to be effective with depression even when it did not influence measured activity level. Moreover, most of the studies are subject to criticism on a number of grounds, such that it could be argued that only in the Turner et al. study did the true state of affairs emerge. However, the burden of proof must rest heavily with advocates of the pleasant-activities model at this time.

### Mixed Behavioral Interventions

Studies reviewed in the present section consist of those that, while in the behavioral tradition, cannot be characterized as having employed a particular commonly used strategy: Either several strategies were used together, the approach was behavioral only in a very general way, or the approach was idiosyncratic to the study. In the absence of a rational way of classifying these studies, presentation is largely chronological.

Heavenrich (1972) assessed the effectiveness of tape-recorded vignettes, varied on dimensions posited as important in depression. Subjects were 43 female undergraduates, solicited by class and media announcements. The screening requirement was a score in excess of one $SD$ above the mean on a locally developed depression questionnaire; subjects with severe psychological problems or recent psychotherapy were excluded. There were four 30-minute sessions over a 2-week span. Subjects met in small groups in a language lab to listen to their tapes. Each tape presented a number of segments, each characterized by three components: description of an event known to lead to depression in college females (same in all conditions); description of a reaction (depressive or nondepressive); and description of a consequence (rewarding, punishing, or neutral). Each subject heard only one of the possible six sequences, though the specific event, reaction, and consequence changed from segment to segment. Results on several measures of depression given pre and post indicated a general lessening of depression, but not differentially as a function of group. The author concluded that the principles of operant conditioning cannot account for the effects of covert sensitization as a method for the treatment of depression.

Shipley (1972; Shipley & Fazio, 1973) reported two studies. In the first, subjects were 22 undergraduates who reported being depressed for at least 3 weeks and had Zung depression scores of at least .45 and MMPI-D scores of 70 or above; MMPI means were in the high 70s and low 80s. No restriction regarding other MMPI elevations was imposed, so depression may not have been the primary problem for some. Eleven were assigned to a control group, and 11 were given three 1-hour sessions of therapy, consisting of the clarification of alternatives, suggestions to emit or cease emitting certain responses, assertiveness training, and the use of isolated depression. Specific techniques varied as a function of the subject's problem. The therapy was effective as indicated by posttreatment MMPI-D scale score differences (reduction of about 15 $T$-score points); controls were subsequently also treated and showed comparable improvement at that time. In the second study, 28 similarly recruited subjects were treated in one of four groups created by the crossing of two variables. Specifically, half were treated behaviorally as in Experiment 1 and half received interest and support; in both, half were told that they were receiving a therapy of proven effectiveness and half were told nothing about effectiveness. Pre- to posttreatment change scores indicated that, while the perceived effectiveness manipulation made no difference, subjects in the behavioral groups became significantly less depressed, whereas those receiving the interest–support treatment did not.

McLean, Ogston, and Grauer (1973) assessed the effectiveness of a treatment that focused on the modification of verbal interaction styles, training in social learning, and behavioral contracting. Patients (10 treated, 10 untreated controls) were referred by physicians and were required to be nonpsychotic and somewhat incapacitated by depressive behaviors and have a spouse also willing to become involved. The patient and her or his spouse were treated together, and considerable effort in treatment was spent on getting the couples to relate to one another in a more rewarding and supportive fashion. Dependent variables included self-reports (DACL), spouse's report of patient's depressive status, and ratings of tapes obtained of conversations in the home. Data both at the end of 8 weeks of treatment and at 3-month follow-up indicated greater improvement for treated subjects.

Hilford (1975) briefly reported a study with 46 depressed inpatient women, including contact and no-contact controls. Experimental subjects were given instructions designed to encourage the emission of behaviors incompatible with depressive behaviors; daily small-group sessions consisted of discussions of patients' experiences vis-à-vis the instructions. Self-reports and ward ratings indicated greater improvement among experimental than among control patients.

Magers (1977) reported a study inspired by the helplessness model and by the observation that female sex-role training in our society tends to encourage helplessness. Subjects were 18 women recruited through clinical referrals and media advertisements; all were nonpsychotic, middle-class mothers. Though the BDI score distribution was not well described, it apparently had a median of about 21. Therapy, which took place over a 6-week period, was in a group context and was directed toward having the women define goals and work toward them and toward developing group support for goal achievement. Techniques used included modeling, cognitive restructuring, reinforcement, assertiveness exercises, role playing, and relaxation techniques. Subjects were assigned to immediate or delayed treatment groups, and all were assessed at three points in time: before the immediate group's therapy, when the immediate group had finished and the delayed group was about to begin, and after the delayed group had completed therapy. Though appropriate statistical analyses are not presented, BDI means apparently shifted downward during therapy and only during therapy.

Fuchs and Rehm (1977) assessed the effectiveness of a group treatment module inspired by a self-control model of depression. Subjects ($N = 36$) were recruited through media announcements and were women who had elevated MMPI-D scores (D $>$ 70 and one of the two highest elevations) but were not psychotic, suicidal, or in treatment elsewhere; pretreatment BDI means were in the low 20s, with MMPI-D means in the low 80s. There were two control conditions: nonspecific therapy (focus on group interaction and empathic reflecting of feelings) and waiting-list. The experimental therapy involved the didactic presentation of the self-control model, monitoring of positive events on a daily basis, setting concrete goals of pleasant-activity increase, and self-reward for the reaching of the goals; there were six weekly 2-hour sessions. BDI results indicated that both the self-control and the nonspecific therapy groups improved more than waiting-list subjects, and the self-control therapy was more successful than the nonspecific therapy. MMPI-D results were similar, as were findings on a number of related measures, including reports of participation in pleasant activities. Indeed, one is tempted to suggest that this treatment may be a model of how the increase-pleasant-activities strategy can be made to work effectively, since it may well circumvent the problems raised by Hammen *et al.* (1979); on the other hand, one cannot assume that the effect upon activity level was an important mediator of the effect upon depression.

Rehm *et al.* (1979) reported what can be viewed as a replication of these findings, but with a different control condition, namely group assertion training.

Procedural details (e.g., subject selection, duration of therapy) were similar to those reported by Fuchs and Rehm (1977). Fourteen self-control and 11 assertion condition subjects completed the study. Briefly, the self-control therapy was more effective than assertion training on a number of measures, including the BDI, the MMPI-D scale, and self-report of participation in pleasant activities. This was the case despite the fact that the assertion training was evidently more effective in increasing assertive behavior.

It will be recalled that four studies were described earlier in the section on cognitive therapy in which a behavioral condition was among those being compared. The findings of those studies can be briefly recapitulated. In Shaw's study (1977), a cognitive treatment appeared more effective than a behavioral treatment; the latter was more effective than a waiting-list control but not more than a nonspecific therapy. In Taylor and Marshall's (1977) study, subjects receiving a combined cognitive plus behavioral treatment improved more than did subjects receiving either a cognitive treatment or a behavioral treatment; the latter two treatments did not differ in efficacy. Weinberg (1977) compared a behavioral group treatment with a cognitive treatment, an emotional awareness treatment, and an assessment-only control. Though there were instances of significant differences among groups, they portrayed no consistent picture of differential effectiveness. Recall, however, that treatment was minimal (4 hours, group format) and subjects were minimally depressed persons who had not sought treatment. Finally, a study by Besyner (1978) was described in which a behavioral group therapy was compared with cognitive, nonspecific, and waiting-list groups. The behavioral group in this case was patterned after the writings of Lewinsohn and involved didactic presentations, modeling, coaching, rehearsal, and homework. As noted earlier, this appeared more effective, especially at 1-month follow-up, than any of the other conditions, on cognitive as well as on affective and self-report variables.

Hussian (1978) reported a study of nursing home residents, most of whom had some serious medical problem; the mean age was in the mid-70s, and the BDI means were in the mid- to upper 30s. Two treatments were evaluated: social reinforcement, in which subjects were prompted to pursue an activity of their choice, with a staff member present to give social approval for the participation; and problem-solving training, with a focus on active ways of solving problems of daily life. There were a total of six conditions in the study: (a) a waiting-list control ($N = 12$); (b) an informational control in which subjects were read an upbeat book on the aging process ($N = 6$); (c) 2 weeks of social reinforcement ($N = 6$); (d) 2 weeks of problem solving $N = 6$); (e) 1 week of each, with social reinforcement first ($N = 6$); and (f) 1 week of each, with problem solving first ($N = 6$). Results indicated that the two treatments had some specific effects on the targeted characteristics. The most reasonable comparisons (since they involve $N$s of 12 each) are between waiting-list controls, social reinforcement, and problem-solving subjects at the end of 1 week;

at this point, both groups showed improved BDI scores relative to controls, with the improvement maintained for the subsequent week (i.e., through crossover for half of each treatment group). There was some evidence that 2 weeks of problem solving was better than 2 weeks of social reinforcement and that, among the groups involving social reinforcement, the reinforcement–problem-solving sequence was most beneficial. These results pertain to depression, but there was evidence that 2 weeks of problem solving resulted in improved hospital adjustment as well.

Harpin (1978) conducted a study of nonpsychotic but chronically depressed individuals who had been unresponsive to antidepressant medication or any other therapy. The typical subject treated had had two previous inpatient hospitalizations. All subjects were put on a subclinical dose of an antidepressant, to fend off requests for medications. Six subjects were treated, and there were six waiting-list controls. The treatment, which consisted of 20 1-hour sessions over a 10-week period was individualized but involved the following components: self-monitoring of pleasant events and constructive activities; role playing; obtaining the cooperation of significant others to ignore depressive behavior and reward healthier behaviors; use of depressive behaviors as contingent outcomes for lower frequency behaviors; thought stopping; self-instructions to combat negative cognitions; social skills training; and anxiety management. In terms of its impact upon depression, the treatment was unsuccessful. In the author's words: "Significant improvements were evidenced in the utilization of the verbal and nonverbal components of skilled social behavior and in self-reports of social anxiety and assertion. Overall, this gain in functioning was not associated with significant improvement in depression [p. 77]."

McLean and Hakstian (1979) have conducted a major study in which 154 depressed subjects were randomly assigned to one of four treatment conditions. Screening requirements included the following: current depression of at least 2 months, resulting in impairment of functioning; not in treatment elsewhere; and specified elevations on at least two of three tests of depression (e.g., BDI cutoff of 23; $M$ = about 27). Treatment consisted of 8–12 weekly sessions, which the spouse was also encouraged to attend. The four conditions were: (a) short-term psychotherapy, which included attempts to develop the patients' insight into the dynamic forces and personality problems behind the depression, and other traditional techniques; (b) relaxation therapy; (c) behavior therapy, involving goal setting and attainment in the areas of communication, behavioral productivity, social interaction, assertiveness, decision making and problem solving, and cognitive self-control (as described elsewhere in McLean's clinical writing); and (d) drug therapy, involving a course of 150 mg/day of amitriptyline at maximum. Dependent variables were numerous, but in general, the pattern was that behavior therapy was most effective and psychotherapy was least effective. The greatest differences appeared to be between behavior therapy and the other three.

Biglan, Craker, and Dow (n.d.) reported a study of 14 subjects assigned to a treatment group or to a self-monitoring control. Subjects (BDI $M = 28$) were recruited through letters to community clincs and through the media. Subjects in both groups were first assessed extensively, such that specific problem areas could be identified and targeted for monitoring and treatment. Controls were encouraged to change targeted events on their own and were told that monitoring alone would help. Treatment in the experimental group was very individualized and carried out through written instructional materials dealing with the problem area. Actual therapy sessions during the 10-week treatment period appear to have served mainly to make sure the subject understood the instructions. Even though controls improved significantly during the period of the study, experimental subjects improved more and were significantly less depressed at posttest than were the controls.

In summary, the studies reviewed in this section differ markedly in scope and import—from academic exercises (the review of which is probably also a minor exercise) to major contributions to the literature. There is a preponderance of studies indicating that multifaceted behavioral approaches are effective, even that they are more effective than other credible treatments. Results are unclear regarding whether effectiveness differs between behavioral and cognitive treatments and, if so, which is better. The best guess, on the basis of Taylor and Marshall's (1977) findings, is that a combination of the two is optimal; supporting this is the observation that, just as some effective cognitive regimes reviewed previously included a behavioral component, a number of the effective behavioral treatments reviewed in this section included a cognitive component. Though not the only one, the most glaring exception to the generally favorable picture painted by the studies reviewed in this section is the study by Harpin (1978); the failure in effectiveness shown in his study may, of course, merely reflect the small sample size, but it may instead indicate that there exists a subset of chronically depressed persons whose condition is intractable in the face even of intensive, individualized behavioral intervention.

The upcoming sections are given over to the review of studies of the efficacy of specific behavioral techniques. Unlike those just discussed, the studies that follow seem not to have come into the mainstream of behavioral thinking about depression. In most cases, just a study or two exist.

## Antidepressive Program

Taulbee and Wright (1971) described a procedure for inpatient treatment in which the depressed person is given a menial and repetitive task to perform, is treated firmly but kindly while doing so, and is kept at the task for long hours until an angry, assertive outburst occurs. Taulbee and Wright reviewed a number of unpublished comparisons between this regime and various other inpatient approaches, and the results were very encouraging. Two controlled tests have since been published. One of them (Barnes, 1977) will not be recounted, since subjects in the study's two experimental conditions differed not only in the treatment to which they were assigned but also in pretreatment diagnosis.

Wadsworth and Barker (1976) compared the antidepressive program with a more traditional hospital approach, in which patients were given imipramine and group therapy and were dealt with in an active and friendly way by staff. Each group contained 16 neurotic and 12 psychotic patients (Zung Self-Rating Depression Scale means in the mid-60s in all instances); psychotic patients in both groups were given antipsychotic drugs. The results indicated that the psychotics did about equally well on the two treatment regimes and that neurotic patients showed substantially more improvement on the antidepressive program than on the control treatment. Given the presumptive efficacy of imipramine, even the results for the psychotic patients are respectable. It would appear that this technique deserves more attention than it has thus far received. Note also that there is a commonality between this approach and assertiveness training, in that the outburst may be seen as an assertive response and the treatment regime specifically directs that it should be rewarded as such by staff.

## Running

Though evidence has existed of positive effects upon mood resulting from structured exercise programs (e.g., Folkins, 1976), no assessment of such an approach in the treatment of depression appears to have been reported until very recently. Greist, Klein, Eischens, Faris, Gurman, and Morgan (1979; see also Greist, Klein, Eischens, & Faris, 1978) reported two studies (Ns of 28 and 24) in which subjects having mild elevations on the depression cluster of the Symptom Check List 90 (SCL-90) and other indications of minor depression were assigned to time-limited psychotherapy, time-unlimited psychotherapy, or a structured, supervised course of running. These interventions lasted 10 weeks in the first study and 12 in the second. In both studies, running was as effective as either kind of psychotherapy; unfortunately, there was no no-treatment control, so the possibility that none of the interventions was helpful cannot be ruled out.

It is possible to construe running simply as a pleasant activity, not necessarily different from other such activities in terms of its impact upon depression. As Greist et al. (1979) noted, however, there are a number of possible mechanisms, including biochemical, that might underlie any effectiveness shown by such a program.

## Flooding

Hannie and Adams (1974) reported a study of the effectiveness of flooding in the treatment of 21 inpatient women with agitated depression. Flooding, in which the therapist described scenes created to elicit an emotional reaction, was compared with supportive, feeling-oriented therapy and with no treatment. The therapy conditions involved nine 45-minute sessions over a 3-week period. Flooding was clearly better than supportive therapy, and it appeared to be better than no treatment as well.

*Helplessness Reduction*

Most studies of helplessness reduction or inoculation are analogue studies and will not be reviewed in detail; the usual procedure involves exposure to a success–contingency experience prior to a failure–noncontingency experience (helplessness inoculation) or following a failure–noncontingency experience (helplessness reduction). Blaney (1977) has reviewed a number of analogue studies in this tradition. Let it merely be noted here that the following conclusions are suggested by studies since that review:

1. Success only is less effective as a helplessness inoculation than mixed success–failure (e.g., Nation, Cooney, & Gartrell, 1979; Nation & Massad, 1978).
2. The effects of success-oriented reduction experiences may vary as a function of subject gender (Sobelman, 1978).
3. The effect of real success experiences is greater than that of recalling past success experiences (Teasdale, 1978).

While a number of the interventions described throughout this chapter can be related to the helplessness model, and while several (e.g., Magers, 1977) were explicitly influenced by the model, there appears to be but one nonanalogue study assessing an intervention that could be said to be uniquely a helplessness treatment. Specifically, Glass (1978) designed a technique that, in his words, would be analogous to "dragging helpless dogs across the shuttle box [p. 23]." Subjects were 29 college students recruited through media who reported depression and manifested no other severe condition; their BDI mean was 20.4. In addition to a waiting-list control, a control focusing on group support, clarification of feelings, and self-monitoring was also used. This latter condition and the helplessness treatment condition involved six sessions of 90 minutes each over a 3-week period, apparently in a group context. The helplessness treatment itself involved helping individuals identify an area in which helplessness was debilitating and prompting them to engage in some active behavior already in their repertoires so that they would learn that responding and outcome in that area were not now independent. As distinguished from a social skills training approach, the experimenter did not suggest solutions but rather encouraged subjects to generate possible alternative behaviors that they could perform in their major helplessness situation. There were a number of dependent variables, and the general pattern was for the helplessness group to show the most improvement, with the treatment control next, and the waiting-list control last; not all of the pairwise comparisons were significant, but a number were. However, a dependent measure of the cognitions of helplessness failed to differentiate treatment groups, and the reason for the greater effectiveness of the helplessness training group remains unclear.

## Comment

Clear evidence exists for the efficacy of both cognitive and behavioral treatments of depression; moreover, evidence indicates that both may be more effective than either antidepressant medication or traditional psychotherapy. With regard to evidence of therapeutic superiority, however, it should be noted that, whenever such evidence is at hand, it is possible and even reasonable to argue that the treatment found to be less effective was not delivered in its optimal form (as did Becker and Schuckit [1978] with regard to the relatively poor showing of imipramine in the Rush *et al.* [1977] results). This may be particularly apt when short-term insight-oriented treatment is found less effective, since it is not unreasonable to argue that such psychotherapy, to be optimal, must involve the possibility of longer courses of therapy than were provided in any of these studies.

I am, of course, reraising the classic argument in the psychotherapy versus behavior therapy controversy: that psychotherapy loses not because it is less effective but because it is made to compete according to ground rules that are alien to it. This argument is considerably less apt in the case of depression than, say, in the case of a discreet symptom like a snake phobia; since depression is molar and not entirely reducible to specifiable behaviors, there is a sense in which it is behavior therapy that is competing in a somewhat alien context. Moreover, perhaps the best response to a claim that the less effective treatment was delivered suboptimally is the one offered by Rush *et al.* (1978): that one cannot assume that the treatment found to be superior was not also delivered suboptimally.

All the foregoing ignores the fact that there are instances reviewed both for behavioral and for cognitive therapy in which treated subjects improved no more than did subjects exposed to no therapy at all. I will offer some possible reasons for the variability in outcomes and discuss them.

An obvious one is sample size. It may be no accident that some of the most encouraging results were obtained in some of the largest studies (e.g., McLean & Hakstian, 1979; Rush *et al.*, 1977). This may, of course, be related to the fact that significance is easier to come by with larger samples. In this vein, it should be noted that the differences shown in successful studies such as these are substantial in an absolute sense, not merely small differences rendered significant by virtue of sample size.

Another consideration is therapist competence. This may, in fact, be confounded with sample size, since many of the smaller studies, often dissertations, employed therapists who were relatively inexperienced and who may not have been supervised by someone with greater experience. Some of the most resounding failures were in studies of this sort.

As noted earlier, there seems to be a pattern for mixed cognitive and behavioral treatments to exceed those limited to one model. This may reflect a general complementarity of these techniques, or it may reflect a situation in which, with heterogeneous samples, mixed treatments are more likely than restricted treatments to offer something that everyone can benefit from.

This raises the question of patient variables. In most instances, about all that is known about the patients is how depressed they were. A close examination of the studies reviewed makes it clear that successes and failures of cognitive and of behavioral therapy were evident throughout the range of severity employed; assertion training is the only exception—with this modality most often shown effective with the more severely depressed. Severity is not the only dimension on which patients could be assessed, of course, and the question remains about what kinds of treatments are optimal for what kinds of depressed persons. Zeiss *et al.* (1979) noted, for instance, that they believed that their overall success rate for three therapies studied would have been higher if subjects had been assigned on a rational (rather than random) basis to a particular therapy; Rehm *et al.* (1979) made a similar observation in their comparison of assertion and self-control therapy.

Regarding depressive subtype, Commorato and Carroll (n.d.) have suggested that there is little evidence that behavioral treatments are effective with endogenomorphic depressives. Since the status of most samples cannot be ascertained vis-à-vis that stereotype, one cannot really either affirm or deny this conclusion from a review of the research, except to note that some samples had group means on such scales as the BDI that were so high as to render it highly likely that a number of patients included did have endogenomorphic symptoms. Rush and Beck (1978) have addressed this specific issue, noting that, in their (Rush *et al.*, 1977) study, patients with a greater preponderance of vegetative symptoms appeared to do well with either chemotherapy or cognitive therapy; the clear superiority of cognitive therapy appeared to be with more reactive patients. On the other hand, Harpin (1978) reported a failure of a comprehensive and intensive behavioral approach with a group of chronic depressed persons, which, as noted earlier, does raise the possibility that there is a subgroup of persons with whom these techniques are of little use.

In any case, in the words with which Rehm and Kornblith (1979) closed their review, "What seems to be most needed now is greater attention to relating therapy strategies to specific subject differences [p. 314]."

## Summary

This chapter briefly summarizes the findings of all or most of the existing studies relevant to the cognitive and behavioral treatment of depression. The cognitive approaches focus on the individual's beliefs and interpretative distortions, which are presumed to underlie his or her depression; the goal is to change these depressogenic thought patterns. Although the primary thrust of behavior therapy is quite straightforward—getting the individual to participate more frequently in rewarding activities—a diverse array of strategies have grown directly or indirectly out of the behavioral tradition. These include: assertion training, social skills training, problem-solving training, reduction in reinforcement of depressive behaviors and increase in reinforcement (from others and from oneself) of prosocial behaviors, relaxation training, thought stopping, and flooding. With both the behavioral and the cognitive approaches, the literature is exceptionally inconsistent, with results of specific studies ranging from very encouraging to very discouraging. Indeed, the only techniques for which conflicting findings are not reported are those that have been evaluated in only one or two studies. While many of the treatment failures can be explained away rather easily, this is not the case for all the treatment successes, particularly those in which mixed cognitive and behavioral strategies have been employed. For this reason, it must be concluded, albeit tentatively, that these techniques are indeed promising, though it is not at all clear which patients can benefit most from a given technique, nor is it even clear which of the specific strategies are in fact sources of any therapeutic benefit at all.

## Acknowledgments

Sara Puga, Edward Murray, and Roxane Head assisted in the process of compiling the bibliography. I also benefited in developing a bibliography from the existing reviews of Commorato and Carroll (n.d.), Rehm and Kornblith (1979), and Rush and Beck (1970).

## References

Barnes, M. R. Effects of antidepressive program on verbal behavior. *Journal of Clinical Psychology,* 1977, *33,* 545–549.

Barrera, M. W. An evaluation of a brief group therapy for depression (Doctoral dissertation, University of Oregon, 1977). *Dissertation Abstracts International,* 1977, *38,* 3842B-2843B. (University Microfilms No. 77–26,483.)

Barrera, M. An evaluation of a brief group therapy for depression. *Journal of Consulting and Clinical Psychology,* 1979, *47,* 413–415.

Beck, A. T., Rush, A. J., Shaw, B. F., & Emery, G. *Cognitive therapy of depression.* New York: Guilford Press, 1979.

Becker, J., & Schuckit, M. A. The comparative efficacy of cognitive therapy and pharmacotherapy in the treatment of depressions. *Cognitive Therapy and Research,* 1978, *2,* 193–197.

Besyner, J. K. The comparative efficacy of cognitive and behavioral treatments of depression: A multi-assessment approach (Unpublished doctoral dissertation, Texas Tech University, 1978). *Dissertation Abstracts International,* 1979, *39,* 4568B.

Biglan, A., Craker, D., & Dow, M. A problem-specific, self-administered approach to the treatment of depression. Unpublished manuscript, University of Oregon, n.d.

Blaney, P. H. Contemporary theories of depression: Critique and comparison. *Journal of Abnormal Psychology,* 1977, *86,* 203–223.

Commorato, A. J., & Carroll, B. J. Behavioral treatment of depression. Unpublished manuscript, University of Michigan, n.d.

Cooke, S. A. An experimental study of the effectiveness of coverant conditioning in alleviating neurotic depression in college students (Unpublished doctoral dissertation, University of Virginia, 1974). *Dissertation Abstracts International,* 1975, *35,* 3574B. (University Microfilms No. 74–29,220.)

Craker, D. Evaluation of a self-reward system for increasing pleasant activities and its relevance to the treatment of depression. Unpublished manuscript, n.d.

Fagan, M. M. Alleviated depression: The efficacy of group psychotherapy and group assertive training. *Small Group Behavior,* 1979, *10,* 136–152.

Folkins, C. H. Effects of physical training on mood. *Journal of Clinical Psychology,* 1976, *32,* 385–388.

Fuchs, C. Z., & Rehm, L. P. A self-control behavior therapy program for depression. *Journal of Consulting and Clinical Psychology,* 1977, *45,* 206–215.

Gioe, V. J. Cognitive modification and positive group experience as a treatment for depression (Doctoral dissertation, Temple University, 1975). *Dissertation Abstracts International,* 1975, *36,* 3039B-3040B. (University Microfilms No. 75–28,219.)

Glass, D. R., Jr. An evaluation of a brief treatment for depression based on the learned helplessness model (Unpublished doctoral dissertation, University of California, Los Angeles, 1978). *Dissertation Abstracts International,* 1978, *39,* 2495B. (University Microfilms No. 78–20,221.)

Graf, M. G. A mood-related activities schedule for the treatment of depression (Unpublished doctoral dissertation, Arizona State University, 1977). *Dissertation Abstracts International,* 1977, *38,* 1400B-1401B. (University Microfilms No. 77–17,868.)

Greist, J. H., Klein, M. H., Eischens, R. R., & Faris, J. T. Running out of depression. *The Physician and Sportsmedicine,* 1978 (December), 49–56.

Greist, J. H., Klein, M. H., Eischens, R. R., Faris, J., Gurman, A. S., & Morgan, W. P. Running as treatment for depression. *Comprehensive Psychiatry,* 1979, *20,* 41–54.

Haeger, T. F. Application of the Premack differential probability hypothesis to the treatment of depression (Unpublished doctoral dissertation, American University, 1977). *Dissertation Abstracts International,* 1978, *38,* 3395B. (University Microfilms No. 77–29,358.)

Hammen, C. L., & Glass, D. R., Jr. Depression, activity, and evaluation of reinforcement. *Journal of Abnormal Psychology,* 1975, *84,* 718–721.

Hammen, C. L., Rook, K. S., & Harris, G. Effects of activities and attributions on depressed mood. Unpublished manuscript, University of California, Los Angeles, 1979.

Hannie, T. J., Jr., & Adams, H. E. Modification of agitated depression by flooding: A preliminary study. *Journal of Behavior Therapy and Experimental Psychiatry,* 1974, *5,* 161–166.

Harpin, R. E. A psychosocial treatment for some forms of depression? (Unpublished doctoral dissertation, State University of New York at Stony Brook, 1978). *Dissertation Abstracts International,* 1979, *39,* 2499B. (University Microfilms No. 78–20,832.)

Hayman, P. M. Effects on depression of assertive training (Unpublished doctoral dissertation, University of Missouri–Columbia, 1977). *Dissertation Abstracts International,* 1978, *38,* 5019B. (University Microfilms No. 78–3,720.)

Head, R. Cognitive therapy with depressed college students. Unpublished master's thesis, University of Miami, 1978.

Heavenrich, R. M. Evaluation of the effect of reward and punishment contingencies in the covert behavioral treatment of depression (Unpublished doctoral dissertation, Wayne State University, 1972). *Dissertation Abstracts International,* 1973, *33,* 5515B-5516B. (University Microfilms No. 73–12,529.)

Hilford, N. G. Self-initiated behavior change by depressed women following verbal behavior therapy. *Behavior Therapy,* 1975, *6,* 703.

Hussian, R. A. Social reinforcement of activity and problem-solving training in the treatment of depressed institutionalized elderly patients (Unpublished doctoral dissertation, University of

North Carolina at Greensboro, 1978). *Dissertation Abstracts International,* 1979, *39,* 3517B–3518B. (University Microfilms No. 78–24,891.)

Kirkpatrick, P. W. The efficacy of cognitive behavior modification in the treatment of depression (Unpublished doctoral dissertation, University of Texas at Austin, 1977). *Dissertation Abstracts International,* 1977, *38,* 2370B.

LaPointe, K. A. Cognitive therapy versus assertive training in the treatment of depression. (Unpublished doctoral dissertation, Southern Illinois University, 1976). *Dissertation Abstracts International,* 1977, *37,* 4689B. (University Microfilms No. 77–6232.)

Lewinsohn, P. M. Engagement in pleasant activities and depression level. *Journal of Abnormal Psychology,* 1975, *84,* 729–731.

Lomont, J. F., Gilner, F. H., Spector, N. J., & Skinner, K. K. Group assertion training and group insight therapies. *Psychological Reports,* 1969, *25,* 463–470.

Lowe, M. R. The use of covert modeling in social skills training with depressed patients (Unpublished doctoral dissertation, Boston College, 1978). *Dissertation Abstracts International,* 1978, *38,* 6163B–6164B. (University Microfilms No. 78–7,239.)

Magers, B. D. Cognitive–behavioral short-term group therapy with depressed women (Unpublished doctoral dissertation, California School of Professional Psychology, San Francisco, 1977). *Dissertation Abstracts International,* 1978, *38,* 4468B. (University Microfilms No. 78–1,687.)

Maish, J. I. The use of an individualized assertive training program in the treatment of depressed in-patients (Unpublished doctoral dissertation, Florida State University, 1972). *Dissertation Abstracts International,* 1972, *33,* 2816B. (University Microfilms No. 72–31,413.)

McDonald, A. C. A cognitive/behavioral treatment for depression with Veterans Administration out-patients (Unpublished doctoral dissertation, University of Utah, 1978). *Dissertation Abstracts International,* 1978, *39,* 2994B. (University Microfilms No. 78–22,829.)

McLean, P. D., & Hakstian, A. R. Clinical depression: Comparative efficacy of outpatient treatments. *Journal of Consulting and Clinical Psychology,* 1979, *47,* 818–836.

McLean, P. D., Ogston, K., & Grauer, L. A behavioral approach to the treatment of depression. *Journal of Behavior Therapy and Experimental Psychiatry,* 1973, *4,* 323–330.

Morris, N. E. A group self-instruction method for the treatment of depressed outpatients (Unpublished doctoral dissertation, University of Toronto, 1975). *Dissertation Abstracts International,* 1978, *38,* 4473B–4474B.

Muñoz, R. F. A cognitive approach to the assessment and treatment of depression (Unpublished doctoral dissertation, University of Oregon, 1977). *Dissertation Abstracts International, 38,* 2873B. (University Microfilms No. 77–26,505.)

Nation, J. R., Cooney, J. B., & Gartrell, K. E. Durability and generalizability of persistence training. *Journal of Abnormal Psychology,* 1979, *88,* 121–126.

Nation, J. R., & Massad, P. Persistence training: A partial reinforcement procedure for reversing learned helplessness and depression. *Journal of Experimental Psychology: General,* 1978, *107,* 436–451.

Nystedt, G. A. Self-monitoring and self-instruction: Therapeutic procedures for the treatment of depression in college students (Unpublished doctoral dissertation, West Virginia University, 1976). *Dissertation Abstracts International,* 1977, *37,* 6342B. (University Microfilms No. 77–12,320.)

Pace, F. R. Behavioral techniques in the treatment of depression (Unpublished doctoral dissertation, University of New South Wales, 1977). *Dissertation Abstracts International,* 1978, *39,* 992B.

Padfield, M. The comparative effects of two counseling approaches on the intensity of depression among rural women of low socioeconomic status. *Journal of Counseling Psychology,* 1976, *23,* 209–214.

Rehm, L. P., Fuchs, C. Z., Roth, D. M., Kornblith, S. J., & Romano, J. M. A comparison of self-control and assertion skills treatments of depression. *Behavior Therapy,* 1979, *10,* 429–442.

Rehm, L. P., & Kornblith, S. J. Behavior therapy for depression: A review of recent developments. In M. Hersen, R. M. Eisler, & P. M. Miller (Eds.), *Progress in behavior modification* (Vol. 7). New York: Academic Press, 1979.

Robinson, J. C., & Lewinsohn, P. M. Experimental analysis of a technique based on the Premack Principle changing the verbal behavior of depressed individuals. *Psychological Reports,* 1973, *32,* 199–210.

Rush, A. J., & Beck, A. T. Behavior therapy in adults with affective disorders. In M. Hersen & A. S. Bellack (Eds.), *Behavior therapy in the psychiatric setting.* Baltimore: Williams and Wilkins, 1978.

Rush, A. J., Beck, A. T., Kovacs, M., & Hollon, S. Comparative efficacy of cognitive therapy and pharmacotherapy in the treatment of depressed outpatients. *Cognitive Therapy and Research,* 1977, *1,* 17–37.

Rush, A. J., Hollon, S. D., Beck, A. T., & Kovacs, M. Depression: Must pharmacotherapy fail for cognitive therapy to succeed? *Cognitive Therapy and Research,* 1978, *2,* 199–206.

Rush, A. J., & Watkins, J. T. Group versus individual cognitive therapy: A pilot study. (Unpublished manuscript, Southwestern Medical School, Dallas, Texas, 1979.)

Sanchez, V. C. Assertion training: Effectiveness in the treatment of depression. (Unpublished doctoral dissertation, University of Oregon, 1978). *Dissertation Abstracts International,* 1979, *39,* 5085B. (University Microfilms No. 79–7502.)

Schmickley, V. G. The effects of cognitive–behavior modification upon depressed outpatients (Unpublished doctoral dissertation, Michigan State University, 1976). *Dissertation Abstracts International,* 1976, *37,* 987B. (University Microfilms No. 76–18,675.)

Shaw, B. F. Comparison of cognitive therapy and behavior therapy in the treatment of depression. *Journal of Consulting and Clinical Psychology,* 1977, *45,* 543–551.

Shipley, C. R. A behavioral treatment for depression (Unpublished doctoral dissertation, University of Wisconsin–Milwaukee, 1972). *Dissertation Abstracts International,* 1973, *33,* 3324B-3325B. (University Microfilms No. 72–32,976.)

Shipley, C. R., & Fazio, A. F. Pilot study of a treatment for psychological depression. *Journal of Abnormal Psychology,* 1973, *82,* 372–376.

Sobelman, L. J. Success only and attribution retraining in the alleviation of depression and learned helplessness (Unpublished doctoral dissertation, University of Massachusetts, 1978). *Dissertation Abstracts International,* 1979, *39,* 4055B. (University Microfilms No. 79–3,840.)

Taulbee, E. S., & Wright, H. W. A psychosocial–behavioral model for therapeutic intervention. In C. D. Spielberger (Ed.), *Current topics in clinical and community psychology* (Vol. 3). New York: Academic Press, 1971.

Taylor, F. G., & Marshall, W. L. Experimental analysis of a cognitive–behavioral therapy for depression. *Cognitive Therapy and Research,* 1977, *1,* 59–72.

Teasdale, J. D. Effects of real and recalled success on learned helplessness and depression. *Journal of Abnormal Psychology,* 1978, *87,* 155–164.

Turner, R. W., Ward, M. F., & Turner, D. J. Behavioral treatment for depression: An evaluation of therapeutic components. *Journal of Clinical Psychology,* 1979, *35,* 166–175.

Wadsworth, A. P., & Barker, H. R. A comparison of two treatments for depression: The antidepressive program vs. traditional therapy. *Journal of Clinical Psychology,* 1976, *32,* 445–449.

Weinberg, L. Behaviorally and cognitively oriented approaches to the alleviation of depressive symptoms in college students (Unpublished doctoral dissertation, SUNY Stony Brook, 1977). *Dissertation Abstracts International,* 1978, *38,* 3422B–3423B. (University Microfilms No. 77–28,140.)

Zeiss, A. M. Interpersonal behavior problems of the depressed: A study of outpatient treatment (Unpublished doctoral dissertation, University of Oregon, 1977). *Dissertation Abstracts International,* 1977, *38,* 2895B–2896B. (University Microfilms No. 77–27,205.)

Zeiss, A. M., Lewinsohn, P. M., & Muñoz, R. F. Nonspecific improvement effects in depression using interpersonal skills training, pleasant activity schedules, or cognitive training. *Journal of Consulting and Clinical Psychology,* 1979, *47,* 427–439.

# 2

# Comparisons and Combinations with Alternative Approaches[1]

## STEVEN D. HOLLON

The last decade has seen a sharp increase in the number of published articles describing behavioral and cognitive–behavioral interventions in the treatment of depression. How effective can these interventions be said to be? Akiskal and McKinney (1975), following a review of intervention efficacy in clinical depression, concluded that "it would appear that no matter what interpersonal factors mobilize depressive behaviors, once the latter reach the melancholic phase, they become biologically autonomous and relatively refractory to psychotherapeutic intervention [p. 293]." Such a judgment, based largely on then existing studies documenting the relative inefficacy of traditional psychotherapies in the amelioration of syndrome depression (see Hollon & Beck, 1978, for a review), appears no longer to hold. By the end of the 1970s, two independent reviews (Hollon & Beck, 1979; Rehm & Kornblith, 1979) had concluded that both behavioral and cognitive–behavioral interventions appeared to have demonstrated evidence of specific efficacy in at least some types of affective populations.

To what extent can the various behavioral and cognitive–behavioral approaches be said to be effective in the amelioration of clinical depression? A considerable portion of the existing studies have been conducted with mildly depressed or subclinical populations. Does treatment efficacy extend to those more severely depressed populations typically treated with pharmacological or somatic interventions? Can the behavioral and cognitive–behavioral approaches provide any protection against relapse or the recurrence of affective

[1] Presentation of this chapter was supported, in part, by a grant from the National Institute of Mental Health (RO1–MH33209) to the Department of Psychology, University of Minnesota, and the St. Paul–Ramsey Medical Education and Research Foundation and the Department of Psychiatry of the St. Paul–Ramsey Medical Center.

33

symptomatology? Depression has traditionally been considered to be an episodic disorder, with the majority of depressed individuals likely to experience at least one or more subsequent episodes at some later point. Given the self-limiting course for any given episode and the probable occurrence of subsequent episodes, questions of prevention and prophylaxis appear to be as important as questions regarding effectiveness during acute phases. Finally, how do the newly developed learning-based approaches compare with the more established pharmacological or somatic interventions? It is not sufficient that a class of interventions be effective in its own right, it is necessary that those interventions be at least as effective as viable alternative approaches.

This chapter examines the efficacy and status of behavioral and cognitive–behavioral interventions for the major affective disorders. It will focus not so much on descriptions of existing studies as on discussions of central conceptual and methodological issues involved in the further development and evaluation of the learning-based approaches. Particular attention will be directed toward attempts to integrate these approaches with major alternative classes of interventions. While it is not clear that such efforts at integration will prove successful, it is evident that they have already begun. While no adequately controlled evaluation of the combined efficacy of learning-based and pharmacological interventions has yet been reported in the literature, widespread interest in the learning-based interventions has already led to pragmatic combinatorial efforts in applied clinical practice. The advisability of such practices, given the dearth of existing experimentation, remains an open question.

## Issues in Outcome Research on Depression

A number of conceptual and methodological issues need to be addressed before reviewing existing outcome literature on depression. Chief among these issues are concerns about sample heterogeneity, the level of assessment, distinctions between treatment comparisons and combinations, the nature of the outcome, the distinction between mechanisms of action and the targets of those mechanisms, and the apparent overlap between the various mechanisms of action.

### Sample Heterogeneity

The various affective disorders appear to be markedly heterogeneous with respect to manifest symptomatology, course, prognosis, probable heritability, and perhaps, response to treatment. The history of descriptive taxonomies in the area has been marked by a series of great debates (e.g., endogenous versus exogenous, endogenous versus reactive, endogenous versus autonomous, and psychotic versus neurotic, to mention only a few [Beck, 1967]). Such debates have frequently contributed more confusion than clarity, particularly when different definitions are given to similar terms. The term *endogenous,* for example, may be used to indicate that a depression is (*a*) of internal origin; (*b*) hereditary; (*c*) of unknown origin; (*d*) psychotic in nature; (*e*) characterized by a particular pattern of manifest behaviors and symptomatology; or (*f*) the depressive phase of a manic–depressive psychosis; or (*g*) any combination of the above definitions (Perris, 1976). The term *neurotic,* similarly, may refer simply to less severe or less "classically" endogenous depressions or may be used to imply a specific subtype of the disorder, with differential etiology, descriptive features, and prognostic implications (Klein, 1974). *Psychotic* may be defined either on the basis of severity and/or the presence of discrete signs or symptoms, as in DSM-II (American Psychiatric Association, 1968), or on the basis solely of those discrete signs or symptoms, as in DSM-III (American Psychiatric Association, 1978). Particularly troublesome has been the dearth of efforts to assess the reliability or stability over time of the various subtypal designations.

The consequence of such heterogeneity is uncertainty as to exactly what types of depressions are being treated in any particular design. Sample characteristics are often left undescribed, or where described, descriptive terms are often left undefined.

The distinction between bipolar and unipolar depressions appears to represent one particularly important, increasingly recognized distinction (Depue & Monroe, 1978).[2] It is unclear whether any controlled study has investigated the efficacy of any behavioral strategy in the treatment of a bipolar depression during a depressive episode, although Sims and Lazarus (1973) have reported using distracting auditory stimuli followed by a redirection of attention in a thought-stopping paradigm to disrupt ruminations in a hypomanic male patient. Bipolar patients may have been represented in selected samples in earlier designs, but there appears to be only one study in the literature in which they were specifically selected for study. In that nonrandomized design (Davenport, Ebert, Adland, & Goodwin, 1977), traditional couples group therapy added to lithium maintenance was compared with lithium maintenance alone. Given the variability associated with the use of the term *manic–depressive,* it is clearly not justifiable to assume that earlier reports involving patients so described refer to bipolar patients. In general, the utility of behavioral approaches in bipolar patients remains a largey unexplored issue.

Distinctions between endogenous and the various alternate descriptions must also be treated carefully. As noted, definitions of the various terms often confound manifest symptomatology with presumed etiology, often with the

---

[2] There are reasons for preferring the term *nonbipolar* to *unipolar* when referring to those individuals who have never experienced, or are unlikely to experience, a manic episode. Genetic investigations (cf. Bertelson, Harvald, & Hauge, 1977; Slater & Cowie, 1971) point toward marked heterogeneity within the nonbipolar depressions with respect to heritability of the disorder. The term *unipolar,* while retaining its descriptive utility, is often applied to those relatively rare nonbipolar samples evidencing multiple hospitalizations. Evidence for heritability in these groups, while not so strong as for the bipolar depressions, appears stronger than for the vast majority of the remaining nonbipolar disorders.

implication that those patients evidencing a classically endogenous manifest symptom pattern (e.g., vegetative symptoms, diurnal variation, anhedonia, early morning insomnia, and behavioral retardation) do so as a consequence of biologic disruption unrelated to and uninfluenced by external or psychosocial events. The status of such an assumption is notably suspect (Mendels & Cochrane, 1968), with little correlation observed between the nature of the symptomatology and the presence or absence of any clear precipitant. Such evidence as is currently available suggests that endogenous patients may respond as readily to learning-based interventions as they do to more traditional tricyclic pharmacological interventions (Hollon, Beck, Kovacs, & Rush, 1977a; Rush, Hollon, Beck, Kovacs, & Weissenburger, 1979). Given the relatively recent emergence of the newer behavioral and cognitive–behavioral interventions, investigators must exercise care not to uncritically accept clinical lore derived from experience with more traditional psychosocial interventions when selecting relevant populations for study.

Overall, heterogeneity in terms of populations and definitions of populations both hinders attempts to review the existing literature and points to the need for care in selecting and describing relevant samples for further study. Clearly, descriptions of samples should include definitions of descriptive labels in terms of specific behavioral signs and/or reported symptoms.

## Level of Assessment

Closely associated to sample heterogeneity is the issue of the level of assessment, in terms of either sample selection or outcome assessment. Depression can be defined as a symptom, syndrome, or nosological entity (Beck, 1967; Lehmann, 1959). As a symptom, the term usually refers to reported dysphoric affect. As a syndrome, *depression* is generally defined as a cluster of affective, behavioral, cognitive, motivational, and vegetative manifestations. As a nosological entity, considerations of presumed etiology, course, prognosis, and probable treatment response become distinguishing features.

Existing measures generally operate at either the symptom (or sign) level (e.g., affect adjective checklists, response latency tasks, or behavioral observation measures limited to single behaviors) or at the syndromal level (e.g., the various depression inventories, such as the Beck Depression Inventory [BDI] [Beck, Ward, Mendelson, Mock, & Erbaugh, 1961], or clinician-rated scales, such as the Hamilton Rating Scale for Depression [HRS-D] [Hamilton, 1960]). For the purposes of sample designation for the comparative outcome studies, syndromal designation appears to be a necessary, but rarely sufficient, level of specification. Evidence from the pharmacological treatment literature (cf. Bielski & Friedel, 1976; Klein & Davis, 1969) points strongly toward heterogeneity with regard to treatment response both within groups sharing nosological classification and, more clearly, across groups sharing clinical levels of syndrome depression but heterogeneous with respect to nosological classification.

Sampling problems are particularly likely to emerge when moving from sub-clinical to clinical populations and from one level of clinical population to another (Hollon & Garber, 1979). The probability of an individual with a high score on a syndrome depression measure being classified as schizophrenic rises sharply when moving from analogue to outpatient to inpatient settings. Much of the current controversy over the generalizability of the findings from one ex-perimental psychopathological study (e.g., Suarez, Crowe, & Adams, 1978) may reflect the problems inherent in drawing different nosological samples when relying on syndromal sampling procedures.

When evaluating treatment effects, symptom (or sign) or syndromal mea-sures are frequently the only readily quantifiable measures available. Potential problems in these studies may arise from relying on symptom–sign levels of measurement to draw inferences regarding change on the syndromal level (e.g., relying solely on an adjective checklist to infer changes across the syn-drome of depression). Specific interventions may well generate changes in specific symptom–behavior clusters that may or may not be reflected in the full syndrome. Changing reported beliefs or specific behaviors may be viewed as desirable, but it is not necessarily evidence that changes across the syndrome have occurred.

## Comparisons and Combinations

Any two effective interventions might logically be expected to enhance one another's effectiveness, especially when the two modalities appear to operate through independent mechanisms or on different targets. Such pragmatic reasoning appears to lie behind efforts to combine presumably effective in-terventions, particularly pharmacological and psychosocial interventions for the affective disorders for which the drugs have been so well established.

While such efforts appear reasonable, benign or advantageous outcomes are by no means guaranteed. Figure 2.1 depicts the type of outcomes possible on any single index when two or more treatments are combined. Additivity, or joint effects equal to the sum of the two independent effects, and potentiation, or joint effects greater than the sum of the two independent effects, represent two classes of possible benign combinatorial outcomes. Inhibition, or joint effects lesser than the least effective single modality, and reciprocation type 2, or joint effects equivalent to the least effective modality, represent relatively undesirable outcomes, while reciprocation type 1, or joint effects equivalent to the more effective modality, represents a curiously neutral outcome. Taylor and Mar-shall's (1977) finding that the combination of cognitive and behavioral techni-ques exceeded the improvement rates associated with either modality alone represents an example of partial additivity. Our own experience, albeit unplan-ned, with the joint effects of electroconvulsive therapy (ECT) and cognitive therapy at the University of Minnesota indicates that the amnesic effects of ECT may produce an instance of reciprocation (whether type 1 or type 2 remains to

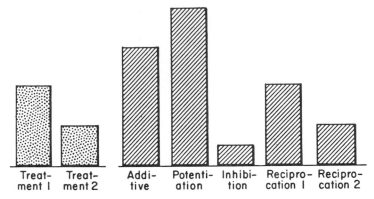

**Figure 2.1.** Possible drug–psychotherapy interactions. (Adapted by permission from E. H. Uhlenhuth, R. S. Lipman, & L. Covi, Combined pharmacotherapy and psychotherapy: Controlled studies. *Journal of Nervous and Mental Disease*, 1969, *148*, p. 60. © 1969, The Williams & Wilkins Co., Baltimore, and reprinted by permission from Hollon & Beck, 1979.)

be determined), producing near total loss of the specific skills associated with the pre-ECT training in cognitive–behavioral techniques. In an earlier review of the drug and psychotherapy comparative literature (Hollon & Beck, 1978), no instance of either positive or negative interaction resulting from the combination of pharmacological and psychosocial interventions could be found among reported outcome studies.

Issues of differential types of outcomes (see the following section, "Nature of the Outcome") would appear to be particularly fruitful areas of research. Behavioral and cognitive–behavioral interventions frequently entail the development of specific skills by treated patients. Such capacities might well be expected to survive the termination of active treatment. Unlike the various pharmaco- and somatic therapies, which do not appear to reduce the probability of relapse or recurrence[3] following withdrawal, the various skills training approaches appear likely candidates to provide prophylaxis against subsequent episodes. The very properties that appear to complicate efforts to utilize single-subject reversal designs may well serve to increase the stability of treatment gains over time. Combinatorial designs should be constructed so as to assess both acute symptom-reduction and maintenance indexes, since the combinatorial treatments may prove superior to single-modality interventions by virtue of producing changes across two or more outcome indexes rather than differential change on any given single outcome measure.

Finally, while the bulk of the studies in the literature involved drug-free behavioral or cognitive–behavioral interventions (e.g., Fuchs & Rehm, 1977;

---

[3] *Relapse* is used to refer to recrudesces of symptomatic states within the expected time-course of a given episode, typically 3–6 months after onset for outpatients or 6–9 months after onset for inpatients. *Recurrence* typically refers to the onset of a subsequent episode following a symptom-free interval following the end of the expected length of the initial episode, as outlined in the text (Prien & Caffey, 1977).

Shaw, 1977; Taylor & Marshall, 1977) or explicitly compared psychosocial interventions versus pharmacological interventions (McLean & Hakstian, 1979; McLean, Ogston, & Grauer, 1973; Rush, Beck, Kovacs, & Hollon, 1977) several studies either examined behavioral intervention efficacy in patients receiving ongoing pharmacotherapy (Hersen, Eisler, Alford, & Agras, 1973) or failed to specify whether drug treatments were or were not provided (e.g., Hannie & Adams, 1974). It is not clear that inferences drawn from these designs can be made without reference to the possible interaction between learning-based and pharmacological interventions. Collateral treatment status clearly needs to be specified and inferences regarding treatment efficacy stated, so as to leave open the possibility that differential interactions between classes of treatments, not specific single-modality effects, may have accounted for observed changes.

## Nature of the Outcome

Treatment outcome can be divided into several relevant components, as shown in Table 2.1. The *magnitude* of the outcome refers to the degree of reduction in manifest symptomatology. *Generality* refers to the range of symptom reduction shown by an individual, either across symptoms or across situations. *Universality* refers to the range of treatment effects across individuals. *Stability* refers to the maintenance of symptom reduction over time, whether the suppression of relapse or the prevention of subsequent recurrence. *Acceptability* refers to the likelihood of program acceptance and/or completion, the latter usually defined in terms of differential attrition (dropout) rates. Pharmacological regimes typically generate strong treatment response rates (e.g., 60–70% response rates in unselected samples [cf. Klein & Davis, 1969; Lehmann, 1977]) but also typically generate high dropout or noncompliance rates (e.g., 20–30% [Hollon & Beck, 1979]). *Safety* refers to the likelihood of undesirable complications associated with specific interventions. It is ironic, given the relationship between suicide and depression (Silverman, 1968), that the tricyclic antidepressants have one of the lowest active dosage to lethal dosage ratios of any of

**TABLE 2.1**

Types of Outcomes in Controlled Trials in the Treatment of Depression

| | |
|---|---|
| Magnitude | Amount of change in target behaviors or symptoms for any given or "average" patient |
| Generality | Across targets—range of target behaviors or symptoms evidencing change |
| | Across situations—range of situations in which changes in target behaviors or symptoms are evidenced |
| Universality | Percentage of individuals evidencing change |
| Stability | Maintenance of change over time |
| Acceptability | Likelihood of completion of treatment program by individuals |
| Safety | Freedom from undesirable complications associated with treatment |

the psychoactive medications in current usage. The potential for long-lasting memory impairment in electroconvulsive therapy may be offset by the reduction in distress in acutely symptomatic, frequently suicidal depressed inpatients, but such potential dangers have spurred the desire to develop more benign interventions.

Distinctions between these various classes of outcomes can provide guides to a more thorough evaluation of intervention efficacy. Different interventions may prove differentially effective with respect to these various types of outcomes, as suggested in the example provided earlier in which learning-based interventions, when effective, might be expected to be more stable over time than pharmacotherapies. Similarly, explicit skills training programs might be expected to be more stable than externally manipulated contingency management programs if those contingencies cannot be continued into the posttreatment environment.

## Mechanisms of Action and Outcomes

Mechanisms of action are those processes presumed to be central to the change process. Typically, relevant mechanisms are specified by a given theory; for example, the goal of an intervention inspired by Seligman's helplessness theory (Seligman, 1975) might be to alter the perception of noncontingency, while the goal of a Lewinsohnian approach (Lewinsohn, 1974) might be to increase the rate of response-contingent reinforcement. In either instance, the ultimate goal involves the reduction in syndrome depression, and this latter goal can be viewed as the major outcome of interest. Documenting changes in the mechanism of interest may be necessary to corroborate theoretical formulations of the change process, but such documentation does not in itself establish the existence of change across the full syndrome. Assessing mechanisms independently of outcomes plays the same role as conducting independent manipulation checks in the typical experiment. The adequate evaluation of any theory of change requires at least three levels of assessment:

1. Was the treatment implemented in an adequate fashion?
2. Did the treatment alter those processes reflective of the mechanisms specified by theory to be central to change?
3. Were the desired outcomes, defined in an atheoretical fashion, produced?

Two articles provide examples of attempts to specify the nature of the mechanism underlying change. Zeiss, Lewinsohn, and Munoz (1979) compared behavioral, (a variation of) cognitive, and interpersonal approaches with a waiting-list control. All three active treatment groups evidenced greater change than did the waiting-list controls on syndrome depression measures, but none of the three differed from one another with respect to change on specific measures targeted at processes that should have changed differentially with the approaches. The lack of evidence for specific mechanisms, combined with the comparable rates of change across the three active treatment groups, led the authors to conclude that change was the product of nonspecific factors. On the other hand, Rush *et al.* (1979) found that changes in cognitive processes were more likely to precede changes in syndrome depression for patients treated with cognitive–behavioral psychotherapy than for patients treated by tricyclic pharmacotherapy, supporting the notion of differential specific mechanisms of action.

### Overlapping Mechanisms of Action and Procedures

Finally, efforts to evaluate treatment efficacy are frequently confounded by the apparent overlap between both the apparent mechanisms of action and the procedures used to produce change. Descriptions of treatment programs frequently involve multiple techniques and less frequently involve efforts at component analyses. Studies by Taylor and Marshall (1977) and Rehm, Kornblith, O'Hara, Lamparski, Romano, and Volkin (1978) provide notable exceptions. Cognitive therapy (Beck, Rush, Shaw, & Emery, 1979) not only involves cognitive change procedures but relies heavily on enactive behavioral techniques. Similarly, McLean and Hakstian (1979) utilized a predominantly behavioral intervention, but incorporated some cognitive change procedures, in a comparison with pharmacotherapy and a variety of alternative psychosocial interventions. This overlap makes it difficult to classify treatment programs with respect to type, frustrating efforts to specify which components, or combinations of components, produced the observed effects.

## Review of the Outcome Literature

Therapeutic interventions in depression can be divided into several basic categories, based largely on distinctions between the processes seen as desirable to alter and the procedures used to produce those alterations (Bandura, 1977). As shown in Table 2.2, the various classes of interventions can be grouped into pharmacological, somatic, dynamic, behavioral, and cognitive approaches. The behavioral interventions can be further subdivided into several broad categories: (*a*) the affect-mediated interventions; (*b*) the outcome-mediated interventions; and (*c*) the self-control approaches. Distinctions between the self-control and the various cognitive approaches are frequently particularly arbitrary; covariant control strategies, typically designed to alter the nature and flow of covert or cognitive events, are sometimes classed with self-control approaches (Rehm & Kornblith, 1979) and at other times classed with cognitive approaches (Hollon & Beck, 1978). Certainly, a distinction between efforts to modify the occurrence of specific covert events can be distinguished from efforts to modify the subjective validity ascribed to that cognition when it occurs. This latter process, typically referred to as "cognitive restructuring," appears to be particularly important to the cognitive approaches.

Cognitive therapy as described by Beck and colleagues (Beck, 1970; Beck *et al.*,

**TABLE 2.2**
Types of Interventions

| Type of treatment | Processes | Procedure | Examples |
|---|---|---|---|
| Pharmacological | Biochemical imbalance | Pharmacotherapy | Tricyclics MAO inhibitors Lithium Other drugs |
| Somatic | Biochemical imbalances | Somatic interventions | Convulsive therapies Sleep deprivation |
| Dynamic | Unconscious motivational processes | Catharsis and/or insight | Traditional supportive Depth psychotherapy |
| Behavioral Affect-mediated | Inhibition of reinforceable behaviors via anxiety | Reduction of conditioned anxiety | Systematic desensitization Flooding Implosion |
| Outcome-mediated | Deficit in reinforcement or excess in punishment | Increase in reinforcement or reinforceable behaviors | Contingency management Skills training |
| Self-control | Deficit in self-reinforcement or excess in self-punishment | Increase in self-administered reinforcement or decrease in self-punishment | Coverant control Anticipatory training Self-control training |
| Cognitive | Maladaptive beliefs and distorted information processing | Hypothesis testing via enactive and empirical procedures | Cognitive therapy |
|  |  | Persuasion via deductive reasoning | Rational–emotive therapy |

1979) is included here as a combined cognitive–behavioral intervention. While the basic theory underlying cognitive therapy focuses on alterations in the flow, content, and subjective validity ascribed to cognition, specific techniques utilized may involve either cognitive or behavioral procedures and may be targeted at either cognitive or behavioral targets. Most typically, an effort is made to integrate both cognitive and behavioral procedures to produce change in any given response–outcome sequence. More strictly cognitive approaches, such as Ellis's rational emotive therapy, appear to share an adherence to a cognitive theory of depression but to utilize enactive procedures to a lesser extent than do approaches following Beck's model.

## Pharmacological Interventions

A massive body of literature exists documenting the efficacy of a variety of pharmacological agents in the treatment of depression. Chief among these agents are the tricyclic antidepressants, the monoamine oxidase inhibitors, and lithium. All three classes of medications have been clearly established as effective agents in the treatment of depression (c.f. American Psychiatric Association Task Force, 1975; Cole, 1964; Klerman & Cole, 1965; Morris & Beck, 1974; Rogers & Clay, 1975), with the various agents apparently evidencing different levels of efficacy with different subtypes of depressives.

Imipramine and amitriptyline appear to be the most widely used and, perhaps, the most effective of the tricyclic agents. Both agents are tertiary amines, although the two compounds appear to have somewhat separate effects on CNS neurotransmitter systems, with imipramine impacting most directly on the andrenonergic systems (e.g., norepinepherine) and amitriptyline appearing to impact most directly on the indoleaminic systems (e.g., serotonin). At this time, it remains uncertain whether either compound can be said to produce clearly superior treatment responses; reviews point toward some small advantage for amitriptyline. Morris and Beck (1974) found amitriptyline superior to imipramine in four of seven direct comparisons, with two ties and one comparison favoring imipramine. Ban (1974), reviewing a similar time span but using somewhat different criteria, found two comparisons favoring amitriptyline, three equivalent outcomes, and one comparison favoring imipramine. Biochemical evidence linking superior imipramine response to initially reduced levels of urinary 3-methoxy-4-hydroxy-phenethylene-glycol (MHPG) and superior amitriptyline response to normal or elevated levels of urine MHPG may provide the basis for future biochemical classificatory and predictive systems (Schildkraut, 1973a, 1973b, 1977), but the available evidence is far from conclusive. More relevant are published reports indicating a disproportionate distribution of "serotonin" depressions in unselected clinically depressed samples (Schildkraut, Orsulak, Schatzberg, Guderman, Cole, Rohde, & LaBrie, 1978a, 1978b). If replicated, such evidence should point toward a greater probability of response for unselected depressives to amitriptyline than to imipramine. However, it is by no means clear that biochemical models are sufficiently well developed at this time to support such speculation. Further, even if borne out, such predictions regarding differential treatment response require corroboration in comparative outcome trials.

Despite their widespread use and the impressive number of studies in which average response rates for the drugs exceeded those for the placebo, the magnitude, generality, universality, stability, acceptability, and safety of the pharmacotherapies can be questioned. The bulk of the reviews of the magnitude of drug-related trials are reported in terms of the percentage of patients evidencing a specific level of response, for example a 50% reduction in initial symptom levels (Klerman, DiMascio, Weissman, Prusoff, & Paykel, 1974) or simple "improvement" versus "unimprovement" designations extracted from clinician ratings (cf. Cole, 1964; Klein & Davis, 1969; Klerman & Cole, 1965; Rogers & Clay, 1975). It is not clear from such reviews what absolute magnitude of symptom reduction can be associated with pharmacological treatment. In both trials comparing drugs with either behavioral or cognitive–behavioral interventions, the modal pharmacotherapy patients ended treatment far less symptomatic than they began but still at least two standard deviations above normative levels on normed syndrome depression measures (McLean & Hakstian, 1979; Rush et al., 1977). While drugs are clearly associated with specific relative reductions in symptom levels, it is not clear that they necessarily produce clinically adequate remission in absolute terms.

Drug efficacy can also be questioned with regard to generality. Greater attention needs to be paid to the rates of change across the various components of syndrome depression. At this time, it is not clear whether symptom reduction is distributed evenly across all components of the syndrome or unevenly across specific clusters of behaviors and symptoms. Universality remains particularly problematic, with predictive studies still contradictory and inconclusive (see Bielski & Friedel, 1976, for a review). One example involves the traditional characterization of "endogenous" depressions as being more responsive to medication than "neurotic" depressions. Table 2.3, calculated from figures provided in a review by Rogers and Clay (1975) of 30 controlled imipramine–placebo comparisons, illustrates this point. Endogenous patients are typically considered more likely to be drug responsive than neurotic patients, yet the percentage of improved versus unimproved patients, based on those studies reviewed by Rogers and Clay, appears almost equal between the two presumed subtypes.

Treatment acceptability also remains problematic, in part related to the existence of small but important subsets of depressed patients who cannot tolerate various medications because of the occurrence of noxious or life-threatening side effects. Further, it is unclear to what extent nonparticipation in

**TABLE 2.3**
Percentage Improvement by Patient Subtype[a]

| Subtype | Imipramine | | | Placebo | | |
|---|---|---|---|---|---|---|
| | Improved | Treated | Percentage | Improved | Treated | Percentage |
| Endogenous | 200 | 318 | 63 | 85 | 289 | 29 |
| Neurotic | 72 | 104 | 69 | 12 | 113 | 11 |
| Mixed sample | 189 | 293 | 64 | 100 | 217 | 46 |
| Total | 461 | 715 | 64 | 197 | 619 | 32 |

[a] Calculated from figures in Rogers & Clay, 1975.

or attrition from controlled trials limits the external validity of claims for pharmacological efficacy. In some trials, dropout rates have approached 50% of the selected sample, and rates of 20–30% of the selected samples are not atypical (Hollon & Beck, 1979). While efforts to determine the precise reasons for treatment termination are always difficult, it is possible that estimates of drug response are inflated by the exclusion of nonresponsive dropouts who have self-selected out of the trials.

Difficulties involving treatment stability and safety have already been discussed. It is clear that pharmacological practice is moving in the direction of increased reliance on maintenance medication strategies, both for bipolar and nonbipolar populations (American Psychiatric Association Task Force, 1975; Davis, 1976; Schou, 1976). While there currently exists little or no evidence suggesting the existence of hazards associated with long-term antidepressant maintenance therapies, the recency of the approach may have had more to do with this absence of evidence than the actual safety of the procedure. The existence of tardive dyskinesia following long-term phenothiazine therapy in schizophrenia did not become evident until after decades of use.

Despite the issues raised in this section, the various pharmacotherapies remain the current standard of treatment for the bulk of the affective populations. However, it is clear that while the various pharmacotherapies are currently the best-established interventions, they remain far from ideal answers to the problems raised by the clinical depressions.

*Electroconvulsive Therapies*

To date, no study has evaluated the comparative efficacy of any behavioral or cognitive–behavioral intervention either in contrast to or in combination with the various convulsive therapies. Several studies have utilized traditional psychotherapy or milieu group therapy approaches as treatment controls in open trials of ECT efficacy with inpatient depressives (Holbrock, 1948; Huston & Locker, 1948; Tillotson & Sulzbach, 1945). All three trials reported comparable rates between groups, but the length of hospitalization proved to be shorter for patients receiving ECT. Postdischarge suicide rates were greater in the non-ECT cell in the Huston and Locker study.

In general, the available outcome literature appears to indicate favorable outcomes in association with ECT (Turek & Hanlon, 1977). Typically, convulsive therapies are applied only to severely depressed patients and generally, but not necessarily, limited to inpatient populations. The notion of differential relative efficacy with different subtypes of depressions (e.g., psychotic versus neurotic, unipolar versus bipolar, endogenous versus reactive) appears firmly entrenched in clinical lore but is not documented by adequately controlled clinical trials. At issue is the apparent tendency for more severe, symptomatically endogenous depressed patients to evidence a greater differential response to any of several active treatments relative to inert controls (Bielski & Friedel,

1976). In general, ECT appears to be superior to chemotherapy in terms of producing remission of acute symptomatology (Greenblatt, Grosser, & Wechsler, 1962; Pickering, Bowlby, & Cochrane, 1965), but predicting differential response by individual patients remains quite problematic. Lehmann (1977), in summarizing the available outcome literature, reports "average" relative response rates for "severely" depressed inpatients as follows: no treatment (20%), pill-placebo (40%), antidepressant pharmacotherapy (70%), and ECT (90%). It should be emphasized that these estimates, even if relatively accurate, reflect the percentage of patients evidencing some set degree of relative improvement, not absolute improvement levels.

Two additional concerns remain regarding ECT: stability over time and relative safety. There is little, if any, indication that ECT provides any prophylactic effect on relapse or recurrence rates beyond the active treatment period. Maintenance ECT has received relatively little investigation. Two existing, albeit relatively uncontrolled, studies (Kerman, 1957; Stevenson & Goegehan, 1951) point toward positive outcomes in terms of reducing postepisode rehospitalizations. It is an open question whether the combination of ECT and a learning-based treatment procedure would improve on stability rates over ECT alone. One pragmatic problem involves the tendency for ECT-treated patients to experience amnesia for recent experiences, for example, recently acquired skills in a behavioral or cognitive–behavioral program.

The relative safety of ECT also remains problematic. Estimates of mortality rates range from .08% to .10% for all treated patients, indicating that iatrogenic mortality is a relatively improbable, but still possible, event. More troubling are reports of memory deficits and impairment in intellectual functioning. Evidence for permanent impairment is inconclusive (Turek & Hanlon, 1977), but the occurrence of temporary amnesia appears clearly documented. The occurrence of fractures and contusions during convulsions appears to have been largely eliminated by the use of muscle relaxants, while the use of unilateral rather than bilateral electrode placement appears to reduce the occurrence of intellectual deficits (Abrams, 1972). While iatrogenic deterioration appears unlikely with behavioral approaches, there is evidence that inadequate treatment may be associated with greater subsequent mortality and stress-related illness (Avery & Winokur, 1976).

Our own experience with ECT-cognitive therapy combinations has been limited to a single case study (DeRubeis, Hollon, & Wiemer, 1979). In this study, a 24-year-old depressed female inpatient with a history of multiple hospitalizations was treated with an intensive regime of cognitive–behavior therapy (four sessions per week for 3 weeks), following 4 months of nonresponse to ECT, tricyclic antidepressants, and a monoamine oxidase (MAO) inhibitor. Self-reported depression scores on the BDI decreased over the 3-week period, leading to discharge to further outpatient treatment. The absence of formal pre-cognitive therapy assessments, the continuation of MAO medications, and the potential placebo effects from initiating a novel treatment effort all prevent attributing benign outcomes to the initiation of cognitive therapy. Nonetheless, the case study clearly demonstrates the feasibility of conducting a cognitive–behavioral intervention with at least one severely depressed, non-ECT responsive inpatient.

### Dynamic Interventions

Traditional dynamic interventions have, in the past, fared poorly in controlled trials, whether compared with nonspecific control conditions or with the various pharmacological or somatic interventions (see Hollon & Beck, 1978, 1979 for reviews). Seven studies have compared traditional dynamic interventions with pharmacotherapy, in terms of either acute symptom reduction (Cole, Patterson, Craig, Thomas, Ristine, Stahly, & Pasamanick, 1959; Covi, Lipman, Derogatis, Smith, & Pattison, 1974; Daneman, 1961; Friedman, 1975; Olson, 1961; Weissman, Prusoff, DiMascio, Neu, Goklaney, & Klerman, 1979) or the prevention of subsequent relapse or recurrence (Klerman *et al.,* 1974).

In the Friedman and the Klerman *et al.* designs (see also Weissman, Klerman, Paykel, Prusoff, & Hanson, 1974, for an extended report), traditional interventions were associated with positive gains on indexes other than syndrome depression. Thus, Friedman found that couples receiving marital therapy reported improvement in their marital relationships, while patients in the Klerman–Weissman studies receiving interpersonally oriented social casework therapy were found to exhibit improved interpersonal skills and to report relationships to be more satisfying. Such findings point toward positive outcomes with combinatorial interventions, in which each respective intervention operates on a different class of outcomes (Klerman, Paykel, & Prusoff, 1973).

Such outcomes may be desirable, but they still do not demonstrate any specific efficacy for the dynamic interventions on syndrome depression. One particularly troublesome conceptual problem that has run across both experimental psychopathological studies and treatment outcome studies of depression has been the tendency to attribute causal status to correlated deficits (Miller, 1975). Identifying some deficit (e.g., unsatisfying interpersonal relationships, suppression of aggression and/or assertive behavior, deficits in self-control skills, or distortions in cognitive content or process) then intervening to alter that deficit may produce desirable changes in both the deficit and syndrome depression, in either alone, or in neither. The issue of change with respect to syndrome depression clearly needs to be addressed independently from the assessment of changes in the deficit. The distinction lies between presumed mechanism and observed outcome.

Only one of these studies, Weissman *et al.* (1979), reportedly documents a specific therapeutic effect for traditional interpersonal psychotherapy (IPT) on syndrome depression as well as on social relations (although problems involving differential attrition may vitiate such a conclusion). Such an outcome is clearly discrepant from the earlier Klerman–Weissman *et al.* trial, which involved a forerunner of IPT. It is not clear whether this greater efficacy is the product of refinements in therapy technique (see Klerman, Rounsaville, Chevron, Neu, & Weissman, 1979, for an expanded IPT manual), the switch from a maintenance to an acute intervention design, or an artifact in experimentation. If this latter report proves replicable, the relatively pessimistic view concerning the lack of efficacy of the traditional dynamic therapist will need to be revised.

## Behavioral Interventions

The behavioral interventions can be divided into the affect-mediated (classical), outcome-mediated (operant), and self-control approaches. The combinatorial cognitive–behavioral interventions will be discussed in the section on cognitive approaches.

### AFFECT-MEDIATED INTERVENTIONS

The affect-mediated approaches are predicated on the theory that conditioned anxiety serves to inhibit the emission of behaviors that might have resulted in satisfying states of affairs (Lazarus, 1968; Wolpe, 1971; Wolpe & Lazarus, 1966). Treatment procedures selected by adherents to this model have typically focused on standard behavioral techniques designed to decondition anxiety—systematic desensitization, flooding, and implosive therapy. Variations have included systematic resensitization (Lazarus, 1968; Sammons, 1974), a combination of relaxation training and imaginal presentation of "reinforcing" hierarchies, and the antidepressive programs (ADPs) (Patterson, Taulbee, Golsom, Horner, & Wright, 1968). The ADPs involve the planned provocation of patients until they rebel in anger against ward conditions. While also couched in assertion training terminology, such programs appear to provide little explicit behavioral skills training, relying rather on provocation to anger and reinforcement of the resultant noncompliant behavior.

*Systematic Desensitization.* In general, the affect-mediated behavioral approaches have been evaluated by means of methodologically inadequate case studies or nonequivalent groups designs (Badri, 1971; Rosenthal & Meyer, 1971; Seitz, 1971; Shapiro, Neufeld, & Post, 1962; Wanderer, 1972; see also Blaney, Chapter 1, and Craighead, Chapter 3, this volume for extended reviews). McLean and Hakstian (1979) provided the only adequately controlled groups design involving relaxation training (sans progressive exposure to hierarchy items). Standard progressive relaxation training proved no more effective than an inadequate dosage of imipramine (150 mg per day), more effective than traditional psychotherapy, and less effective than behavioral skills training in reducing syndrome depression.

*Systematic Resensitization.* Systematic resensitization (Lazarus, 1968; Sammons, 1974) involves relaxation paired with imaginal rehearsal of positive outcomes and subsequent behavioral assignments. Only case descriptions were provided, and it is not clear that reported benign treatment outcomes can be attributed to the specific aspects of the interventions.

*Flooding.* Flooding procedures, designed to elicit maximum exposure to arousing stimuli, have been utilized in attempts to reverse anxiety presumed to mediate depressions. Ramsay (1977) described using contact and imaginal flooding to treat severe grief reactions, describing a successfully treated patient exhibiting a severe grief reaction (Ramsay, 1976). In the only adequately controlled equivalent groups design evidencing a favorable outcome for the anxiety-reduction techniques, Hannie and Adams (1974) compared flooding, nonspecific supportive group therapy, and no-treatment (standard ward milieu) conditions with depressed–anxious inpatient females. Subjects in the flooding condition evidenced greater reductions on the Multiple Affect Adjective Checklist (MAACL) (Zuckerman & Lubin, 1965). Differences on relevant items from the Mental Status Schedule (MSS) (Spitzer, Burdock, & Hardesty, 1964) favored the flooding cell over the nonspecific control, but neither cell differed from the milieu-only condition. Attrition rates and follow-up data were not reported.

While somewhat supportive of the efficacy of flooding in this population, several problems are apparent with the study. First, all subjects were selected on the basis of being both anxious and depressed. The major outcome measure, the MAACL, in addition to being a solely symptomatic measure, combined indexes of anxiety and depression. Given the probable beneficial effects of flooding on anxiety per se, it is not clear from the reported analyses that syndrome depression (or even symptom depression) was directly impacted by treatment. Further, it is not clear whether patients in the trial were or were not on medications.

*Implosion.* Beutler (1973) and Hogan (1966) reported utilizing implosive therapy, involving the use of dynamically relevant hierarchy content, in a flooding-type intervention to reduce anxiety presumably mediating depression. As with the systematic desensitization approaches, only inadequately controlled case reports are presented to support claims of treatment efficacy. At this time, there appears to be little documentation of any specific effectiveness.

*Antidepressive Programs (ADPs).* Initial tests of the ADPs have generated generally positive outcomes (Barnes, 1977; Patterson *et al.,* 1968; Taulbee & Wright, 1971a, 1971b; Wadsworth & Barker, 1976) but have yet to be conducted in an adequately controlled groups or single-subject design. It should be noted that the ADPs involve several components, including provocation to the point of anger, behavioral assertion (spontaneously emitted by the patient), and successful modification of the previously aversive environment. Given the demonstrated effects of personal efficacy on subsequent performance and affect (Klein & Seligman, 1976; Loeb, Beck, & Diggory, 1971), controlled studies are clearly needed to deconfound anger provocation from the experience of success before concluding that the provocation strategies produce desirable treatment effects.

Overall, despite the existence of several clinical case descriptions, non-equivalent groups designs, and two adequately controlled groups designs, the efficacy of the various behavioral approaches targeted at reducing anxiety that presumably mediates depressive reactions remains uncertain. While some evidence does exist pointing to the efficacy of flooding as a short-term intervention for anxious–depressed patients in an inpatient sample (Hannie & Adams, 1974), it is not clear that that treatment impacted either directly or indirectly on depression per se. Further, with medication status left unspecified, it is difficult to determine whether treatment effects reflect the behavioral interventions only or the interaction of drugs and behavior therapy. In the only other controlled groups design (McLean & Hakstian, 1979), progressive relaxation training was superior only to traditional psychotherapy and decidedly less effective than an operantly oriented behavior skills training approach. The available evidence does not appear to offer strong support for the utility of the affect-mediated approaches.

OUTCOME-MEDIATED APPROACHES

The outcome-mediated approaches typically seek to alter the amount of response-contingent reinforcement available, by means of contingency management procedures and/or behavioral skills training procedures (see Rehm & Kornblith, 1979, for a review). Contingency management procedures have ranged from the less structured, within-session procedures, usually combined with behavioral feedback and skills training, to the more structured environmental management programs. The nature of the program frequently reflects practical management considerations, with the bulk of the less structured and/or informational-skills training categories being conducted with outpatients and the bulk of the studies involving token management procedures being conducted in inpatient settings.

*Instructional and In-Session Contingency Management.* Several studies have explored the utility of instructional and contingency management procedures with depressed patients (Burgess, 1969; Lewinsohn, 1976; Lewinsohn & Atwood, 1969; Lewinsohn & Shaffer, 1971; Lewinsohn & Shaw, 1969; Liberman, 1970; Liberman & Raskin, 1971; Mogan & O'Brien, 1972). While generally supportive, none of these designs incorporated adequate controls to document treatment efficacy. In three other studies (Johansson, Lewinsohn, & Flippo, 1969; Robinson & Lewinsohn, 1973a, 1973b), operant procedures were used to modify speech content in depressives. No index of depression other than speech content was assessed. Controlled group comparisons between behavioral approaches designed to increase pleasant activities have typically provided little support for this approach (Barrera, 1977; Lewinsohn & Biglan,

1975; Lewinsohn, Munoz, Youngren & Zeiss, 1976; Padfield, 1976; Zeiss et al., 1979).

Padfield (1976) compared a behavior therapy program modeled on Lewinsohn's programs with a nondirective relationship therapy, designed to provide noncontingent positive regard. All clients were depressed females recruited via newspaper ads and physician referral. The sole difference observed across four measures—the Zung Self-Rating Depression Scale (SDS) (Zung, 1965), the Lubin Depression Adjectives Checklist (DACL) (Lubin, 1967), the Pleasant Events Schedule (PES) (MacPhillamy & Lewinsohn, 1975), and the Grinker Feelings and Concerns Checklist (GFCC) (Grinker, Miller, Sabshin, Nunn, & Nunnally, 1961)—occurred on the GFCC and favored the behavior therapy program.

Finally, Zeiss et al. (1979) have provided a particularly thorough comparison of behavior therapy (focused on increasing the rate of pleasant activities), a cognitive intervention developed at Oregon, an interpersonal skills training program, and a waiting-list control. As described in the section on "Mechanisms of Action and Outcomes," measures were also taken of those processes that should have mediated change in the various interventions. All modalities were superior to the waiting-list control, but none differed from one another with regard to the apparent mechanism of action. All were clearly effective, but it is unclear from the data whether this effectiveness was due to nonspecific mechanisms or to different specific mechanisms that uniformly impacted syndrome depression and all mechanism measures. The issue of specificity has implications for outcome, since nonspecific control groups have typically produced marginal but detectable improvement in depression.

Overall, the available outcome literature relative to these various approaches is not overwhelmingly supportive. Combined with the relatively weak demonstrated efficacy in two other controlled groups designs (Shaw, 1977; Taylor & Marshall, 1977; reviewed in the section on cognitive therapies), one must begin to question the efficacy of these various techniques in effecting changes in syndrome depression.

*Environmental Contingency Management.* Several studies have evaluated the direct manipulation of external reinforcements in contingency management procedures (Hanaway & Barlow, 1975; McQueen, 1973; Reisinger, 1972; Thompson, Errickson, Pickens, Heston, & Eckert, 1978). Findings have generally been supportive of the utility of this approach, although the relatively uncontrolled nature of these designs prevent drawing strong conclusions.

Hersen, Eisler, Alford, and Agras (1973) utilized a token economy system to modify work, responsibility, occupational therapy, and personal hygiene behaviors in three neurotically depressed male inpatients. Experimental control over the target behaviors was demonstrated by means of an ABA design. Concurrent changes in rates of smiling, talking, and motor activity as measured by nurses' ratings on the Behavioral Rating Scale (BRS) (Williams, Barlow, & Agras, 1972) paralleled contingency-related increases and decreases in target behaviors. While the BRS was found to covary with syndrome depression measures (both the HRS-D and the BDI) in the earlier Williams *et al.* study, the ratings served as the sole syndromal-level depression measure in the Hersen *et al.* design. While the demonstration of contingency-related changes in discrete behaviors in depressed patients is in itself noteworthy, it is not clear that syndrome depression per se as opposed to specific behaviors, was brought under experimental control. Inclusion of syndromal or, minimally, additional affective, vegetative, and/or cognitive indexes would have strengthened the conclusions that could have been drawn from this otherwise well-executed design. Further, all three patients were on one or another form of medication during all treatment phases. It is not clear whether observed effects could be attributed solely to the effects of imposed contingencies or to the interaction of drug treatment and imposed contingencies.

In general, these studies are somewhat encouraging. Evidence that depressed patients respond to reinforcement contingencies (at least positive reinforcement and response cost) provides a guide to pragmatic management techniques. None of the studies examined relative response between depressed and nondepressed patients. Little evidence exists, as yet, indicating that operant techniques differentially influence syndrome depression, while existing evidence speaks against the stability of treatment effects following the termination or reversal of explicit therapeutic contingencies.

*Assertion Training.* Assertion training programs seek to enhance assertive interpersonal skills, as in studies by Lazarus (1968); Lewinsohn, Weinstein, and Alper (1970); Rimm (1967); and Wells, Hersen, Bellack, and Himmelhoch (1977). All four sets of investigators reported associated reductions in depressive symptoms, although methodological deficits precluded attributing such outcomes to treatments. In the only controlled groups evaluation, assertion training proved less effective than self-control training in reducing syndrome depression (Rehm, Fuchs, Roth, Kornblith, & Romano, 1979).

*Problem-Solving Training.* Caple and Blechman (1976) reported a single case study in which modeling, prompting, selective verbal praise, and between-session homework assignments were used to improve problem-solving skills in a depressed female outpatient. While desirable changes in life circumstances were reported, the extended length of treatment (17 months) and use of concurrent pharmacotherapy precluded attributing outcomes to specific interventions.

Shipley and Fazio (1973) reported two studies involving the teaching of problem-solving skills to psychometrically identified depressed college students. In Study 1, student volunteers were assigned to either "functional problem solving" (FPS), which included both cognitive and behavioral components, or a waiting-list control. As shown in Figure 2.2, pre- and posttreatment comparisons on the MMPI clearly favored the FPS cell. In Study 2, FPS versus a

nonspecific treatment control condition was crossed with outcome expectational manipulation versus no outcome expectational manipulation. Whereas
the relatively weak expectational manipulation had no demonstrable effect, both
FPS cells evidenced greater symptom reduction than either nonspecific control
condition.

Figure 2.2 provides a graphic illustration of relative pre- and posttreatment
effects on major syndrome depression measures. All comparative group studies published up until the time of the Hollon and Beck (1979) review providing
pre- and posttreatment means have been included (with the exception of the
Hannie and Adams [1974] design, which provided no sole measure of depression), in an effort to facilitate a crude comparison of treatment effects across
studies. While efforts at parametric comparisons of treatment effects across
disparate populations remain premature, the inclusion of standardized outcome
measures across trials can at least provide some initial guidelines. Perhaps the
most striking feature of the figure, discussed in greater detail in a later section, is
the consistent emergence of superior results for those interventions combining
behavioral and cognitive techniques over other modalities.

*Marital Skills Training.* McLean *et al.* (1973) provided one of the few
adequately controlled group comparisons supporting the efficacy of primarily
behavioral techniques. Twenty couples were identified in which one spouse
exhibited a clinical level of nonpsychotic depression. The couples either received 8 weeks of social learning therapy designed to enhance marital skills and
increase positive interactions or were referred back to the initial referral source
for treatment. Interventions in this latter cell were not controlled, varying from
supportive psychotherapy to pharmacological treatments. Social learning therapy consisted of weekly sessions involving training in social learning principles,
utilization of spouse feedback boxes (in which different-colored lights indicated
whether an interaction was seen as friendly or hostile, and reciprocal behavioral contracting. Scores on the DACL and summed scores on ratings of five target
problems indicated greater positive changes for the social learning treatment
group, both at treatment termination and at a 3-month follow-up. While inclusion of a depression measure at the syndromal rather than symptom level
would have strengthened the inferences that could be drawn, the study
nonetheless represents a clear instance of specific treatment efficacy.

In a second major comparative study, McLean and Hakstian (1979) compared behavior therapy with couples therapy, psychotherapy, pharmacotherapy,
and relaxation therapy in the treatment of 178 moderately depressed outpatients. Patients were selected on the basis of both syndromal and nosological
criteria. Clients in the behavior therapy cell were trained in self-monitoring
techniques and encouraged to engage in daily skill development activities.
Specific hierarchies of treatment goals were developed, and graded practice
and modeling were used to facilitate goal attainment in communicational,
behavioral, interactional, assertive, decision-making, problem-solving, and

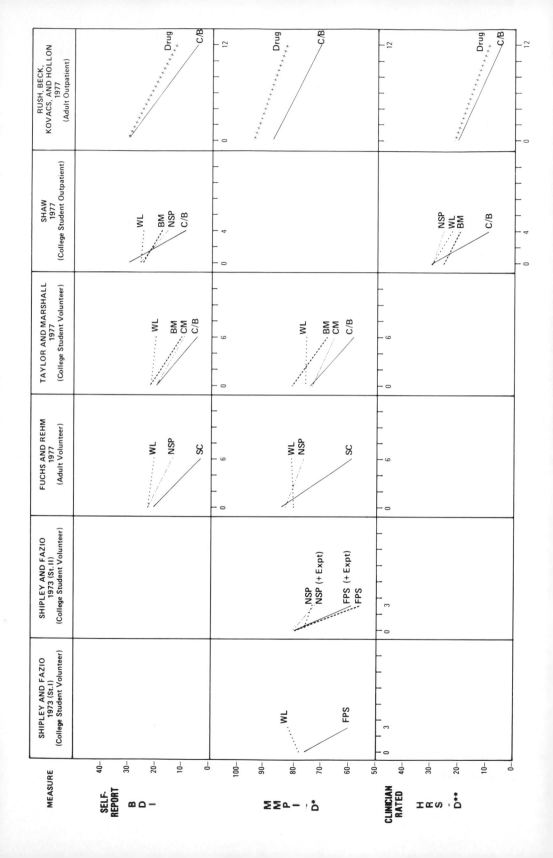

cognitive self-control domains. Patients in the pharmacotherapy cell were treated on a fixed dosage ratio of 125 mg of imipramine per day. Psychotherapy was directed at the relief of symptom complaints and the development of insight into the psychodynamic forces presumably initiating the episode. Relaxation training involved 10 1-hour sessions of structured relaxation training, with instructions to practice self-relaxation between sessions.

Outcome measures included the BDI and a variety of client ratings. Posttreatment results clearly favored the behavioral intervention over other treatment cells, while the psychotherapy cell evidenced the least change. Drug and relaxation cells did not differ from one another. Follow-up assessments at 3 months posttreatment evidenced marginal superiority for the behavior therapy cell. Therapist experience was not related to outcome.

This study represents a significant contribution to current knowledge regarding the efficacy of behavior therapies. The presence of differential gains for behavior therapy over traditional psychotherapy and the relaxation training control condition speaks directly to outcome specificity. Clearly, the behavior therapy produced greater change than was associated with the alternate interventions, controlling for contact, expectations, and extraneous change factors.

What the study does not do is speak to the relative comparability of drugs versus behavior therapy. The dosage utilized, a maximum of 125 mg per day, is well below typical dosage levels. It is not clear why a clearly inadequate drug dosage level was selected. The selection of an inadequate dosage level is particularly curious given the relative sophistication of the investigators, as indicated by the drawing of blood samples to provide checks on serum dosage levels.

One final comment involves differential dropout. As in the Rush et al. (1977) comparison between drugs and cognitive therapy, markedly differential attrition occurred between the pharmacotherapy and the learning-based treatment cells: 36% for drug therapy versus 5% in the McLean and Hakstian design, and 32% for drug versus 5% for cognitive therapy in the Rush et al. study. It is not clear whether such dropout rates are truly representative of pharmacotherapy trials or if they reflect difficulties in adequately implementing drug treatments by basically behaviorally oriented researchers. In the former case, differential acceptability may represent yet another, largely unrecognized, outcome index favorable to the learning-based approaches. In the latter instance, greater attention would need to be directed to the adequate implementation of pharmacotherapies

**Figure 2.2.** Pre–post group means in studies comparing cognitive–behavioral with alternative treatments. BDI = Beck Depression Inventory; MMPI-D = Minnesota Multiphasic Personality–Depression Scale; HRS-D = Hamilton Rating Scale for Depression; WL = Waiting List; NSP = Nonspecific; BM = Behavior Modification; CM = Cognitive Modification; FPS = Functional Problem Solving; SC = Self-Control; C/B = Cognitive Therapy;* = MMPI-D in Taylor and Marshall is MMPI-D(30);** = HRS-D in Shaw based on 21 items—in Rush et al. on 17 items, FPS, SC, and C/B are cognitive–behavioral interventions. (Reprinted from Hollon & Beck, 1979).

within the comparative trials. Evidence of differential ability to implement different cells in comparative trials is not new. In a recent reanalysis of drug–psychotherapy comparisons covered by Luborsky, Singer, and Luborsky (1975), psychotherapy proved superior to various control conditions in 67% of the instances in which the comparison occurred in the context of a study not involving any pharmacotherapy cell but in only 33% of the instances in which the comparison was embedded in a larger drug versus psychotherapy comparative study (DeRubeis & Hollon, 1979).

## SELF-CONTROL INTERVENTIONS

Self-control interventions typically involve attempts to train clients to apply behavior control strategies to modify their own overt and covert response processes. Techniques range from applications of Homme's coverant control strategies (Homme, 1966), typically utilized to alter the probability of various covert self-statements, to Rehm's more fully elaborated self-control therapy (Rehm, 1977), incorporating self-monitoring, self-evaluative, and self-reinforcement components.

*Coverant Control.* Coverant interventions have generally been evaluated in relatively inadequate single-case or nonequivalent groups designs. Mahoney (1971) reported the successful use of covert control strategies to alter obsessional thinking in a depressed male. Todd (1972) combined covert control strategies with various other behavioral techniques to reduce depressive symptoms in a female outpatient. Vasta (1976) and Johnson (1971) both utilized coverant control strategies to increase the frequency of positive self-statements in a depressed male college student.

*Anticipational Training.* The use of covert rehearsal of positive imagery to prompt behavioral activation was reported by Anton, Dunbar, and Friedman (1976) to reduce syndrome depression in nine female outpatient volunteers. This approach is somewhat similar to the use of time projection with positive imagery described by Lazarus (1968). It is not clear whether this approach best belongs with the self-control or the cognitive–behavioral techniques. In either instance, the approach appears to be an interesting innovation, but one that has yet to receive an adequately controlled trial.

*Self-Control.* Explicit self-reinforcement training was evaluated by Jackson (1972), working with a single female outpatient, while Tharp, Watson, and Kaya (1974) reported four case studies utilizing, respectively, self-monitoring of events, self-reinforcement, positive imagery, and the self-reinforcement of positive self-statements. In general, positive outcomes were reported, although design limitations limit the nature of the conclusions that can be drawn from these studies. In general, the studies demonstrate the feasibility of such interventions rather than clearly documenting treatment efficacy.

Three studies by Rehm and colleagues provide the most adequately controlled evaluations of self-control interventions in the literature. Fuchs and Rehm (1977) recruited female community volunteers for a comparison between self-control, nonspecific control, and waiting-list conditions. All treatment was conducted in a group format over a 6-week period. Treatment efficacy was evaluated by means of both the BDI and the MMPI-D scales.[4] As evidenced in Figure 2.2, subjects in the self-control treatment group exhibited greater improvement on both measures than either other treatment cell. A 1-month follow-up indicated that treatment gains were maintained, although differences between groups were significant for the MMPI only, with a trend on the BDI.

In a second controlled study, Rehm et al. (1979) compared self-control therapy with assertion skills training in a similar sample of female volunteers. Twenty-four females between the ages of 21 and 60 were assigned to weekly group sessions in either modality over a 6-week interval. Outcome criteria included the MMPI-D scale and BDI as syndrome depression measures, with mechanism of action measures provided by self-control questionnaires, role-play measures of social skills, and the PES. The assertion skills training evidenced greater change on the role-play measures, whereas the self-control cells evidenced greater change not only on self-control measures but also on syndrome depression. Treatment gains were maintained at a 6-week posttermination follow-up.

One cautionary note is in order. While the two controlled studies just reviewed speak directly to the issue of treatment efficacy for Rehm's self-control approach, an effort at component analysis appears to have provided a somewhat surprising outcome (Rehm et al., 1978). Rehm and colleagues compared self-monitoring versus self-monitoring plus self-evaluation versus self-monitoring plus self-evaluation plus self-reinforcement components of the self-control approach. Interestingly, the maximum therapeutic gain was associated with the self-monitoring alone cell; the addition of self-evaluative and self-reinforcement components appeared to be associated with lesser treatment efficacy.

Overall, the self-control strategies appear to have generated rather impressive supportive evidence in a relatively brief period of time. Specific comparative and/or combinative studies involving alternate interventions (e.g., pharmacotherapy or cognitive therapy) appear indicated. Similarly, attention should be directed to testing the generality of the treatment's efficacy for more clearly clinical populations.

---

[4] The MMPI has frequently been considered to be an insensitive change measure. McNair (1974), for example, labeled the performance of the depression subscale "disappointing" after reviewing the percentage of studies utilizing various self-report measures evidencing significant drug–placebo or drug–drug differences. In addition to simply miscounting, McNair's procedures confounded measure sensitivity with study design factors. In a review focused on concordance between measures used in the same studies, the MMPI proved at least as sensitive as any of the standard self-report syndrome depression measures (Hollon & Mandell, 1979).

*Cognitive Therapies*

The cognitive therapies include those approaches that adhere to a cognitive theory in depression and that involve the use of cognitive and, in some instances, behavioral interventions in the treatment of depression. Two major types of interventions are typically included: variations of Beck's cognitive therapy (Beck, 1970; Beck et al., 1979) and variations of Ellis's rational emotive therapy (RET) (see Hauck, 1971, for a description of an RET model of depression). Despite its name, cognitive therapy, as described by Beck and colleagues, clearly involves the use of both cognitive change and behavior change techniques. In addition to such behavioral procedures as activity scheduling, graded task assignment, training in self-monitoring skills, role playing, skills training, and covert control strategies, heavy emphasis is placed on such cognitive change procedures as cognitive restructuring, hypothesis testing (using the client's beliefs and expectations as the hypotheses to be tested), alternative therapy, and attributional reevaluations. A key factor differentiating such procedures from coverant control strategies lies in the attention paid to the subjective validity ascribed to the covert events by the client, rather than restricting attention to the occurrence–nonoccurrence of the covert event in the functional chain. Cognitive and behavioral procedures are typically integrated around specific single response–outcome units rather than simply applied independently to different targets. A major distinction between cognitive therapy and RET lies in the strategies used to alter cognitions. In RET, change is typically pursued by means of persuasive communications and reasoned debate, as opposed to the greater reliance on the use of enactive procedures to test the client's beliefs in an empirical fashion typical of cognitive therapy.

COGNITIVE THERAPY

Rush, Khatami, and Beck (1975) provided an early description of three outpatient depressives treated with cognitive therapy. Although decreases in syndrome depression were observed, the lack of experimental controls precluded attributing improvement to the specific interventions. Studies by Schmickly (1976), Morris (1975), and Gioe (1975) provided partially controlled groups designs showing some evidence, albeit vitiated by design limitations, for treatment efficacy. Two doctoral dissertations, Kirkpatrick (1977) and Harpin (cited in Marks, 1978), reportedly did not find any treatment advantage with cognitive therapy, but the brevity of the treatment (four sessions) in the Kirkpatrick study and the small sample size (six per cell) in the Harpin design may have reduced the probability of finding such differences.

Studies by Shaw (1977) and Taylor and Marshall (1977) provided stronger evidence for treatment efficacy (see Figure 2.2). Shaw assigned college students requesting therapy at a university counseling center to either cognitive therapy, behavior therapy (following Lewinsohn and colleagues' program), a nondirective treatment control, or a waiting-list control. All active therapy modalities were conducted in small-group formats, with the investigator serving as the sole therapist for all subjects. Treatment efficacy was assessed by means of the BDI and clinician ratings on the HRS-D. Ratings on the HRS-D were made by raters blind to treatment conditions, operating from videotaped interviews. Results, as shown in Figure 2.2, clearly favored cognitive therapy over either the behavior therapy or the nondirective cells on both measures, with each of those two groups superior to the waiting-list control. Follow-up assessment at 1 month posttreatment evidenced a maintenance of treatment gains, although group differences no longer reached statistical significance.

Taylor and Marshall (1977) compared cognitive–behavioral treatment versus a strictly cognitive versus a strictly behavioral therapy in the treatment of psychometrically identified college student volunteers. A fourth cell consisted of a no-treatment control. Treatment, conducted by relatively inexperienced graduate student therapists, consisted of six sessions over 6 weeks. Outcome was assessed on three measures, including the BDI; MMPI-D 30 (Dempsey, 1964), a shortened version of the 60-item depression scale; and the Visual Analogue Scale (VAS) (Aiken, 1969). Posttreatment differences favored the combined cognitive–behavioral cell over either single modality alone. Both individual modalities evidenced greater symptom reduction than the no-treatment cell. Treatment gains were maintained at a 5-week follow-up, although mean differences were no longer statistically significant.

Combined with the relative dearth of successful outcomes in controlled group comparisons for programs modeled after Lewinsohn's behavioral program (cf. Barrera, 1977; Lewinsohn & Biglan, 1975; Lewinsohn et al., 1976; Padfield, 1976), the lesser efficacy of the strictly behavioral cells in the Shaw and the Taylor and Marshall studies speaks poorly for the relative efficacy of this type of intervention. To date, only McLean's more elaborate versions of behavioral interventions (McLean & Hakstian, 1979; McLean et al., 1973) have demonstrated greater efficacy than alternative-treatment control (as opposed to waiting-list control) conditions.

A study by Rush et al. (1977) compared cognitive therapy with imipramine pharmacotherapy. In the initial report, 41 depressed outpatients, defined both by syndromal and nosological criteria, were assigned to 12 weeks of either cognitive therapy or imipramine pharmacotherapy, in doses of up to 250 mg per day. Patients in the cognitive therapy cell were seen up to a maximum of 20 times over the 12-week treatment period. Therapists were, in general, relatively inexperienced psychiatric residents (although several psychologists and one clinical psychology intern also participated), and the typical treatment preference held by the modal therapist was for combined pharmacotherapy plus supportive contacts during acute episodes of depression.

Outcome was assessed by means of the BDI, MMPI, HRS-D, and Raskin Rating Scale for Depression (Raskin, Schulterbrandt, Reatig, & Rice, 1967). Posttreatment results indicated that, while both groups evidenced striking symptomatic improvement, change was significantly greater for the cognitive therapy patients. At the end of treatment, the mean cognitive therapy patient scored within a standard deviation of the mean for normative groups on the BDI and within two standard deviations on the MMPI-D scale, whereas the mean drug patient remained several standard deviations above the mean for normative groups on both measures. These results were paralleled by changes on the independent clinician-rated scales, although only the HRS-D reached significance (missing data points reduced the available sample sizes for the Raskin analyses).

Periodic reports of sample survival during follow-up (Hollon, Beck, Kovacs, & Rush, 1977a, 1977b; Hollon, Kovacs, Beck, & Rush, 1977; Kovacs, Rush, Beck, & Hollon, in press) included three additional cases in the pharmacotherapy cell, added to replace earlier dropouts. The Kovacs et al. report represents the most up-to-date follow-up report, taking the full sample through 1 year posttreatment. Results indicated that, while treatment gains were maintained, on the average, across both groups, considerable individual variability occurred within both cells in terms of clinical course. Group differences, while not always significant at all points during follow-up, did favor the cognitive therapy cell throughout the full 12-month posttreatment period. Individual relapse (recurrence?) rates for patients treated by pharmacotherapy were about twice those for cognitive therapy, and greater numbers of patients in the drug cell than in the cognitive therapy cell returned to therapy earlier during the follow-up period.

Despite the relatively adequate controls in the Rush et al. design, several problems are evident. First, raters were not blind to treatment group. Efforts to maintain a single blind evaluation were discarded when it became evident that raters were reliably detecting drug-treated patients on the basis of visible pharmacotherapy side effects. Second, the level of medication utilized, 250 mg per day, while near the upper limit of recommended daily dosage for imipramine, still falls below levels often utilized by more aggressive pharmacotherapists, particularly with initially nonresponsive patients. Third, the absence of blood serum drug levels leaves open the possibility that medication levels were inadequate for those specific individuals or that unreported noncompliance undermined the implementation of the pharmacotherapy. The ratio between oral dosage and blood serum levels of the tricyclics can vary by more than a factor of 30 across individuals, largely because of differential absorption potentials (Hammer, Idestrom, & Sjoquiat, 1966).

Somewhat more troublesome was the design calling for the initiation of drug withdrawal at the end of 10 weeks, with the final assessment point at 12 weeks. Currently available evidence (Prien & Caffey, 1977) suggests that postwithdrawal relapse following tricyclic therapy may well be forestalled by maintenance medication therapy. Clearly, the Rush et al. design must be interpreted as indicating the superiority of cognitive therapy over pharmacotherapy as typically practiced (at least at the time the comparison was conducted) not as might most aggressively be practiced. A distinction needs to be made between trials utilizing pharmacotherapy as an active control condition, in which it is argued that placebo controls can be assumed to have been unnecessary if the novel modality exceeds the improvement evidenced by an already established modality, and those trials comparing some intervention with pharmacotherapy to establish relative superiority.

Hollon, Bedrosian and Beck, (1979) have recently reported preliminary findings based on a controlled comparison between cognitive therapy and combined cognitive–pharmacotherapy. The tricyclic utilized in this trial was amitriptyline, up to 300 mg per day. Treatment lasted over 12 weeks, with subject selection and assessment procedures similar to those used in Rush *et al.* (1977). While posttreatment follow-up data are not yet available, end-of-treatment scores on the BDI and HRS-D indicate that both cells were associated with significant reductions in depression. The groups did not differ from one another at the end of treatment, nor did they differ from the cognitive therapy cell in Rush *et al.* in terms of the magnitude of change evidenced. Both cells did show a greater absolute change than the pharmacotherapy-alone cell in the Rush *et al.* study. These data appear to provide both a replication for Rush *et al.* and an indication that the addition of drugs to cognitive therapy adds nothing over cognitive therapy alone, at least with respect to the magnitude of symptom change.

Finally, initial efforts have been made to evaluate the efficacy of cognitive therapy conducted in a group format (see Hollon & Shaw, 1979, for a review). While treatment in the Shaw (1977) study was conducted in group sessions, no individual cognitive therapy format was available for comparative purposes. Shaw and Hollon (1978) have compared patients drawn from the same research setting with patients treated in the Rush *et al.* study. Group cognitive therapy patients responded at a level intermediate between the pharmacotherapy treated and the individually treated cognitive therapy patients. However, the essentially nonequivalent groups design precluded drawing any firm interpretations. Rush and Watkins (1978) have reported superior results with individual as opposed to group cognitive therapy in the treatment of depressed outpatients. However, some patients in the individual treatment cell received adjunctive pharmacotherapy, at the treating physician's discretion. The confounding of drug and individual cognitive therapy makes it impossible to compare individual versus group treatment modalities independently of interaction effects, and the confounding with the individual therapy cell makes comparisons between drug plus cognitive therapy versus cognitive therapy alone largely correlational in nature.

Overall, the evidence supporting the efficacy of cognitive therapy appears to be fairly strong, in terms of magnitude, acceptability, and stability of the intervention. Clearly, additional replications and extensions are indicated. Evaluation of the joint effects of drugs and cognitive therapy, as well as attempts at evaluation with as yet unevaluated populations (e.g., inpatients, bipolar depressives) appear desirable.

STRESS INOCULATION

Novaco (1977) described the application of a stress inoculation training strategy to a case involving a 38-year-old depressed male inpatient, described

as being neurotically depressed. Stress inoculation consists of three components: cognitive preparation, skills acquisition and behavioral rehearsal, and
application practice. All techniques were designed to enhance skills in handling
previously anger-provoking situations. Presumably, anger arousal, with episodic
inhibition and explosive behavior, produced depressive affect. Treatment was
reported to be followed by gains in appropriate anger-modulation skills. Unfortunately, no syndrome depression measures were obtained.

## RATIONAL EMOTIVE THERAPY

No controlled comparison of rational emotive therapy for depression appears
to exist, unless the strictly cognitive therapy cell in the Taylor and Marshall
(1977) is taken as being representative. In that design, the cognitive-only cell
proved superior to a waiting-list control, equivalent to behavior therapy only, and
less effective than a cognitive–behavioral combination. In a separate case study,
Greene (1973) described utilizing hypnotic techniques to facilitate the process
of implementing RET with a 38-year-old depressed female outpatient. Similarly,
Oliver (1977) described using a variant of RET to treat a female patient
depressed after her children had grown and left home.

Overall, there appears to be little evidence speaking either for or against the
utility of RET in depression. If the Taylor and Marshall study provides any guide,
those interventions emphasizing primarily cognitive procedures (persuasion,
discussion) without also incorporating enactive procedures appear to be relatively ineffective, perhaps superior to no treatment but less effective than
viable alternatives.

## Conclusions

Given the availability of several adequately controlled single-subject and
controlled groups designs, some tentative statements regarding the efficacy
and relative efficacy of the behavioral and cognitive–behavioral interventions
can now be made. These statements must be qualified with respect to type of
intervention, characteristics of the population, and nature of the outcome.

Overall, McLean's behavioral marital skills training, Rehm's self-control, and
Beck's cognitive therapy appear to have generated the most adequate indications of efficacy, at least with outpatient populations. It is still not clear whether
the samples studied by Rehm and colleagues are representative of clinical
outpatient samples, although available indexes point toward relative comparability. Behavioral approaches other than those listed have either remained
largely underevaluated (e.g., assertion training), untested in clinical samples
(e.g., problem solving), or restricted to specific populations (e.g., token economy programs in inpatient settings). Strictly behavioral programs do not
appear to have fared well relative to self-control or cognitive therapy procedures.
Affect-mediated approaches may prove particularly advantageous with clearly
mixed anxious and depressed patients, but specific efficacy in depression per se
remains unproven.

Comparisons with alternate types of interventions are few in number but relatively supportive of the efficacy of the learning-based approaches. Cognitive therapy was superior to pharmacotherapy or equal to combined cognitive–pharmacotherapy in terms of magnitude, universality, acceptability, and stability outcome indexes (Hollon *et al.,* 1979; Rush *et al.,* 1977; Rush & Watkins, 1979), while behavioral marital skills training was superior to pharmacotherapy (albeit at an inadequate dosage level) in terms of magnitude, acceptability, and, perhaps, stability indexes. However, caution must be exercised in generalizing from these results. Four studies do not justify strong statements, particularly when questions remain concerning the representativeness of the pharmacotherapy implementation in those studies. They should, however, stimulate an acceleration of the rate of comparative research, and they clearly raise questions concerning the validity of Akiskal and McKinney's conclusions regarding the impotence of psychosocial interventions in the affective disorders. Traditional psychosocial interventions appear to have fared poorly in comparisons with either drugs or the learning-based therapies, although the most recent Weissman *et al.* (1979) trial may suggest that the refined IPT approach has a specific treatment effect. The proposed NIMH collaborative trial, involving a comparison between cognitive, interpersonal dynamic, and pharmacologic interventions, might prove of interest. Comparisons with the somatic therapies have yet to be attempted, although the feasibility of implementing any of several types of behavioral or cognitive–behavioral interventions with the specific populations in the specific settings most likely to receive somatic interventions has been clearly established.

At this time, nothing is known (using *known* to indicate evidence derived from observations based on controlled interventions) about potential interactions between the learning-based and alternate interventions. Potential interactions between drugs and the behavioral and/or cognitive–behavioral interventions appear to be particularly likely candidates for investigation. Particular attention should be given to isolating different types of outcomes; combinatorial treatments may affect some, but not all, types of goals. Interactions, if they occur, may not be benign. For example, a drug and learning-based therapy combination may prove superior to either modality alone in terms of the magnitude of the reduction produced, yet no more effective than drugs alone and less effective than the learning-based intervention alone in preventing relapse or recurrence. The follow-up portion of the Hollon *et al.* (1979) design may test this concern. Similarly, nuisance side effects may be less well tolerated by patients who are in combinatorial treatment simply because they feel less compelled to depend on the medications, a consequence leading to greater refusal rates of the medications. Too little is currently known about the mechanisms of action of the various interventions to safely predict the effects of combining treatments.

The bulk of the work has been conducted with nonbipolar outpatient or subclinical populations. Clearly, additional adequately controlled trials need to be attempted with various populations of interest (e.g., bipolar, schizoaffective, psychotic, or other severely depressed inpatients). In these efforts, it must be remembered that, while etiological concepts can serve to guide the development of interventions, effective interventions need not be directly linked to probable etiological factors. Specifically, evidence pointing toward genetic or biological factors in the etiology of some of the depressive subtypes should not inhibit efforts to develop and evaluate learning-based interventions with those subtypes.

Finally, greater attention needs to be directed toward the way in which treatment stability has been assessed. The typical follow-up design, in which depression levels are assessed within 1–2 months after treatment termination, may inadvertently underestimate the potential efficacy of the learning-based interventions. Given the average length of an episode of depression of from 6 to 9 months in outpatients (Beck, 1967), differential group effects may decay over time as control-group subjects begin to remit spontaneously. Short-term follow-up designs can only detect the reversibility of effective interventions (e.g., pharmacotherapy) if factors related to the natural course of the disorder play a major role. If the only effective intervention in a design is a relatively nonreversible (stable over time) intervention, then a longer-term follow-up, one that spans several years, may be required to allow sufficient time for the occurrence of subsequent episodes in the less stably treated cells. Follow-up strategies clearly must be designed to fit the special nature of a largely episodic disorder, one typically marked by prolonged symptom-free intermorbid periods.

## Summary

The available evidence regarding the learning-based interventions is clearly promising but far from conclusive. Pharmacotherapies (and, perhaps for the most severe depressions, somatic therapies) remain the current standards of efficacy, but a standard erected on relative, rather than absolute, indexes. At least several of the specific behavioral and cognitive–behavioral interventions appear to have survived initial tests of efficacy, and several others have yet to receive adequate trials. At this time, it seems fair to conclude that, for nonbipolar, nonpsychotic samples, indications of treatment efficacy have been documented and the potential for treatment superiority has been suggested. What is needed now are attempts at replication and extension.

## Acknowledgments

The author wishes to express his appreciation to Kelly Bemis, Robert J. DeRubeis, Mark D. Evans, and Judy Garber for their comments on an earlier version of this chapter.

## References

Abrams, R. Recent clinical studies of ECT. *Seminars in Psychiatry*, 1972, *4*, 3–12.
Aiken, R. C. B. Measurement of feeling using visual analogue scales. *Proceedings of the Royal Society of Medicine*, 1969, *62*, 989–993.

Akiskal, H. S., & McKinney, W. T. Overview of recent research in depression: Ten conceptual models. *Archives of General Psychiatry*, 1975, *32*, 285–305.

American Psychiatric Association. *Diagnostic and statistical manual of mental disorders* (2nd ed.). Washington, D.C.: American Psychiatric Association, 1968.

American Psychiatric Association. *Diagnostic and statistical manual of mental disorders* (3rd ed.). Washington, D.C.: American Psychiatric Association, 1978. (Draft version)

American Psychiatric Association Task Force. The current status of lithium therapy: Report of an APA Task Force. *American Journal of Psychiatry*, 1975, *132*, 997–1001.

Anton, J. L., Dunbar, J., & Friedman, L. Anticipation training in the treatment of depression. In J. D. Krumboltz & C. E. Thoresen (Eds.), *Counseling methods*. New York: Holt, Rinehart & Winston, 1976.

Avery, D., & Winokur, G. Mortality in depressed patients treated with electroconvulsive therapy. *Archives of General Psychiatry*, 1976, *33*, 1029–1037.

Badri, M. B. A new technique for the systematic desensitization of pervasive anxiety and phobic reactions. *Journal of Psychology*, 1967, *65*, 201–208.

Dan, T. A. *Depression and the tricyclic antidepressants*. Montreal: Ronalds Federated Graphics Limited, 1974.

Bandura, A. Self-efficacy: Toward a unifying theory of behavioral change. *Psychological Review*, 1977, *84*, 191–215.

Barnes, M. R. Effects of antidepressive program on verbal behavior. *Journal of Clinical Psychology*, 1977, *33*, 545–549.

Barrera, M. An evaluation of a brief group therapy for depression. Paper presented at the Annual Meeting of the Western Psychological Association, Seattle, Washington, April 1977.

Beck, A. T. *Depression: Clinical, experimental, and theoretical aspects*. New York: Harper & Row, 1967.

Beck, A. T. Cognitive therapy: Nature and relation to behavior therapy. *Behavior Therapy*, 1970, *1*, 184–200.

Beck, A. T., Rush, A. J., Shaw, B. F., & Emery, G. *Cognitive therapy of depression: A treatment manual*. New York: Guilford, 1979.

Beck, A. T., Ward, C. H., Mendelson, M., Mock, J. E., & Erbaugh, J. K. An inventory for measuring depression. *Archives of General Psychology*, 1961, *4*, 561–571.

Bertelson, A., Harvald, B., & Hauge, M. A Danish twin study of manic–depressive disorders. *British Journal of Psychiatry*, 1977, *130*, 330–351.

Beutler, L. E. A self-directed approach to the treatment of a complex neurosis with implosive therapy. *Journal of Clinical Psychology*, 1973, *29*, 106–108.

Bielski, R. J., & Friedel, R. O. Prediction of tricyclic antidepressant response: A critical review. *Archives of General Psychiatry*, 1976, *33*, 1479–1489.

Burgess, E. P. The modification of depressive behaviors. In R. D. Rubin & C. M. Franks (Eds.), *Advances in behavior therapy, 1968*. New York: Academic Press, 1969.

Caple, M. A., & Blechman, E. A. Problem-solving and self-approval training with a depressed single mother: Case study. Paper presented at the Annual Meeting of the Association for the Advancement of Behavior Therapy, New York, December 1976.

Cole, C. E., Patterson, R. M., Craig, J. B., Thomas, W. E., Ristine, L. P., Stahly, M., & Pasamanick, B. A controlled study of iproniazid in the treatment of depression. *Archives of General Psychiatry*, 1959, *1*, 513–518.

Cole, J. O. Therapeutic efficacy of antidepressant drugs. *Journal of the American Medical Association*, 1964, *190*, 448–455.

Covi, L., Lipman, R. S., Derogatis, L. R., Smith, J. E., & Pattison, J. H. Drugs and group psychotherapy in neurotic depression. *American Journal of Psychiatry*, 1974, *131*, 191–197.

Daneman, E. A. Imipramine in office management of depressive reactions (a double-blind study). *Diseases of the Nervous System*, 1961, *22*, 213–217.

Davenport, Y., Ebert, M. H., Adland, M. L., & Goodwin, F. K. Couples group therapy as an adjunct to lithium maintenance of the manic patient. *American Journal of Orthopsychiatry*, 1977, *47*, 495–502.

Davis, J. M. Overview: Maintenance therapy in psychiatry: II. Affective disorders. *American Journal of Psychiatry,* 1976, *133,* 1–14.

Dempsey, P. An unidimensional depression scale for the MMPI. *Journal of Consulting Psychology,* 1964, *28,* 364–370.

DePue, R. A., & Monroe, S. M. The unipolar–bipolar distinction in the depressive disorders. *Psychological Bulletin,* 1978, *85,* 1001–1029.

DeRubeis, R., & Hollon, S. D. Are pharmacotherapies really superior to psychotherapies? A further examination of Luborsky, Singer, and Luborsky. Unpublished manuscript, University of Minnesota, Minneapolis, 1979.

DeRubeis, R., Hollon, S. D., & Wiemer, M. J. Cognitive therapy following ECT failure: A case report. Unpublished manuscript, University of Minnesota, Minneapolis, 1979.

Friedman, A. S. Interaction of drug therapy with marital therapy in depressed patients. *Archives of General Psychiatry,* 1975, *32,* 619–637.

Fuchs, C. Z., & Rehm, L. P. A self-control behavior therapy program for depression. *Journal of Consulting and Clinical Psychology,* 1977, *45,* 206–215.

Gioe, V. J. Cognitive modification and positive group experience as a treatment for depression (Doctoral dissertation, Temple University, 1975). *Dissertation Abstracts International,* 1975, *36,* 3039B–3040B.

Greenblatt, M., Grosser, G. H., & Wechsler, H. A comparative study of selected antidepressant medications and EST. *American Journal of Psychiatry,* 1962, *119,* 144–153.

Greene, R. J. Combining rational–emotive and hypnotic techniques: Treating depression. *Psychotherapy: Theory, Research, and Practice,* 1973, *10,* 71–73.

Grinker, R. R., Miller, J., Sabshin, M., Nunn, J., & Nunnally, J. D. *The phenomena of depression.* New York: Hoeber, 1961.

Hamilton, M. A rating scale for depression. *Journal of Neurology, Neurosurgery, and Psychiatry,* 1960, *23,* 56–62.

Hammer, W., Idestrom, C. M., & Sjoquist, F. Chemical control of antidepressant drug therapy. *Proceedings of the 1st International Symposium on Antidepressant Drugs.* S. Garattini & M. N. G. Dukes (Eds.), Excerpta Medica International Congress Serial Number 122: 301–310, 1966.

Hanaway, T. P., & Barlow, D. H. Prolonged depressive behaviors in a recently blinded deaf mute: A behavioral treatment. *Journal of Behavior Therapy and Experimental Psychiatry,* 1975, *6,* 43–48.

Hannie, T. J., & Adams, H. E. Modification of agitated depression by flooding: A preliminary study. *Journal of Behavior Therapy and Experimental Psychiatry,* 1974, *5,* 161–166.

Hauck, P. A. A RET theory of depression. *Rational Living,* 1971, *6,* 32–35.

Hersen, M., Eisler, D., Alford, G., & Agras, W. S. Effects of token economy on neurotic depression: An experimental analysis. *Behavior Therapy,* 1973, *4,* 392–397.

Hogan, R. A. Implosive therapy in the short-term treatment for psychotics. *Psychotherapy: Theory, Research, and Practice.* 1966, *3,* 25–32.

Holbrock, C. S. What we expect from electroshock treatment. *Southern Medical Journal,* 1948, *41,* 441–449.

Hollon, S. D., & Beck, A. T. Psychotherapy and drug therapy: Comparison and combinations. In S. L. Garfield & A. E. Bergin (Eds.), *The handbook of psychotherapy and behavior change: An empirical analysis* (2nd ed.). New York: Wiley, 1978.

Hollon, S. D., & Beck, A. T. Cognitive therapy for depression. In P. C. Kendall & S. D. Hollon (Eds.), *Cognitive–behavioral interventions: Theory, research, and procedures.* New York: Academic Press,1979.

Hollon, S. D., Beck, A. T., Kovacs, M., & Rush, A. J. Cognitive therapy of depression: An outcome study with six-month follow-up. Paper presented at the Annual Meeting of the Society for Psychotherapy Research, Madison, Wisconsin, June 1977. (a)

Hollon, S. D., Beck, A. T., Kovacs, M., & Rush, A. J. Cognitive therapy versus pharmacotherapy of depression: Outcome and follow-up. Paper presented at the Annual Meeting of the American Psychological Association, San Francisco, August 1977. (b)

Hollon, S. D., Bedrosian, R. C., & Beck, A. T. Combined cognitive–pharmacotherapy vs cognitive therapy in the treatment of depression. Paper presented at the Annual Meeting of the Society for Psychotherapy Research, Oxford, England, July 1979.

Hollon, S. D., & Garber, J. Base rate effects on sample selection in depression as a function of clinical setting and level of assessment. Unpublished manuscript, University of Minnesota, Minneapolis, 1979.

Hollon, S. D., Kovacs, M., Beck, A. T., & Rush, A. J. Cognitive therapy of depression: An outcome study. Paper presented at the Annual Meeting of the Eastern Psychological Association, Boston, April 1977.

Hollon, S. D., & Mandell, M. The MMPI as a measure of treatment outcome. In J. N. Butcher (Ed.), New developments in MMPI research. Minneapolis: University of Minnesota Press, 1979.

Hollon, S. D., & Shaw, B. F. Group cognitive therapy with depressed patients. In A. T. Beck, A. J. Rush, B. F. Shaw, & G. Emery (Eds.), Cognitive therapy of depression: A treatment manual. New York: Guilford, 1979.

Homme, L. E. Contiguity theory and contingency management. Psychological Record, 1966, 16, 233–241.

Huston, P. E., & Locker, L. M. Manic–depressive psychosis: Course when treated and untreated with electric shock. Archives of Neurology and Psychiatry, 1948, 60, 37–48.

Jackson, B. Treatment of depression by self-reinforcement. Behavior Therapy, 1972, 3, 298–307.

Johansson, S., Lewinsohn, P. M., & Flippo, J. F. An application of the Premack Principle to the verbal behavior of depressed subjects. Paper presented at the Annual Meeting of the Association for the Advancement of Behavior Therapy, Washington, D.C., 1969.

Johnson, W. G. Some applications of Homme's coverant control therapy: Two case reports. Behavior Therapy, 1971, 2, 240–248.

Kerman, E. G. Prevention of recurrence of mental illness with modified prophylactic electroshock therapy. Diseases of the Nervous System, 1957, 18, 189–191.

Kirkpatrick, P. W. The efficacy of cognitive behavior modification in the treatment of depression. (Doctoral dissertation, University of Arizona, 1977). Dissertation Abstracts International, 1977, 38, 2370B. (University Microfilms No. 77–22,978)

Klein, D. C., & Seligman, M. E. P. Reversal of performance deficits and perceptual deficits in learned helplessness and depression. Journal of Abnormal Psychology, 1976, 85, 11–26.

Klein, D. F. Endogenomorphic depression: A conceptual and terminological revision. Archives of General Psychiatry, 1974, 31, 447–454.

Klein, D. F., & Davis, J. M. Diagnosis and drug treatment of psychiatric disorders. Baltimore, Maryland: Williams & Wilkins, 1969.

Klerman, G. L., & Cole, J. O. Clinical pharmacology of imipramine and related antidepressant compounds. Pharmacological Review, 1965, 17, 101–141.

Klerman, G. L., DiMascio, A., Weissman, M., Prusoff, B., & Paykel, E. Treatment of depression by drugs and psychotherapy. American Journal of Psychiatry, 1974, 131, 186–191.

Klerman, G. L., Paykel, E. S., & Prusoff, B. Antidepressant drugs and clinical psychopathology. In J. O. Cole, A. M. Freedman, & A. J. Friedhoff (Eds.), Psychopathology and psychopharmacology. Baltimore: Johns Hopkins University Press, 1973.

Klerman, G. L., Rounsaville, B., Chevron, E., Neu, C., & Weissman, M. Manual for short-term interpersonal psychotherapy (IPT) of depression. Unpublished manuscript, New Haven, Connecticut, 1979.

Kovacs, M., Rush, A. J., Beck, A. T., & Hollon, S. D. A one year follow-up of depressed outpatients treated with cognitive therapy or pharmacotherapy. Archives of General Psychiatry, in press.

Lazarus, A. Learning theory and the treatment of depression. Behaviour Research and Therapy, 1968, 6, 83–89.

Lehmann, H. E. Psychiatric concepts of depression: Nomenclature and classification. Canadian Psychiatric Association Journal Supplement, 1959, 4, 51–52.

Lehmann, H. E. Depression: Somatic treatment methods, complications, failures. In G. Usdin (Ed.), Depression: Clinical, biological and psychological perspectives. New York: Bruner/Mazel, 1977.

Lewinsohn, P. M. A behavioral approach to depression. In R. M. Friedman & M. M. Katz (Eds.), *The psychology of depression: Contemporary theory and research.* Washington, D.C.: Winston/Wiley, 1974.

Lewinsohn, P. M. Activity schedules in the treatment of depression. In J. D. Krumboltz & C. E. Thoresen (Eds.), *Counseling methods.* New York: Holt, Rinehart, & Winston, 1976.

Lewinsohn, P. M., & Atwood, G. E. Depression: A clinical-research approach. *Psychotherapy: Theory, Research and Practice,* 1969, *6,* 166–171.

Lewinsohn, P. M., & Biglan, A. Behavioral treatment of depression. Paper presented at the Annual Meeting of the Association for the Advancement of Behavior Therapy, San Francisco, 1975.

Lewinsohn, P. M., Munoz, R. F., Youngren, M. A., & Zeiss, A. M. Assessment and treatment of depression: A social learning perspective. Paper presented at the Annual Meeting of the American Psychological Association, Washington, D.C., September 1976.

Lewinsohn, P. M., & Shaffer, M. The use of home observations as an integral part of the treatment of depression: Preliminary report and case studies. *Journal of Consulting and Clinical Psychology,* 1971, *37,* 87–94.

Lewinsohn, P. M., & Shaw, D. A. Feedback about interpersonal behavior as an agent of behavior change: A case study in the treatment of depression. *Psychotherapy and Psychosomatics,* 1969, *17,* 82–88.

Lewinsohn, P. M., Weinstein, M. S., & Alper, T. A behavioral approach to the group treatment of depressed persons: Methodological contributions. *Journal of Clinical Psychology,* 1970, *26,* 525–532.

Liberman, A. Behavioral approaches to family and couple therapy. *American Journal of Orthopsychiatry,* 1970, *40,* 106–118.

Liberman, R. P., & Raskin, D. E. Depression: A behavioral formulation. *Archives of General Psychiatry,* 1971, *24,* 515–523.

Loeb, A., Beck, A. T. & Diggory, J. Differential effects of success and failure on depressed and nondepressed patients. *Journal of Nervous and Mental Disease,* 1971, *152,* 106–114.

Lubin, B. *Manual for the Depression Adjective Check Lists.* San Diego: Education and Industrial Testing Service, 1967.

Luborsky, L., Singer, B., & Luborsky, L. Comparative studies of psychotherapies: Is it true that "Everyone has won and all must have prizes"? *Archives of General Psychiatry,* 1975, *32,* 995–1008.

MacPhillamy, D. J., & Lewinsohn, P. M. Manual for the Pleasant Events Schedule. Unpublished manuscript, University of Oregon, Eugene, 1975.

Mahoney, M. J. The self-management of covert behavior: A case study. *Behavior Therapy,* 1971, *2,* 575–578.

Marks, I. Behavioral psychotherapy of adult neurosis. In S. L. Garfield & A. E. Bergin (Eds.), *Handbook of psychotherapy and behavior change: An empirical analysis* (2nd ed.). New York: Wiley, 1978.

McLean, P. D., & Hakstian, A. R. Clinical depression: Comparative efficacy of outpatient treatments. *Journal of Consulting and Clinical Psychology,* 1979, *47,* 818–836.

McLean, P. D., Ogston, K., & Grauer, L. A behavioral approach to the treatment of depression. *Journal of Behavior Therapy and Experimental Psychiatry,* 1973, *4,* 323–330.

McNair, D. M. Self-evaluations of antidepressants. *Psychopharmacologia,* 1974, *37,* 281–302.

McQueen, R. The token economy and a target behavior. *Psychological Reports,* 1973, *32,* 599–602.

Mendels, J., & Cochrane, C. The nosology of depression: The endogenous–reactive concept. *American Journal of Psychiatry* (Suppl. No. 11), 1968, *124,* 1–11.

Miller, W. R. Psychological deficit in depression. *Psychological Bulletin,* 1975, *82,* 238–260.

Mogan, M. J., & O'Brien, J. S. Counterconditioning of a vomiting habit by sips of ginger ale. *Journal of Behavior Therapy and Experimental Psychiatry,* 1972, *3,* 135–137.

Morris, J. B., & Beck, A. T. The efficiency of anti-depressant drugs: A review of research 1958–1972. *Archives of General Psychiatry,* 1974, *30,* 667–674.

Morris, N. E. A group self-instruction method for the treatment of depressed outpatients. Unpublished doctoral dissertation, University of Toronto, 1975.

Novaco, R. W. Stress inoculation: A cognitive therapy for anger and its application to a case of depression. *Journal of Consulting and Clinical Psychology,* 1977, *45,* 600–608.

Oliver, R. The "Empty Nest Syndrome" as a focus of depression: A cognitive treatment model based on rational emotive therapy. *Psychotherapy: Theory, Research and Practice,* 1977, *14,* 87–94.

Olson, G. W. Application of an objective method for measuring the action of "antidepressant" medications. *American Journal of Psychiatry,* 1961, *25,* 178–179.

Padfield, M. The comparative effects of two counseling approaches on the intensity of depression among rural women of low socioeconomic status. *Journal of Counseling Psychology,* 1976, *23,* 209–214.

Patterson, W. E., Taulbee, E. S., Golsom, J. C., Horner, R. F., & Wright, H. W. Preliminary report: Comparison of two forms of milieu therapy in the treatment of depression. Unpublished manuscript, VA Hospital, Tuscaloosa, Alabama, 1968.

Perris, C. Frequency and hereditary aspects of depression. In D. M. Gallant & G. M. Simpson (Eds.), *Depression: Behavioral, biochemical, diagnostic and treatment concepts.* New York: Spectrum, 1976.

Pickering, G., Bowlby, J., & Cochrane, A. L. Clinical trial of the treatment of depressive illness. *British Medical Journal,* 1965, *1,* 881–886.

Prien, R. F., & Caffey, E. M. Long-term maintenance drug therapy in recurrent affective illness: Current status and issues. *Diseases of the Nervous System,* 1977, *164,* 981–992.

Ramsay, R. W. A case study in bereavement therapy. In H. J. Eysenck (Ed.), *Case studies in behaviour therapy.* London: Routledge & Kegan Paul, 1976.

Ramsay, R. W. Behavioral approaches to bereavement. *Behaviour Research and Therapy,* 1977, *15,* 131–136.

Raskin, A., Schulterbrandt, J., Reatig, N., & Rice, C. E. Factors of psychotherapy in interview, ward behavior, and self-report ratings of hospitalized depressives. *Journal of Consulting Psychology,* 1967, *31,* 270–278.

Rehm, L. P. A self-control model of depression. *Behavior Therapy,* 1977, *8,* 787–804.

Rehm, L. P., Fuchs, C. Z., Roth, D. M., Kornblith, S. J., & Romano, J. A comparison of self-control and assertion skills treatments of depression. *Behavior Therapy,* 1979, *10,* 429–442.

Rehm, L. P., & Kornblith, S. J. Behavior therapy for depression: A review of recent developments. In M. Hersen, R. M. Eisler, & P. M. Miller (Eds.), *Progress in behavior modification* (Vol. 7). New York: Academic Press, 1979.

Rehm, L. P., Kornblith, S. J., O'Hara, M. W., Lamparski, D. M., Romano, J. M., & Volkin, J. An evaluation of major elements in a self-control therapy program for depression. Paper presented at the Annual Meeting of the Association for the Advancement of Behavior Therapy, Chicago, November 1978.

Reisinger, J. J. The treatment of "anxiety–depression" via positive reinforcement and response cost. *Journal of Applied Behavioral Analysis,* 1972, *5,* 125–130.

Rimm, D. C. Assertive training used in treatment of chronic crying spells. *Behavior Research and Therapy,* 1967, *5,* 373–374.

Robinson, J. C., & Lewinsohn, P. M. Behavior modification of speech characteristics in a chronically depressed man. *Behavior Therapy,* 1973, *4,* 150–152. (a)

Robinson, J. C., & Lewinsohn, P. M. Experimental analysis of a technique based on the Premack Principle changing verbal behavior of depressed individuals. *Psychological Reports,* 1973, *32,* 199–210. (b)

Rogers, S. C., & Clay, P. M. A statistical review of controlled trials of imipramine and placebo in the treatment of depressive illness. *British Journal of Psychiatry,* 1975, *127,* 599–603.

Rosenthal, T. L., & Meyer, V. Case report: Behavioral treatment of clinical abulia. *Conditioned Reflex,* 1971, *6,* 22–29.

Rush, A. J., Beck, A. T., Kovacs, M., & Hollon, S. D. Comparative efficacy of cognitive therapy versus pharmacotherapy in outpatient depressives. *Cognitive Therapy and Research,* 1977, *1,* 17–37.

Rush, A. J., Hollon, S. D., Beck, A. T., Kovacs, M., & Weissenburger, J. Does cognitive therapy change cognitions? Paper presented at the Annual Meeting of the Society for Psychotherapy Research, Oxford, England, July 1979.

Rush, A. J., Khatami, M., & Beck, A. T. Cognitive and behavior therapy in chronic depression. *Behavior Therapy*, 1975, *6*, 398–404.

Rush, A. J., & Watkins, J. T. Group versus individual cognitive therapy: A pilot study. Unpublished manuscript, Southwestern Medical School, Dallas, Texas, 1978.

Sammons, R. A. Systematic resensitization in the treatment of depression. Paper presented at the Annual Meeting of the Association for the Advancement of Behavior Therapy, Chicago, November 1974.

Schildkraut, J. J. Norepinephrine metabolites as biochemical criteria for classifying depressive disorders and predicting responses to treatment—preliminary findings. *American Journal of Psychiatry*, 1973, *130*, 695–699. (a)

Schildkraut, J. J. Norepinephrine metabolism in the pathophysiology and classification of depressive and manic disorders. In J. O. Cole, A. M. Freedman, & A. J. Friedhoff (Eds.), *Psychopathology and psychopharmacology*. Baltimore: Johns Hopkins Press, 1973. (b)

Schildkraut, J. J. Biochemical research in affective disorders. In G. Usdin (Ed.), *Depression: Clinical, biological and psychological perspectives*. New York: Brunner/Mazel, 1977.

Schildkraut, J. J., Orsulak, P. J., Schatzberg, A. F., Gudeman, J. E., Cole, J. O., Rohde, W. A., & Labrie, R. A. Toward a biochemical classification of depressive disorders. I. *Archives of General Psychiatry*, 1978, *35*, 1427–1435. (a)

Schildkraut, J. J., Orsulak, P. J., Schatzberg, A. F., Gudeman, J. E., Cole, J. O., Rohde, W. A., & LaBrie, R. A. Toward a biochemical classification of depressive disorders. II. *Archives of General Psychiatry*, 1978, *35*, 1436–1439. (b)

Schmickley, V. G. The effects of cognitive–behavior modification upon depressed outpatients. Unpublished doctoral dissertations, Michigan State University, 1976.

Schou, M. Prophylactic and maintenance therapy in recurrent affective disorders. In D. M. Gallant & G. M. Simpson (Eds.), *Depression: Behavioral, biochemical, diagnostic, and treatment concepts*. New York: Spectrum Publications, 1976.

Seitz, F. C. A behavior modification approach to depression: A case study. *Psychology*, 1971, *8*, 58–63.

Seligman, M. E. P. *Helplessness*. San Francisco: Freeman, 1975.

Shapiro, M. B., Neufeld, I. L., & Post, F. Note: Experimental study of depressive illness. *Psychological Report*, 1962, *10*, 590.

Shaw, B. F. Comparison of cognitive therapy and behavior therapy in the treatment of depression. *Journal of Consulting and Clinical Psychology*, 1977, *45*, 543–551.

Shaw, B. F., & Hollon, S. D. Cognitive therapy in a group format with depressed outpatients. Unpublished manuscript, University of Western Ontario, London, Ontario, 1978.

Shipley, C. R., & Fazio, A. F. Pilot study of a treatment for psychological depression. *Journal of Abnormal Psychology*, 1973, *82*, 372–376.

Silverman, C. *The epidemiology of depression*. Baltimore: Johns Hopkins University Press, 1968.

Sims, G. K., & Lazarus, A. A. The use of random auditory stimulation in the treatment of a manic–depressive patient. *Behavior Therapy*, 1973, *4*, 128–133.

Slater, E., & Cowie, V. *The genetics of mental disorders*. London: Oxford University Press, 1971.

Spitzer, R. L., Burdock, E. I., & Hardesty, A. S. *Mental Status Schedule*. New York: Biometrics Research, 1964.

Stevenson, G. H., & Geogehan, J. J. Prophylactic electroshock. *American Journal of Psychiatry*, 1951, *107*, 743–746.

Suarez, Y., Crowe, M. J., & Adams, H. E. Depression: Avoidance learning and physiological correlates in clinical and analog populations. *Behavior Research and Therapy*, 1978, *16*, 21–31.

Taulbee, E. S., & Wright, H. W. Attitude therapy: A behavior modification program in a psychiatric hospital. In H. C. Rickard (Ed.), *Behavioral interventions in human problems*. New York: Macmillan, 1971. (a)

Taulbee, E. S., & Wright, H. W. A psychosocial–behavioral model for therapeutic intervention. In C. D. Spielberger (Ed.), *Current topics in clinical and community psychology* (Vol. 3). New York: Academic Press, 1971. (b)

Taylor, F. G., & Marshall, W. L. Experimental analysis of a cognitive–behavioral therapy for depression. *Cognitive Therapy and Research*, 1977, *1*, 59–72.

Tharp, R. G., Watson, D., & Kaya, J. Self-modification of depression. *Journal of Consulting and Clinical Psychology*, 1974, *42*, 624.

Thompson, T., Errickson, E., Pickens, R., Heston, L., & Eckert, E. A behavior therapy unit for acute psychiatric inpatients. Paper presented at Symposium on Behavior Theory and Modification, First Conference, Associazione Italiano Analisiz e Modificazione d' Comportamente, Venice, Italy, June 1978.

Tillotson, J. J., & Sulzbach, W. A comparative study and evaluation of electric-shock therapy in depressive states. *American Journal of Psychiatry*, 1945, *101*, 455–459.

Todd, F. J. Coverant control of self-evaluation responses in the treatment of depression: A new use for an old principle. *Behavior Therapy*, 1972, *3*, 91–94.

Turek, I. S., & Hanlon, T. E. The effectiveness and safety of electroconvulsive therapy (ECT). *Journal of Nervous and Mental Disease*, 1977, *164*, 419–431.

Uhlenhuth, E. H., Lipman, R. S., & Covi, L. Combined pharmacotherapy and psychotherapy: Controlled studies. *Journal of Nervous and Mental Disease*, 1969, *148*, 52–64.

Vasta, R. Coverant control of self-evaluations through temporal cueing. *Journal of Behavior Therapy and Experimental Psychiatry*, 1976, *7*, 35–37.

Wanderer, Z. W. Existential depression treated by desensitization of phobias: Strategy and transcript. *Journal of Behavior Therapy and Experimental Psychiatry*, 1972, *3*, 111–116.

Wadsworth, A. P., & Barker, H. R. A comparison of two treatments for depression; The antidepressive program vs. traditional therapy. *Journal of Clinical Psychology*, 1976, *32*, 445–449.

Weissman, M. M., Klerman, G. L., Paykel, E. S., Prusoff, B., & Hanson, B. Treatment effects on the social adjustment of depressed patients. *Archives of General Psychiatry*, 1974, *30*, 771–778.

Weissman, M. M., Prusoff, B. A., DiMascio, A., Neu, C., Goklaney, M., & Klerman, G. L. The efficacy of drugs and psychotherapy in the treatment of acute depressive episodes. *American Journal of Psychiatry*, 1979, *136*, 555–558.

Wells, K. C., Hersen, M., Bellack, A. S., & Himmelhoch, J. Social skills training for unipolar depressive females. Paper presented at the Annual Meeting of the Association for the Advancement of Behavior Therapy, Atlanta, Georgia, December 1977.

Williams, J. G., Barlow, D. H., & Agras, W. S. Behavioral measurements of severe depression. *Archives of General Psychiatry*, 1972, *72*, 330–337.

Wolpe, J. Neurotic depression: Experimental analog, clinical syndromes and treatment. *American Journal of Psychotherapy*, 1971, *25*, 362–368.

Wolpe, J., & Lazarus, A. A. *Behavior therapy techniques.* New York: Pergamon Press, 1966.

Zeiss, A. M., Lewinsohn, P. M., & Munoz, R. F. Nonspecific improvement effects in depression using interpersonal skills training, pleasant activity schedules, or cognitive training. *Journal of Consulting and Clinical Psychology*, 1979, *47*, 427–439.

Zuckerman, M., & Lubin, B. *Manual for the Multiple Affective Adjective Check List.* San Diego: Educational and Industrial Testing Service, 1965.

Zung, W. W. A self-rating depression scale. *Archives of General Psychiatry*, 1965, *12*, 63–70.

# 3

# Issues Resulting from Treatment Studies

W. EDWARD CRAIGHEAD

Depression is a psychological problem of profound personal and social significance. Its impact on individuals who experience it has been vividly portrayed in the lives, poetry, and writings of many major historical, political, and literary figures. The same emotional, motivational, behavioral, and cognitive dysfunctions of depression are just as devastating in the lives of millions of other individuals. Illustrating the personal catastrophe of clinical depression, the National Institute of Mental Health has suggested that depression is second only to schizophrenia as a national mental health problem (Secunda, Friedman, & Schuyler, 1973).

The social significance of the problem is underscored by the President's Commission of Mental Health estimate that approximately 20% of the U.S. population will have an affective disorder during their lifetime (*Task Panel Reports Submitted to the President's Commission on Mental Health*) (Vol. 4, Appendix, 1978). Since it occurs most frequently during the adult years of family development and career productivity, depression is a family and social as well as a personal problem.

Despite its long history, prevalence, and personal and social impact, we have limited scientific knowledge regarding the etiology and treatment of depression. Varied and numerous descriptive case reports and theoretical explanations of depression have been offered; however, it is only in recent years that depression has even begun to be scrutinized by empirical investigation.

It is probably not accidental that behavior therapists have been among the most recent to join the expanding group of clinical scientists studying depression. Behavior therapists have until recently eschewed the study of depression for a number of reasons, among them are the following.

73

BEHAVIOR THERAPY FOR DEPRESSION

1. None of the early behavior therapy leaders were concerned with depression but rather with more circumscribed problems that were more amenable to study in the experimental–clinical laboratory.
2. Depression traditionally has not been defined in terms of somatic–motor behaviors, which until the 1970s were the verbalized *sine qua non* of behavioral assessment and intervention.
3. It was difficult to fit depression within the "learning theory" definition of behavior therapy as espoused in the late 1950s and in the 1960s.

However, shifts in emphases within the behavioral clinical framework have resulted in a broader perspective for behavior therapists and a greater inclusion of the problem areas considered to be appropriate for study (cf. Craighead, Kazdin, & Mahoney, 1981). It was within this framework that behavior therapists earnestly began the study of depression during the 1970s.

Implied in the preceding brief discussion is an assumption that behavior therapy and depression are clearly defined; in fact, neither is clearly defined in operational terms. Thus, at the risk of being pedantic to some and presumptuous to others, I will first discuss definitions of behavior therapy and depression. Then, within the context of those definitions I will summarize the outcome studies. Third, I will offer some observations regarding those studies, and, finally, I will discuss the major issues resulting from the summarized outcome data.

## Definitions of Behavior Therapy and Depression

Although behavior therapy is frequently viewed as a well-defined enterprise based on a single theoretical or atheoretical model, no such monolithic condition exists. Definitions of behavior therapy have ranged from the "application of principles of learning" (cf. Ullmann & Krasner, 1975) to "an armamentarium of clinical intervention strategies in want of a conceptual model" (London, 1972). While there would not be total concurrence on any definition among behavior therapists, there is considerable convergence on the following two definitional characteristics. Behavior therapy derives its rationale and intervention procedures from psychological theory and empirical findings of psychological research. In order for a therapy procedure to be considered behavioral, it must be testable according to the currently acceptable criteria for scientific investigation. This definition represents the broadened conceptualization of contemporary behavior therapy. It is a rigorous definition for clinicians and probably more often an ideal toward which they aspire than one they achieve. On the other hand, it defines the minimum criteria for acceptability for behavior therapy research.

It is within this framework that behavior therapy has been expanded to include findings from cognitive psychology on the role of cognition in behavior change (Beck, 1976; Mahoney, 1974; Meichenbaum, 1977) and the role of physiological variables in such areas as anxiety management (Borkovec, 1976) and behavioral medicine (Schwartz & Weiss, 1977). Other behaviorally oriented clinicians have suggested that findings from social psychology may be relevant to behavior change (Craighead & Craighead, 1980) and that findings in cognitive—developmental psychology may be critical to behavior therapy with children (Craighead, Craighead, & Meyers, 1978; Ross, 1978). It is this perspective that allows us to view the self-control and cognitive therapies for depression on equal footing with the more socioenvironmental approaches in the behavior therapy arena (Wilcoxon, Schrader, & Nelson, 1976).

It is also within the context of this definition that the generally accepted "three-channel" approach to behavior therapy assessment has developed. From this viewpoint, many of the traditional psychological or psychiatric disorders are believed to be represented in three response classes: somatic—motor, self—report, and physiological. Within each of these classes, specific relevant measures are defined, and each of the defined variables is assessed. Treatment of choice is then determined by the specific areas of deficit or surplus responses and their interactions. The label for the disorder is relatively meaningless in the absence of assessment of the specific variables of the three response classes. It is these variables that give the label its meaning, provide operational definitions for the behavioral researcher, and suggest the locus of intervention and the intervention strategy for the behavioral clinician.

Because the emphasis of behavior therapy in the 1950s and 1960s was on somatic—motor behaviors, the only responses acceptable for experimental clinicians to study or change were overt observable ones. As the field of behavior therapy has matured and its conceptual boundaries have enlarged, self-report measures have become more acceptable. Self-report measures have ranged from more traditional self-reports regarding overt behaviors to more recent attempts to assess such ongoing cognitive activity as thoughts, internal verbal responses, and self-statements (Craighead, Kimball, & Rehak, 1979; Kendall & Korgeski, 1979). Concurrently, increased sophistication in both the conceptual issues and measurement procedures has led to an increased assessment of physiological processes, which have long been postulated to be central to behavioral explanations of the etiology and treatment of the traditional "adult neurosis."

It is within this broadened conceptual and assessment context that behavior therapists have begun the study of depression. But it is also within this context that the traditional conceptualization of depression as a mood disorder defined by a global score on a single self-report measure is considered inadequate. As I have suggested elsewhere (W. E. Craighead, 1980), the major immediate contribution of the behavior therapist to the study of depression is a move away from a unitary model to a reconceptualization of the disorder as a multifaceted problem. Each facet of the problem and its interaction with the other facets must be assessed if we are to advance our understanding of the etiology of depression and successfully modify the maladaptive responses.

Drawing from this contemporary view of behavior therapy and the empirical work on depression (Beck, 1967; Becker, 1974), I offer the following definition of depression: *Depression is a label for a feeling or affective state of dysphoria as experienced by a person. This affective state may be precipitated by, occur simultaneously with, or result in a specific set of maladaptive or dysfunctional somatic–motor, cognitive, and physiological responses.* Since emotional responses (classical characteristics of depression) as we can currently measure them are subsumed by the other three categories of responses encompassed in the definition, they were not included as a separate class of responses. Classical behavioral characteristics of depression include withdrawal or a reduction in social interaction, retardation of response speed, reduced verbal output, and increased crying. Cognitive responses include self-reports of perceptions of behaviors and emotions, guilt, self-blame, negative distortion of the environment, diurnal mood variations, helplessness, and hopelessness. Physiological responses include a loss of appetite, a loss of interest in sexual behavior, fatigue, insomnia, and early morning awakening.

These variables are noted here to provide some specificity for the behavioral definition of depression. Recent research has demonstrated that a number of other variables are also implicated by clients or patients who identify themselves as depressed. We shall return to further discussion of these variables and the need for their assessment later in the chapter. However, with these definitions of behavior therapy and depression, it seems appropriate now to turn our attention to the current status of behavior therapy for depression. In doing so, we can determine what behavior therapists have contributed to assessment and treatment procedures, how these satisfy or fail to satisfy the definitions presented here, and how and what behavior therapists may contribute to the further understanding and treatment of depression.

## Review of the Treatment Studies

In order to evaluate the outcome studies according to our definitions of behavior therapy and depression, this review is organized by the three response classes. Since others (Blaney, Chapter 1, this volume; Hollon, Chapter 2, this volume; Rehm & Kornblith, 1979) have provided exhaustive summaries and critiques of the extant studies of behavioral treatment for depression, I have adopted the following format for this chapter. I will first describe the measures that investigators using behavioral treatments for depression have employed and then summarize the *published* experimental studies that have utilized those measures. Case studies will not be included. It is felt that this approach to summarizing the research will provide a clearer picture of the strengths and weaknesses of the current data and will indicate some of the directions research needs to take.

## Somatic–Motor Responses

The overt motor behaviors that have been included as outcome measures in the treatment of depression may be divided into five groups, according to the settings in which they have been observed: (a) institutional settings (i.e., mental hospital wards or units); (b) home; (c) clinical interviews; (d) therapy groups; and (e) laboratory role-play settings.

### INSTITUTIONAL SETTINGS

The behaviors that have been observed in institutional situations include some that have historically been associated with depression as well as some that have generally been associated with behavioral deficits occurring with chronic hospitalization (Paul & Lentz, 1978). The Behavioral Rating Scale developed by Williams, Barlow, and Agras (1972) includes observational ratings of smiling, talking, and movement or activity level. The only other behaviors that have been reported under the rubric of depression in behavioral studies in this setting are time spent smiling or crying, attendance at work or occupational therapy (work training), and personal hygiene or self-care skills, such as dressing and shaving.

Utilizing a reversal design, Reisinger (1972) demonstrated that a token system of reinforcement for smiling and response cost (token loss) for crying was an effective contingency management procedure to increase the frequency of smiling and to reduce crying in a mildly retarded, 20-year-old, institutionalized female. Hanaway and Barlow (1975), using an ABA design, assessed the effects of a token economy program on several behaviors of a 35-year-old multiple-handicapped male, whom they described as depressed. The target behaviors included grooming, personal hygiene (self-care responses), and attendance at occupational therapy sessions. The target behaviors increased with token reinforcement, but the failure of the grooming and personal hygiene behaviors to reverse make the data difficult to interpret. Further, a 17-month follow-up conducted after the patient's discharge from the institution indicated that all behaviors had reverted to initial baseline levels.

In another study using an ABA design in an institutional setting, Hersen, Eisler, Alford, and Agras (1973) studied the effects of a token economy on the behavior of three "neurotically depressed" inpatients. Token reinforcement led to an increase in work behaviors and a decrease in the depressive behaviors rated on the Williams et al. (1972) Behavioral Rating Scale. All behaviors returned to baseline levels during the reversal phase of the study.

### HOME

Home observations of specific behaviors associated with depression were developed first by operantly oriented clinicians and have been utilized in the study of the relationship between such behaviors and moods, to identify goals for treatment, and as treatment outcome measures (Lewinsohn & Shaffer,

1971; Lewinsohn & Shaw, 1969; Liberman & Raskin, 1971). Two methods of recording home behaviors have been employed. In one case, researchers go into the home and observe, and in the second case, audio recordings are taken in the home, and later in the laboratory, researchers rate the specific behaviors of interest from the tape recordings.

Two treatment studies that meet the criteria for inclusion in this review have employed home observations. Reports from Liberman's operant treatment program for depression were summarized by Liberman and Raskin (1971). With one depressed person an ABAB reversal design was employed to demonstrate that family social reinforcement affected the depressed and coping behaviors of a 37-year-old housewife. The depressive behaviors—crying, complaining about somatic symptoms, pacing, and withdrawal—were recorded in the home by the therapist. While the adaptive behaviors were not specified, they appeared to include such activities as cooking, cleaning house, and attending to children's needs. The treatment consisted of "instant and frequent attention" by the family to adaptive behaviors and ignoring of depressive behaviors. Adaptive behaviors increased and depressive behaviors decreased as a function of the social reinforcement treatment program.

McLean, Ogston, and Grauer (1973) employed observations based on tape recordings in the home as a dependent measure in an outcome study comparing a behavior therapy approach to a group assigned to receive the usual therapy from the referral source. In order to assess verbal interactions with spouses, tape recordings of a 30-minute problem-oriented discussion were made before and following treatment. The recordings were rated according to Lewinsohn's (1968) scoring system and yielded frequency data for positive and negative initiations and responses. Two raters independently scored three randomly selected tapes and obtained an average interrater agreement of 88%. The method of calculating observer agreement was not reported. Subjects also completed the Depression Adjective Check List (DACL) at pre-, post-, and follow-up-testing and rated themselves at pre-, mid-, and posttreatment and follow-up on five target behaviors considered to be problematic and attributable to depression.

Twenty nonpsychotic patients between 21 and 51 years of age who exhibited "incapacitating" depressive behaviors were randomly assigned to behavior therapy or to a "usual treatment" therapy. The usual treatment was conducted at the original referral source and consisted of a hodgepodge of treatment procedures, including antidepressant medication, group therapy, irregular office consultations, and even no treatment. Whatever treatment the client received was allowed to continue during the follow-up period. This comparison group hardly qualifies as more than a no-treatment control group. The behavior therapy program consisted of eight weekly sessions composed of the following procedures: (a) training in principles of social learning (basically principles of operant conditioning); (b) therapy and 20-minute daily home practice sessions for the first 4 weeks using spouse feedback boxes on which a red light signaled that the spouse had perceived the communication as negative and a green light signaled that the spouse had perceived it as positive; and (c) training in the construction and use of reciprocal behavioral contracts during all eight sessions. Pre–post comparisons for the observational data indicated that the experimental group decreased their frequency of negative reactions and negative initiations and reactions combined but that the comparison group did not. Unfortunately, no relative comparisons of change were made between the two groups, and thus the advantages of including a control group for comparison purposes were negated. The outcome data for the DACL and self-report of specific depressive behaviors will be summarized within their respective sections.

## CLINICAL INTERVIEWS

Speech behaviors, namely content and rate, within a clinical interview setting have been employed in Lewinsohn's work in depression (Robinson & Lewinsohn, 1973a, 1973b). In the treatment program for a chronically depressed adult male (Robinson & Lewinsohn, 1973b), rate of verbal behavior was the focus of treatment and the sole dependent variable. Utilizing an ABCAB design, the authors demonstrated that the rate of verbal output could first be increased by making therapy time contingent on increased rate of speech (B) and then be maintained by presentation of an aversive stimulus, a buzzer (C), when speech rate dropped below the criterion level.

## THERAPY GROUP

In two studies, better known for their effects on measures to be discussed later, Rehm and his colleagues (Fuchs & Rehm, 1977; Rehm, Fuchs, Roth, Kornblith, & Romano, 1979) have studied the effectiveness of treatment based on Rehm's (1977) self-control model of depression. Both studies included observational data taken from 10 minutes of therapy group interactions (sans therapist) near the beginning of the first and the last therapy sessions. These group interactions were also videotaped.

Fuchs and Rehm (1977) compared the effectiveness of a self-control treatment for depression to a nonspecific treatment condition and a waiting-list control group. Rehm and Kornblith (1979) described the self-control program as follows:

> Teaching self-monitoring emphasizes the importance of monitoring positive rather than negative events. Participants are instructed to keep a log of their mood and positive activities each day. In the self-evaluation phase, each person selected behaviors which they wished to engage in more frequently. Following the presentation of information on how to define goals in behavioral terms and establish realistic, attainable subgoals that are within their control, participants are aided in selecting and monitoring their own goals and subgoals in subsequent weeks. During the self-reinforcement phase of the program, individuals are exposed to concepts of self-administered reinforcement programs which specified reward contingencies for performing target behaviors [pp. 30–31].

The nonspecific therapy consisted of discussion of past and current problems. The therapist kept the discussion active by empathetic reflection and clarification and the use of unspecified group activities. No evaluation of treatment credibility was obtained.

Thirty-six female volunteer clients, who met criteria for depression on the Minnesota Multiphasic Personality Inventory (MMPI), were randomly assigned to the self-control therapy, nonspecific therapy, or waiting-list control group. Therapy was conducted in a group format with six weekly 2-hour sessions.

Observations of the pre–post group interactions were made for the number of speeches emitted and for the response elicitation (the percentage of group members who responded to a person's verbalization). Three observers independently rated these measures. Interobserver agreement was not reported separately for each measure, but the reported data (presumably for both measures combined) ranged from 83% to 100% with an average of 87%. The data indicated that the self-control therapy produced greater increases in activity level than did the nonspecific therapy; the two groups did not differ on changes in response elicitation. Because of the situation (therapy groups) in which the observations were obtained, no comparisons with the waiting-list control were possible.

In the second study in Rehm's laboratory (Rehm et al., 1979), the relative effectiveness of self-control therapy and an assertion skills program was determined. The assertion training program was composed of six 2-hour weekly sessions designed to help the client increase refusal behaviors, make requests, and express criticism and disapproval, and express approval and affection. The therapy procedures included instruction, behavioral rehearsal, group and therapist feedback, and occasional therapist modeling.

The 27 women in this study, like those in the Fuchs and Rehm (1977) study, were volunteers and met the MMPI criteria for depression. Within the constraints of time schedules, they were randomly assigned to either the self-control or assertion skills program. Fourteen subjects completed the self-control program, and 10 completed the assertion skills program.

Although the observations were obtained in a similar manner and in the same setting, the behaviors being rated in this study differed from those rated by Fuchs and Rehm (1977). Near the beginning of the first group therapy session and near the end of the last session, each client was asked to say something about her current level of functioning. This presentation was rated for nine variables: duration, eye contact, loudness, expressivity, overall depression, positive self-references, negative self-references, positive other-references, and negative other-references. Each scale was rated by three "blind" raters, and, even using stringent criteria for defining an agreement, interobserver agreement ranged from 83% to 100%. This rating scale, which was based on several findings from the broader social skills (Hersen & Bellack, 1977) and depression literature, represents the most adequate attempt to develop a rating scale of depressive behaviors.

Analyses of covariance on the posttest scores, with the respective pretest score as the covariate, indicated that the self-control treatment resulted in significantly greater improvement on overall depression and negative references to self and others. Since the self-control program included considerable attention to social functioning and the assertion skills therapy was limited to assertion training, the data suggest that the greatest treatment effect was demonstrated on those variables toward which the treatment was directed.

LABORATORY ROLE-PLAY SETTINGS

As a part of their multifaceted pre–post assessment package Rehm *et al.* (1979) obtained subjects' responses to eight tape-recorded verbal stimuli on the Taped Situation Test. These responses were tape recorded and rated by the client and independent raters for a number of variables typically employed as measures of assertion training effectiveness (Hersen & Bellack, 1977). These measures included self-ratings of adequacy of the response and observer ratings of latency, duration, compliance, requests for new behaviors from other persons, statements of subjects' opinion, loudness, appropriate affect, fluency, and overall assertiveness. Adequate interobserver agreement (above 80%) was reported for all measures, except the marginal agreement figure (72%) for statements of opinion.

The self-control condition produced greater pre–post positive changes on the self-ratings of adequacy. The assertion skills program produced significantly greater improvement on duration of response, requests for new behavior from another person, statements of opinion, loudness of responses, fluency, and overall assertiveness. It is clear that the assertion training was effective for those behaviors toward which that therapy was directed, whereas the self-control program produced a greater effect on the overall self-evaluation, which is an important aspect of that therapy strategy. The data are consistent with the pattern of findings on the previously discussed behavioral ratings.

## Self-Report Measures

A number of self-report measures of depression have been employed to evaluate the effectiveness of treatment procedures. Frequently these measures serve the dual role of defining the population to be studied and measuring pre–post change. There are three types of self-report measures: (*a*) global ratings, or self-reports of occurrences of the classical characteristics of depression (Beck, 1967); (*b*) clinician ratings of self-reports of occurrences of the classical characteristics of depression; and (*c*) self-ratings of specific behaviors and thought processes (e.g., self-control skills).

GLOBAL SELF-REPORT MEASURES

The Beck Depression Inventory (BDI) (Beck, Ward, Mendelson, Mock, & Erbaugh, 1961) rivals the MMPI for the most frequently used self-report measure of depression, with the BDI being used in 7 of the 17 studies summarized in this chapter and the MMPI being used in 6.

*Depression Inventory.* In a study published only in abstract form, (1975), utilizing mildly depressed college students, compared the effec-tiveness of four treatment conditions: (a) positive group experience; (b) a combination of relaxation training and rehearsal of positive self-statements (labeled cognitive therapy); (c) a combination of positive group experience and cognitive therapy; and (d) a no-treatment control. No data regarding treatment session parameters were reported, and no statistics were presented. However, the author reported that analysis of variance on BDI change scores indicated that the combination treatment was more effective than either treatment alone or the no-treatment condition. Shaw (1977) compared Beck's earlier cognitive therapy (cf. Beck, Rush, & Kovacs, 1975) with a behavior therapy program modeled after Lewinsohn (1974a), a nondirective group, and a waiting-list control group. College students who requested services at the university health services or who were self-referred served as subjects. Criteria for inclusion in the study included self-reported current depression of 3 weeks duration, desire to participate in the study, a BDI score of 18 or greater, an interview that eliminated psychotic and serious suicide risk subjects and indicated that depression was the primary problem, and clinical ratings of the taped standardized interview. Thirty-two male and female subjects who met these criteria were randomly assigned to the four treatment conditions, with eight subjects in each. The investigator served as the therapist for all treatment, which consisted of four weekly group sessions. Pre–post assessment on the BDI indicated that the cognitive therapy was more effective than the behavioral and nondirective therapies, which were more effective than the waiting-list control. One-month follow-up data for the behavioral and cognitive therapy groups indicated a maintenance of treatment effects, but, because of a slight increase in depression in the cognitive group, the difference between the two groups was smaller and no longer significant.

Taylor and Marshall (1977) reported a study designed to compare the relative effects of cognitive and behavior therapy alone and in combination for the treatment of depression. The pre–post–follow-up assessment package was composed of several self-report measures, including the BDI. The cognitive therapy was based on the writings of Beck (1963), Ellis (1970), Bandura (1971), and Marston (1964), while the behavioral program was based on the predominantly (but not exclusively) operant procedures suggested by Ferster (1965), Lazarus (1968), and Lewinsohn (1974b). The use of the combined treatment approach had been suggested by Wilcoxon, Schrader, and Nelson (1976). Twenty-eight subjects who met the following criteria were selected from 45 who applied following an advertisement of the study in the university newspaper: (a) self-reported depression of at least 2 weeks; (b) BDI of 13 or greater; (c) MMPI-D-30 *T* score of 70 or greater; (d) not receiving other treatment or medication; and (e) willingness to participate in the study. Seven subjects were randomly assigned to each of the following conditions: cognitive therapy alone, behavior therapy alone, cognitive and behavior therapy in combination, and a waiting-list control. Active therapy consisted of weekly individual therapy sessions, all conducted by the senior author, who was an advanced graduate student. Although the number of treatment sessions was not specified, it seems reasonable to conclude that there were four weekly sessions, since subjects in the waiting-list control were told they must wait 4 weeks for treatment. Results for the BDI indicated that the combination of treatment procedures was more effective than either therapy alone and that either therapy alone produced greater changes than the waiting-list control. Although delayed treatment precluded a waiting-list comparison at a 5-week follow-up, the obtained treatment differences favoring the superiority of the combined treatment approach were maintained.

Rush, Beck, Kovacs, and Hollon (1977) used the BDI as a criterion for inclusion in their study and as a dependent variable to evaluate treatment effectiveness of cognitive therapy. Subjects who requested treatment in Beck's program at the University of Pennsylvania Department of Psychiatry and who scored above 20 on a screening BDI received a 3-hour pretreatment assessment package. Patients who met the following criteria were included in the study: (a) BDI of 20 or greater; (b) a minimum score of 14 on the Hamilton Rating Scale for Depression (Hamilton, 1960); and (c) clinical evaluation of depression according to Feighner's criteria (Feighner, Robins, Guze, Woodruff, Winokur, & Munoz, 1972). Subjects who had a primary diagnosis of other psychiatric disorders, contraindications for tricyclic medication, or a previous failure on a clinical trial with a tricyclic medication were excluded. Forty-one subjects were randomly assigned within the constraints of time availability of therapists; 19 patients were assigned to cognitive therapy and 22 to a pharmacotherapy condition. The cognitive therapy was based on a standard cognitive therapy manual (Beck, Rush, Shaw, & Emery, 1979). Each patient was treated individually by a psychiatric resident or a psychology intern for 20 sessions during a 12-week period. Pharmacotherapy consisted of doses of up to 250 mg per day of imipramine, and the patient was seen in 20-minute sessions once per week for 12 weeks.

While both groups showed significant decreases in depression, pre–post analysis of covariance on the BDI with the pretest as the covariate indicated that the cognitive therapy produced larger decreases on the BDI than did the imipramine condition. Significantly more cognitive therapy than imipramine patients scored in the normal range on the BDI at posttest. One-year follow-up data, including three replacement subjects in the imipramine condition, showed essentially the same effects as the posttest data (Kovacs, Rush, Beck, & Hollon, 1979). More subjects dropped out of treatment in the imipramine condition. Although depression remained lower in the cognitive therapy condition during the follow-up period and more people fell into the normal range on the BDI, approximately equal numbers of subjects from each condition sought additional treatment. Because of the effectiveness of this brief cognitive therapy procedure relative to such a well-established antidepressant medication with a clinically depressed population, this study has made a major impact in the area of depression treatment research.

Another study of major importance, which used the BDI as part of a multiple criterion for inclusion in the study and as an outcome measure, has been reported by McLean and Hakstian (1979). In initial screening, each subject had to be between 20 and 60 years of age, depressed for at least 2 months, functionally impaired by the depression (e.g., unable to work), fluent in English, not receiving treatment elsewhere, and, if recently pregnant, at least 3 months postpartum. Subjects who met those criteria participated in a clinical interview and completed several self-report measures, including the BDI. In order to participate in the study, subjects had to meet the criteria for primary depression as specified by Feighner et al. (1972) and be at least moderately depressed on two of the following three self-report measures—the BDI, the MMPI, or Lubin's DACL (1965).

A total of 196 subjects who met the criteria were randomly assigned to a psychotherapy, relaxation training, behavior therapy, or drug therapy condition. Psychotherapy was based on the work of Marmor (1974, 1975) and Wolberg (1967) and was an insight approach to therapy. "The specific goals of psychotherapy were to relieve symptomatic complaints and to restore the client's pre-episode level of functioning, through the development of insight into the psychodynamic forces that initiated the current depression and through the recognition of personality problems as they related to past experiences and the current depression [McLean & Hakstian, 1979, p. 821]." Relaxation training consisted of standard progressive muscular relaxation training presented via audiotaped instructions. In addition to the therapy sessions, clients practiced relaxation at home six days per week. Behavior therapy utilized graduated practice and modeling, with the therapy focus on goal attainment in the following areas: communication, behavioral productivity, social interaction, assertiveness, decision making, problem solving, and cognitive self-control. It was a comprehensive program incorporating parts of the operant, cognitive, and self-control treatments of depression. Drug therapy consisted of 11 weeks of tricyclic (amitriptyline) medication at a maximum dosage of 150 mg per day, with phase-in and phase-out dosage increases and decreases. Clients had 15-minute weekly sessions to allow blood samples to be drawn occasionally and to participate in a physiological review. Clients in the three psychological treatment procedures participated in 10 (range 8–12) weekly individual therapy sessions. Treatments were crossed with an experienced–inexperienced therapist factor, which produced no effects in the study, and thus for outcome analysis, the data were pooled across this factor.

Use of complex multivariate data analysis procedures and appropriate follow-up comparisons revealed that for the 178 subjects who completed posttest assessment the behavior therapy procedures produced a greater decrease on the BDI than did any of the other treatment procedures, with more subjects in the behavior therapy group falling into the normal range at posttest. However, differential treatment effects had largely dissipated at a 3-month follow-up because of a slight increase in depression in the behavior therapy group and a slight decrease in depression in the other treatment groups.

Fuchs and Rehm (1977) found significantly greater reductions on the BDI for their self-control treatment procedures relative to their nonspecific therapy at posttest. The difference was maintained at a marginally significant level at follow-up. Interestingly, all 8 of the self-control subjects fell within the normal range (less than 11) at posttest, whereas only 3 of the 10 nonspecific therapy subjects fell within this range.

Rehm et al. (1979) found that both self-control subjects and assertion skills subjects showed significant decreases on the BDI. However, the self-control subjects changed significantly more than did the assertion skills subjects.

*MMPI-D Scale.* A few studies have employed the MMPI-D scale as the major dependent variable (Lewinsohn & Biglan, 1975; Shipley & Fazio, 1973), while a few others have used the MMPI-D scale as one of several global self-report measures of depression (Fuchs & Rehm, 1977; Rehm et al., 1979; Rush et al., 1977; Taylor & Marshall, 1977).

Lewinsohn and Biglan (1975) used the MMPI (cf. Lewinsohn, Biglan, & Zeiss, 1976) both as a criterion for subject identification and as a pre- and posttreatment measure. Subjects were assigned to groups that used the following techniques: (a) therapy time as a reinforcer for mood-related activities; (b) therapy time as a reinforcer for non-mood-related activities; (c) therapy time as a reinforcer for general activity; (d) instructions to increase activities; and (e) no-instructions, no-contingency control. All groups demonstrated equal, significant pre–post decreases on the MMPI. It is not possible to determine what produced the treatment effect, but these data seem to be inconsistent with Lewinsohn's suggestion (1974a) that treatment should focus primarily on the increase of behaviors associated with positive moods.

Shipley and Fazio (1973) reported two studies designed to evaluate a problem-solving approach to the treatment of college students identified as depressed on the MMPI. In the first study, clients were assigned to three weekly sessions of functional problem solving, which focused on the modification of inappropriate behaviors or cognitive distortions in social situations, or to a waiting-list control. In the second study, problem-solving treatment and a support group treatment were crossed with a positive expectancy manipulation or no expectancy manipulation factor. The MMPI data indicated that the problem-solving procedure produced greater reductions on the MMPI than did the waiting-list control of the first study or the nonspecific treatment control of the second study. No significant treatment or interaction effects were obtained for the expectancy manipulation.

Fuchs and Rehm (1977) found that their self-control program produced greater MMPI decreases at posttest than did their nonspecific and waiting-list controls. This difference was maintained at the 6-week follow-up for the self-control as versus the nonspecific treatment; waiting-list controls were treated during the follow-up, which precluded their being included in the follow-up comparison.

Rehm *et al.* (1979) found that the self-control group showed significantly greater reductions on the MMPI-D scale than did the assertion skills group. The pre–post change for the self-control group was significant, but the assertion skills group did not demonstrate a significant decrease on this global rating of depression.

Rush *et al.* (1977) found MMPI-D scale changes to correspond to changes on the BDI, with both the cognitive therapy and the imipramine therapy producing significant decreases. The decreases for cognitive therapy were significantly greater than those for imipramine therapy.

Taylor and Marshall (1977), using the MMPI-D-30 scale, found that the cognitive, behavioral, and combined cognitive–behavioral groups demonstrated greater pre–post decreases than did the waiting-list control, but the greater decrease for the combined group over either treatment alone was only marginally significant ($p < .10$). It should be remembered that this latter comparison demonstrated the superiority of the combined group on the BDI.

*Zung Self-Rating Depression Scale.* Only one treatment study (Padfield, 1976) has utilized the Zung Self-Rating Depression Scale (Zung, 1965) and Grinker's Feelings and Concerns Checklist. Padfield compared Lewinsohn's operant approach with a reflective-listening relationship development approach modeled after Carkhuff (1971). Rural, low SES women, identified as depressed on the Zung and Grinker scales, were randomly assigned to one of the treatment conditions. No pre–post differences were reported for the Zung SRDS.

CLINICAL RATINGS OF SELF-REPORT DATA

Behavioral researchers have used three clinical rating scales of depression: (a) Grinker's Feelings and Concerns Checklist (GFCC); (b) the Hamilton Rating Scale for Depression; and (c) the Raskin Depression Scale. The only study to use the Grinker scale was by Padfield (1976). Data for the GFCC indicated that Lewinsohn's approach was superior to the reflective-listening treatment; however, pretreatment differences on the GRCC were not taken into account in the analyses and may partially explain the obtained effect.

Two studies (Shaw, 1977; Rush *et al.*, 1977) utilized a clinical interview and ratings on the Hamilton Rating Scale for Depression (HRS-D) (Hamilton, 1960). Shaw found that his cognitive group showed greater improvement on the HRS-D than did the nonspecific and waiting-list groups and a marginally significant ($p < .06$) greater improvement for the cognitive group relative to the operant group. As with the BDI, this significant difference did not appear at follow-up. Rush *et al.* (1977) found that both cognitive therapy and imipramine produced a significant decrease in depression as rated on the HRS-D and that this decrease was significantly greater for the cognitive therapy. Neither group showed a significant change from posttreatment scores at the 1-year follow-up (Kovacs *et al.*, 1979).

Only Rush *et al.* (1977) have employed the Raskin Depression Scale (Raskin, Schulterbrandt, Reatig, & McKeon, 1970) as a pre–post measure of treatment outcome. Cognitive therapy and imipramine therapy both showed significant pre–post changes in the direction of improvement; however, only a nonsignificant trend showed the cognitive therapy to be superior to imipramine. This latter finding was significant for the BDI, the MMPI, and the HRS-D scales. Treatment effects were maintained at the 1-year follow-up (Kovacs *et al.*, 1979).

SPECIFIC SELF-REPORT SCALES

A number of self-report measures regarding specific behaviors or thoughts have been developed. These include Lewinsohn's Pleasant Events Schedule (PES), McLean's rating of target behaviors, Rehm's Self-Control Questionnaire, and the Wolpe–Lazarus Assertiveness Scale.

The most widely used of these scales is the PES. Fuchs and Rehm (1977) found that their self-control treatment produced a greater increase in pleasant events than did their nonspecific therapy and waiting-list groups. Rehm *et al.* (1979) found that the self-control subjects increased their participation in pleasant events, whereas the assertion skills group did not. Neither Lewinsohn and Biglan (1975) nor Padfield (1976) found significant differential treatment effects for participation in pleasant events.

McLean *et al.* (1973) used the self-rating of five target behaviors (i.e., social withdrawal, sleep disturbance, etc.) as a pre–post measure of change. The experimental group showed significant improvements on these ratings, whereas the "usual therapy" groups did not. McLean and Hakstian (1979) developed this self-report measure into a questionnaire with 32 items designed to tap seven dimensions: cognitive, coping, personal activity, social, and somatic indicators; mood; and overall general satisfaction. In general, the data favored the superiority of the behavior therapy procedure, but not on all measures.

Rehm has developed three self-control measures—for self-evaluation, for self-reinforcement, and for self-control statements. Both Fuchs and Rehm (1977) and Rehm *et al.* (1979) have demonstrated the superiority of self-control treatment in change scores on these specific measures of self-control.

The other specific self-report measure used in the assessment of treatment effectiveness is the Wolpe-Lazarus Assertiveness Scale (Wolpe & Lazarus, 1966). Rehm *et al.* (1979) found that assertion skills training produced greater pre–post changes on this measure than did self-control therapy. These two findings of Rehm and his colleagues with regard to self-control and assertion measures highlight the significant relationship between specific treatment and outcome effects.

OTHER SCALES

A number of other scales, such as the Visual Analogue Scale (Aitken, 1969), the Tennessee Self-Concept Scale, Kelly's Repertory Grid, the Multiple Affect Adjective Checklist (Zuckerman & Lubin, 1965), and the Depression Adjective

Check List (Lubin, 1965) have been employed in one or two studies, but the findings are not of sufficient import to warrant discussion in this chapter.

## Observations on the Outcome Data

The first observation is that calculating actual numbers associated with the treatment studies summarized in this chapter is a very revealing and humbling experience. Seventeen studies met the criteria for inclusion in this review by virtue of their use of single-subject or group comparison experimental designs. Three of those studies were single-subject designs with inpatients; two studies using one subject each and the other showing replication across three subjects. Thus, behavioral researchers have systematically evaluated behavior therapy on a total of five inpatients, who, according to even liberal criteria, were questionably labeled depressed.

The remainder of the studies were concerned with outpatient populations, with two of the studies (Liberman & Raskin, 1971; Robinson & Lewinsohn, 1973b) employing single-subject designs without replication (the hallmark of operant intervention procedures) and 12 utilizing group comparison designs. It seems safe to estimate that at most 300 people who have been defined by various criteria as depressed have received systematically evaluated, broadly defined, behavior therapy. These figures are all the more striking when one realizes that behavior therapy probably ranks second only to pharmacological therapies in systematic evaluation of treatments for depression. In spite of these meager figures, it is clear that substantial progress has been made and a number of issues, which are badly in need of practical and empirical resolution, have been generated. These will be discussed in the next section of this chapter.

The second observation is that each treatment approach appears to be most effective when the therapy is conducted in the laboratory of the originator or a staunch supporter of the respective orientation of a particular type of therapy. Thus, self-control therapy seems to work best in Rehm's laboratory, cognitive therapy to work best for Beck and the people he has trained, and more classical behavior therapy to work best for McLean. *This is not to suggest any duplicity on the part of any investigator.* The role of such nonspecific effects as therapist enthusiasm and newness of the therapy approach as well as a plethora of other unknown factors may inadvertently affect treatment outcome. This observation does, however, underscore the importance of determining the exportability of these various treatment procedures.

The third observation is that there exists an alarming paucity of adequate assessment devices. This observation is germane to the major issues raised by this review: the relationship of the theoretical orientation to assessment and the need for a more standardized assessment battery. These issues will be discussed in the next section. Suffice it at this point to note that not one single overt motor behavior (other than smiles and crying in studies with inpatients) has been employed in more than one study. Not one study has evaluated physiological variables such as facial EMG (cf. Schwartz, Fair, Mandel, Salt, Mieske, & Klerman, 1975) or sleep changes associated with therapeutic changes. Not even the global self-report measures of occurrences of characteristics of depression have been used in all of the reported studies.

The fourth observation is that the treatment effects have been clearest and most pronounced on those measures that are directly related to the focus of the therapy. Thus, operant programs have shown changes in target behaviors. This would have been predicted. However, this observation has been substantiated in other ways. For example, Rehm and his colleagues (Fuchs & Rehm, 1977; Rehm et al., 1979) have shown that assertion training has a greater effect than self-control on assertive responses. On the other hand, self-control therapy has a greater effect than assertion training on self-control behaviors. The more broadly aimed self-control program produced greater effects than did the more narrowly focused assertion training on the more broadly based measures of social behavior skills and global self-ratings. This last finding introduces the final observation.

The fifth observation is that, the more comprehensive the treatment program, the greater its effect will be on global rating scales. The data are consistent with this conclusion in that the strongest effects on the so-called symptom checklists or global self-rating scales of depression have been with Beck's cognitive behavior therapy (Rush et al., 1977); McLean's behavioral program, which has a major cognitive component (McLean & Hakstian, 1979); Taylor and Marshall's (1977) combined cognitive–behavioral group; and Rehm's self control therapy, which is posited to encompass both cognitive and behavioral approaches (cf. Rehm, 1977). The most parsimonious explanation for these findings is that the more broadly based programs are designed to produce specific changes in more of the types of response surpluses and deficits that are characteristic of depression. These are the very responses that are rated on the global depression scales. As I have suggested elsewhere (W. E. Craighead, 1980), each of the behavioral models of depression has emphasized a subset of the characteristics of depression. Thus, it is posited that a greater number of these subsets change in the more comprehensive therapies and that this produces changes on the corresponding items of the rating scale rather than changes on some pathological entity, depression. The discussion of this last point introduces one of the major issues resulting from the treatment outcome studies.

## Issues

The first major issue is: Is there a syndrome of depression? The behavioral approach outlined in the introduction to this chapter would suggest that, at least for those who have traditionally been labeled outpatient, unipolar, or neurotic depressives, no clear syndrome exists. (In fact, such a model would question the utility of a syndromal approach to bipolar and psychotic depression.) It would further suggest that depression has become a label in our society (cf. Mischel, 1978) to refer to any one or a combination of a number of responses, which may or may not be interrelated. However, the data for the studies summarized in this chapter, in addition to the more general literature on depression (Becker, 1974; Friedman & Katz, 1974), clearly demonstrate that adequate measures have not been developed to allow us to even begin to evaluate the interrelationships of the various responses associated with the label depression.

This research might take a number of directions, including the development of adequate assessment devices for each response, so that the interrelationships among these variables might be determined. An alternative approach might be to determine via the use of discriminate function analyses if successful responders to a particular treatment exhibit a particular pattern of "depressive" responses. To develop a symptom checklist and have people distribute themselves on total scores on that checklist does not solve the problem—a global score on a self-report checklist does not a syndrome make. A self-report checklist is only one type of assessment device needed to study the characteristics of depression and their interrelationships. On the other hand, to argue for specific assessment devices for target behaviors without studying the interrelationships of those responses and developing a theoretical model to explain those empirically determined relationships will probably limit our understanding of depression and our ability to treat it effectively.

The second issue is inextricably tied to the first, and that is the evident need for the development of a standardized or at least multifaceted set of assessment devices. Some investigators, most notably Rehm and McLean, have begun to move in this direction in their recent treatment studies. Such assessment devices could be developed from the current literature regarding the etiology of depression and studies evaluating hypotheses of the various models of depression.

Based on the current state of the literature, I will offer a few suggestions for responses that seem important to consider. The primary recommendation here is not that these particular measures be used but that more attention be devoted to systematic development of these assessment devices. The behavioral measures that currently seem to be of most use would be real-life ratings of specific behaviors (e.g., crying, time in bed) by a significant other, activity measures (e.g., pedometer, class or work attendance), observations of performance in social interactions, and, possibly, differential learning to positive reinforcement and punishment (cf. Kennedy & Craighead, 1980). The physiological measures of most immediate possible use include objective measures of sleep disturbance, facial EMG, and, possibly, bilateral differences in skin conductance. To date, these measures have only been tapped, if at all, as one item on a global self-report scale such as the BDI. The third area of assessment is self-report measures. These may take the form of global rating scales, such as the BDI, MMPI, or Zung, or clinical ratings based on interviews, such as the HRS-D, the

Raskin Depression Scale, and the combined use of the Schedule of Affective Disorders and Schizophrenia (Endicott & Spitzer, 1978) and the Research Diagnostic Criteria (Spitzer, Endicott, & Robins, 1978). Another type of self-report measure would be for specific thoughts or behaviors. These might include such measures as Rehm's Self-Control Questionnaires or Hollon and Kendall's (1979) Automatic Thoughts Questionnaire. Perhaps it would be best to develop these measures to be used in conjunction with specific settings, such as the social interaction situation that was suggested as a method of obtaining behavioral ratings; this method of assessment of self-statements has worked well in the assertion training literature (L. W. Craighead, 1979; Schwartz & Gottman, 1976). Other measures are sorely needed, for example, easy to use measures of selective attention (which almost every model suggests is characteristic of depression) and the well-established phenomenon of distortion of recall of positive feedback. In light of the relationship between participation in pleasant events and depression, refinement and continued use of the PES seems warranted.

The third issue is the relationship between depression and other psychological disorders, especially anxiety. While the current assessment procedures may eliminate schizophrenic or psychotic individuals from the depressive population, little effort is made to eliminate individuals with other problems more characteristic of outpatient populations. An especially thorny problem at both a conceptual and a practical level is the relationship between anxiety and depression. While the BDI may do a good job of discriminating anxious from more severely depressed patients, serious questions may be raised as to whether it accomplishes that objective with the more moderately depressed patients (cf. Kennedy & Craighead, 1980). In testing over 3000 individuals with the BDI over the past few years in our laboratory, we have found that fewer than 2% are depressed but not anxious as measured by Endler's S-R Inventory of General Trait Anxiousness (Endler & Okada, 1975), whereas 10–12% are both depressed and anxious. Further, additional work needs to be done to establish the psychometric properties of the BDI, which was developed to be completed in an interview setting but is now most frequently used in questionnaire form (Honn, 1979).

The final issue raised by the treatment studies is: Are we focusing our attention in the most expedient place by doing treatment outcome studies? As indicated in the introduction, we have a high percentage of depressed individuals in our society, and certainly effort must go into developing effective treatment procedures for those people. What I would like to suggest, however, is that we need to devote more effort to the study of the development and prevention of depression, or at least preventative treatment approaches for high-risk populations, particularly children and adolescents. Very little has been offered by way of theoretical behavioral models to explain the development of depression, and virtually no empirical work has been done to determine the environmental and cognitive factors that may produce depression in children and adolescents. Given our limited success in the alleviation of depression and in general the inability to maintain treatment effects, there seems to be a strong need for programmatic research regarding factors affecting the development and prevention of depression.

## Summary

Although depression has been known virtually throughout recorded history, only in recent years has it been investigated empirically. Behavior therapists have been among the social scientists most recently to take up the study of depression and its treatment.

Behavior therapy derives its rationale and intervention procedures from psychological theory and empirical findings of psychological research. For a procedure to be considered behavioral, it must be testable according to the currently acceptable criteria for scientific investigation. *Depression* is defined as a label for a feeling or affective state of dysphoria as experienced by a person. This affective state may be precipitated by, occur simultaneously with, or result in a specific set of maladaptive or dysfunctional somatic–motor, cognitive, and physiological responses.

Within these definitions, the published behavior therapy outcome studies were reviewed and organized according to and with an emphasis upon the specific measurements of depression. The somatic–motor response measures included those taken in institutional settings, in clinical interviews, in the home, in therapy group interactions, and in laboratory role-play settings. The outcome on self-report measures were reviewed under global measures of depression (e.g., BDI, MMPI-D, and the Zung SRDS), clinical ratings of self-report data (e.g., HRS-D and the Raskin Depression Scale), and specific self-report measures (e.g., PES and Rehm's self-control measures).

Several observations were made on the basis of the summarized outcome data. The total number of subjects included in these studies was small but larger than the number of subjects studied by most approaches to the treatment of depression. Specific behavior therapy approaches to the treatment of depression have been studied primarily in the laboratories of their originators; thus, exportability of the therapy procedures needs to be investigated. There is a paucity of adequately developed assessment devices. Treatment effects have been clearest and most pronounced on those measures that are directly related to the focus of the therapy. In general, the more comprehensive the treatment program, the greater its effect on global rating scales of depression.

Four issues were raised by the treatment studies. The first is: Is there a syndrome of depression? This question cannot currently be answered; however, a research strategy based on a multifaceted assessment package and focusing on the interrelationships of the various somatic–motor, self-report, and physiological measures of depression was suggested to help resolve this question.

The second issue centers on a discussion of the assessment strategies suggested in response to the first issue. The third issue concerns the relationship between depression and other types of psychopathology, especially anxiety. The final issue is whether treatment studies should receive the primary attention of behavior therapists. It was suggested that in the final analysis the deleterious effects of depression may be better understood and overcome by the study of its development and prevention.

# References

Aitken, R. C. B. Measurement of feeling using visual analogue scales. *Proceedings of the Royal Society of Medicine,* 1969, *62,* 989–993.

Bandura, A. Psychotherapy based on modeling principles. In A. E. Bergin & S. L. Garfield (Eds.), *Handbook of psychotherapy and behavior change: An empirical analysis.* New York: Wiley, 1971.

Beck, A. T. Thinking and depression. *Archives of General Psychiatry,* 1963, *9,* 324–333.

Beck, A. T. *Depression: Causes and treatment.* Philadelphia: University of Pennsylvania Press, 1967.

Beck, A. T. *Cognitive therapy and the emotional disorders.* New York: International Universities Press, 1976.

Beck, A. T., Rush, A. J., & Kovacs, M. Individual treatment manual for cognitive/behavioral psychotherapy of depression. Unpublished manuscript, Department of Psychiatry, University of Pennsylvania, 1975.

Beck, A. T., Rush, A. J., Shaw, B. F., & Emery, G. *Cognitive therapy of depression: A treatment manual.* New York: Guilford Press, 1979.

Beck, A. T., Ward, C. H., Mendelson, M., Mock, J., & Erbaugh, J. An inventory for measuring depression. *Archives of General Psychiatry,* 1961, *4,* 561–571.

Becker, J. *Depression: Theory and research.* New York: Wiley, 1974.

Borkovec, T. D. Physiological and cognitive processes in the regulation of anxiety. In G. E. Schwartz & D. Shapiro (Eds.), *Consciousness and self-regulation: Advances in research* (Vol. 1). New York: Plenum, 1976.

Carkhuff, R. R. *The development of human resources: Education, psychology, and social change.* New York: Holt, 1971.

Craighead, L. W. Self-instructional training for assertive-refusal behavior. *Behavior Therapy,* 1979, *10,* 529–542.

Craighead, L. W., & Craighead, W. E. Implications of persuasion communication research for the modification of self-statements. *Cognitive Therapy and Research,* 1980, *4,* 117–134.

Craighead, W. E. Away from a unitary model of depression. *Behavior Therapy,* 1980, *11,* 123–129.

Craighead, W. E., Craighead, L. W., & Meyers, A. W. New directions in behavior modification with children. In M. Hersen, P. Miller, & R. Eisler (Eds.), *Progress in behavior modification* (Vol. 6). New York: Academic, 1978.

Craighead, W. E., Kazdin, A. E., & Mahoney, M. J. *Behavior modification: Principles, issues, and applications* (2d ed.). Boston: Houghton Mifflin, 1981.

Craighead, W. E., Kimball, W. H., & Rehak, P. J. Mood changes, physiological responses, and self-statements during social rejection imagery. *Journal of Consulting and Clinical Psychology,* 1979, *47,* 385–396.

Ellis, A. *The essence of rational psychotherapy: A comprehensive approach to treatment.* New York: Institute for Rational Living, 1970.

Endicott, J., & Spitzer, R. L. A diagnostic interview: The Schedule for Affective Disorders and Schizophrenia. *Archives of General Psychiatry,* 1978, *35,* 837–844.

Endler, N. S., & Okada, M. A multidimensional measure of trait anxiety: The S–R Inventory of General Trait Anxiousness. *Journal of Consulting and Clinical Psychology,* 1975, *43,* 319–329.

Feighner, J. P., Robins, E., Guze, S. B., Woodruff, R. A., Winokur, G., & Munoz, R. Diagnostic criteria for use in psychiatric research. *Archives of General Psychiatry,* 1972, *26,* 57–63.

Ferster, C. B. Classification of behavioral pathology. In L. Krasner & L. P. Ullmann (Eds.), *Research in behavior modification.* New York: Holt, 1965.

Friedman, R. J., & Katz, M. M. (Eds.). *The psychology of depression: Contemporary theory and research.* New York: Wiley, 1974.

Fuchs, C. Z., & Rehm, L. P. A self-control behavior therapy program for depression. *Journal of Consulting and Clinical Psychology,* 1977, *45,* 206–215.

Gioe, V. J. Cognitive modification and positive group experience as a treatment for depression (Doctoral dissertation, Temple University, 1975). *Dissertation Abstracts International,* 1975, *36,* 3039B–3040B.

Hamilton, M. A rating scale for depression. *Journal of Neurology, Neurosurgery, and Psychiatry,* 1960, *23,* 56–62.

Hanaway, T. P., & Barlow, D. H. Prolonged depressive behaviors in a recently blinded deaf mute: A behavioral treatment. *Journal of Behavior Therapy and Experimental Psychiatry,* 1975, *6,* 43–48.

Hersen, M., & Bellack, A. S. Assessment of social skills. In A. R. Ciminero, K. S. Calhoun, & H. E. Adams (Eds.), *Handbook of behavioral assessment.* New York: Wiley, 1977.

Hersen, M., Eisler, D., Alford, G., & Agras, W. S. Effects of token economy on neurotic depression: An experimental analysis. *Behavior Therapy,* 1973, *4,* 392–397.

Hollon, S. D., & Kendall, P. C. Cognitive self-statements in depression: Development of an Automatic Thoughts Questionnaire. Unpublished manuscript available from S. D. Hollon, Department of Psychology, University of Minnesota, Minneapolis, Minnesota, 1979.

Honn, S. A. A methodological study of the Beck Depression Inventory: The effect of group versus individual testing conditions and repeated testing upon depression scores. Unpublished master's thesis, Pennsylvania State University, 1979.

Kendall, P. C., & Korgeski, G. P. Assessment and cognitive–behavioral interventions. *Cognitive Therapy and Research,* 1979, *3,* 1–21.

Kennedy, R. E., & Craighead, W. E. Differential effects of positive and negative feedback on learning, expectations, and recall in depression and anxiety. Unpublished manuscript available from W. E. Craighead, Department of Psychology, Pennsylvania State University, University Park, Pa., 1980.

Kovacs, M., Rush, A. J., Beck, A. T., & Hollon, S. P. A one year follow-up of depressed outpatients treated with cognitive therapy or pharmacotherapy. Paper presented at the meetings of the Eastern Psychological Association, Philadelphia, April 1979.

Lazarus, A. A. Learning theory and the treatment of depression. *Behavior Research and Therapy,* 1968, *6,* 83–89.

Lewinsohn, P. M. Manual for instructions for the behavior rating used for the observation of interpersonal behavior. Unpublished manuscript available from P. M. Lewinsohn, Department of Psychology, University of Oregon, Eugene, Oregon, 1968.

Lewinsohn, P. M. A behavioral approach to depression. In R. J. Friedman & M. M. Katz (Eds.), *The psychology of depression: Contemporary theory and research.* New York: Wiley, 1974. (a)

Lewinsohn, P. M. Clinical and theoretical aspects of depression. In K. S. Calhoun, H. E. Adams, & K. M. Mitchell (Eds.), *Innovative treatment methods in psychopathology.* New York: Wiley, 1974. (b)

Lewinsohn, P. M., & Biglan, A. Behavioral treatment of depression. Paper presented at the meetings of the Association for the Advancement of Behavior Therapy, San Francisco, 1975.

Lewinsohn, P. M., Biglan, A., & Zeiss, A. M. Behavioral treatment of depression. In P. O. Davidson (Ed.), *The behavioral management of anxiety, depression and pain.* New York: Brunner-Mazel, 1976.

Lewinsohn, P. M., & Shaffer, M. The use of home observations as an integral part of the treatment of depression: Preliminary report and case studies. *Journal of Consulting and Clinical Psychology,* 1971, *37,* 87–94.

Lewinsohn, P. M., & Shaw, D. A. Feedback about interpersonal behavior as an agent of behavior change: A case study in the treatment of depression. *Psychotherapy and Psychosomatics,* 1969, *17,* 82–88.

Liberman, R. P., & Raskin, D. E. Depression. A behavioral formulation. *Archives of General Psychiatry,* 1971, *24,* 515–523.

London, P. The end of ideology in behavior modification. *American Psychologist,* 1972, *27,* 913–920.

Lubin, B. Adjective checklists for the measurement of depression. *Archives of General Psychiatry,* 1965, *12,* 57–62.

Mahoney, M. J. *Cognition and behavior modification.* Boston: Ballinger, 1974.

Marmor, J. *Psychiatry in transition.* London: Butterworth, 1974.

Marmor, J. Academic lecture: The nature of the psychotherapeutic process revisited. *Canadian Psychiatric Association Journal,* 1975, *20,* 557–565.

Marston, A. Personality variables related to self-reinforcement. *Journal of Psychology,* 1964, *58,* 169–175.

Meichenbaum, D. M. *Cognitive behavior modification.* New York: Plenum, 1977.

McLean, P. D., & Hakstian, A. R. Clinical depression: Comparative efficacy of outpatient treatments. *Journal of Consulting and Clinical Psychology,* 1979, *47,* 818–836.

McLean, P. D., Ogston, K., & Grauer, L. A behavioral approach to the treatment of depression. *Journal of Behavior Therapy and Experimental Psychiatry,* 1973, *4,* 323–330.

Mischel, W. Personality, cognition, and behavior. Paper presented at the meetings of the American Psychological Association, Toronto, Ontario, Canada, August 1978.

Padfield, M. The comparative effects of two counseling approaches on the intensity of depression among rural women of low socioeconomic status. *Journal of Counseling Psychology,* 1976, *23,* 209–214.

Paul, G. L., & Lentz, R. J. *Psychosocial treatment of chronic mental patients.* Cambridge, Mass.: Harvard University Press, 1978.

Raskin, A., Schulterbrandt, J. G., Reatig, N., & McKeon, J. J. Differential response to chlorpromazine, imipramine, and placebo: A study of subgroups of hospitalized depressed patients. *Archives of General Psychiatry,* 1970, *23,* 164–173.

Rehm, L. P. A self-control model of depression. *Behavior Therapy,* 1977, *8,* 787–804.

Rehm, L. P., Fuchs, C. Z., Roth, D. M., Kornblith, S. J., & Romano, J. M. A comparison of self-control and assertion skills treatments of depression. *Behavior Therapy,* 1979, *10,* 429–442.

Rehm, L. P., & Kornblith, S. J. Behavior therapy for depression: A review of recent developments. In M. Hersen, R. M. Eisler, & P. M. Miller (Eds.), *Progress in behavior modification* (Vol. 7). New York: Academic Press, 1979.

Reisinger, J. J. The treatment of "anxiety-depression" via positive reinforcement and response cost. *Journal of Applied Behavior Analysis,* 1972, *5,* 125–130.

Robinson, J. C., & Lewinsohn, P. M. Behavior modification of speech characteristics in a chronically depressed man. *Behavior Therapy,* 1973, *4,* 150–152. (a)

Robinson, J. C., & Lewinsohn, P. M. Experimental analysis of a technique based on the Premack Principle for changing verbal behavior of depressed individuals. *Psychological Reports,* 1973, *32,* 199–210. (b)

Ross, A. O. Behavior therapy with children. In S. L. Garfield & A. E. Bergin (Eds.), *Handbook of psychotherapy and behavior change: An empirical analysis* (2nd ed.). New York: Wiley, 1978.

Rush, A. J., Beck, A. T., Kovacs, M., & Hollon, S. D. Comparative efficacy of cognitive therapy versus pharmacotherapy in outpatient depressives. *Cognitive Therapy and Research,* 1977, *1,* 17–37.

Schwartz, G. E., Fair, P. L., Mandel, M. R., Salt, P., Mieske, M., & Klerman, G. L. Facial electromyography in the assessment of improvement in depression. *Psychosomatic Medicine,* 1975, *40,* 355–360.

Schwartz, G. E., & Weiss, S. M. What is behavioral medicine? *Psychosomatic Medicine,* 1977, *39,* 377–381.

Schwartz, R. M., & Gottman, J. M. Toward a task analysis of assertive behavior. *Journal of Consulting and Clinical Psychology,* 1976, *44,* 910–920.

Secunda, R., Friedman, R. J., & Schuyler, D. Special report, 1973: *The depressive disorders* (DHEW Publication No. HSM73–9125). Washington, D.C.: U.S. Government Printing Office, 1973.

Shaw, B. F. Comparison of cognitive therapy and behavior therapy in the treatment of depression. *Journal of Consulting and Clinical Psychology,* 1977, *45,* 543–551.

Shipley, C. R., & Fazio, A. F. Pilot study of a treatment for psychological depression. *Journal of Abnormal Psychology,* 1973, *82,* 372–376.

Spitzer, R. L., Endicott, J., & Robins, E. Research Diagnostic Criteria: Rationale and reliability. *Archives of General Psychiatry,* 1978, *35,* 773–782.

Taylor, F. G., & Marshall, W. L. Experimental analysis of a cognitive–behavioral therapy for depression. *Cognitive Therapy and Research,* 1977, *1,* 59–72.

Ullmann, L. P., & Krasner, L. *A psychological approach to abnormal behavior* (2nd ed.). Englewood Cliffs, N.J.: Prentice Hall, 1975.

Wilcoxon, L. A., Schrader, S. L., & Nelson, R. E. Behavioral formulations of depression. In W. E. Craighead, A. E. Kazdin, & M. J. Mahoney (Eds.), *Behavior modification: Principles, issues, and applications.* Boston: Houghton Mifflin, 1976.

Williams, J. G., Barlow, D. H., & Agras, W. S. Behavioral measurement of severe depression. *Archives of General Psychiatry,* 1972, *72,* 330–337.

Wolberg, L. R. *Short-term psychotherapy.* New York: Grune and Stratton, 1967.

Wolpe, J., & Lazarus, A. A. *Behavior therapy techniques.* New York: Pergamon, 1966.

Zuckerman, M., & Lubin, B. *Multiple Affect Adjective Checklist.* San Diego: Education and Industrial Testing Service, 1965.

Zung, W. W. K. A self-rating depression scale. *Archives of General Psychiatry,* 1965, *12,* 63–70.

# 4

# Toward a Second-Generation Model: A Problem-Specific Approach

ANTHONY BIGLAN
MICHAEL G. DOW

This chapter advocates the development of a "second-generation" model of depression treatment. Such a model is needed because there are diverse theories of depression but striking similarities among the treatment programs they have spawned. An effective second-generation model would specify treatment components at a fairly operational level. It would prompt us to identify the problems that a client is experiencing and the treatment procedures that are likely to affect those events. It would promote more effective communication among investigators.

The difficulty with trying to discuss depression treatment programs in terms of current theories is illustrated by the diverse ways in which treatment programs can be interpreted. Here are a few examples. In a review that we wrote for a grant proposal to the National Institute of Mental Health (Biglan & Dow, 1977), we classified the treatment program of Fuchs and Rehm (1977) as a pleasant-activities treatment, since a central component involved monitoring, planning, and executing pleasant activities. We could perhaps be accused of expedience or perversity, since Fuchs and Rehm (1977) presented a cogent argument for construing their procedures in terms of the self-control processes of the individual (Kanfer & Karoly, 1972; Rehm, 1977). But we are not alone. Hollon and Beck (1979, p. 35) suggest that we consider Fuchs and Rehm's (1977) program as a type of cognitive intervention similar to Beck's cognitive therapy. They contend that the self-control model (Rehm, 1977) is "at best . . . a semantic rewording of cognitive theory into behavioral terminology [p. 21]."

Another example: Rush, Beck, Kovacs, and Hollon (1977) describe their treatment program as a cognitive intervention, but the program involves, among other procedures, self-monitoring and increase of pleasant activities. As McLean and Hakstian (1979) noted, "The useful distinction between cognitive

97

and behavior therapy fades in this study, inasmuch as an examination of treatment procedures clearly indicates that both behavioral and cognitive techniques were deployed [p. 819]."

Finally, consider the treatment program described by Shipley and Fazio (1973). They derived their procedures from Ferster's (1966) analysis of depression as being due to a low rate of reinforcement. The treatment program employed a functional problem-solving technique that was designed to ameliorate personal and social problems and consequently increase the amount of reinforcement obtained from the subject's environment. Yet Hollon and Beck (1979) characterize the program as cognitive.

We suspect that most of the contributors to the present volume could, with little difficulty, construct an argument that any given treatment procedure affects cognitive processes, or manipulates contingencies of reinforcement, or affects the self-control processes of the individual, or alters the person's perception of helplessness. Criteria for choosing among these interpretations are not obvious. Therefore, it may be more fruitful to enumerate the specific components of each program in fairly operational terms and suppress our desire to subsume treatment elements under more general theoretical headings.

## The Framework of Behavior Analysis

The experimental analysis of behavior (Sidman, 1960; Skinner, 1970) provides a useful framework for talking about depression treatment and research. Biglan and Kass (1977) have described how this approach is much more generally applicable to clinical phenomena than has been realized. The basic features of the experimental analysis of behavior involve identifying all the variables that affect the occurrence of behavior (Skinner, 1970). The probability of a specific event or class of events can be studied in relation to any well-defined independent variable. The efficacy of any intervention is a question of the effects of an independent variable on the probability of certain behaviors.

This version of behaviorism makes no reference to specific learning principles. In fact, it is not committed to the preeminence of any specific set of independent variables. Its value lies in the precise and empirical way in which any organismic event, *including private events,* can be formulated as behavior and in its empirical program for the identification of any variables that affect those behavioral events.

The approach is of particular value in studying depression, since it prompts us to specify the private and observable events that occur in depression and the specific events that may create, maintain, or remediate each of these problems. Research on the treatment of depression is a matter of determining the effects of specific independent variables on each of the problematic events that make up the depression syndrome. A list of independent variables that are relevant to treatment is presented in the left-hand column of Table 4.1. We identified these variables by reviewing depression treatment programs. Any independent variable could be added to our list. For example, pharmacological agents would be included if they were germane to our review. Behavioral events could themselves be studied as independent variables that affect one or more classes of depressive behaviors. For example, increasing pleasant activities could be thought of as an independent variable that may affect questionnaire responses, insomnia, and so on.

The dependent variables in this model are the specific depressive events that have been enumerated by others (Lewinsohn, Biglan, & Zeiss, 1976; McLean, 1976b; Feighner, Robins, Guze, Woodruff, Winokur, & Munoz, 1972). They are presented in the right-hand column of Table 4.1. We can only enumerate depressive events at this point, because we know little about their covariance or their centrality to depression. When we know more about the covariance among these events and the extent to which clusters of problems respond to particular interventions, we may be able to solve the elusive problem of identifying types of depressions (Hersen, Himmelhoch, & Bellack, 1977; Mendels, 1968). Simply enumerating depressive events keeps before us the assessment problems involved in depression treatment research. Current assessment relies largely on questionnaire measures (Rehm, 1976). Questionnaires are samples of verbal behavior. When such measures change, we cannot be sure whether we have actually affected the problem events in question or simply affected the person's verbal behavior.

## A Taxonomy of Treatment Components

The ideal treatment model would indicate the specific procedures that have been empirically demonstrated to affect one or more of the constituents of the depression syndrome. Given a depressed client, the model would specify the particular interventions that are most likely to remediate each of the problems that person is experiencing. Although a number of total treatment programs have been found to be superior to comparison conditions (McLean & Hakstian, 1979; Rush et al., 1977; Shaw, 1977; Taylor & Marshall, 1977), we know little about which specific components affect which depressive events.

In the absence of such a data-based organization, we will enumerate the components that current evidence suggest are the most relevant to treating one or more depression problems. In this analysis, we will consider two types of components. *Setting conditions* are the circumstances under which treatment is delivered, such as the number of sessions and the characteristics of therapists. *Major treatment components* are the main elements of treatment, such as social skills training or the modification of activity. In addition, each of the major components are made up of a number of *fine-grained techniques,* such as modeling, self-monitoring, therapist empathy, and identifying automatic thoughts. Many of these techniques are part of several different major treatment components. For example, self-monitoring and between-session assignments

**TABLE 4.1**
Independent and Dependent Variables in Depression Treatment Research

| Independent variables | Dependent variables |
|---|---|
| **Setting conditions** | **Overt behavior** |
| Arrangements for treatment delivery | Nonsocial |
| Group treatment | Inactivity |
| Timing of sessions | Insomnia |
| Money deposits | Suicidal behavior |
| Charges for treatment | Social |
| Therapist characteristics | Low rate or range of interactions |
| Intake and assessment procedures | Avoidance of others |
| Goal setting | Skill deficits |
| Extent and content of assessment | Conflict with others |
| | Sexually inactive |
| **Major treatment components** | Verbal |
| Modification of activities | Complaints (including questionnaire responses) |
| Self-monitoring of activity and mood | |
| Planning small increases in activities | **Covert behavior** |
| Instructions | Feelings |
| Rewards for activities | Anxiety |
| Modification of social behavior | Dysphoria |
| Social skills interventions | Fatigue |
| Target skills: "Assertive" responses: smiling, gesturing, | Verbal–cognitive events |
| eye contact, voice, loudness, questions | Worry |
| Target procedures: Covert and overt modeling, instruction, | Indecisiveness |
| social reinforcement, coaching, behavior rehearsal, | Negative self-talk |
| bibliotherapy, token reinforcement | Suicidal thoughts |
| Increasing social activity | Somatic events |
| (Same as for Modification of activities) | Weight loss |
| Marital interventions | Headaches |
| Feedback about interpersonal behavior | Pain |
| Contracting with spouse | Gastrointestinal problems |
| Communications training | Dizziness |

Modification of verbal—cognitive events
Suppression of negative self-talk
    Self-monitoring
    Thought stopping
    Flooding
    Punishment
    Systematic desensitization
    Paradoxical intention
    Delay between thoughts and overt behavior
    Extinction
    Geographical control (restrict thinking to certain places)
    Temporal control (restrict thinking to certain times)
Analysis of thought content
    Self-monitoring
    Identifying themes or content
    Distancing thoughts by labeling them as hypotheses
    Evaluating evidence for thoughts, then implications if true
    Identifying other ways to look at them
    Testing validity of thoughts or beliefs
    Bibliotherapy
    Writing and saying rational refutations of thoughts
Anxiety treatment
    Systematic desensitization
    Flooding
    Relaxation training with coping skill instructions
Insomnia treatment
    Relaxation training
    Stimulus control procedures

have been used with social skills training (Zeiss, Lewinsohn, & Munoz, 1979), activities programs (Lewinsohn, 1976), and cognitive modification procedures (cf. Hollon & Beck, 1979).

## Setting Conditions

We include three categories under setting conditions: (*a*) arrangements for treatment delivery; (*b*) therapist characteristics; and (*c*) intake and assessment procedures. Some of the things we are characterizing as setting conditions may themselves be active ingredients in treatment. For example, we may ultimately find that group treatment is more effective than individual treatment in re-mediating the social deficits of depressed clients.

Although these conditions usually do not vary within a single treatment study, they vary considerably across studies. Indeed, some of these conditions, such as the content of assessment instruments, appear to be confounded with research programs. When setting conditions vary across projects and between research and nonresearch treatment settings, it is possible that treatment programs that appear to be effective will not be generalizable to other settings (cf. Campbell & Stanley, 1963).

### ARRANGEMENTS FOR TREATMENT DELIVERY

Some relevant issues regarding arrangements for treatment delivery are group versus individual treatment, timing of sessions, whether money deposits are required of patients, and whether clients are charged for treatment. There is little empirical evidence about the extent to which these specific facets of treatment affect outcome.

### THERAPIST CHARACTERISTICS

Reviewers have differed on the importance of therapist characteristics for treatment outcome (Lambert, DeJulio, & Stern, 1978; Truax & Mitchell, 1971). Most of this research has not been done on depressed clients.

There is one outstanding exception to this general summary. McLean and Hakstian (1979) systematically varied the experience of their therapists in a study comparing behavior therapy, psychotherapy, drug therapy, and relaxation training. They found that therapist experience was not associated with outcome when considered over all treatments and therapists. There was a trend for clients of the more experienced behavior therapists to show greater improve-ment on the Beck Depression Inventory (Beck, Ward, Mendelson, Mock, & Erbaugh, 1961) than clients of the less experienced therapists. If solid evidence is generated about the effectiveness of certain therapist characteristics, the most fruitful approach would be to pinpoint the relevant behaviors and teach them to the less experienced therapists.

INTAKE AND ASSESSMENT PROCEDURES

Intake and assessment procedures have often been ignored in the description and empirical evaluation of treatment programs. These procedures may interact with treatment programs and affect the generalizability of treatment. Intake may be important because program effectiveness may depend in part on how well specific target problems are identified and prioritized. The intake session could also sensitize some clients to the interventions that follow.

*Goal Setting.* Goal setting may contribute to the success of treatment and may prompt us to be precise about the components of depression for each individual. A number of treatment programs have included goal setting. McLean (1976a) emphasizes the importance of depressed individuals learning to set reasonable goals. In our own work, we ask clients to enumerate the specific problems they want to change. We let clients decide the priorities among the goals, since we believe it enhances their involvement and because they may be better able to predict which problems are most amenable to treatment. There is some evidence from our work with anxious clients that they can predict treatment outcome (Lewis, Biglan, & Steinbock, 1978).

It is noteworthy that the behavior therapy treatment condition in the study by McLean and Hakstian (1979) had a significantly lower client dropout rate than did either the drug or psychotherapy group. This condition included goal-setting procedures. Other factors, such as side effects in the drug treatment group, may account for these differences, but it is interesting that the main reason for dropout given by the relaxation and general psychotherapy groups was that they could not see the relevance of treatment procedures to their current problems.

Finally, goal specification could improve our research. It would force us to enumerate and treat the specific depressive problems of the individual rather than adopt the implicit assumption that our treatment program, as a whole, affects all constituents of the depression syndrome.

*Extent and Content of Assessment.* Assessments in research studies have ranged from a few brief questionnaires (e.g., Shipley & Fazio, 1973) to extensive assessment of the social and psychological functioning of the individual, including direct observation of social behavior (Zeiss, Lewinsohn, & Munoz, 1979).

Rehm (1976) has already made a good case for extensive assessment. Surely, if we are ever to determine what treatment components affect which problem areas, we shall need extensive data on the specific problems of the individual. However, extensive assessment could interact with treatment and affect the generalizability of results. The type of assessment instrument is also important. For example, social skills training may produce improvement on a behavioral interaction but not on certain questionnaire measures.

Finally, the content of assessments is relevant to our learning how to improve treatment. Unless we assess each of the specific events that are problematic for a client, we cannot elaborate the effects of specific components of our treatment program.

## Major Treatment Components

### MODIFICATION OF ACTIVITIES

Modification of activities is a component of virtually every treatment program we have reviewed. Although increasing pleasant activities is primarily identified with Lewinsohn's approach to depression treatment, some form of activity increase is usually targeted in cognitive and self-control treatments. A review of available correlational evidence suggests that there are good reasons for attempting to modify activities, although experimental evidence is inconclusive regarding whether manipulating activity level produces improvement in depression.

*The Relevance of Activity to Depression.* By using the Pleasant Events Schedule (MacPhillamy & Lewinsohn, 1971), Lewinsohn and MacPhillamy (1974; MacPhillamy & Lewinsohn, 1974) found that depressed individuals engage in fewer pleasant activities and have a lower subjective evaluation of the enjoyability of these events than either nondepressed normal controls or nondepressed psychiatric control subjects.

In two additional studies (Lewinsohn & Graf, 1973; Lewinsohn & Libet, 1972), a significant association was found between self-monitored records of the number of pleasant activities engaged in each day and daily rated mood. However, across subjects, the magnitude of these correlations varied considerably. Lewinsohn and Libet (1972) also examined whether activity one or two days previous to a given day predicted mood on that day and conversely whether the mood ratings one or two days prior to a given day predicted activity. The means for these lead and lag correlations were not significantly different from zero. This finding is inconsistent with the hypothesis that lower activity rates cause dysphoria.

The generally significant correlations that have been found between pleasant activity and mood measures may be due in part to common method variance. The Pleasant Events Schedule (PES) requires subjects to report only on the occurrence of activities that were at least somewhat pleasant. Thus, mood ratings and activity ratings are both verbal reports of the extent to which the subject feels positive about something. We need additional sources of data about activities in order to test the role of activities themselves as opposed to reports of feelings about activities.

A second difficulty is that mood measures and activity measures are probably autocorrelated across time for particular subjects. This violates an important assumption of correlational analyses. Traditional significance tests are not appropriate, and adjustment of the degrees of freedom should be made (Bartlett, 1935).

A high frequency of unpleasant events may also be relevant to depression. Grosscup and Lewinsohn (1980) developed a measure of the rate of unpleasant events—the Unpleasant Events Schedule (UES) (Lewinsohn, 1975). In general, persons diagnosed as depressed report higher rates of events on the UES, and daily self-monitored rates of these events are correlated with mood ratings. It may be important to help some depressed individuals reduce the frequency of unpleasant events or cope with them more effectively.

*Methods of Increasing Activities.* The techniques used to increase activities have varied considerably. They are listed in Table 4.1. Most procedures include some method of pinpointing situations where increased activity may be relevant or of pinpointing activities that are associated with mood. This is done through daily self-monitoring of mood and activity (e.g., Barrera, 1979; Fuchs & Rehm, 1977; Lewinsohn, 1976) and through discussions about situations that create difficulties for the client (Shipley & Fazio, 1973). Most treatment programs have the client monitor daily activities throughout treatment (Craker & Biglan, 1979; Fuchs & Rehm, 1977; Hollon & Beck, 1979; Lewinsohn, 1976). Self-monitoring may itself produce changes in behavior, although such changes may be short lived (Kazdin, 1974).

Not all treatment programs focus strictly on increasing pleasant activities. McLean (1976a, 1976b) also emphasizes encouraging the client to engage in productive, problem-solving activities that may not be immediately pleasant but may be incompatible with rumination and likely to improve the person's situation. A similar emphasis is seen in the programs described by Hollon and Beck (1979) and Fuchs and Rehm (1977).

Perhaps the main method of attempting to increase activities involves planning small increases between treatment sessions. This was done by Lewinsohn (1976), Zeiss et al. (1979), Fuchs and Rehm (1977), Taylor and Marshall (1977), and Shipley and Fazio (1973). It appears to have been the strategy for McLean and Hakstian (1979) and for Rush et al. (1977). Hammen and Glass (1975) simply instructed subjects to increase the frequency of pleasant activities.

A number of programs have provided reinforcement contingent on activity level. Lewinsohn (1976) made time with the therapist contingent on the frequency of targeted activities. Significant increases in targeted activities were found for the 10 subjects in his study. Craker and Biglan (1979), in a series of withdrawal designs with six clients, had clients reward themselves for meeting daily activity goals. In comparison with baseline and daily goal setting, definite increases in self-monitored activity level are obtained during self-reward phases, but self-monitored mood was not affected. Hersen, Eisler, Alford, and Agras

(1973) used an ABA design to evaluate token reinforcement of ward work behavior in three hospitalized depressed males. Subjects were rated as less depressed on the Behavioral Rating Scale (Williams, Barlow, & Agras, 1972) during contingent reinforcement phases.

*Problems in Evaluating Pleasant-Activities Interventions.* There are three types of problems in deciding on the value of activity interventions. First, few treatment programs are exclusively designed to change activities. For example, in the study by Zeiss *et al.* (1979), the pleasant-activities treatment included relaxation training. In the cognitive treatment described by Hollon and Beck (1979), alteration of activities is only one of a number of components. Even if these treatment programs prove superior to comparison conditions, we cannot tell to what extent the superiority was due to the activity component.

Second, the pleasant activities targeted in treatment usually include cognitive and social events. Inspection of PES items reveals this similarity. Lewinsohn and Libet (1972) identified items that were significantly associated with mood for at least 10% of their subjects. The largest single group consisted of 21 items involving social interaction (e.g., being with happy people; having people show interest in what you have said). Fifteen involved cognitive and emotional states (e.g., laughing, being relaxed). It seems important in further work to examine separately the effects of changing social, cognitive, and nonsocial activities. Similarly, we will need to examine whether simply targeting increases in these activities is sufficient or whether additional interventions are needed.

A third problem was pointed out by Zeiss *et al.* (1979). If we are specifically interested in the effects on depression of changing pleasant activities, we should demonstrate that we have actually increased the rate of pleasant activity. Only when we are able to manipulate pleasant-activity level as an independent variable can we experimentally evaluate the efficacy of pleasant-activities changes in the treatment of depression. Some studies have not succeeded in increasing pleasant activities (e.g., Hammen & Glass, 1975, Experiment 2; Zeiss *et al.,* 1979). These studies have generally shown significant changes between pre- and posttreatment assessment of pleasant activity, but it has not been possible to conclude that the changes were due to treatment manipulation.

Where pleasant activities have been successfully manipulated as an independent variable, the results have been equivocal. One control group design that was successful in achieving greater increases in pleasant activities for its treatment group than for other groups (Fuchs & Rehm, 1977) did find significantly greater improvement on depression measures as well. However, the study contained self-control training in addition to the pleasant-activities focus. In a second control group design that was successful in manipulating pleasant activities (Hammen & Glass, 1975, Experiment 1) improvements on depression measures were not achieved. In a series of single-case experiments we conducted (Craker & Biglan, 1979), significant increases in pleasant activities were not consistently associated with improvements in mood.

In summary, pleasant activities are clearly an important factor in depression, and a general strategy for increasing activity level may be useful in treating depressed individuals. However, specific techniques may be needed to deal with the particular classes of activities that are problematic for each person. Treatment procedures that focus on increasing social skill, decreasing social anxiety, increasing the individual's ability to manage his or her time, reducing obsessional thinking, reducing anxiety, and increasing approaches to phobic stimuli may all be relevant for particular clients. In further work, the effects of intervening separately on different classes of activities should be evaluated.

SOCIAL BEHAVIOR COMPONENTS

*Relevance of Social Behavior to Depression.* There is ample evidence that the social behavior of depressed individuals is different from that of others. Persons meeting diagnostic criteria for depression report fewer social activities and less comfort in social interactions than do nondepressed psychiatric controls (persons with elevations on MMPI scales other than the depression scale [Youngren & Lewinsohn, 1977]). In at least some studies (Libet & Lewinsohn, 1973; Libet, Lewinsohn, & Javorek, 1973), specific deficits in social behavior of depressed subjects have been identified. Depressed persons have been found to emit fewer positive responses in small-group interactions (Libet & Lewinsohn, 1973) and fewer responses that have been empirically demonstrated to be social reinforcers (Libet, Lewinsohn, & Javorek, 1973). Even when specific deficits in social behavior have not been identified among depressed subjects, it has been found that their social behavior has a negative impact on those who observe them or interact with them (Coyne, 1976; Youngren & Lewinsohn, 1977).

In our own work (Biglan, Glaser, & Dow, 1979), we compared socially anxious and nonanxious women who were selected as high and low scorers on the Social Avoidance and Distress Scale (Watson & Friend, 1969). The socially anxious women were significantly more depressed than the nonanxious women on both the Center for Epidemiological Studies Depression Scale (CES-D) (Radloff, 1977) and the Beck Depression Inventory.

Marital relationships may be particularly problematic among depressed persons (Patterson & Rosenberry, 1969; Weissman & Paykel, 1974). Coleman and Miller (1975) found that among men, marital discord as measured by the Locke–Wallace Marital Adjustment Test (Locke & Wallace, 1959) is related to scores on the Beck Depression Inventory. Weiss and Aved (1978) found the same relationship for men using the Zung Self-Rating Depression Scale (SDS) (Zung, 1965). For women, the Locke-Wallace and the SDS were correlated, but when a measure of health status was partialed out, no relationship was found. Lewinsohn and his colleagues conducted a series of home observation studies of marital interaction (Lewinsohn & Atwood, 1969; Lewinsohn & Shaffer, 1971; Lewinsohn, Weinstein, & Shaw, 1969; Shaffer & Lewinsohn, 1971). In general, the depressed partner appeared to receive less attention for social behaviors, more negative reactions, and fewer positive reactions from the spouse and family members.

There may be considerable heterogeneity in the extent and type of social relationship problems among depressed individuals. One person may be involved in continued marital conflict, another may lack skills in interacting with fellow workers. Thus, even where social relationships are problematic, an assessment must be done that pinpoints the specific situations that are problematic and the specific skills that the individual lacks.

*Varieties of Social Skills Interventions.* We have been able to find surprisingly few social behavior treatments for depression (McLean & Hakstian, 1979; Reisinger, 1972; Wells, Hersen, Bellack, & Himmelhoch, 1977; Zeiss *et al.,* 1979).

Zeiss *et al.* (1979) evaluated a social behavior program for depression. Two of three components of the program involved skills training: assertiveness training and modification of interpersonal style. Target responses for interpersonal style included responding to others, reducing complaints, and increasing social communication. There was no evidence that this treatment was more effective than a self-monitoring-only control condition, but there was also no evidence that the social behavior of this group had changed more than that of the controls.

Hersen and his coworkers (Hersen & Bellack, 1976; Hersen, Eisler, & Miller, 1973) have reported a number of careful single-case experimental designs evaluating methods of teaching assertiveness skills. A report by Wells *et al.* (1977) illustrates their use of social skills training with depressed persons. Behaviors that were taught included identifying an appropriate verbal response, maintaining eye contact while talking, gesturing, smiling, and speaking louder. All subjects evidenced improvement on observer ratings of assertiveness on the Behavioral Assertiveness Test (Eisler, Miller, & Hersen, 1973) as well as improvements in eye contact and response latency. Similar improvements were found on all self-report and rating measures of assertiveness and depression. This study is only a series of four AB designs (Hersen & Barlow, 1976). Better control for extraneous factors is needed in order to be sure that social skills training was indeed the effective ingredient in the improvement of these women.

McLean and Hakstian's (1979) behavior therapy depression treatment program included components directed at three aspects of social skill: communication, social interaction, and assertiveness. According to McLean's (1976b) earlier discussion of his treatment program, the problems addressed under communication often involve aversive marital exchanges and a restricted range and quantity of interactions. Problems in social interaction include unfamiliarity with social possibilities in the community, unrewarding social interactions, and avoidance of social situations "due to anxiety" (McLean, 1976b, p. 73). In general, the three social skill areas are treated through graduated assignments and therapist modeling (McLean & Hakstian, 1979). A great strength of McLean's treatment program is its tailoring of treatment to the specific deficits of each client.

Finally, Reisinger (1972) examined the effects of token reinforcement of smiling in a reversal design with one hospitalized depressed woman. Reinforcement of smiling produced increases in this behavior that were associated with other improvements in her functioning.

*Marital Interventions.* Lewinsohn and Shaw (1969) presented a case study where feedback about interpersonal behavior between a depressed woman and her husband was used as an agent of behavior change. Results showed a substantial drop in the depression scale of the Minnesota Multiphasic Personality Inventory (MMPI-D), as well as in the Hs and Hy scales. There were also favorable changes on the Interpersonal Checklist (Leary, 1957).

McLean, Ogston, and Grauer (1973) systematically evaluated a treatment program based on social learning theory that included a marital therapy component. The comparison group represented a cross-section of available community treatments. All subjects in both groups were married. Social learning treatment included: (a) training in behavioral principles (for example, the use of positive and negative reinforcers in reinforcing other people's behaviors); (b) training in the development and use of behavioral contracts; and (c) training to interact positively with the marital partner.

Patients receiving the social learning treatment improved significantly more than the comparison group on their ratings and their spouse's ratings of targeted problematic behaviors. Recordings of conversations at home showed that couples in the experimental groups significantly decreased their frequency of negative reaction by the end of treatment, whereas this was not true for the comparison group. However, the difference between these two groups was not significant.

A study by Friedman (1975) bears on the possible usefulness of marital interventions, although it is difficult to know precisely what that intervention involved. In a 2 × 2 factorial design, he compared drug and placebo treatments with marital therapy versus minimal contact. Both drug and marital therapies were more effective than mere control conditions. The drug therapy was generally more effective in achieving symptom relief. However, marital therapy produced greater improvement on "family role task performance and perception of the marital relationship [p. 619]." The marital intervention involved the spouse (and sometimes children) participating in all sessions. Friedman indicated that the central focus in this treatment was "on the marital relationship." He does not indicate what specific techniques were used.

*Comments.* It seems premature to draw conclusions about the usefulness of social behavior interventions for depression. The results of Wells *et al.* (1977) look promising, but the results of Zeiss *et al.* (1979) do not support the value of intervening on social behavior. Interventions that focus on marital interactions do appear to be useful, but "more research is needed."

As we have discussed, there is substantial overlap between social behavior interventions and pleasant-activities interventions. Both types of interventions often focus on increasing the rate of social activity. But even where social behavior programs do not target social activity increases, the social reinforcement derived from newly developed social skills may increase the rates of these activities anyway.

In intervening on social behavior, it may be important to pinpoint the particular social behaviors that should be changed and the particular situations that are problematic. Clearly one intervention does not fit all clients. The most appropriate test of a program's effectiveness is to administer it to clients who have the specific problems that are addressed by the program.

It may be useful in further research to distinguish between treatment components that are focused on nonsocial pleasant activity and those that focus on social activities and social skills. Similarly, it will be necessary to assess changes in social and nonsocial events separately if we are going to determine the effects of each intervention on each depressive event. It will also be important to discover the precise way in which changes in targeted social behavior affect other aspects of depression.

Considering the amount of social skills research that has been done, we really have not scratched the surface in applying social behavior treatment technology to the social problems of depressed individuals. A number of promising treatment procedures have not yet been tried with depressed clients, including desensitization for social situations and a number of marital interventions (Weiss & Birchler, 1978).

## MODIFICATION OF VERBAL–COGNITIVE EVENTS

*Distinction between Occurrent Events and Constructs.* A good deal of confusion has been created by the ambiguity of cognitive terms. These terms refer both to specific occurrent events and to constructs or theoretical concepts. The distinction has usually not been clear in cognitive literature (e.g., Shaw & Beck, 1977), although Hollon and Beck (1979) do make such a distinction.

The term *cognition* can refer to specific events such as thinking or saying "I am not a good person" (Beck, 1967, p. 230). Hollon and Beck (1979) refer to these behaviors as "automatic thoughts." These problematic events can be assessed in terms of their frequency, and interventions can presumably be designed to alter their occurrence. We can examine the effects of altering these behaviors on other aspects of depression. Similarly, we can alter the frequency of positive verbal–cognitive events and examine the effects of these changes.

As constructs, cognitive terms apparently refer to assumed mediational structures that are taken to determine behavior. Shaw and Beck (1977) state that cognitive therapy is directed toward overt symptomatology and toward the silent assumptions or beliefs "from which the patient operates" (p. 311). When Beck (1967, 1976) speaks of the cognitive triad, he appears to be speaking of negative organizational sets about the self, the world, and the future. Hollon and Beck (1979) refer to this kind of cognition as the "silent assumptions," or inferred beliefs, derived from a person's experience of the world.

Cognitive contructs are one type of theoretical or paradigmatic (Kuhn, 1962) approach to all the phenomena of depression. Such constructs can and are construed in other ways by other theorists. For example, if depressed subjects respond to social situations by interacting less than nondepressed subjects (Libet & Lewinsohn, 1973), they may be said to expect rejection, feel helpless, have unnecessarily high standards of self-evaluation, or be on an extinction schedule for social initiations. These are rival explanations of the same empirical relationship—namely, the relationship between diagnosed depression and social initiation. Rival theorists are not pointing to different explanatory variables; they are using different paradigms (Kuhn, 1962) or language games (Wittgenstein, 1958). For this reason, interventions that are said to be cognitive in the sense of affecting constructs are not dealt with in this section. Rather, each of their components is described in the relevant section of the chapter, according to the specific target events they seem designed to affect.

*Relevance of Verbal–Cognitive Events.* We are concerned here with occurrent events, not cognitive constructs. That negative self-statements are an important problem among depressed individuals is well established. Questionnaire measures are themselves verbal statements to which depressed individuals respond in a negative way. Beck (1963) has presented evidence that depressed patients differ from nondepressed patients in the frequency of negative self-evaluations, ideas of deprivation, self-criticism, and exaggeration of problems. Munoz (1977) found that depressed subjects agreed more with irrational beliefs than either normals or psychiatric controls. They also indicated that they had more negative expectations regarding themselves. Finally, the frequency of self-monitored positive and negative thoughts were correlated with mood in the expected directions.

*Varieties of Intervention.* The literature abounds with reports of techniques to control negative thoughts. These have included thought stopping, flooding, punishment, systematic desensitization, paradoxical intention, delay between thoughts and overt behavior, and extinction. However, only the thought-stopping and the flooding procedures have been systematically evaluated (Hackmann & McLean, 1975; Stern, Lipsedge, & Marks, 1973), and the support for their efficacy was limited. Moreover, it is unclear whether the subjects in these studies were depressed.

McLean (1976b) has reported several techniques for suppressing negative thoughts of depressed patients. He has clients self-monitor successful attempts to suppress negative thoughts. In the temporal control procedure, a client suppresses thoughts for a fixed period of time and is later free to think them. In geographic control, the client must go to a certain place whenever worrying and remain until the worrying stops.

None of the techniques addresses the specific content or meaning of the negative thoughts. It may be critical to do so, since the probability of a particular thought may be a function of its association with other thoughts or statements (Quine & Ullian, 1970; Watts, Powell, & Austin, 1973). Beck and his colleagues have developed a number of promising techniques that get at the content of a person's negative thoughts (cf. Hollon & Beck, 1979). Clients self-monitor automatic thoughts. They are then assisted to evaluate the content of those thoughts. Clients are taught to "distance" themselves from the thoughts by thinking of them as hypotheses, not as facts. Hollon and Beck (1979, pp. 55–56) indicate that repetition, practice, and a gradual emphasis on generalization "appear to be at least adequate procedures" for achieving distancing. Clients are then taught to ask some standard questions to evaluate the thought or belief, such as:

1. What's my evidence?
2. Is there another way of looking at that?
3. Even if it is true, is it as bad as it seems?

Clients are prompted to ask these questions in sessions and between sessions, "in the head" or in written assignments. In the written assignments, clients list "rational responses" to the questions they ask concerning their automatic thoughts and they note whether the rational response produces any improvement in their emotion. Although Hollon and Beck (1979) do not say so, presumably the therapist prompts, shapes, and reinforces question asking and "rational" responding. Clients are also prompted to test the validity of some of their beliefs by gathering further information about them. Finally, an attempt is made to identify underlying assumptions and to test them. These procedures have been components in a number of cognitive treatments of depression. In general, the total program has been found to be more effective than the conditions it has been compared with, at least on questionnaire measures (Rush et al., 1977; Shaw, 1977; Taylor & Marshall, 1977).

*Comments.* Many cognitive treatments of depression are not limited to changing or eliminating specific thoughts. Thus, while these studies do tend to support the efficacy of the overall treatment programs, they do not clarify the importance of focusing on an individual's cognitive behaviors. Furthermore, most interventions are sufficiently complex to be characterized in a variety of ways. One investigator may consider an intervention cognitive, while another may construe it to be prompting and reinforcing new patterns of overt and covert behavior.

Studies that effectively manipulate problematic thoughts and that evaluate the effects of such manipulation on other aspects of the depression syndrome are needed. Before we can conclude that cognitions play a casual role in the occurrence of other depressive events, we must show that we can unambiguously manipulate those cognitive events and that changes in these events result in changes in other depressive behaviors.

ANXIETY TREATMENT

*Relevance of Anxiety to Depression.* Surprisingly little attention has been given to the role that anxiety may play in the depression syndrome. Although some researchers have included anxiety as a symptom of depression (cf. Cronholm, Schalling, & Asberg, 1974), it has typically been treated as a quite distinct clinical entity. Indeed, most recent depression treatment studies do not include measures of anxiety (cf. Lewinsohn, Muñoz, Youngren, & Zeiss, 1976; Fuchs & Rehm, 1973; Shipley & Fazio, 1973). To some extent, the role of anxiety in depression may have been obscured simply by our failure to inquire about it.

Recent evidence suggests that a substantial proportion of the people who fit diagnostic criteria for depression also have serious anxiety problems. Cronholm *et al.* (1974) reported that psychiatrists' ratings of depressed mood and anxiety were significantly correlated for both outpatient and inpatient samples. In a sample of college undergraduates, Stehouwer and Rosenbaum (1977) found that scores on the Beck Depression Inventory (BDI) were significantly correlated ($r = .582$) with the Short Form Manifest Anxiety Scale (Bendig, 1956). In our own work, we have found similar relationships. The Pt scale of the MMPI was correlated with the BDI ($r = .609$, $N = 19$, $p < .01$) for a series of depressed outpatients whom we have treated. Perhaps a more significant indication of the importance of anxiety among these patients is the fact that during intake, 8 of the 19 identified anxiety as a recurrent problem for which they wanted help.

That anxiety may contribute to other problems among depressed individuals is suggested by relationships between anxiety measures and measurement of the frequency of activity. Stehouwer and Rosenbaum (1977) found that scores on their anxiety measure were as highly correlated with subjects' ratings of the frequency of pleasant activities ($r = -.510$, $N = 151$, $p < .01$) as were BDI scores ($r = .522$, $N = 151$, $p < .01$). Similarly, in our own sample of depressed clients, MMPI-Pt scores were significantly related to the rated frequency of pleasant activities ($r = -.578$, $N = 19$, $p < .01$). These results *suggest* that anxiety is a factor in leading some depressed patients to become less active and perhaps, as a consequence, more depressed.

*Treatment of Anxiety among Depressed Patients.* We are unaware of any controlled evaluations of the effects of treating anxiety on the other problems of depressed individuals. Some form of anxiety management training has been included in a few depression treatment programs (McLean, 1976b; Lewinsohn, Biglan, & Zeiss, 1976), including our own. But, to date, no one appears to have systematically evaluated the effects of treating anxiety on such depressive problems as inactivity, worry, dysphoria, and social isolation.

*Critique and Conclusions.* The evidence reviewed in this section is entirely based on correlational studies of self-report measures. We need to replicate the findings of relationships between anxiety and depression with data derived from self-monitoring, direct observations of behavior, and the reports of significant others. More importantly, we need to examine the functional relationships between carefully pinpointed anxiety events and other facets of the depression syndrome. Unless we can successfully manipulate anxiety as an independent variable, we cannot study its effects on other problems.

It will be necessary to distinguish between social and nonsocial anxieties in future research. In order to remediate social anxiety, it appears essential to teach the person specific skills; relaxation training and desensitization appear to be less successful with these forms of anxiety than they are with nonsocial anxieties (Arkowitz, 1979). However, in treating anxiety for which no specific antecedent stimuli can be identified, teaching relaxation as a coping skill may be an effective intervention (Lewis *et al.,* 1978).

INSOMNIA TREATMENT

*Relevance of Insomnia to Depression.* Sleeping difficulties are common among depressed individuals (Levitt & Lubin, 1975). Many patients report frequent trouble in falling asleep or frequent awakening during the night. Moreover, diagnostic criteria for depression usually include such problems (Feighner *et al.,* 1972).

*Treatment of Insomnia among Depressed Patients.* Progressive relaxation and stimulus control procedures have been successfully employed in the treatment of sleep onset insomnia. Bootzin and Nicassio (1978) have presented a thorough review of these studies. However, we know of no studies that have evaluated the effects of those interventions on the sleep problems of depressed clients. Perhaps one of the reasons for this is that no current theory of depression emphasizes sleep disturbances as a cause of depression. Thus, global approaches would presumably ignore this problem or hope that it would be indirectly affected through other treatment procedures. Future research should examine at least three empirical questions:

1. Would relaxation or stimulus control interventions affect insomnia among depressed clients?
2. Would other depression treatments be more effective than these procedures in remediating insomnia among depressed clients?

3. Would amelioration of insomnia produce improvements in other aspects of depression?

## Implementation of a Problem-Specific Model

*Recommendations*

*Examine the effects of well-specified treatment components on each depressive problem.* This is the next logical step given the initial successes of behavioral and cognitive treatment programs (e.g., Fuchs & Rehm, 1977; McLean & Hakstian, 1979; Rush *et al.*, 1977). It will strengthen treatment programs by identifying effective ways of dealing with all of the most common problems of depression. It will help us to eliminate ineffective components. It will identify depressive problems that are central in the sense that their remediation will produce improvements in other aspects of the depression syndrome. It will enable us to tailor treatment to the specific needs of the individual. It will improve our classification of depressions.

*Develop combined single-organism and group designs.* The research strategy needed to pursue this course involves combinations of single-organism and control group designs (Hersen & Barlow, 1976). For example, we might examine the effects of a social skills program for depressed individuals who are socially isolated. We could use a multiple baseline design over subjects with a similar number of depressed isolates assigned (in multiple baseline fashion) to a relaxation training control condition. We could assess the effects of the intervention on social behavior, nonsocial pleasant activities, negative thoughts, questionnaire measures, and any other specific targets that were identified in initial assessment. Multiple sources of data, such as peer reports, direct observation, and self-monitoring, would obviously be needed.

*Set priorities among components.* The major treatment components that appear useful involve increasing pleasant activities, changing social behavior, modifying cognitive–verbal events, reducing anxiety, and alleviating insomnia. Each of these addresses a problem area that is significant for many, though not all, depressed individuals. The first three of these components have been parts of larger treatment programs that have proven superior to comparison conditions. However, it is impossible to judge the individual contribution of each component or the priority it should have in planning treatment. It does appear that each component "gives you what you pay for" in the sense that it is most likely to affect the behavior for which it is targeted. Pleasant-activities interventions increase pleasant activities, though they may not affect mood or other aspects of depression. Cognitive–verbal modifications may produce changes in covert and overt verbal behavior (including questionnaire measures), but they may not affect dysphoria or physiological symptoms.

Social interventions affect social behavior, though they may not affect cognitive events or other activities.

The components that seem to deserve more attention than they have received as yet include anxiety interventions, such as coping skills training, relaxation training, social skills training, and insomnia treatment.

## The Heuristic Value of a Problem-Specific Model

*Makes no unfounded assumptions.* Untested assumptions about depression could hinder further research. The approach we are advocating makes no unfounded assumptions about the nature of depression or its determinants. The model does not assume homogeneity among depressed clients or covariance among depressive problems. Rather, we examine the specific events that are problematic for the individual and keep before us the heterogeneity of depressions. The model does not assume that any single intervention (independent variable) is effective across all depressive problems. We must evaluate the effects of our interventions on each problem separately.

*Places questionnaire measures in an appropriate light.* A number of quite valuable questionnaire measures are available in depression treatment research (BDI, PES, CES-D), but as Rehm (1977b) has pointed out, the relationship of these measures to other aspects of the depression syndrome is not well understood. We cannot assume that questionnaires are valid assessments of the effects of our interventions on the social, recreational, productive, and physiological behaviors of the people we work with. Data about these events will need to be obtained through self-monitoring, direct observation, and physiological assessment.

*Prompts us to elaborate which procedures affect which specific problems.* As Hollon and Kendall (1979) suggested, "increasingly, attention can be turned away from questions involving 'does it work?' to questions involving 'what are the necessary and sufficient procedures?' and 'what are the mechanisms through which these procedures operate?' [p. 5]." The types of studies we are recommending would enable us to discover if there are treatment components that are central in the sense that they affect all or most depression symptoms. We have argued in the preceding pages that interventions on social behavior appear particularly promising.

This strategy will also enable us to test whether the component actually affected the target problem that it was presumed to affect. Before we can conclude that an intervention, such as social skills training, remediated depression because of its specific effect on social behavior, we must first show that it has, in fact, affected social behavior.

*Is open to the examination of any intervention.* We have only reviewed the major treatment components of behaviorally oriented depression treatment programs. Yet, the model of examining the effects of well-specified interventions on specific depressive events is open to the introduction of any new independent variable, including pharmacological interventions.

The work of Greist and his colleagues suggests that running may be as effective and less costly in the treatment of depression than traditional psychotherapy (Greist, Klein, Eischens, Faris, Gurman, & Morgan, 1977). As Greist *et al.* acknowledge, there are a number of distinct methodological weaknesses in their study. However, this intervention deserves more study. The possibility that running could be an effective intervention for depressive problems was not anticipated by any of the existing theoretical treatment models, although it could undoubtedly be explained in terms of them. Greist *et al.* identified nine different possible explanations for the apparent efficacy of the intervention, ranging from producing a sense of increased mastery to biochemical effects. With such a large range of theoretical possibilities, it should be clear that "deciding" which explanation seems most reasonable adds very little to the actual results of the study. Moreover, entrenched theoretical positions may make us hesitant to investigate otherwise promising areas of research.

### Similarities to Other Models

McLean's work is an excellent example of the type of approach we are advocating (McLean, 1976b; McLean & Hakstian, 1979). He has enumerated the areas of skill deficit that appear to be most frequently found among depressed individuals. For each of the specific problem areas associated with these skill deficits, he describes a specific treatment intervention. McLean's treatment program is designed to specify the precise problem areas that each depressed individual has. Treatment is then a matter of bringing to bear on each of those problems the intervention that appears most likely to affect that problem. Although analyses of the effects of their specific treatment components have not been published, McLean and Hakstian (1979) carefully evaluated the effects of the overall program, in comparison with psychotherapy, a relaxation control, and amitriptyline. Their results favored the behavior therapy program. Thus, this problem-specific approach to depression treatment appears to be fruitful.

Hollon and Kendall (1979) present a cognitive–behavioral model that is quite compatible with the present approach. Cognitive processes are conceived of as specific occurrent events. These events can be affected by both antecedent and consequent events just as overt behavior can. Moreover, their model includes the possibility that the cognitive events can function as stimuli for other cognitive events, autonomic behavior, and overt behavior. These models help us specify the particular events occurring in depression. They also prompt us to consider the relationships among depressive events and help us isolate the relationships between these events and environmental variables.

# References

Arkowitz, H. The measurement and modification of minimal dating behavior. In M. Hersen, R. Eisler, & P. Miller (Eds.), *Progress in behavior modification* (Vol. 7). New York: Academic Press, 1979.

Barrera, M. An evaluation of a brief group therapy for depression. *Journal of Consulting and Clinical Psychology*, 1979, *47*, 413–415.

Bartlett, M. S. Some aspects of the time-correlation problem in regard to tests of significance. *Journal of the Royal Statistical Society*, 1935, *98*, 536–543.

Beck, A. T. Thinking and depression. I. Idiosyncratic content and cognitive distortions. *Archives of General Psychiatry*, 1963, *9*, 36–40.

Beck, A. T. *Depression: Causes and treatment.* Philadelphia: University of Pennyslvania Press, 1967.

Beck, A. T. *Cognitive theory and emotional disorders.* New York: International Universities Press, 1976.

Beck, A. T., Ward, C. H., Mendelson, M., Mock, J., & Erbaugh, J. An inventory for measuring depression. *Archives of General Psychiatry*, 1961, *4*, 561–571.

Bendig, A. W. The development of a short form of the manifest anxiety scale. *Journal of Consulting Psychology*, 1956, *20*, 384.

Biglan, A., & Dow, M. G. Self-administered treatment for depression. Unpublished grant proposal, University of Oregon, 1977.

Biglan, A., Glaser, S. R., & Dow, M. G. Conversational skills training for social anxiety: An evaluation of its validity. Unpublished manuscript.

Biglan, A., & Kass, D. J. The empirical nature of behavior therapies. *Behaviorism*, 1977, *5*, 1–15.

Bootzin, R. R., & Nicassio, P. M. Behavioral treatments for insomnia. In M. Hersen, R. Eisler, & P. Miller (Eds.), *Progress in behavior modification* (Vol. 6). New York: Academic Press, 1978.

Campbell, D. T., & Stanley, J. C. Experimental and quasi-experimental designs for research on teaching. In N. L. Gage (Ed.), *Handbook of research on teaching.* Chicago: Rand-McNally, 1963.

Coleman, R. E., & Miller A. G. The relationship between depression and marital maladjustment in a clinic population: A multitrait–multimethod study. *Journal of Consulting and Clinical Psychology*, 1975, *43*, 647–651.

Coyne, J. C. Depression and the response of others. *Journal of Abnormal Psychology*, 1976, *85*, 186–193.

Craker, D., & Biglan, A. Evaluation of a self-reward system for increasing pleasant activities and its relevance to the treatment of depression. Unpublished manuscript, Oregon Research Institute, 1979.

Cronholm, B., Schalling, D., & Asberg, M. Development of a rating scale for depressive illness. Psychological Measurements in Psychopharmacology. *Modern Problems Pharmacopsychiatry*, 1974, *7*, 139–150.

Eisler, R. M., Miller, P. M., & Hersen, M. Components of assertive behavior. *Journal of Clinical Psychology*. 1973, *29*, 295–299.

Feighner, J. P., Robins, E., Guze, S. B., Woodruff, R. A., Jr., Winokur, G., & Munoz, R. Diagnostic criteria for use in psychiatric research. *Archives of General Psychiatry*, 1972, *26*, 57–63.

Ferster, C. B. Animal behavior and mental illness. *Psychological Record*, 1966, *16*, 345–356.

Friedman, A. S. Interaction of drug therapy with marital therapy in depressive patients. *Archives of General Psychiatry*, 1975, *32*, 619–637.

Fuchs, C. Z., & Rehm, L. P. A self-control behavior therapy program for depression. *Journal of Consulting and Clinical Psychology*, 1977, *45*, 206–215.

Greist, J. H., Klein, M. H., Eischens, R. R., Faris, J., Gurman, A. S., & Morgan, W. P. Running as treatment for depression. Unpublished manuscript, Department of Psychiatry, University of Wisconsin, 1977.

Grosscup, S. J., & Lewinsohn, P. M. Unpleasant and pleasant events, and mood. *Journal of Clinical Psychology*, *36*, 1980, 252–259.

Hackmann, A., & McLean, C. A comparison of flooding and thought stopping in the treatment of obsessional neurosis. *Behavior Research*, 1975, *13*, 263–269.

Hammen, C. L., & Glass, D. R. Depression, activity and evaluation of reinforcement. *Journal of Abnormal Psychology*, 1975, *84*, 718–721.

Hersen, M., & Barlow, D. *Single case experimental designs: Strategies for studying behavior change.* New York: Pergamon Press, 1976.

Hersen, M., & Bellack, A. S. Social skills training for chronic psychiatric patients: Rationale, research findings, and future directions. *Comprehensive Psychiatry*, 1976, *17*, 559–580.

Hersen, M., Eisler, R. M., Alford, G. S., & Agras, W. S. Effects of token economy on neurotic depression: An experimental analysis. *Behavior Therapy*, 1973, *4*, 392–397.

Hersen, M., Eisler, R. M., & Miller, P. M. Development of assertive responses: Clinical, measurement and research considerations. *Behavior Research and Therapy*, 1973, *11*, 505–521.

Hersen, M., Himmelhoch, J., & Bellack, A. S. *Pharmacological and social skills treatment for unipolar (non-pychotic) depression.* Unpublished grant proposal, Univeristy of Pittsburgh, 1979.

Hollon, S. D., & Beck, A. T. Psychotherapy and drug therapy: Comparisons and combinations. In S. L. Garfield & A. E. Bergin (Eds.), *The Handbook of Psychotherapy and Behavior Change* (2nd ed.). New York: John Wiley and Sons, 1979.

Hollon, S. D., & Kendall, P. C. Cognitive–behavioral interventions: Theory and procedure. In P. C. Kendall & S. D. Hollon (Eds.), *Cognitive–behavioral interventions: Theory, research, and procedures.* New York: Academic Press, 1979.

Kanfer, F. H. & Karoly, P. Self control: A behavioristic excursion into the lion's den. *Behavior Therapy*, 1972, *3*, 398–416.

Kazdin, A. E. Self-monitoring and behavior change. In M. J. Mahoney & C. E. Thoresen (Eds.), *Self-control: Power to the person.* Montery, California: Brooks/Cole, 1974.

Kuhn, T. S. *The structure of scientific revolutions* (Vol. 1 & 2). Chicago: University of Chicago Press, 1962.

Lambert, M. J., DeJulio, S. S., & Stern, D. M. Therapist interpersonal skills process, outcome, methodological considerations and recommendations for future research. *Psychological Bulletin*, 1978, *85*, 476–489.

Leary, T. *Interpersonal diagnosis of personality.* New York: Ronald Press, 1957.

Levitt, E. E., & Lubin, B. *Depression.* Indianapolis: Bobbs-Merrill, 1975.

Lewinsohn, P. M. Engagement in "pleasant" activities and depression. *Journal of Abnormal Psychology*, 1975, *85*, 729–731.

Lewinsohn, P. M. Activity schedules in the treatment of depression. In C. E. Thoresen & J. D. Krumboltz (Eds.), *Counseling Methods.* New York: Holt, Rinehart, & Winston, 1976.

Lewinsohn, P. M., & Atwood, G. E. Depression: A clinical–research approach—The case of Mrs. G. *Psychotherapy: Theory, Research and Practice*, 1969, *6*, 166–171.

Lewinsohn, P. M., Biglan, A., & Zeiss, A. S. Behavioral treatment of depression. In P. O. Davidson (Ed.), *The behavioral management of anxiety, depression, and pain.* New York: Brunner/Mazel, 1976.

Lewinsohn, P. M., & Graf, M. Pleasant activities and depression. *Journal of Consulting and Clinical Psychology*, 1973, *41*, 261–268.

Lewinsohn, P. M., & Libet, J. Pleasant events, activity schedules, and depression. *Journal of Abnormal Psychology*, 1972, *79*, 291–295.

Lewinsohn, P. M. & MacPhillamy, D. J. The relationship between age and engagement in pleasant activities. *Journal of Gerontology*, 1974, *29*, 290–294.

Lewinsohn, P. M., Munoz, R. F., Youngren, M. A., & Zeiss, A. M. Assessment and treatment of depression: A social learning perspective. Paper presented at the meeting of the American Psychological Association, Washington, D. C., September 1976.

Lewinsohn, P. M., & Shaffer, M. Use of home observations as an integral part of the treatment of depression: Preliminary report and case studies. *Journal of Consulting and Clinical Psychology*, 1971, *37*, 87–94.

Lewinsohn, P. M., & Shaw, D. A. Feedback about interpersonal behavior as an agent of behavior change: A case study in the treatment of depression. *Psychotherapy and Psychosomatics,* 1969, *17,* 82–88.

Lewinsohn, P. M., Weinstein, M. S., & Shaw, D. A. Depression: A clinical–research approach. In R. D. Rubin & C. M. Franks (Eds.) *Advances in Behavior Therapy 1968.* New York: Academic Press, 1969.

Lewis C. E., Biglan, A., & Steinbock, E. Self-administered relaxation training and money deposits in the treatment of recurrent anxiety. *Journal of Consulting and Clinical Psychology,* 1978, *46,* 1274–1283.

Libet, J. M., & Lewinsohn, P. M. Concept of social skill with special relevance to the behavior of depressed persons. *Journal of Consulting and Clinical Psychology,* 1973, *40,* 304–312.

Libet, J. M., Lewinsohn, P. M., & Jovorek, F. *The construct of social skill: An empirical study of several behavioral measures on temporal stability, internal structure, validity and situational generalizability.* Unpublished manuscript, University of Oregon, 1973.

Locke, H. J., & Wallace, K. M. Short marital adjustment and prediction tests: Their reliability and validity. *Journal of Marriage and Family Living,* 1959, *21,* 251–255.

MacPhillamy, D. J., & Lewinsohn, P. M. *The pleasant events schedule.* University of Oregon, 1971. (Mimeo)

MacPhillamy, D. J., & Lewinsohn, P. M. Depression as a function of levels of desired and obtained pleasure. *Journal of Abnormal Psychology,* 1974, *83,* 651–657.

McLean, P. D. Depression as a specific response to stress. In I. G. Sarason & C. D. Spielberger (Eds.), *Stress and Anxiety.* New York: Wiley & Sons, 1976. (a)

McLean, P. Therapeautic decision-making in the behavioral treatment of depression. In P. O. Davidson (Ed.), *Behavioral management of anxiety, depression, and pain.* New York: Brunner/Mazel, 1976. (b).

McLean, P. D., & Hakstian, A. R. Clinical depression: Comparative efficacy of outpatient treatments. *Journal of Consulting and Clinical Psychology,* 1979, *47,* 818–836.

McLean, P. D., Ogston, K., & Grauer, L. A behavioral approach to the treatment of depression. *Journal of Behavior Therapy and Experimental Psychiatry,* 1973, *4,* 323–330.

Mendels, J. Depression: The distinction between syndrome and symptom. *British Journal of Psychiatry,* 1968, *114,* 1549–1554.

Munoz, R. F. *A cognitive approach to the assessment and treatment of depression.* Unpublished doctoral dissertation, University of Oregon, 1977.

Patterson, G. R., & Rosenberry, C. A social learning formulation of depression. Paper presented at the meeting of the International Conference on Behavior Modification, Banff, Alberta, 1969.

Quine, W. V., & Ullian, J. S. *The web of belief.* New York: Random House, 1970.

Radloff, L. S. The CES-D scale: A self-report depression scale for research in the general population. *Applied Psychological Measurement,* 1977, *1,* 385–401.

Rehm, L. P. Assessment of depression. In M. Hersen & A. S. Bellack (Eds.), *Behavioral assessment: A practical handbook.* Oxford: Pergamon Press, 1976.

Rehm, L. P. A self-control model of depression. *Behavior Therapy,* 1977, *8,* 787–804.

Reisinger, J. J. The treatment of "anxiety depression" via positive reinforcement and response cost. *Journal of Applied Behavior Analysis,* 1972, *5,* 125–130.

Rush, A. J., Beck, A. T., Kovacs, M., & Hollon, S. Comparative efficacy of cognitive therapy and pharmacotherapy in the treatment of depressed out-patients. *Cognitive Therapy and Research,* 1977, *1,* 17–37.

Shaffer, M., & Lewinsohn, P. M. *Interpersonal behaviors in the homes of depressed versus non-depressed psychiatric and normal controls: A test of several hypotheses.* Paper presented at the meeting of Western Psychological Association, San Francisco, 1971.

Shaw, B. F. Comparison of cognitive therapy and behavior therapy in the treatment of depression. *Journal of Consulting and Clinical Psychology,* 1977, *45,* 543–551.

Shaw, B. F., & Beck, A. T. The treatment of depression with cognitive therapy. In A. Ellis & R. Grieger, *Handbook of rational emotive therapy.* New York: Springer, 1977.

Shipley, C. R., & Fazio, A. F. Pilot study of a treatment for psychological depression. *Journal of Abnormal Psychology,* 1973, *82,* 372–376.

Sidman, M. *Tactics of scientific research: Evaluating experimental data in psychology.* New York: Basic Books, 1960.

Skinner, B. F. What is the experimental analysis of behavior? In R. Ullrich, T. Stachnik, & J. Mabry (Eds.), *Control of human behavior* (Vol. 2). Glenview, Illinois: Scott, Foresman, & Co., 1970.

Stehouwer, R. S., & Rosenbaum, G. *Role of frequency and potency of reinforcing events in depression and anxiety.* Paper presented at the Association for Advancement of Behavior Therapy, Atlanta, December 1977.

Stern, R. S., Lipsedge, M. S., & Marks I. M. Obsessive ruminations: A controlled trial of thought-stopping technique. *Behavior Research and Therapy,* 1973, *11,* 659–662.

Taylor, F. G. & Marshall, W. L. Experimental analysis of a cognitive–behavioral therapy for depression. *Cognitive Therapy and Research,* 1977, *1,* 59–72.

Traux, C. B., & Mitchell, K. M. Research on certain therapist interpersonal skills in relation to process and outcome. In A. E. Bergin & S. L. Garfield (Eds.), *Handbook of psychotherapy and behavior change.* New York: John Wiley & Sons, 1971.

Watson, D., & Friend, R. Measurement of social evaluation anxiety. *Journal of Consulting and Clinical Psychology,* 1969, *33,* 448–457.

Watts, F. N., Powell, G. E., & Austin, S. V. The modification of abnormal beliefs. *British Journal of Medical Psychology,* 1973, *46,* 359–363.

Weiss, R. L., & Aved, B. M. Marital satisfaction and depression as predictors of physical health status. *Journal of Consulting and Clinical Psychology,* 1978, *46,* 1379–1384.

Weiss, R. L., & Birchler, G. R. Adults with marital dysfunction. In M. Hersen & A. S. Bellack (Eds.), *Behavior therapy in the psychiatric setting.* New York: Williams & Wilkins, 1978.

Weissman, M. M., & Paykel, E. S. *The depressed woman: A study of social relationships.* Chicago: University of Chicago Press, 1974.

Wells, K. C., Hersen, M., Bellack, A. S., & Himmelhoch, J. *Social skills training for unipolar depressive females.* Paper presented at the meeting of the Association for Advancement of Behavior Therapy, Atlanta, December 1977.

Williams, J. G., Barlow, D. H., & Agras, W. S. Behavioral measurement of severe depression. *Archives of General Psychiatry,* 1972, *27,* 330–333.

Wittgenstein, L. *The blue and brown notebooks.* New York: Harper & Row, 1958.

Youngren, M. A., & Lewinsohn, P. M. *The functional relationship between depression and problematic interpersonal behavior.* University of Oregon, 1977. (Mimeo)

Zeiss, A., Lewinsohn, P. M., & Munoz, R. F. Nonspecific improvement effects in depression using interpersonal skills training, pleasant activity schedules, or cognitive training. *Journal of Consulting and Clinical Psychology,* 1979, *47,* 427–439.

Zung, W. K. A self-rating depression scale. *Archives of General Psychiatry,* 1965, *12,* 63–70.

# 5

# A Learned Helplessness Point of View[1]

MARTIN E. P. SELIGMAN

In this chapter, I will first outline what the reformulated learned helplessness model of depression says (Abramson, Seligman, & Teasdale, 1978) and mention some new evidence that supports it. Then I will deduce four therapeutic strategies from this model. I will then look at the major "tactics" that make up the behavioral and cognitive treatments of depression, dividing them into those that the model predicts would be active ingredients and those that should, from my theoretical perspective, be inert. In the course of this, I will suggest some other techniques that follow from the model that have not been explicitly incorporated into the behavioral and cognitive repertoire. Finally, I shall attempt to show that cognitive "theory" and cognitive therapy are best viewed within the more rigorous framework of learned helplessness.

## The Reformulated Helplessness Model of Depression

The reformulated helplessness model of depression has four premises, and their co-occurrence is deemed sufficient (but emphatically not necessary) for depression to occur. Depression, itself, is defined by four sets of deficits: motivational, cognitive, affective–somatic, and self-esteem.

*Premise 1 (expected aversiveness):* The individual expects that highly aversive outcomes are probable or that highly desired outcomes are improbable.

*Premise 2 (expected uncontrollability):* The individual expects that no response in his or her repertoire will change the likelihood of these events.

[1] Research for this chapter was supported by MH 19604 and by NSF grant BNS76-22943 A02 to the Center for Advanced Study in the Behavioral Sciences.

BEHAVIOR THERAPY FOR DEPRESSION

*Premise 3 (attributional style):* The individual possesses an insidious attributional style that governs the duration and the breadth of the depressive deficits and whether self-esteem is lowered. The depressive attributional style consists of a tendency to make internal attributions for failure, but external attributions for success; stable attributions for failure, but unstable attributions for success; and global attributions for failure, but specific attributions for success. Internal attributions for failure (and external ones for success) produce long-lasting depressive deficits, and global attributions for failure (and specific ones for success) produce depressive deficits over a variety of situations.

*Premise 4 (severity):* The strength of the motivational and cognitive deficits of depression depends jointly on the strength (i.e., the certainty) of the expectation of the aversive outcome (Premise 1) and the strength of the uncontrollability expectancy (Premise 2). The severity of the affective and self-esteem deficits is governed by the importance of the uncontrollable outcome.

Put in a nutshell, depression will occur when the individual expects that bad events will occur, expects that he or she can do nothing to prevent their occurrence, and construes the cause of this state of affairs as resulting from internal, stable, and global factors.

## New Evidence for the Reformulation

Some recent evidence has been obtained that supports the reformulated model, and since the evidence is new, I shall briefly mention it here. We developed an attributional style scale to test whether or not depressives have the attributional style that the model predicts (Premise 3). The scale consists of 12 questions of the form shown in Table 5.1.

Half of the situations are about good events, and half are about bad events. As you can see from the table, subjects are asked to vividly imagine each of the situations and to state what the major cause would have been if it occurred to them. They then rate the internality of the cause, its stability, its globality, and the importance of the event.

We found a clear depressive attributional style. Using a sample of 143 undergraduates in Psychology 1 at the University of Pennsylvania, we correlated the Beck Depression Inventory (Beck, 1967) with our attributional style scale. For bad outcomes, depression (as measured by the Beck Depression Inventory) correlated with internality ($p < .0001$), stability ($p < .0001$), and globality ($p < .0001$). As for good outcomes, depression correlated with externality ($p < .01$), instability ($p < .002$), but not significantly with specificity (Seligman, Abramson, Semmel, & von Baeyer, 1979).

We then went on to ask whether this insidious way of construing causality actually causes depression or merely correlates with it. In a prospective pilot study, students of various attributional styles faced our Psychology 1 midterm examination and were asked before they took the exam to rate what grade they

**TABLE 5.1**
Sample Questions from the Attributional Style Scale[a]

---

You have been looking for a job unsuccessfully for some time.
1. Write down *one* major cause. _____
2. Is the cause of your unsuccessful job search due to something about you or something about other people or circumstances? (Circle one number).

| Totally due to other people or circumstances. | 1 2 3 4 5 6 7 | Totally due to me. |

3. In the future when looking for a job, will this cause again be present? (Circle one number).

| Will never again be present. | 1 2 3 4 5 6 7 | Will always be present. |

4. Is the cause something that just influences looking for a job or does it also influence other areas of your life? (Circle one number).

| Influences just this particular situation. | 1 2 3 4 5 6 7 | Influences all situations in my life. |

5. How important would this situation be if it happened to you? (Circle one number).

| Not at all important. | 1 2 3 4 5 6 7 | Extremely important. |

---

[a]Seligman, Abramson, Semmel, & Von Baeyer, 1979.

would consider a failure. We then looked at those students who actually got a grade low enough for them to consider it a failure. Who became depressed and who did not? We found that the students who 8 weeks before had made stable and global attributions for failure on the attributional style questionnaire tended to become depressed ($r = .63$, $p < .05$). Lyn Abramson and I are presently replicating this experiment on a larger sample. Our prediction is that the combination of a preexisting internal, stable, and global way of construing causality for negative events followed by an actual encounter with failure will be sufficient to cause depression.

## Therapeutic Implications of the Reformulated Model

Four therapeutic strategies follow from the reformulation: environmental enrichment, personal control training, resignation training, and attribution re-training. Table 5.2 outlines the treatment strategies (and examples of tactics) implied by the reformulated hypothesis.

## Strategy One: Environmental Enrichment

Since Premise 1 (of the sufficiency conditions for depression) is that the individual expects that bad outcomes will occur, changing the individual's estimate of the probability of bad outcomes for the better should be therapeutic. One way of reducing the expected probability of aversive outcomes and increasing the expected probability of desired outcomes is by actual environmen-

**TABLE 5.2**

Treatment Strategies and Examples of Tactics Implied by the Reformulation

---

A. **Environmental enrichment**

Change the estimated probability of the relevant event's occurrence; reduce estimated likelihood for aversive outcomes, and increase estimated likelihood for desired outcomes.

1. Environmental manipulation by social agencies to remove aversive outcomes or provide desired outcomes (for example, rehousing, job placement, financial assistance, provision of nursery care for children).
2. Provision of better medical care to relieve pain, correct handicaps (for example, prescription of analgesics, provision of artificial limbs and other prostheses).

B. **Personal control training**

Change the expectation from uncontrollability to controllability.

1. When responses are not yet within the person's repertoire but can be, train for the necessary skills.
2. When responses are within the person's repertoire, modify the distorted expectation that the responses will fail.

C. **Resignation training**

Make the highly preferred outcomes less preferred.

1. Reduce the aversiveness of highly aversive outcomes.
   a. Provide more realistic goals and norms (for example, "Failing to be at the top of your class is not the end of the world; you can still be a competent teacher and lead a satisfying life").
   b. Assumption challenging to modify the significance of outcomes perceived as aversive (for example, challenge "If I fail in anything, it means that I am unsuccessful") (Beck, 1976; Ellis, 1962).
   c. Assist acceptance and resignation.
2. Reduce the desirability of highly desired outcomes.
   a. Assist the attainment of alternative available desired outcomes (for example, encourage the disappointed lover to find another boy or girl friend).
   b. Assist reevaluation of unattainable goals.
   c. Assist renunciation and relinquishment of unattainable goals.

D. **Attribution retraining**

To the extent reality permits, change unrealistic attributions for failure toward external, unstable, specific; change unrealistic attributions for success toward internal, stable, global.

1. For failure:
   a. External (for example: "The system minimized the opportunities for women. It is not that you are incompetent").
   b. Unstable (for example: "The system is changing. Opportunities that you can snatch are opening at a great rate").
   c. Specific (for example: "Marketing jobs are still relatively closed to women, but publishing jobs are not").
2. For success:
   a. Internal (for example, "He loves you because you are nurturant and not because he is insecure").
   b. Stable (for example, "Your nurturance is an enduring trait").
   c. Global (for example, "Your nurturance pervades much of what you do and is appreciated by everyone around you").

tal manipulation. (The other is by personal control training, see next section.) The reformulation therefore holds that changing the environment for the better, and getting the individual to see this, should be antidepressive. This is a therapeutic strategy omitted not only in psychodynamic therapies, which rely on a passive therapist, but also in behavioral and cognitive therapies, which rely on a more active therapist.

From the helplessness point of view, part of a therapeutic package for depression should include environmental manipulation. In principle, it would be useful to have an "expediter" at the service of the therapist whose expertise included such areas as job placement, rehousing, sources of financial assistance, night courses, nursery care, better medical care, finding dates and friends, and the like.

One caveat: The therapist's enriching the environment may antagonize the second therapeutic strategy implied by the reformulation—that of changing the expectation from uncontrollability to controllability. To the extent that patients perceive that it was not their own actions, but the therapist's, that bettered the environment, the expectations of uncontrollability may be strengthened even though the expectations of future aversiveness may decrease. This balance is a delicate one, but should tilt toward environmental enrichment when the patient's trainable skills are low and the availability of reinforcers is also low.

### Strategy Two: Personal Control Training

Change the expectation from uncontrollability to controllability. This is the heart of the therapeutic suggestions made by the original learned helplessness model and is also a strategy that best describes many of the tactics of behavioral therapy in dealing with depression. The tactics of social skills training, child management skills, problem-solving skills, depression management skills, graded task assignment, assertiveness training, and decision-making training are all examples of therapies that may well be antidepressive and that work, both helplessness models claim, by changing the expectation from uncontrollability to controllability.

In addition to modifying expectancies about the controllability of bad events, such training, when successful, thereby modifies expectations about the probability of the bad events themselves (environmental enrichment). When depressed patients learn new social skills, they will not only come to expect that they can affect friendship by their own actions, but that their social life will be richer as well. It will take fine-grained research designs to tell us whether or not such tactics, when effective for depression, work by changing expectations of controllability of the outcomes or by making the individual more optimistic about the outcomes. Although the topic is beyond the scope of this chapter, the question of whether the beneficial effects of coming to expect more control over outcomes merely reduces to coming to expect better outcomes is theoretically of crucial importance (Miller, 1979).

*Strategy Three: Resignation Training*

Reduce the aversiveness of expected aversive outcomes and reduce the desirability of unobtainable desired outcomes. It is not uncommon for helplessness to be realistic. Patients may not have, nor be able to acquire, the skills necessary to obtain the outcomes they want. In addition, the therapist, using the tactics of environmental enrichment, may not be able to provide these outcomes for the patient. When this is so, a variety of techniques are available to the therapist to aid in acceptance and resignation. The reformulated model deduces that the affective and self-esteem deficits will be reduced when the importance of the expected outcomes is reduced.

Resignation seems to be a natural process. It usually occurs in the months following bereavement, and it may be assisted by working through the loss. It has been argued, based on rather striking clinical examples, that failure to work through the loss results in failure of resignation to occur and in subsequent depression (Ramsay, 1977). The cognitive mechanisms that underlie resignation have been largely unexplored, and this is a matter of both therapeutic and theoretical importance. One year following the death of a child, the helplessness cognition still seems to be present—"She's gone and there's nothing I can do about it"—but the affect has changed. Is this because of an endogenous process, or have other cognitions (tag lines) changed—a change from "She's dead, and I can't go on" to "She's dead, but I was able to go on living. My world didn't end"?

Among the techniques of resignation training are (*a*) helping to provide more realistic norms; (*b*) helping to find alternative desirable outcomes; and (*c*) assumption challenging (Beck, 1976; Ellis, 1962).

*Strategy Four: Attribution Retraining*

Premise 3 of the reformulation argues that there is an insidious attributional style that makes one prone to depression. Individuals who make internal, global, and stable attributions for failure, and external, unstable, and specific attributions for success, will—when they encounter failure—have long-lasting depressions with self-esteem deficits that occur in a wide variety of situations. Particular attributions and even attributional style may be changeable, and as we shall see in the following discussion, many of the techniques of cognitive therapy seem to be effective, but theoretically unfocused, attempts to do just this.

Table 5.2 gives some examples of countering particular attributions for failure and success. In addition, attributional style itself may be modifiable. While very little work has been done on this to date, Layden of the University of Wisconsin gave attribution retraining to a group of depressed and low self-esteem women. She tried to change only the internality of failure attributions, but in principle the stable and global dimensions could be modified in analogous ways. Each week these women were instructed to write down several bad things that had happened to them and then to give external, rather than internal, reasons for them. Layden (1978) reported that merely being forced to see that there might be external ways of construing the cause of the bad events that had happened (e.g., "My boyfriend shouted at me not because I said stupid things, but because he was in a bad mood") changed the attributions that these women made, raised their self-esteem, and reduced depression.

In addition, certain kinds of confrontation with reality itself may change particular attributions and perhaps attributional style. As Carol Dweck has shown (Dweck, 1975; Dweck & Reppucci, 1973), trying harder and then succeeding may, with appropriate help in seeing the connection, alleviate helplessness and perhaps change attributions. When individuals successfully broaden their repertoires so that more outcomes become controllable, their attributions for success and possibly for failure may change as well. So, for example, individuals who learn assertive training may come to construe the causes of their newly won social successes as more internal and stable and the causes of their failures as more external and unstable.

## Antidepressive Tactics of Behavioral and Cognitive Therapy

Table 5.3 presents the four therapeutic strategies—environmental enrichment, personal control training, resignation training, and attribution retraining—that are deduced from the reformulated learned helplessness model of depression, and then reviews the tactics that behavioral and cognitive therapists have used that fit the model. The table draws heavily on the excellent review of the literature by Rehm and Kornblith (1979), adding to their enumeration whether and why each particular tactic should be antidepressive. Incidentally, it is not intended that the enumeration of tactics should be exclusive or exhaustive. Such a project will require a closer analysis.

Two things should be noted about Table 5.3: Many, but not all, of the tactics used in behavioral and cognitive therapy can be placed within the table. The table does not attempt to review whether or not, in fact, these actually are effective tactics but merely commits itself to the assertion that by the reformulation they should be antidepressant.

The second thing to note—and this will be elaborated in the final section of the chapter—is that cognitive therapy, and indeed cognitive "theory," which can be seen as unsystematic and diffuse, receives systematic and parsimonious underpinnings in this table. Cognitive therapy and rational emotive therapy boil down to a variety of tactics of attribution retraining and resignation training.

**TABLE 5.3**
Tactics of Behavioral and Cognitive Therapy, as Reported in the Literature, That Should Be Antidepressant Based on the Reformulation of Helplessness

A. Environmental enrichment
   Increase the expectation that positive outcomes will occur, and decrease the expectation that negative outcomes will occur.
   1. *See Section B, "Personal Control Training."* All tactics that increase control over outcomes will tend to make expectations of future outcomes more positive (e.g., marital contracting produces expectancies of more control over affection and thereby produces stronger expectancies that future affection will occur; assertiveness training produces expectancies of control over being exploited and thereby produces stronger expectancies that exploitations will not occur.
      a. Noncontingent positive outcome comparison groups. Whether such "personal control" tactics are antidepressant because of increased expectation of control or because of increased expectations of positive outcomes and decreased expectations of negative outcomes can be determined by a noncontingent comparison group (i.e., a group that gets the same increase in positive outcomes but not via increased personal control). Such noncontingent treatment should be antidepressant, relative to untreated controls.
   2. *Monitoring positive events rather than negative events* (Fuchs & Rehm, 1977; Rehm, Fuchs, Roth, Kornblith & Romano, 1979). More positive outcome expectations are partially determined by what outcomes are attended to and remembered. An individual who attends to and remembers only negative events will tend to expect negative outcomes, as individuals trained to attend to and remember positive events will tend to expect more positive outcomes.
   3. *Increased pleasant activities* (Lewinsohn, 1976; contra Hammen & Glass, 1975).
   4. *Develop positive future expectancies via imagery* (Anton, Dunbar, & Friedman, 1976; Lazarus, 1968).
B. Personal control training
   Change the expectation from uncontrollability to controllability.
   1. *Reinforcement* for engaging in *previously enjoyable activities* (e.g., Anton, Dunbar, & Friedman, 1976; Burgess, 1969; Liberman & Raskin, 1971; Sammons, 1974).
   2. Perform *new coping behavior* (Anton, Dunbar, & Friedman, 1976; Caple & Blechman, 1976; Shipley & Fazio, 1972).
   3. *Therapy time contingent on patient's behavior* (Lewinsohn, 1976; Robinson & Lewinsohn, 1973). Patient learns control over therapist.
   4. *Assertiveness training* (Lazarus, 1968; Lewinsohn, Biglan, & Zeiss, 1976; Shaw, 1977).
   5. *Social skill training* (Lewinsohn, Biglan, & Zeiss, 1976; Lewinsohn, Weinstein, & Alper, 1970; Taylor & Marshall, 1977; Wells, Hersen, Bellack & Himmelhoch, 1977).
   6. *Token economy* (Hersen, Eisler, Alford, & Agras, 1973; Reisinger, 1972). Patient learns that his or her own actions will lead to valued tokens.
   7. *Family reinforces adaptive behaviors* (Liberman & Raskin, 1971).
   8. *Problem-solving training* (Caple & Blechman, 1976; Shipley & Fazio, 1973).
   9. *Marital communications training* (Lewinsohn & Atwood, 1969; McLean, 1978; McLean, Ogston, & Grauer, 1973). Patient learns that his or her actions will control family behavior.
   10. *Reinforcing interruption of negative rumination and replacing with pleasant fantasy* (Hilford, 1975; Tharp, Watson, & Kaya, 1974). Patient learns depression management skills.
   11. *Graded task assignment* and task completion (Hilford, 1975; Kovacs & Rush, 1976; Rush, Beck, Kovacs, & Hollon, 1977).
   12. *Self evaluation:* selecting and defining obtainable subgoals (Fuchs & Rehm, 1977; Rehm, Fuchs, Roth, Kornblith, & Romano, 1979). By setting obtainable goals, the probability of personal control increases.
   13. *Desensitization* should *only* be effective with depressed patients who are anxious as well (learning that anxiety can be controlled will reduce depression); it should be inert otherwise. (Badri, 1967; Wanderer, 1972; Wolpe, 1971).

*(continued)*

**TABLE 5.3** (*continued*)

14. *Decision-making training.* Start with a small decision (choose anchovies versus pepperoni on your pizza) and work up to large, meaningful decisions (see *graded task assignment*).

C. **Resignation training**

Make expected, uncontrollable aversive outcomes less aversive, and make desirable but unattainable outcomes less desirable.

1. *Assumption challenging* (Beck, Rush, Shaw, & Emery, 1979; Ellis, 1962), for example, to challenge: "In order to be happy, I must always be accepted," make acceptance less desirable; "I can't live without love," make love less desirable; and "If someone disagrees with me, it means she doesn't like me," make disagreement less aversive.
2. *Grief flooding* (Ramsay, 1977).

D. **Attribution retraining**

To the extent that reality permits, instill more external, unstable, specific attributions for failure and more internal, stable, global attributions for success.

1. *See Section B, "Personal Control Training" tactics.* All such tactics that work will tend to change success attributions to internal and stable ones (i.e., "I now have the *ability* to, for example, assert myself").
2. *Change failure attribution from ability to effort* (Dweck, 1975; Dweck & Reppucci, 1972.) Actual experiences with effort increase after failure, producing success.
3. Weekly listing of *external reasons for failure* (Layden, 1978). Can be applied to success, stability, and globality as well.
4. *Increase frequency of positive self-statements* (Vasta, 1976). Make internal, global, stable attribution for success ("I handled that awkward situation really skillfully," for example). This should only be antidepressive when the individual comes to believe the self-statement and not merely to mouth it (see Inert techniques below).

(5–9 are the basic techniques of cognitive therapy)

5. *Identify and criticize* negative self-statements, obsessional ruminations, and "automatic thoughts" (for example, "The teacher didn't give me a C because she thinks I'm stupid [internal, global, stable] but to prod me into working harder [external, global, unstable].") (Beck, 1976; Beck, Rush, Shaw, & Emery, 1979; Kovacs & Rush, 1977; Mahoney, 1971; Rush, Beck, Kovacs, & Hollon, 1977).
6. Substitute *reality oriented interpretations for distorted negative cognitions* (Beck, 1976; Beck, Rush, Shaw and Emery, 1979; Rush, Beck, Kovacs, & Hollon, 1977).
7. *Recognize* and self-monitor *connection between negative cognition and low mood* (Beck, 1976; Rush, Beck, Kovacs, & Hollon, 1977). For example, "My depressed mood is caused by my distorted thinking (unstable, specific) and not by actual worthlessness, unattractiveness, stupidity, etc. (stable, global)."
8. *Identifying* and self-monitoring *social situations* and activities *that lead to depression* (Beck, Rush, Shaw, & Emery, 1979; Taylor & Marshall, 1977; Tharp, Watson, & Kaya, 1974). Make more external, unstable, specific attributions for low mood.
9. *Correct the "errors in logic"* of depressed patients (Beck, Rush, Shaw, & Emery, 1979). All are instances of attributional bias.
   a. Arbitrary inference: drawing a negative conclusion without basis. (Making an internal, stable, or global negative causal inference on insufficient evidence.)
   b. Selective abstraction: focusing on one detail out of context. (Making an internal, stable, or global negative causal inference on insufficient evidence.)
   c. Overgeneralization: drawing a sweeping negative conclusion based on a single incident. (Making global negative causal inference on insufficient evidence.)
   d. Magnification and minimization: magnifying bad events, minimizing good events. (Stable, global attributions for failure and unstable, specific attributions for success.)
   e. Personalization: taking undue responsibility for bad outcomes. (Internal attributional bias for failure.)

## Inert Tactics of Behavioral and Cognitive Therapy

According to the reformulated learned helplessness model of depression, several of the therapies commonly employed by behavioral and cognitive therapists should be inert. The following are all examples of therapies that, according to the model, should not be effective antidepressants.

*Restricting the emission of depressive speech.* There is no direct reason in the model why this should be antidepressant. This tactic might have secondary effects by making other people avoid depressives less and therefore exposing them to enriched environment, but in itself, it should be inert (Robinson & Lewinsohn, 1972).

*Inducing depressed individuals to engage in positive self-statements.* This tactic should also probably be inert; there is no direct reason why getting depressives to mouth good things about themselves should be effective. When mouthing such statements causes depressed individuals to believe them, then their causal analysis of their failures and successes, and therefore their attributions, will change, and the therapy will be antidepressive (see Table 5.3, c. 5–9). Those special circumstances under which inducing and reinforcing depressives for engaging in good statements about themselves actually changes belief are unknown, but we can safely say that reinforcement of such statements is not a sufficient condition of belief change.

*Self-reinforcement.* Merely getting depressives to say "good boy" to themselves more often and to say "bad boy" to themselves less often should not directly lower depression, according to the reformulated model. When self-reinforcement, either external or internal, increases the probability of certain personal control responses, and only insofar as it does so, if should be an antidepressive tactic. Self-monitoring and self-evaluation phases of self-control training should both be active (self-monitoring should be an effective environmental enrichment tactic [Table 5.3, A.2] as well as an effective attribution retraining tactic [D.7 and D.8], and self-evaluation [B.12] should be an effective personal control training tactic). I see no theoretical reason why the rate of self-reinforcement alone should affect depression. Only its response-enhancing consequences should directly be antidepressive (Fuchs & Rehm, 1977; Rehm *et al.*, 1978).

*Coverant control therapy* (Hannie & Adams, 1974; Taylor & Marshall, 1977; Wanderer, 1972) should also be inert. Increasing the probability of positive self-statements by reinforcing each statement with a more desired outcome (or with high-probability responses) should have no direct effect on depression. The important matter is getting depressed patients to change their attributions about the causes of their successes and failures, not getting them to mouth such statements. Insofar as inducing patients to mouth such statements actually changes attribution, this will be antidepressant; but I know of no theoretical reason why reinforcing the utterance of statements should increase the belief in such statements.

*Desensitization* should also be inert with respect to depression. Desensitization might have indirect antidepressive effects, but only in individuals who are both anxious and depressed, by producing personal control over the symptoms of anxiety.

*Flooding* should also be an inert tactic for depression. Insofar as the individual is both anxious and depressed, flooding may relieve anxiety (environmental enrichment), but there is no theoretical reason why flooding should directly reduce depression.

I realize that I am going out on a limb by predicting inertness for certain commonly used behavioral and cognitive tactics in therapy. I know of no evidence that disconfirms their inertness, however, since all the studies that show some effectiveness for them use a package of tactics with the allegedly inert ones only part of the package. To the extent that we are interested in finding out what the active ingredients are in therapy, controlled studies that use the allegedly inert tactics, uncontaminated by the allegedly active tactics of Table 5.3, would be useful.

## Relationship of Cognitive Theory to the Reformulated Model

I shall now argue that cognitve theory are subsumed by the reformulated helplessness model of depression. According to cognitive "theory," two "mechanisms" produce depression (Beck, 1976; Beck, Rush, Shaw, & Emery, 1979). The first is the cognitive triad—negative thoughts about the self, negative thoughts about ongoing experience, and negative thoughts about the future.

The depressive's *negative thoughts about the self* consist of the belief that he or she is defective, worthless, and inadequate. The symptom of low self-esteem derives from the belief that he or she is defective, and when depressives have unpleasant experiences, they attribute them to personal unworthiness. Since depressed persons are defective, they believe that they will never attain happiness.

Depressives' *negative thoughts about ongoing experience* consist of the interpretation that what happens to them is bad. They misinterpret neutral interaction with people around them as meaning defeat. They misinterpret small obstacles as impassable barriers. Even when positive views of an experience are more plausible, they are drawn to the most negative possible interpretation of what has happened.

Depressives' *negative view of the future* is one of hopelessness. When they look to the future, they see that the negative things that are now happening to them will continue unabated and that continuance will result from their personal defects.

Three of the major classes of symptoms of depression—motivational, cognitive, and self-esteem—are deducible from the negative cognitive triad. The motivational deficit of passivity results from the depressives' hopelessness: even if they do something, they believe a negative outcome will surely occur. The cognitive and self-esteem symptoms are direct expressions of the depressives' negative views of self, experience, and the future. Beck claims that the other class of symptoms (emotional–somatic) also results from the depressives' belief that they are doomed to failure. It is both a strength and a weakness of the theory that its basic theoretical entity, the negative cognitive triad, is such an accurate description of the basic symptoms of depression. The strength is the good fit into the cognitive and self-esteem symptoms of depression, but the weakness is that the theory can be seen as shallowly descriptive rather than deeply explanatory.

The other "mechanism" of depression is the systematic errors in logic. Depressives make five different logical errors in thinking, and each of these darkens their experiences: arbitrary inference, selective abstraction, overgeneralization, magnification and minimization, and personalization. *Arbitrary inference* refers to drawing a conclusion when there is little or no evidence to support it. An intern became discouraged when she received an announcement that said that in the future all patients worked up by interns would be reexamined by residents. She thought, "The chief doesn't have any faith in my work." *Selective abstraction* consists of focusing on one insignificant detail while ignoring the more important features of a situation. An employer praised an employee at length about her work, but midway through the conversation he suggested that she need not make extra carbon copies of his letters anymore. Her selective abstraction was, "He is dissatisfied with my work." In spite of all the good things said, only this was remembered. *Overgeneralization* refers to drawing global conclusions about worth, ability, or performance on the basis of a single fact. A man notices a leaky faucet in his house and overgeneralizes, thinking "I am a poor husband." *Magnification and minimization* are gross errors of evaluation in which a small bad event is magnified and large good events are minimized. The inability to find the right color dress is a disaster, but a large raise and praise for good work is trivial. *Personalization* refers to incorrectly taking responsibility for bad events in the world. A friend slips and falls on her own icy walk, and the depressed neighbor next door blames himself unremittingly for not having alerted his friend to her icy walk and insisting that she shovel it.

Beck's model has two main strengths. It accurately describes the state of the mind of the typical depressive, and it has generated a set of therapies that appear to be at least as successful as somatic treatment. But the model's main weaknesses are the looseness of its terms, its descriptive and shallowly explanatory cast, and its loose contact with any scientific base.

Put more baldly, the "theory" is ad hoc. Its main terms and mechanisms are made up in lockstep with the descriptions of depression and are not rooted anywhere else in scientific psychology. The mechanisms are not deduced from any simple or elegant set of premises. Put another way, while it is descriptively true that depressed individuals have a negative view of self, a negative view of their future, and a negative view of ongoing experience, these three terms are not well defined nor are they rooted in an experimental literature. How does the negative view of self differ from the negative view of experience? How does the negative view of the future differ from the negative view of the self? What is a "view"?

I believe that the negative cognition triad simply reduces to the better-defined and experimentally rooted terms of the reformulated helplessness model: The negative view of the future equals the fact that the individual expects that negative events will occur, the individual expects that they will be uncontrollable, and he or she attributes this to stable and global causes. The negative interpretations of ongoing experiences equal the perception of independence between ongoing outcomes and responding, with the concomitant misinterpretations equivalent to the specific attributional style. The negative attitude towards self equals the expectancy for future aversive uncontrollable outcomes attributed to internal causes.

The same lack of definition and the parallel reduction arise for the other "mechanism" of depression, the logical errors that Beck so accurately describes in depressed individuals. How do these errors differ from one another? Are they exclusive and exhaustive? How do they relate to the negative cognitive triad? How does personalization differ from the negative view of self? How is overgeneralization different from magnification? How is minimization of credit different from the negative view of the self? How is arbitrary inference different from selective abstraction? And so on. While Beck's description of the errors depressives make is an insightful one, theoretical advance may now come from more analytically defined mechanisms.

The helplessness framework provides a simpler and better-defined account of these errors, because it reconstructs the five errors of logic and shows their interrelationship. Each follows from the attributional style postulated by the reformulation. The error of overgeneralization results from a bias toward internal attributions for failure. The errors of magnification of faults and minimization of credits result from biases toward attributions in which failure is stable and global but attributions for success are unstable and specific. Both arbitrary inference and selective abstractions are instances of a tendency to make global, stable, internal attributions about failure and specific, unstable, and external attributions about success from minimal evidence.

So I would suggest the following. The main mechanisms of depression in cognitive "theory" reduce to the mechanisms of the reformulated learned helplessness model of depression. Thus, learned helplessness provides a more parsimonious, better-defined, and experimentally based framework for cognitive theory, by subsuming the cognitive triad and the logical errors of depression under the expectancy of aversive outcomes that will be uncontrollable accompanied by the depressogenic attributional style. If a slogan is necessary, it is: "The cognition model of depression is subsumed by the reformulated learned helplessness model of depression."

## Relationship of Cognitive Therapy to Learned Helplessness

It is often and carelessly said that the effectiveness of a therapy is not a test of the theory that underlies it. I believe that this is true only of a primitive theory of a disorder, but that one criterion of adequacy of a more complete theory of a disorder is that it deduce the effective therapeutic procedures from its etiological considerations. The techniques of cognitive therapy are only loosely deduced from cognitive "theory," and part of the reason for this has to do with the lack of definition of the terms of cognitive theory and the lack of underpinnings in experimentation. Since I have just gone through the exercise of attempting to show that cognitive theory is reducible to the simpler assumptions of the reformulated learned helplessness model of depression, I shall now do the same with cognitive therapy.

I believe that the basic tactics of cognitive therapy are deducible from the four strategies of therapy of the reformulated learned helplessness model of depression and that helplessness theory provides a well-defined rationale for these tactics.

While cognitive therapy uses such behavior therapy techniques as activity raising, graded task assignment, and assertiveness training for depression (personal control tactics), these are an adjunct to a set of "highly specific learning experiences" that according to Beck teach the patient to: (a) monitor negative automatic thoughts; (b) examine the evidence for and against distorted automatic thoughts; (c) substitute more reality-oriented interpretations for these negative cognitions; (d) recognize the connections between cognition, affect, and behavior; and (e) learn to identify and alter the dysfunctional beliefs that predispose the patient to distort experiences.

I should like now to recast these five basic tactics of cognitive therapy under the therapeutic strategies of the learned helplessness model. The basic principle that I believe underlies these techniques is the attempt to change attributions away from the bias of making internal, global, and stable attributions for negative events and external, unstable and specific attributions for positive events.

Table 5.3 includes the various tactics of cognitive therapy under attribution retraining (D.5–9) and under resignation training (C.1). Distorted negative automatic thoughts, I believe, consist almost entirely of internal, global, and stable attributions for failure and external, unstable, and specific attributions for success. We can call them something much more specific than "thoughts," for they are causal attributions. From the helplessness point of a view, what patients learn to do is to discover that they make particular internal, global, and stable attributions for negative events and particular external, unstable, and specific attributions for positive events (monitor negative automatic thoughts). They are taught to look at the evidence for and against these depressogenic attributions (examine the evidence for the negative automatic thoughts) and to change them toward particular external, specific, unstable failure attributions and internal, global, and stable success ones (substitute more reality-oriented cognitions). Thus, Beck's tactics a, b, and c are included in tactics D.5 and D.6 from the strategy of attribution retraining of Table 5.3.

A glance at what counts for Beck as "automatic thoughts" suggests that they are indeed exactly these depressogenic attributions: "I am a worse mother than my mother was"; "My therapist is rejecting me when he cancels an appointment"; "I won't be able to get into any good university because my grades are not so hot"; "I am worthless"; "If I don't get into college it really means I am stupid."

Beck's tactic of substituting more reality-oriented interpretations for negative automatic thoughts consists of learning to substitute internal, global, and stable attributions for success for the depressogenic external, unstable, and specific ones and to substitute external, unstable, and specific attributions for failure for the depressogenic internal, stable, and global ones. The patient who is convinced that his therapist is rejecting him is shown that the therapist's obligation to speak to a meeting of the American Psychological Association caused the cancellation (internal and global replaced by external and specific). The patient who is convinced that she is a worse mother than her own mother finds out that it is only a particularly bad time of day, the morning (changing from an internal and global source of failure to an external and specfic one).

Beck's tactics of helping a patient to recognize the connection between cognition, affect, and behavior boils down to helping the patient to see that depressed mood is caused by distorted thinking—an unstable and specific attribution for depression as opposed to a stable and global one such as being a bad person—and also helps the patient to see that various situations (usually external, unstable, and specific ones) set off depression. This technique also shows patients that the way they "interpret" situations, and not the situations themselves, produces maladaptive feelings and behavior. "Interpretations" are more changeable (unstable) than are "situations" themselves.

The final technique of cognitive therapy is to identify and alter the dysfunctional beliefs that predispose the patient to distort experience. This parallels "challenging of depressogenic assumptions" (Ellis, 1962), which is a principle technique of Rational Emotive Therapy (RET). Such challenges change attributional style (as discussed earlier) but more importantly are instances of resignation training. Among the assumptions that both Beck and Ellis attempt to uncover and change are: (a) "In order to be happy I have to be successful in whatever I undertake"; (b) "To be happy I must be accepted by all people at all times"; (c) "If I make a mistake I am inept"; (d) "I can't live without love"; (e) "If someone disgrees with me, it means he doesn't like me"; and (f) "My value as a person depends on what others think of me." Changing these assumptions boils down to reducing the aversiveness of highly aversive, but inevitable, outcomes and reducing the desirability of highly desired, but unobtainable, outcomes. Patients learn to devalue having to be successful in whatever they undertake, having to be accepted by all people, the seriousness of making mistakes, the overwhelming importance of love, the seriousness of disagreement, and the importance of the disparaging opinions of others.

In summary, both the therapeutic techniques and the "theory" underlying cognitive therapy can be subsumed under the simple and better-defined principles of the reformulation of the helplessness model of depression. I do not believe that this reduction of cognitive theory and therapy to learned helplessness omits any of the salient factors in cognitive therapy. Lest I be misunderstood, let me emphasize that I think that the development of cognitive theory and therapy has been the single most important advance within the psychology of depression. What I am attempting to do here is to provide a more systematic, better-defined, and experimentally rooted basis for cognitive theory and therapy, to simplify the field by integrating it with learned helplessness.

## A Technology without a Science

The more practical minded among you may have found this chapter to be an empty exercise. Why, after all, should we care whether or not a simple, well-defined, and experimentally rooted theory deduces certain therapeutic strategies? Why should we care if cognitive theory and therapy can be subsumed by learned helplessness? Why don't we content ourselves with testing the effectiveness of a variety of therapeutic techniques, as we have been doing, using the ones that are effective and discarding the ones that prove themselves ineffective in well-designed comparison studies? Does it matter if we don't have a coherent psychological theory of depression?

There is good reason to believe that some techniques of both behavior and cognitive therapy are effective against depression, but these therapies run the risk of being a technology without a science. The connections between behavior therapy and the experimental psychology of learning are tenuous, and the connections between cognitive therapy and the experimental psychology of cognition and learning are almost nonexistent.

What are the advantages of having a science underlying an effective technology, as opposed to merely having an effective technology with no scientific underpinnings? The first is aesthetic: Many of us prefer the interplay of deduction and induction, of testing the hypotheses in the laboratory, applying them in the clinic, and refining the hypotheses back in the laboratory, and so on, to mere clinical intuition. The second is flexibility: Explicit statements of the premises on which effective therapies are deduced allows flexibility in new situations. The therapist who realizes that the heart of cognitive therapy is the change of attributional style will be better able to deduce the appropriate tactics in a novel situation than if the therapist merely has a diffuse repertoire of techniques. The third reason is practical and long term: Preventative techniques, pharmacology, and physiology can be examined from a well-defined model but not from a set of clinical intuitions, however accurate. I hope it is more than an accident that learned helplessness not only deduces effective psychological strategies but also is reversed in the laboratory by tricyclics, monoamine oxidase inhibitors, and electroconvulsive shock, as well as by several other drugs that have yet to be tested out on depressed clinical populations. The fourth reason is understanding: Even if we had a set of tactics that were effective against depression in every instance, I doubt if we would be satisfied. For what counts as understanding depression is not merely having effective therapies but having a theory of how it comes about.

## Summary

I have stated the premises of the reformulated learned helplessness theory of depression. I have laid out four therapeutic strategies that are deduced from the premises of the theory. I have then reviewed the literature on behavioral and cognitive treatments of depression, attempting to sort the tactics actually used into those predicted by the theory to be effective and those predicted to be inert. Finally, I have examined the premises of cognitive "theory" and the techniques of cognitive therapy and have argued that learned helplessness provides a well-defined, parsimonious, and experimentally rooted framework for the cognitive and behavioral treatment of depression.

## References

Abramson, L. Y., Seligman, M. E. P., & Teasdale, J. D. Learned helplessness in humans: Critique and reformulation. *Journal of Abnormal Psychology*, 1978, *87*, 49–74.

Anton, J. L., Dunbar, J., & Friedman, L. Anticipation training in the treatment of depression. In J. D. Krumboltz & C. E. Thoresen (Eds.), *Counseling methods*. New York: Holt, Rinehart & Winston, 1976.

Badri, M. B. A new technique for the systematic desensitization of pervasive anxiety and phobic reaction. *Journal of Psychology*, 1967, *65*, 201–208.

Beck, A. T. *Cognitive therapy and emotional disorders.* New York: International Universities Press, 1976.

Beck, A. T., Rush, A. J., Shaw, B. F., & Emery, G. *Cognitive Therapy of Depression.* New York: Guilford Press, 1979.

Burgess, E. P. The modification of depression behaviors. In R. D. Rubin & C. M. Franks (Eds.), *Advances in behavior therapy*, 1968. New York: Academic Press, 1969.

Caple, M. A., & Blechman, E. A. *Problem-solving and self-approval training with a depressed single mother: Case study.* Paper presented at the meeting of the Association for the Advancement of Behavior Therapy, New York, December 4, 1976.

Dweck, C. S. The role of expectations and attributions in the alleviation of learned helplessness. *Journal of Personality and Social Psychology*, 1975, *31*, 674–685.

Dweck, C. S., & Reppucci, N. D. Learned helplessness and reinforcement responsibility in children. *Journal of Personality and Social Psychology*, 1973, *25*, 109–116.

Ellis, A. *Reason and emotion in psychotherapy*. New York: Lyle Stuart, 1962.

Fuchs, C. Z., & Rehm, L. P. A self-control behavior therapy program for depression. *Journal of Consulting and Clinical Psychology*, 1977, *45*, 206–215.

Hammen, C. L., & Glass, D. R. Depression, activity, and evaluation of reinforcement. *Journal of Abnormal Psychology*, 1975, *84*, 718–721.

Hannie, T. J., & Adams, H. E. Modification of agitated depression by flooding: A preliminary study. *Journal of Behavior Therapy and Experimental Psychiatry*, 1974, *5*, 161–166.

Hersen, M., Eisler, R. M., Alford, G. S., & Agras, W. S. Effects of token economy on neurotic depression: An experimental analysis. *Behavior Therapy*, 1973, *4*, 392–397.

Hilford, N. G. Self-initiated behavior change by depressed women following verbal behavior therapy. *Behavior Therapy*, 1975, *6*, 703.

Kovacs, M., & Rush, J. Cognitive—behavior psychotherapy versus antidepressant medication in the treatment of depression. In A. T. Beck (Chair.), Current developments in the psychotherapy of depression. Symposium at the meeting of the Eastern psychological Association, New York, April 1976.

Layden, M. A. *Attributional retraining of low self-esteem women*. Unpublished study, University of Wisconsin, 1978.

Lazarus, A. A. Learning theory and treatment of depression. *Behavior Research and Therapy*, 1968, *6* 83–89.

Lewinsohn, P. M. Activity schedules in treatment of depression. In J. D. Krumboltz & C. E. Thoresen (Eds.), *Counseling methods*. New York: Holt, Rinehart & Winston, 1976.

Lewinsohn, P. M., & Atwood, G. E. Depression: A clinical research approach. *Psychotherapy: Theory, Research and Practice*, 1969, *6*, 166–171.

Lewinsohn, P. M., Biglan, A., & Zeiss, A. M. Behavioral treatment of depression. In P. O. Davidson (Ed.), *The behavioral management of anxiety, depression, and pain*. New York: Brunner/Mazel, 1976.

Lewinsohn, P. M. Weinstein, M. S., & Alper, T. A behavioral approach to the group treatment of depressed persons: Methodological contribution. *Journal of Clinical Psychology*, 1970, *26*, 525–532.

Liberman, R. P., & Raskin, D. E. Depression: Behavioral formulation. *Archives of General Psychiatry*, 1971, *24*, 515–523.

McLean, P. D. Panel presentation. In L. P. Rehm (Chair.), New results on treatment of depression. Panel presented at the meeting of the Society for Psychotherapy Research, June 1978.

McLean, P. D., Ogston, K., & Grauer, L. A behavioral approach to the treatment of depression. *Journal of Behavioral Therapy and Experimental Psychiatry*, 1973, *4*, 323–330.

Mahoney, M. J. The self-management of covert behavior: A case study. *Behavior Therapy*, 1971, *2*, 575–578.

Miller, S. M. The stress reducing effects of uncontrollability. In M. Seligman & J. Garber (Eds.), *Human helplessness: Theory and application*. New York: Academic Press, 1979.

Ramsay, R. Flooding with grief: A treatment for depression. Paper presented at the International Congress of Behavior Therapy, Uppsala, Sweden, 1977.

Rehm, L. P., Fuchs, C. Z., Roth, D. M., Kornblith, S. J., & Romano, J. A comparison of self-control and assertion skills treatments for depression. *Behavior Therapy*, 1979, *10*, 429–442.

Rehm, L. P., & Kornblith, S. J. Behavior therapy for depression: A review of recent developments. In M. Hersen, R. M. Eisler, & P. M. Miller (Eds.), *Progress in behavior modification* (Vol. 7). New York: Academic Press, 1979.

Reisinger, J. The treatment of "anxiety-depression" via positive reinforcement and response cost. *Journal of Applied Behavior Analysis*, 1972, *5*, 125–130.

Robinson, J. C., & Lewinsohn, P. M. An experimental analysis of a technique based on the Premack Principle for changing the verbal behavior of depressed individuals. *Psychological Reports,* 1973, *32,* 199–210. (a)

Robinson, J. C., & Lewinsohn, P. M. Behavior modification of speech characteristics in a chronically depressed man. *Behavior Therapy,* 1973, *4,* 150–152. (b)

Rush, A. J., Beck, A. T., Kovacs, M., & Hollon, S. Comparative efficacy of cognitive therapy and pharmacotherapy in the treatment of depressed outpatients. *Cognitive Therapy and Research, 1977, 1,* 17–38.

Sammons, R. A. Systematic desensitization in the treatment of depression. Paper presented at meeting of Association for Advancement of Behavior Therapy, Chicago, 1974.

Seligman, M. E. P., Abramson, L. Y., Semmel, A., & Von Baeyer, C. Depressive attributional style. *Journal of Abnormal Psychology,* 1979, *88,* 242–247.

Seligman, M., & Miller, S. M. The psychology of power. In L. Perlmuter & R. Monty (Eds.), *Choice and perceived control.* Hillside, N. J.: Erlbaum, 1979.

Shaw, B. F. Comparison of cognitive therapy and behavior therapy in the treatment of depression. *Journal of Consulting and Clinical Psychology,* 1977, *45,* 543–551.

Shipley, C. R., & Fazio, A. F Pilot study of a treatment for psychlogical depression. *Journal of Abnormal Psychology,* 1973, *82,* 372–376.

Taylor, F. G., & Marshall, W. L. Experimental analysis of a cognitive–behavioral therapy for depression. *Cognitive Therapy and Research,* 1977, *1,* 59–72.

Tharp, R. G., Watson, D. L. & Kaya, J. Self-modification of depression. *Journal of Consulting and Clinical Psychology,* 1974, *42,* 624.

Vasta, R. Coverant control of self-evaluations through temporal cueing. *Journal of Behavior Therapy and Experimental Psychiatry,* 1976, *7,* 35–38.

Wanderer, Z. W. Existential depression treated by desensitization of phobias: Strategy and transcript. *Journal of Behavioral Therapy and Experimental Psychlatry,* 1972, *3,* 111–116.

Wells, K. C., Hersen, M., Bellack, A. S., & Himmelhoch, J. Social skills training for unipolar depressive females. Paper presented at the meeting of the Association for the Advancement of Behavior Therapy, Atlanta, Georgia, December 11, 1977.

Wolpe, J. Neurotic depression: An experimental analog, clinical syndromes, and treatment. *American Journal of Psychotherapy,* 1971, *25,* 362–368.

# 6

# The Role of Self-Regulation

FREDERICK H. KANFER
SUE HAGERMAN

Since their earliest application, behavioral approaches to psychopathology
have rejected traditional diagnostic schemata for several reasons:

1. Some categories suggest that similar syndromes represent the end result
   of similar pathogenic processes in all members of the class.
2. An underlying assumption of the infamous medical model is that the
   function of assessment is to isolate the characteristic manifestations of a
   continuing disease process. The diagnostic statement is then related to
   presumed evidence on etiological factors and serves as a base for planning therapeutic interventions. The goal of therapy is to undo, remove, or
   reduce the pathogenic factors.
3. It is the implicit assumption in the current classification schemata that
   many behavior pathologies are mental representations of organic processes.
4. There is an inherent implication of a discontinuity between normal behaviors, gauged in relation to dominant social norms, and pathological
   behaviors.

At first glance, it is embarrassing to note that depression seems to be the
exception in behavior pathology. Although the importance of a functional
analysis (Ferster, 1965; Kanfer & Saslow, 1965) has been widely accepted as a
basis for treatment formulation, depression has often been described by modern behavioristic approaches as a unified syndrome. Except for some attempts
to relate development of intense fear reactions to phobias, no other behavior
deviation has been explained as a result of a particular developmental pattern.
The largest proportion of research and behavioral treatment has been reported
for patients who were nonpsychotic, had no prior manic phases, and often were

143

BEHAVIOR THERAPY FOR DEPRESSION

Copyright © 1981 by Academic Press, Inc.
All rights of reproduction in any form reserved.
ISBN 0-12-585880-9

not hospitalized. In the conceptual model for these patients, the developmental features include a sudden change in the rate of available reinforcers, prolonged interpersonal skills deficits, or a perceived inability to control important features of one's life. But the emerging quality of the complaint rather than the elements derived from individual assessment appears to be of greater relevance in depression than in other disorders. Consequently, most treatment programs have not been individualized but have been based on broadly generalized statements about the central problem of depressive patients. The standard programs appear to have enjoyed fairly successful therapy outcomes. However, the relative effectiveness of therapeutic methods derived from the conceptual models of depression does not validate the etiological part of the model.

A review of behavioral models of depression suggests many common elements. All emphasize disruption, unpredictability, or cumulative inefficiencies in important response–reinforcement contingencies as antecedents of depression onset. Variations in the theoretical models basically stem from disagreements about the psychological processes by which a dearth of positive reinforcement comes about. Each approach tends to focus on one central mechanism, then takes account of some other problematic issues. But many widely reported common features in depressive disorders are dismissed as lying outside the scope of the proposed theory. For example, neither the bipolar nature of some depressive patterns nor the common self-limiting clinical course of the disabling state is handled. Models concern themselves with tracing the genesis of the symptomatic behavior and its maintenance. But little attention has been paid to discovering the differential features of situations or experiences (or biological constitution) that permit some persons with equivalent histories to adjust to various losses or limitations while others require assistance. The models remain postdictive until these factors are accommodated.

In the present chapter, we will review some of the central issues to which any model of depression must address itself. We will not summarize the main features of current models, because reviews and comparisons of the various behavioral theories of depression are available in several excellent articles (Blaney, 1977; Friedman & Katz, 1974; and others). In the following sections, we will propose a tentative heuristic conceptualization of the various processes alleged to relate to the development of depressive behavior. Derived from Kanfer's three-stage self-regulation model, the schema points up some research implications and provides a broader base for examining the multiple and interrelated psychological processes that might eventuate in the manifestation of a depression syndrome.

There are several messages that we would like to convey in this chapter. First, a comprehensive model of depressive behavior can at best offer only a general sketch of psychological processes and events that may occur in some but not all patients who are called depressed. Even the best general model still does not obviate a functional analysis in each case to assess the degree to which the model's numerous central variables and processes are relevant in the development of the particular patient's depressive reaction and what other non-model-related factors require consideration. Our second theme is to remember the inescapable necessity of evaluating behavior in the context of biological and sociological interrelationships, even though only one level of analysis may be of primary concern to psychologists. Finally, we hope to convey our belief that therapeutic effectiveness may be increased by an expanded analysis of the contributing historical, biological, cognitive,[1] and behavioral processes and their articulation with the patient's social and physical environment. Such a broader framework should permit the therapist to individualize programs, with the goal to remedy the weakest components in the multimatrix to reduce current inefficient behavior and also to prevent recurrence of future depressive episodes. The orientation of the chapter differs from a cognitive view (Beck, 1976; Kovacs & Beck, 1978) and from an operant reinforcement model (Ferster, 1973) in that it stresses the interplay between cognitive, interpersonal, and biological events as critical determinants of the process.

## Issues to Be Accommodated by Depression Models

### The Diagnosis of Depression

Behavioral models of depression have focused heavily on dysfunctions associated with reduction of effective interpersonal behaviors, loss of environmental control over behaviors that previously were at high strength, and self-reports of dysphoric mood and anger. This focus limits the generality of the models. The clinical literature and nonbehavioral theorists point to many other common features in depressed patients. Motor agitation, insomnia, a pessimistic outlook, suicidal thoughts, dwelling on past events, assumption of responsibility for distress of others, and inability to concentrate are among major common complaints. The alternate choices are either to propose that the behavioral models are applicable for a specified subgroup of depressed patients or to work toward increased comprehensiveness of the models. Despite the variety of classificatory schemata, there are some major features that tend to differentiate among groups of patients who are diagnosed as depressed.

In a proposal for reclassification of depressive disorders in DSM-III, Spitzer, Endicott, Woodruff, and Andreason (1977) suggested several criteria for classification. First, the disorder may be episodic or chronic. The episodic groups are further divided into major and minor. In turn, a distinction is made on the basis of recurrence and the mix of manic and depressive episodes. Distinctions between major and minor disorders are made primarily on the basis of intensity.

---

[1] In this chapter, the term *cognitive* is used primarily to describe intrapersonal activities, such as thinking, fantasizing, and perceiving, determined in content and form heavily by learning, by the characteristic parameters of human perception, by availability of language, by information processing, and by concurrent biological events.

The authors also note the frequent occurence of depressed mood in almost all psychiatric disorders. A differential diagnosis is made only when, in addition to the depressive pattern, symptoms from other categories are present or dominant.

The critical triad of the syndrome involves mood, disturbed or inhibited thought processes, and central and psychomotor functional disturbances. Widely used descriptions differentiate among somatogenic, endogenic, and psychogenic types. The problem is diagnosed as somatogenic when the depressed patient also has demonstrated organic brain changes, due to tumors, arteriosclerosis, or epilepsy, postinfectious diseases, cardiac insufficiencies, endocrine disorders, or similar disturbances. The endogenous group has generally been described as including both unipolar and bipolar manic and depressive disorders, and depressive reactions in which the first episode occurs around age 50 (involutional). The psychogenic group includes the neurotic depressions, associated with long-term distrubances in interpersonal relationships, anxiety, and insecurity. Exhaustion depressions, or neurasthenic neuroses, show strong somatic components in all systems but especially in complaints of exhaustion, fatigue, loss of concentration, and indecision. The reactive depressions are characterized as long-standing personal inadequacies, exacerbated by a precipitating event and resulting in reduced activity, apathetic or hostile behaviors, dysphoric mood, and guilt; they are characterized by durations that average 5–7 days before age 30 or up to 60 days at age 65–70.

Although all categories show overlapping behavior patterns, reasonable consistencies have been pointed out that differentiate them on the basis of the predominance of various components (Hoffmann, 1976; Kielholz, 1971; Usdin, 1977). Patient populations vary in the presence of a prodromal phase, importance of somatic complaints, degree of disorganization of interpersonal and cognitive behaviors, anxiety, reduction in activity frequency and appropriateness, presence of suicidal thoughts, and anger and hostility (Depue & Monroe, 1978). As a result, the presence of the characteristic triad of mood, cognitive, and behavioral patterns alone is insufficient to differentially predict patient response to a therapeutic program. Since some behavioral programs focus specifically on particular social skills, activity level, or self-reactions, it is necessary to examine correlations between improvement on the training program and on other criterion dimensions and between these measures and relevant and initial psychological and biological functions in order to obtain a base for predictions of treatment response. The data on age of onset of first episode, duration of untreated episodes, and relative presence and nature of long-standing interpersonal difficulties or precipitating factors lead one to suspect that assignment to a common treatment program may overlook important moderator variables, the consideration of which could further enhance treatment effectiveness. Scores on paper-pencil inventories describe how members of a population respond to questions and can pinpoint one source of variation. But the similarity in self-reports and behavioral patterns may also reflect the end result of a shaping of common forms and contents of behavior by social demands and practices. If the common observed behavior has been developed or maintained by different psychological mechanisms, the analysis of individuals could further contribute toward effectiveness by suggesting treatment components to be added to the modification program for common problem behaviors.

### Biological, Genetic, and Pharmacological Factors

A second cluster of problematic issues concerns the interrelationships between changes in biochemical functions, somatic complaints and behavior, the covariation of familial and genetic factors and behavioral patterns, and the differential responses to pharmacological treatment. Researchers have reported differences in familial histories among subgroups that suggest that different genetic transmission mechanisms could be involved (Cadoret & Tanna, 1977). Data reviewed by Depue and Monroe (1978), Akiskal and McKinney (1975), Usdin (1977), and others also note varying biochemical and neurophysiological characteristics of different subgroups.

Especially disturbing to a unitary psychological formulation of depressive disorders are the reports of differential responsiveness to lithium carbonate and tricyclic antidepressants among various subgroups, since they suggest that different complex biochemical processes may constitute the critical components that determine mood and activity changes. Purely pragmatically, chemotherapy research is progressing toward a catalogue of clinical and biochemical indicators on which treatment choice can be based (Klein, 1974; Lehmann, 1977; Schildkraut, 1977). However, neither psychological nor biochemical data have sufficed for a theory that satisfactorily relates clinical outcomes to a knowledge of the processes by which biochemical agents exercise their therapeutic effects.

Biochemical and pharmacological factors can also influence the behavioral picture of depression. Psychological treatment for depression usually follows far behind initial pharmacological interventions by self-medication or family physicians and short-term intervention programs. Even when medication is stopped at the beginning of the behavioral treatment, the prior interactive effects of medical treatments may continue to modify both the patient's neurochemistry and his or her attitudes toward psychological treatment. For instance, particular expectations of treatment effects, health-relevant role models, and shifts in centrality of somatic complaints and in perceived control over symptoms because of medical intervention can substantially affect responsiveness to behavioral intervention.

### Emotions, Cognitive Behavior, and Interpersonal Actions

A third cluster concerns the comprehensiveness of the psychological models in integrating relatively inaccessible interactions between cognitive processes, affective states, and reinforcement-related (motivated) behaviors. The interdependence of cognitive behaviors and interpersonal and motor actions has been the subject of much debate. Prior assumptions about the directional sequence of thinking and doing dictate different treatment strategies. For example, assuming cognitive behaviors to be precursors of motor and interpersonal actions suggests a treatment focus on altering self-reactions and thought patterns (Beck, 1976), whereas the reverse sequence suggests that changes in actions result in subsequent changes in self-perception and attitudes (Bem, 1972). This problem has been central in discussions of awareness in conditioning and of the limitations of externally controlled behavior modification programs. The data and arguments suggest that for different situations and responses either sequence or a bidirectional effect may occur. Consequently, treatment would best include intervention in both domains (Kanfer, 1968, 1977; Kanfer & Phillips, 1970).

If the incentive function of reinforcing stimuli is presumed to depend also on healthy biological functioning (e.g., Akiskal & McKinney, 1973, 1975) or if the controls over functions needed for motivated behavior (arousal, activation, and effort) reside in normal brain processes (Pribram, 1963; Pribram & McGuinness, 1975), the therapeutic effects of psychological programs may well be limited to the degree that psychological events can in turn affect brain processes. Thus, it becomes critical to know for what patients and for which therapy goals the most promising intervention is at the neurophysiological level, at the behavioral level of the reinforcement system, or in a combined attack on both.

The effects of physical states on behavior can also be indirect by influencing self-evaluations and attributional processes (Rodin, 1978), by enhancing attention to physical irregularitires (symptoms) (Pennebaker & Skelton, 1978), or by cognitive reactions both to automatic feedback and to situational cues, leading in turn to changes in arousal (Coyne, 1976; Holroyd & Appel, 1979). The consequences of these processes can affect the patient's actions with respect to the perceived "illness," as well as the evaluation of his or her own status. The latter can serve as a basis of self-reports, as a cue for interpersonal behaviors, and as the basis for increased self-preoccupation and general decrease of attention and activities that relate a person to the surrounding world.

The changed susceptibility to primary reinforcers, noted by most reserachers, has been attributed to learning histories, cognitive appraisals of the reinforcing events, unavailability of other reinforcers previously associated with them, or disturbances in the underlying biological reinforcement system. Knowledge of the manner in which decreased reinforcement susceptibility developed may aid in constructing treatment programs. But there is no logical reason to assume that therapeutic procedures to restore susceptibility to common reinforcers require such knowledge. Most problematic behaviors, including fears, subassertive responses, and anorexias have been successfully treated without recourse to etiology.

If mood is regarded as a correlate of emotional states, it is expected that the depressed patient's dysphoric mood can serve as a trigger for the complex and cyclic interactional sequences described earlier for emotional and physical states, as they are experienced (perceived) by the patient. Scattered data suggest that mood affects self-regulatory processes, as well as the perception of persons and situations.

Depression has been called an affective disorder, highlighting the crucial role of emotions in the diagnostic picture. Current theorists have begun to recognize the close interdependence of emotional states and (cognitive and interpersonal) behavior. In the operant reinforcement models, the affective features are introduced in the models mainly in connection with the affective by-products of nonreinforcement (Ferster), of a low rate of response-contingent reinforcement (Lewinsohn), or of loss of reinforcer effectiveness (Costello), or with the cognitive consequence—a sense of helplessness and hopelessness—of perceived loss of control over behavior consequences (Seligman). Beck (1967) offers a more abstract conceptual model and states "the affective response is determined by the way an individual structures his experience [p. 287]." But Beck also recognizes the inadequacy of a linear model from cognition to emotion and notes the circular feedback of affective events on cognitive behavior. What is missing is the inclusion of overt behaviors and their consequences in the feedback system.

The cognitive influence on interpersonal and emotional behaviors and perception of emotional states has been widely noted, as has the effect of emotional arousal on performance and on cognitive events. It is reasonable to speculate that these "reverberatory" interaction sequences can eventuate in a spiral effect that maintains the patient's report of his or her mood, self-perceptions, and judgments that affect self-reactions and interpersonal behavior in a direction that further increases a spiral effect.

The recognition of the interdependence of cognitive, overt behavioral, and affective events and their frequent covariations suggests that an array of variables (at any or all levels) may interrupt or alter the sequence with success, as has been shown in various drug and psychological intervention programs. Research is badly needed (a) to pinpoint the most easily altered components in the chain of events; and (b) to determine whether such weak links are common or different for identifiable patient groups.

## Methodological Problems

A fourth cluster of issues is methodological. The particular events on which a diagnosis of depression is based involve more than observation of such clearly definable behavioral characteristics as response frequency, latencies, and functional relationships to common biological and social reinforcers. They also include behavior topographies, the selection of which is not independent of the observer or social context; self-reports, which are notoriously reactive to the context in which they are given; and inferences about such emotional states as anger, dysphoric mood, and hopelessness, often inferred by an observer from a combination of the content of verbal behaviors in a particular stimulus context. While behavioral approaches can handle classification of interpersonal behaviors of varying content, affective elements are more difficult to describe, assess, and attack directly in a behavioristic framework. Current treatment programs rely heavily on self-report for assessment of initial status and progress. Behavioral psychologists accept such reports as interpersonal behavior, influenced not only by the events that they presumably describe but also by the context in which they are given (Kanfer & Phillips, 1970; Natsoulas, 1967). Reviews suggest (Nisbett & Wilson, 1977) that self-reports, especially about a person's own cognitive processes, may be accurate only to the extent that influential stimuli are salient and plausible causes of the responses they produce. Otherwise the report may consist mainly of inferences about the event rather than the observation of the internal process itself.

Retrospectively reported verbal information may be valid when care is taken to eliminate inferential processing by structuring the inquiry to minimize probing that would suggest the interviewer's interest and by use of procedures that discourage the patient from making inferences or from drawing on prior information rather than on recall of the event or process itself. Since the patient's memory for internal states of cognitive processes deteriorates after a lapse of time and lacks detail and since cognitive processes tend to become automated over time (Ericsson & Simon, 1978), the validity of retrospective self-reports is seriously limited. These limitations do not necessarily speak against the use of self-reports or the reinforcement of positive self-reports as a therapeutic device. The social demands made of the depressed patient and the behavioral treatment procedures that clearly reinforce self-reports of increased pleasurable activities may in turn serve as cues to the patient for reassessment of his or her behavioral effectiveness and state of well-being. Thus, self-reports obtained from interviews, questionnaires, or paper-pencil tests may not be valid per se. But, depending on the functional context in which they are given, they can elicit solicitous social support and increase self-preoccupation or they can increase the patient's self-perception of improvement and competence.

Another related set of methodological problems concerns the manner in which populations for research and treatment are selected, the criterion measures for outcome, and the generalization from the results. Experimental tests of models have involved selection of particular populations and different procedures for soliciting participation. Subjects have been selected by advertising in newspapers, by assignment of hospitalized populations, and by personality tests administered to college students. Such diversity in the recruitment of subjects is likely to affect outcome data, not only because of differences in population parameters, but also because the full context in which treatment is offered is known to influence such important outcome determinants as outcome expectations, role relationships, availability of alternative programs, compliance with program demands, and motivation for change. Recruitment procedures vary in the required self-initiated effort and in the number of preliminary hurdles (such as screening tests or interviews), and these variations in turn affect both the sample characteristics and responsiveness to treatment. When "normal" subjects are recruited for analogue studies or when animals are used, the findings are clearly limited. Ideally, these studies are best suited for testing broad hypotheses and require later validation if the results are to be applied to clinical populations. As Blaney (1977) has pointed out, longitudinal studies are essential for such validation.

The multiplicity of behavioral and biochemical dysfunctions in depressed patients confront the researcher with a choice of the appropriate criteria of dependent variables for the measure of therapeutic effectiveness. Characteristically, the choice of dependent variables depends on the researcher's underlying theory about the nature of the depressive reactions. Researchers who employ biochemical interventions favor the choice of dependent variables at the biological level or at the psychological level closely associated with it. Behavioral programs that focus on changes in assertive behavior, self-reinforcement, or increased interactional behaviors tend to select measures relevant to the contents of the treatment program. A broader range of outcome measures would greatly facilitate comparability among treatments. It would further permit statements about cross-behavioral and cross-modality changes that characterize the breadth of impact of target-specific treatments.

Some attention has recently been given to preparing for posttreatment generalization of changes (Goldstein & Kanfer, 1979). Ideally, evidence of treatment effectiveness should include the patient's ability to maintain himself or herself at a "recovered" level after therapeutic supports are withdrawn. However, no uniform criteria have been established for assessing overall treatment effectiveness nor have the domains been pinpointed in which recovery or treatment success should be assessed.

The recent emphasis on the importance of the patient's active participation in treatment (Kanfer, 1979, 1980) and on the role of compliance (Davison, 1973) also speaks against limiting the collection of outcome measures to the time when the patient is still under the influence of the treatment setting and therapist. An important criterion of successful treatment is whether the client can later "spontaneously" put into effect what he or she has learned in treatment and can resume a satisfactory life when external controls are no longer present. Other methodological problems in research on treatment effectiveness include the selection of appropriate control gorups, design decisions about the required length of a clinical experiment to establish reliable differential changes between control and experimental group, and control over nonsystematic beneficial influences of treatment contexts.

## A Model for the Development of Depressive Behavior

In this section, we present a descriptive model that attempts to apply an extension of our earlier model of self-regulation to the particular behavioral and emotional events associated with serious disruption or loss of reinforcers and incentives, commonly defined as a critical antecedent for depressed behavior. Rehm (1977) and his coworkers (Fuchs & Rehm, 1977) have previously applied our general model of self-regulation (Kanfer, 1971) to depression and demonstrated its utility as a basis for a self-control treatment program (Rehm, Fuchs, Roth, Kornblith, & Romano, 1979). In the present chapter, we have extended this application in two ways. First, on the basis of accumulating research on the original model, we have refined the model by including additional variables to achieve greater predictive utility. Second, we present an articulation between the revised model and the behavior patterns recently described in research on depression to increase its heuristic value for explaining the interrelationship between interpersonal behaviors, self-reactions, and emotional arousal in the development of depression. Our formulation essentially attempts to show how disturbing life events can result in a self-maintaining sequence of increasing failures to achieve goals, increasing preoccupation with these failures leading to future failures, and critical shifts in the person's attempts to cope with the resultant distress and behavioral ineffectiveness. While common sequences are proposed, the content and the parameters of important variables affecting the onset and each subsequent stage in the development of depression are presumed to vary in individuals.

We present flowcharts for illustration of the text. However, their use does not imply that the model portrays a rational decision-making sequence or a simulation of information processing structures. The presentation offers a conceptual model, admittedly speculative at this stage and based on research findings developed from other sources than the model itself. Its aim is to order the sequences in which critical variables may influence the flow of behavior in a predictable (and testable) manner. The model strives only to incorporate some diverse experimental findings and theoretical statements in an integrated framework and to provide a basis for further research and for experimental treatment programs. At this stage, the model appears to be sufficiently open to allow eventual accommodation of the issues raised in the first part of the chapter, once sufficient experimental evidence has been accumulated.

The remainder of this section is divided into three parts. The first section will acquaint the reader with our viewpoint and with the revision of our model for the general case. We then examine the role of the model in the development of depressive reactions. Finally, we suggest some implications for research and treatment.

Since the model has been discussed elsewhere in detail (Kanfer, 1970, 1971; Kanfer & Karoly, 1972; Rehm, 1977), we will only briefly summarize some underlying assumptions needed to give the reader the necessary context for following our presentation.

1. Human behavior represents a continuous flow of transactions between various levels of organization, especially the biological, behavioral, and social–environmental. Most psychological models are static and selectively focus on

some aspects of an organism interacting with its environment at $t = 0$. The criteria for inclusion of events and objects depends on the purpose for which the observer makes the analysis. Because of the nearly unmanageable complexity of events required for a full account of interacting variables and their flux in a time continuum, some attention must be paid to defining the limitations of a model in which levels of analysis and temporal continuums are restricted. In a static representation of a constantly changing interbehavioral field (cf. Kantor, 1924), we emphasize the probabilistic character of any generalization from the model. Specifically, we have assumed that the probability of occurrence of a particular response continuously fluctuates as a function of three sources of control: (a) environmental stimulation (alpha variables); (b) psychological events that are relatively independent of momentary environmental or biological inputs and can serve both cue and reinforcing functions (beta variables); and (c) biological variables that alter or limit both input and output functions of the other systems (gamma variables). As described elsewhere (Kanfer, 1970, 1971, 1977b), the relevant contribution of each of these clusters of variables vary from moment to moment and their joint effects determine response probabilities. Further, variables within each of these clusters may affect events in the domain of the other clusters. For example, fatigue can affect the relevance and effectiveness of both environmental and self-generated stimuli; through biofeedback, self-generated psychological behaviors can alter biological variables; and self-generated variables can compete with or shut out environmental sources of input. While the psychological model focuses on the behavioral level, it cannot disregard other sources of variables that affect behavior.

In the case of depression, a psychological model need not incorporate the full range of the biological substratum. It need only account for the psychological processes at the interface. Only an ideal model might incorporate data from all levels and systems. But even a working model of behavior cannot disregard significant biological events as they might affect psychological functioning (cf. Akiskal & McKinney, 1973, 1975; Graham, 1971; and others). Further, a psychological theory need not account for the societal context in which behavior occurs. However, it must attempt to describe the mechanisms at the interface between sociocultural events and behavior (e. g., Arieti, 1959; Paykel, 1973; Rahe, Meyer, Smith, Kjaer, & Holmes, 1964).

2. Despite philosophical and methodological impasses, we believe that a model of human behavior must in some way account for the role of verbal–symbolic events that codetermine or mediate the effects of external and biological stimulation on observable actions. Human propensities for supplementing external and biological stimulation, organizing such experiences in orderly ways, and generating possible future events and outcomes by symbolic behaviors cannot be excluded when behavioral determinants are investigated. In essence, it is believed that self-regulatory mechanisms, both as cues for behavior and as sources of reinforcement, determine a wide range of human actions that are not under direct and total control of alpha or gamma variables.

3. We assume that cognitive, social, and biological variables supplement rather than invalidate the relationships described by learning theorists. We assume that self-regulatory behaviors and acquired self-reactions play a dominant role in human behavior but do not necessarily preempt the contributions of environmental or biological influences.

We have speculated elsewhere (Kanfer, 1977a) that self-regulatory processes are especially critical when well established, newly learned, or reflexively determined behavior patterns are ineffective. Early stages of learning a new behavior, failure of a well-established response to function in obtaining a reinforcement, conflict situations, or disconfirmatory feedback about the expected effect of a behavioral sequence are examples of such situations that trigger operation of self-regulatory processes.

4. It is presumed that a person's engagement in self-regulatory activities serves as a reinforcing event for actions, supplementing (or modifying) the effects of external or biological consequences.

The pursuit and attainment of self-generated goals and the maintenance of standards that a person sets for himself or herself are viewed as critical sources of motivation, and self-regulatory effectiveness per se is a major motivating factor. Similar assumptions are found in Bandura's self-efficacy theory (1977), Rotter's (1954, 1978) generalized expectancies, Mischel's (1973) subjective stimulus values and self-regulatory systems, and other theorists' note of the importance of the "mastery motive." In our model, it is operationalized by the person's capability for generating and successfully meeting personal standards for various behaviors.

## The Revised Self-Regulation Model

Motivational theorists of various persuasions agree that human activities are oriented toward the achievement of goals that vary in the extent to which they control behavior. This conclusion may be reached on the basis of a model of a hierarchy of reinforcers that differ in the priority and effort of the instrumental behaviors needed for their attainment; or a central "state" may be presumed to organize orienting and perceptual behaviors as well as instrumental activities with reference to a current motivational state (Klinger, 1975, 1977; Klinger, Barta, & Maxeiner, 1979a, 1979b). In another view, the ranking of goals is related to the value, the probability of attainment, and the presence of competing obtainable reinforcers (Rotter, 1954). Which of these models, if any, serves as the basis of a motivational argument is immaterial to the present discussion.

As we have stated, the self-regulatory process is assumed to have motivational properties because it provides direction and an end state for behaviors that attain expected reinforcement. (An overview of the revised model is presented schematically in Figure 6.1. Details of the model are presented in subsequent figures in the order mentioned in the text.) It is activated when the smooth flow of ongoing behaviors is disrupted. The disruption can occur for many reasons, such as an uncertainty about the next step, as in early learning or conflict, or a failure to produce expected consequences due to interference from the environment or the person's biological system. The disruption serves as a signal to engage the self-regulatory cycle, beginning with the self-monitoring (SM) stage. Figure 6.2 schematically diagrams this stage. Once engaged in SM, the situation is categorized in terms of the source of the input variables that are presumed to exercise dominant control (see Figure 6.3). Differentiation between alpha, beta, and gamma control is a preparatory step for determining whether self-regulation proceeds. If the disruption is attributed to external variables, responsibility for the "breakdown" in the behavior chain is not assumed by the person. The self-regulation sequence terminates, and the behavioral chain is resumed, either in trial-and-error fashion or according to previous experiences of what one does when encountering unalterable situations. If the situation is categorized as one in which disruptions mainly result from the person's behavioral incompetence or inability, then the self-monitoring continues.

Categorizing situations as being determined by external versus personal control is essential to establish the behavioral standards against which the act is compared. For example, winning at a roulette wheel may be classified as a result of luck, whereas winning at poker may be viewed by a person as involving certain strategic skills. Failure experiences in the first situation would result in little self-regulatory behavior. In the second case, we would expect a person to evaluate the preceding behavior and to self-reinforce (positively or negatively) his or her gambling strategy.

Figure 6.4 illustrates the next sequence in the self-regulatory process leading to the self-evaluation stage (SE). Prior to comparing the current behavior with a standard, a particular criterion for that behavior must be selected. The first point at which different variables can affect the outcome of self-evaluation is symbolized as the decision about the importance of the behavior to the person's motivational state. We have chosen to use Klinger's (1979) definition for this motivational state, which is called a "current concern." "A 'current concern' is defined simply as the state of an organism between the time that it becomes committed to pursuing a particular goal and the time that it either consummates the goal or abandons its pursuit and disengages from the goal [Klinger, Barta, & Maxeiner 1979a, p. 2]. This definition suggests the important influence of such a state upon the person's actions, thoughts, and perceptions. If the monitored behavior is not salient to a current concern, even though it may be judged to be under beta control, it is expected that the self-regulatory process is terminated at this point. For instance, a slight stumble while running to catch a bus may be a trivial interruption that has no further effect. But the same stumble for a runner on elimination trials may result in lengthy self-evaluation.

If the behavior has been judged to be relevant to a current concern, our model differentiates between short-term (ST) and long-term (LT) concerns. ST concerns center around the performance of behaviors relevant only to the

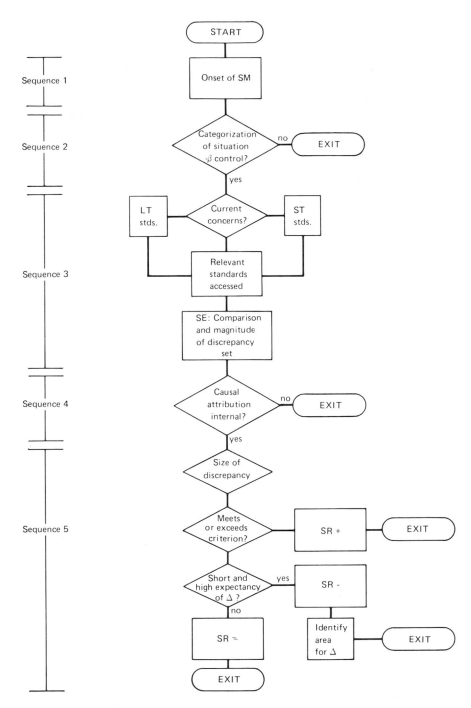

**FIGURE 6.1** Overview of the model.

KEY TO FIGURES

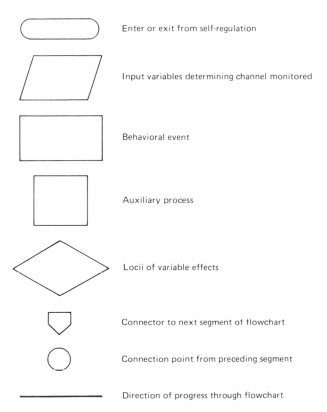

Enter or exit from self-regulation

Input variables determining channel monitored

Behavioral event

Auxiliary process

Locii of variable effects

Connector to next segment of flowchart

Connection point from preceding segment

Direction of progress through flowchart

immediate situation or to specific limited goals. In contrast, LT concerns relate to the maintenance of enduring personal goals, especially as they affect the person's standards for personal conduct in a wide range of situations. LT concerns thus relate to self-perceptions regarding critical personal capabilities and repertoires.[2]

To illustrate, a situation-specific standard may be involved in telling the truth in traffic court or in performing routine quotidian job tasks, such as filing sales reports correctly. In either case, small lapses in performance might not be expected to have far-reaching effects on the person's self-reactions or future

[2] It is important to note that in labeling and classifying concerns as either ST or LT, we do not wish to imply that the length of time during which the concern is active is the critical dimension on which they differ. Nor do we wish to imply that the difference is one of instrumentality, with one achieved goal required before reaching others. The salient difference lies in the scope of the self-reactions that are included in the sequence before disengagement occurs. Labeling the two types of concerns as person relevant and situation relevant instead of LT and ST more clearly elucidates the distinctions we wish to make.

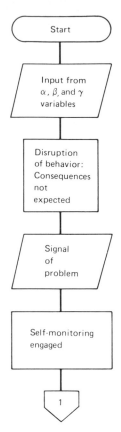

**FIGURE 6.2** Sequence 1: Onset of self-monitoring. See Figure 6.1 for key.

life. But LT concerns could involve considering oneself an ethical person or giving a sales presentation on which one's promotion and job status depend. Deviations from the relevant standards in the latter cases would be presumed to involve a broader range of self-reactions and life spheres. It can thus be seen that differences in the standards selected to judge the adequacy of the monitored behavior and the subsequent impact of self-evaluation can clearly be of some importance to the person.

Performance criteria against which behavior is compared in this stage represent personal norms but are heavily influenced by past experiences, the person's reinforcement history, physical skills and abilities, and prevailing social norms (Bandura, 1976; Kanfer & Karoly, 1972; Mischel, 1973). It is important to note that both the contents and importance of the criteria in the SE stage will differ for ST and LT concerns. For the former, the standards relate only to the situation, whereas LT concerns often provide an idealized perception of the person's behavioral potentials against which the monitored behavior is com-

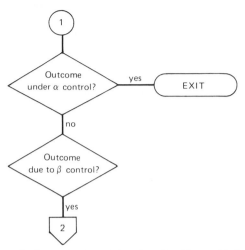

**FIGURE 6.3** Sequence 2: Categorization of situation. See Figure 6.1 for key.

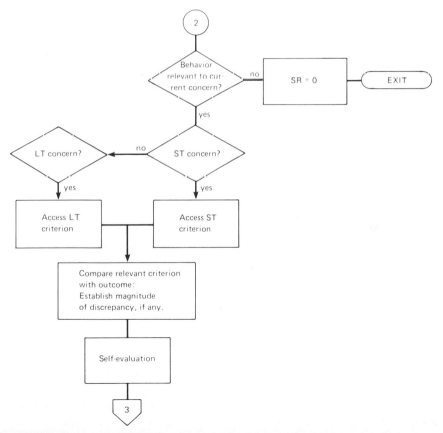

**FIGURE 6.4** Sequence 3: Criterion selection and performance evaluation. See Figure 6.1 for key.

pared. In either case, the appropriate standard is accessed for comparison with the monitored behavior in the self-evaluation stage.[3]

A further note on the differential consequences for subsequent behavior is needed to explicate the importance that we place on the decision whether ST or LT standards are accessed. It is assumed that all persons share one overriding LT concern, that of living up to one's perceived level of competence and skill to handle life situations as well as is possible under given circumstances. Such a LT concern is viewed as an incentive, and obtaining confirmation of such competence is considered as an important basis for self-reinforcement. In this assumption, our model resembles Bandura's (1977) model of the role of efficacy expectations on behavior. Although LT concerns may be accessed relatively infrequently in moment-to-moment behaviors, their presumed importance to the individual suggests a proportionally greater intensity of the associated motivational state. Greater personal involvement and importance of the event would also be accompanied by greater emotional arousal than is the case in ST concerns, especially if discrepancies were to be noted between the performance criterion and the monitored performance. The distinction between ST and LT criteria thus sets up the intensity and importance of the self-reinforcement provided in the subsequent self-regulation stage. When a substantial change (especially a negative one) occurs in the discrepancy between criterion and performance in a situation that involves LT concerns, a large arousal effect would be predicted. This parallels the observation of increased emotional behavior in laboratory animals following either cessation of reinforcement after a long period of reinforcement or provision of reinforcement following long deprivation and nonreinforced trials.

Once a distinction is made during SE between ST and LT concerns, the sequence continues to the next stage, illustrated in Figure 6.5. The monitored behavior is further evaluated with regard to the causal attribution of its consequences either to the person or to situational components. As Rehm (1977) has pointed out, our earlier self-regulation model lacked specification of the point at which attributions can affect both the self-evaluative and self-reinforcement processes. Empirical research from various laboratories suggests that subsequent behavior may differ when the individual attributes discrepancy in reaching the self-set standard either to him or herself or to external events.[4] Attributions, in turn, are influenced by many of the variables described in the relevant literature. Of special interest to us is the higher probability that failure will be attributed to external components when previous efforts in similar situations have been successful than when unsuccessful performance occurs in new situations or when a large personal component characterizes the demand characteristics of the situation. But it should be noted that causal attributions

---

[3] Klinger (1975) suggests that while the content of ST concerns can be explained by using an operant analysis, the explanation of the content and standards of LT concerns is more complex. We concur.

[4] Of course, differentiating internal and external attributions, like the differentiation between ST and LT concerns, does not suggest the existence of "pure types." We invoke arbitrary dichotomies primarily for heuristics and utility rather than as true descriptions of the world.

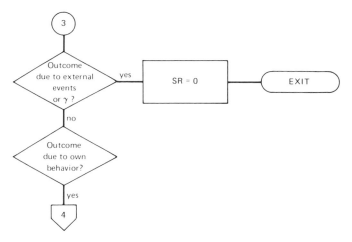

**FIGURE 6.5** Sequence 4: Causal Attribution. See Figure 6.1 for key.

differ from the categorization of the situation (see Figure 6.2). The latter represents an initial assessment of the degree to which external or personal factors can affect the monitored type of situation in general, whereas the causal attribution decision made at the later stage reflects the person's decision of the degree to which external factors or personal actions have brought about the consequences of the specific monitored behavior. If behavioral outcomes are attributed to external causes, then a comparison against self-set standards becomes irrelevant even if an LT concern is involved. In effect, this portion of our model suggests that there should be no significant self-evaluation, regardless of the degree and direction of the observed discrepancy from the self-imposed standard, once the behavioral outcome has been assigned to external causes. On the other hand, if the behavioral consequences are attributed to personal factors, the self-regulation process should proceed.

At this point, it is important to note that causal attributions for the outcome in a situation need not correspond to the actual state of affairs. In fact, environments that encourage behavioral patterns that permit self-labeling of inferiority or helplessness can generate self-descriptions and standards that erroneously provide attributions of helplessness and inadequacy in situations in which the person is not responsible for outcomes. These self-labels and standards can further cue escape and avoidance responses that prevent persons from engaging in behavior in which they have previously been successful or which they could carry out effectively (Langer & Benevento, 1978). Gamma variables may also exert an important influence on causal attributions. The monitored state of one's physical or mental well-being and of current medication may be viewed as a factor beyond the person's control. The perception that the behavioral disruption that initially instigated self-regulation is due to gamma control.

Once the behavioral consequences are attributed internally, the self-regulatory process continues to the self-reinforcement (SR) stage. Figure 6.6

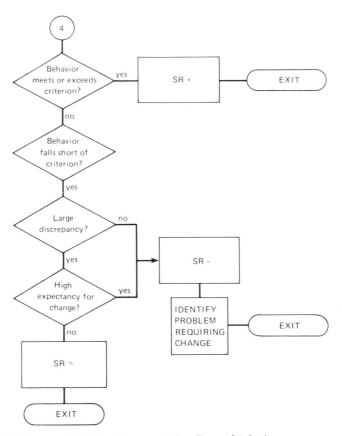

**FIGURE 6.6** Sequence 5: Self-reinforcement. See Figure 6.1 for key.

illustrates the relationship between SE and SR. The first section of the figure indicates that the monitored behavior is compared against previously accessed criteria appropriate to the current concern. The result of this comparison is then evaluated. If the behavior meets or exceeds the accessed standard, positive self-reinforcement would follow, as described in earlier versions of the model. The magnitude, kind, and rate of positive self-reinforcement depend upon the person's past history of reinforcement, base rate of SR, and the level of the criterion against which the performance is compared. It is assumed that continuing accumulation of the results of SE occur. Repeated successes or failures in meeting the criterion in similar situations should alter the level of the standard and may also change the criterion from the ST to the LT category or the reverse. For example, if the person has experienced a series of successes with behaviors instrumental in achieving a ST goal, the ST standard against which the outcome of the behavior is compared will be set higher than if the person had had fewer successes or a varied outcome history. If the person then experiences a failure in an area of high competence, the result may be a switch to an LT standard of general competence. Thus, in a situation in which an ST standard was previously accessed, the new behavioral criterion may now refer to competence in a major life sphere. Conversely, in a situation where standards previously had reflected a competence evaluation (LT), repeated successful outcomes can shift the accessed standards to a more limited, situation-specific (ST) criterion. The number of successes required for alteration of the criterion level will differ, depending on whether the accessed criterion is ST or LT in the current pass through the self-regulation cycle. Each successive self-regulation experience constitutes a previous experience and item in the person's reinforcement history that affects the relevant criterion level on the next occasion. The self-regulatory process then is seen as a frequently repeated process in which parameter values continuously vary as a function of previous experiences in similar situation.

If the behavior falls short of the criterion, the extent of the discrepancy becomes important. A small discrepancy may be met with negative self-reinforcement. The self-regulatory process then shifts to a problem-solving routine (not described here) by which the situation is examined, the problem area is identified, and corrective action is planned and taken. This shift to problem solving constitutes an exit from the self-regulation cycle.

A large discrepancy between the behavior and the criterion is further evaluated for the probability that either the behavior or the situation can be changed to reduce future discrepancies between performance and standard. If the expectation for change is high, some negative self-reinforcement is administered and the problem-solving routine is begun. However, if the expectation for internally attributed change is low, we hypothesize that the person administers severe negative SR, with the results that the entire situation is later avoided or behavior is suppressed on future similar occasions. There may be situations in which, because of externally attributed constraints on options, the expectancy for change is low. In such cases, we expect mild negative SR to be administered. The person then faces the task of having to cope with a situation he or she cannot change. Of course, if the external attribution of constraints is such that a person comes to perceive a widespread lack of options for change, despair and hopelessness may result (Seligman, 1975).

The combination of the selection of self-referred standards and causal self-attributions thus results in prediction of two different outcomes for failure situations in the last stages of the self-regulation process. If ST standards have been accessed and causal attribution is made to the person's current effort rather than to general ability or skill, a mild discrepancy between monitored performance and the standard should result in self-criticism of a constructive nature. Repetition of the sequence and attempts to resolve the situation by increased effort or by attempts to alter the situation toward a more favorable situation would be expected. The consequence of such failure experiences and their evaluation should therefore be temporary and constructive. However, if there has been repeated failure in similar situations or if there is a large change, such as a loss of a person or a job, a physical disability or an incapacity due to increased age or physical illness, the individual's repertoire is seriously limited and previously successful coping can no longer by carried out. With increasing frustrations, disappointments, and failures, the person is more likely to invoke criteria that reflect personal characteristics or competence. Invocation of such standards that results in a comparison between current performance and a general criterion of adequacy, and any outcome that reflects a serious failure to attain the self-generated standard, would further confirm the person's attributed inadequacy and discourage the individual from positive action to ameliorate the situation. As we have stated in our presentation of the original model, a large discrepancy between performance standards and monitored performance should result in self-criticism and discouragement. Just as persons who observe models much more competent than themselves give up in discouragement, the evaluation of a large discrepancy between current performance and the person's "model" of himself—as represented in the standard—should lead to termination of the behavioral sequence with strong self-criticism, negative affect, and reduced activity. The result is a reduction in the frequency of behaviors that have previously had high potential for reinforcement (Ferster, 1973).

We have noted the effects of success and positive SR in changing performance criteria. Similarly, repeated failures should also affect the level of the standard to an extent depending on the situational and behavioral attributions and whether the behavior is relevant to an ST or an LT concern. The important point for the discussion of self-regulatory processes and depression is that a change in criterion level and a switch from ST to LT concerns can occur and further affect the entire self-regulation process.

## The Model Applied to Depression

In applying the self-regulation model to depression, we propose the following speculative sequence of events as a point of departure for a closer analysis and research of the social, psychological, and biological processes that may occur at each point of our flow chart.

1. A person is faced with an unobtainable goal in a life sector that is of major importance. The unattainability of the goal need not be due to a sudden loss of a person or state of affairs that has previously facilitated the attainment of satisfaciton. Cumulative or sudden confirmatory evidence that an important LT goal is unattainable leads all theorists to predict serious behavior disruption. The postulated explanations for the disturbance vary. The cause may be conceptualized as a perceived loss of control (Seligman, 1975); an attribution of personal responsibility for the evanescence of the reinforcer to oneself (Miller & Norman, 1979); the straining of a reinforcement schedule already at a high ratio of work expended to reinforcement gain, changes in the environment, habituation, or adaptation (Ferster, 1965; 1973); the changes in the relative availability

of the reinforcer to others and to oneself (Crosby, 1976); or the various other factors that, as in extinction, produce a low rate of positive reinforcement (Lewinsohn, 1974, 1975; Lewinsohn & Amenson, 1978). In the animal literature, the effect of such a reduction of positive reinforcement has been described as an increase in random-activity level following the termination of positive reinforcement at the beginning of an extinction interval. At the human level, Klinger (1975) described it as a phase of invigoration.

In our model, we conceptualize this event as a failure to obtain the behavioral criterion—indicated by a discrepancy between what is self-monitored and what is expected—and followed by self-criticism (see Figure 6.6). We hypothesize that there is an initial increase in activity, designed either to modify the individual's own behavior or to change the situation in a way that reinstates the previous level of positive reinforcement—either self or externally adminstered (Baron, 1966).[5] If, however, on successive repetitions of the self-regulatory cycle it becomes obvious that the behavioral standard cannot be reached, the person will eventually give up. This should be manifested in a decrement in the variety and rate of activities that had earlier been associated with the attainment of the person's standards for his or her own behaviors (Ferster, 1965).

2. The content and level of the standards against which behavior is compared on each successive cycle can undergo a shift from ST to LT goals, or the converse, on the basis of earlier experience related to achieving the standard. That is, successive failure (or success) experiences, and the concomitant SR, may alter the level and value and/or the content of the criteria for the behavior (see Figure 6.4). The criterion level generated for future performances is not always lowered after failure. For some persons (e.g., high achievers) and during frustration following nonreinforcement, the level may be increased or the blocked incentive may become more attractive (Klinger, 1975). Further, causal attribution may shift from external to internal responsibility for the consequences (see Figure 6.5). We also postulate that a change in the expectation that one can alter one's own behavior or the situation may then occur and lower the expectations that an acceptable resolution can be found (see Figure 6.6).

Failure experiences attributed to oneself or associated with perceived inability (loss of control) to remedy the situation (as in an unexpected loss of vocational security or of physical health) should result in a reduction of constructive efforts to overcome the serious limitations created by the perceived change in competence. This stage is similar to what has been described as the stage of disen-

---

[5] This increase in activity and search for restitutive behaviors could also serve as an antecedent of manic episodes. Attempts to ward off impending loss by excessive preoccupation with actions relevant to the threatened loss increase the probability that the person will reenter the self-regulation cycle. With increased emotional arousal and narrowed attention to the central concern, overactivity and inappropriate corrective actions may result. The hyperactive behavior can also result from the exaggerated evaluation of the chances that one can alter either the situation or one's behavior, thus avoiding future negative self-evaluation and reducing guilt and self-reproach. Finally, realization that even this maximal effort does not reinstate the desired reinforcing conditions may introduce the person into the depressive side of the cycle. In this way, our model could tentatively account for the episodic nature of bipolar depressions.

gagement (Klinger, 1975) and is postulated to be a transition phase from a high level of activity and emotional arousal to a gradual reduction of constructive interactional behaviors. Our assumption of the motivational character of successful self-regulatory activities (as supported by the literature on the beneficial effect of perceived freedom to choose, to originate actions, and to control outcome [Kanfer, 1979; Kanfer & Grimm, 1978]) also leads us to expect that the previously described cycle results in reduced motivation, perception of loss of control, and increased feeling of incapacity and helplessness. This would be further facilitated if the blocked incentive had become more attractive and "especially if [the person's] self-worth was predicated on effectiveness in controlling incentives [Klinger, 1975, p. 151]." At this stage, the characteristics of the depressed client are similar to those described by Seligman (1975), the dysphoria cluster reported by Lewinsohn (1975), and the development of a negative self-view emphasized by Beck (1976).

It should be noted that this critical transition in the contents of the self-regulatory processes (e.g., in level of standards, in an ST-to-LT shift, in increased internal attribution, and in expectation of ability to change) can occur gradually or suddenly and cannot always be easily correlated with specific and observable precipitating factors. For example, we do not expect the loss of a good job or of a beloved person necessarily to cause the immediate onset of the critical changes in self-regulatory processes. On the other hand, an imaginary failure after a long-coveted business promotion can occasion the changes. What is crucial in these examples is the person's reaction to a perceived loss or failure rather than to its actual occurrence. (See Costello, 1972a, for a description of the result of the loss of a distant other who has not been a source of reinforcement for some time.)

Subsequent repeated failures, albeit situationally determined, to find suitable alternatives for the attainment of reinforcements associated with the lost person or event can result, we postulate, in an increasing confirmation of personal incompetence and a shift from ST to LT concerns. A variety of predispositional and person variables affecting each of the component stages in self-regulation can contribute to this outcome. Individuals with high personal standards for achievement in a particular life sector, persons with limited interpersonal skill repertoires, persons who have a long-term high rate of self-criticism, and individuals whose life patterns center primarily about the very same area in which the competency decrement has occurred would be expected to be more vulnerable to this deterioration. Indeed, Muñoz (cited in Zeiss, Lewinsohn, & Muñoz, 1979) has shown that depressives report more irrational beliefs related to guilt, failure, their degree of control over problems, and sources of unhappiness and upset than do normal and nondepressed psychiatric controls. Depressed clients also report lower expectancies of positive thoughts and higher frequencies of negative thoughts than do the controls. Once changes occur in the level of the standards, the shift from ST to LT concerns, and/or the decrease in the expectation that change in one's behavior or situation can be effected, any further perceived failures, increased self-doubts, and the lack of constructive coping strategies increase the stress that the individual experiences. As Akiskal and McKinney (1975) have put it, increased stress has both neuroendocrine and psychological consequences. They produce heightened arousal and can disrupt the functional integrity of the reinforcing system. Thus, "more arousal, more hopelessness and more evidence of purposeless psychomotor activity [p. 299]" result. The increased emotional arousal associated would result further in a shift in the balance between external (alpha), self-generated (beta), and biological (gamma) sources of control (see Figure 6.2). Specifically, a transition is expected to occur in which the person's cognitive self-evaluations and attendant emotional arousal starts the spiral of increased attention to one's own cognitive and bodily processes and a gradual decrement or distortion of behavioral control by external events. This hypothesis is consistent with Klinger's (1975) statement that, "with the marked weakening of current concerns about external incentives, one would expect a relative increase in attention to interoceptive stimuli, which would then elicit a larger share of fantasy segments concerning them [p. 16]." This implies a steadily increasing discrepancy between potential significance of external events, as consensually judged, and how they are perceived and evaluated by the person. Nelson and Craighead (1977) found empirical support for such selective attention in depressives and relate their findings to the self-regulation model of depression. They found that depressives generally reinforced themselves less than nondepressives. They also recalled the amount of positive and negative feedback differentially at high and low rates of feedback, respectively.

3. The shift toward increased self-preoccupation should result in the following changes in the various components of self-regulation. In SM, three changes can be expected. First, an increased selective monitoring of "what did I do wrong" should focus the person's attention on negative outcomes, even when of little importance, and on behavioral inadequacies relevant to self-generated LT standards of personal competence. Therefore, what were originally ST cues are now LT cues. To the observer, this behavior appears as an overgeneralization; it is seen by Beck (1967, 1976) as a central type of dysfunctional depressive cognition. Nelson and Craighead (1977) found that depressed students attend to negative feedback and overestimated the amount of such feedback more than nondepressed students. Such behavioral patterns are consistent with what Beck has called the negative view of oneself and of the world.

Second, the increased frequency and aversiveness of the emotional correlates of negative outcomes should result in the person's increased attention to initially minor somatic and affective (gamma) cues. This pattern is consistent with the self-reports of feeling bad and the increased focusing on somatic disturbances that have been characterized as hypochondriasis and general excessive attention to bodily functioning in depressives. The change in the content of self-monitored behaviors should also result in increased verbal control by the contents of these self-preoccupations over the person's interpersonal behavior (as described by Ferster, 1973; Lewinsohn, 1975), increased intraverbal behavior related to the dysphoric mood, and attempts to escape or terminate this aversive state. As has been described in detail by Ferster (1973), Lewinsohn (1975), and others, this pattern of increased complaints develops into a vicious circle. The attempt to gain sympathy and support in social interactions leads to short-term social support and reinforcement for the complaining and self-attending behavior, on the one hand, but alienates support by the elicitation of negative affect in other persons, on the other hand (Coyne, 1976; Lewinsohn, 1975).

The third consequence of the critical shift toward self-preoccupation is increased attention to immediate events, since other, long-term goals no longer constitute the behavioral standards against which performance is compared. It is now not the successful execution of a task but considerations of the person's self-adequacy that are at stake. Self-monitoring should thus selectively focus on cognitive and interpersonal performances related to the confirmation of the person's momentary behavioral (in)effectiveness. Failure experiences and the shift to self-preoccupation also tend to threaten well-organized goal-oriented behavior patterns, since new goals must be established before commitment to them can occur. The result of such a shift would appear to be related to what Lazarus (1968, 1972) has called the loss of the future perspective and has been noted by Rehm (1977) and others in the assessment of depressed clients.

4. It is immaterial to our current argument to know the mechanisms by which biochemical changes occur at the onset of a depression. Whether they represent antecedents or consequences of critical life events or whether they are simply by-products of increased levels of stress (independent of the content of associated events), one would expect the increased tendency to self-monitor bodily activity level to make the person more cognizant of the biochemical substratum in the process of SE. Perception of a dysphoric mood in oneself can contribute to the maintenance of a spiraling effect by confirming one's inadequacies and reducing one's potential for constructive activity. Thus, the person's state of lowered well-being becomes the primary problem providing the basis for further negative self-reactions and confirmation of personal inadequacy.

The newly developed concern over maintaining control over internal processes, enhanced by such previously unaccustomed events as suicidal thoughts, seemingly uncontrollable recurrence of thoughts, or unusual associations, can increase the urgency of what have been called metacognitive processes (the attempt to observe one's own verbal-symbolic behavior). This increased concern over personal functioning also sets the occasion to test the popular fears about loss of control, going crazy, suffering brain deterioration, or losing responsibility, by evaluating closely how one functions. Such self-observation is time-, energy-, and attention-consuming and frightening to the depressed individual.

5. Continuing daily experiences, negative self-evaluations, bodily discomfort,

and similar generalized personal ineffectiveness should lead individuals to a shift in the dominant current concern (the content of a person's most important motivational state) from concern with factual objective events to a concern about one's well-being. Clearly, increased attention to evidence of personal effectiveness and bodily well-being should result in further failure to act appropriately in a variety of situations (Ferster, 1973), leading to an increased spiral of negative self-evaluations. For example, lack of concentration, failure to attend and respond appropriately in social situations, or failure to plan effective strategies for overcoming the blocking or unattainability of important goals create secondary problems for the depressed person. Thus, it is no longer the original difficulty that is central to the person's moment-to-moment activity, but the concern with his or her own current state. The most important goals, reinforcers, and instrumental behavior should therefore focus mainly around the patient's testing hypotheses about the gap between current behavior, mood, and thoughts and the standard of how "I used to be" or how "I should be." If, as Klinger suggests, fantasy and thinking behaviors provide incentives that stimulate constructive actions, then the depressed person's lack of various long-term goals and the preoccupation with his or her current insufficiencies set the stage for constant comparisons between what the patient views as "normal" standards and current behaviors, as well as for comparisons from past events. Recapitulation of past failure experiences and of actions that could have avoided them can seriously interfere with constructive action to terminate the person's current plight.

6. The depressed person's preoccupation with his or her difficulties, the various disturbances in the conduct of effective behaviors, and the shift to problem-related LT criteria provide little opportunity for either positive external reinforcement or positive SR. Both the behavioral and biological states of affairs should give rise to increased negative SR, especially if positive outcomes are now attributed to external events, rather than to the person's competence. Escape responses (e.g., lowered activity, interpersonal behaviors that solicit sympathy and caretaking, increased nonproductive fantasy related to lost goals, or decreased attention to external events) should increase negative self-evaluations and, therefore, negative self-reinforcements.

7. Depressive reactions have been described as self-limiting in their clinical course. It is apparent that both systematic psychological and pharmacological treatments are designed to interfere with the vicious circle described earlier. The treatment regimen attempts to provide for the development of new incentives, for the increase of evidence of personal competence in some life areas, and for simple adjustive reactions to a different set of self-perceptions. However, it is not at all clear how spontaneous remissions occur without external intervention in the self-defeating circle.

It is tempting to rely upon biological speculations about the "wisdom of the body" to explain a gradual reversibility of biochemical processes, or on postulation of a maximal self-limiting aversiveness of the depressive state to explain gradual activation of the patient toward constructive behaviors and resumption of at least a minimally acceptable life pattern. However, we have found no mention, nor even speculation, in any of the current formulations of depression per se about the mechanisms involved in spontaneous recovery. There are serious ethical problems in research on the "natural" course of depressive reactions without treatment (and even control procedures related to an experiment may have some therapeutic effects). But at least observations, retrospective accounts, and demographic data may provide a clue to whatever curative mechanism(s) nature has provided. Such research would appear to be critical for a better conceptualization of depressive reactions and effective therapeutic interventions. Costello (1972a) argues that depression due to loss of significant others is of survival value. After a loss, usual behaviors may decrease in frequency while restitutive behaviors increase as the person attempts to replace valued social reinforcements. These restitutive behaviors reintegrate the person in the social group and thereby provide the individual with the reinforcers he or she seeks and guarantee the social group the continuing participation of its members. The implications of Costello's argument for spontaneous remission in clinical depression (rather than the mourning form of depression to which Costello refers) is that, the fewer the sources of social reinforcement available to an individual, the more likely he or she is to develop a serious depressive reaction. We might speculate that the restitutive behaviors necessary for social reintegration occur only after an extended period of inactivity, that is, after the person is "clinically depressed." "Spontaneous remission" might be interpreted as the normal pattern of increased restitutive behaviors. What separates "normal" grief reactions from reactive depression is therefore the gap between decreased frequency of usual behaviors and the increased frequency of restitutive behaviors. Our model attempts to explain why there might be such a gap.

Klinger (1975) also suggests that depression has potentially beneficial effects both for the individual and for the survival of the species. For the individual, the ability to disengage from an incentive is crucial to prevent total exhaustion in pursuing the blocked goal. However, if the activity reduction following the "giving up" carries positive incentive value, it would be important that the disengagement process be aversive to prevent failure from resulting in a net positive incentive value, surely a dangerous state of affairs for the species. Depression provides such a mechanism. Klinger thus considers that some degree of depression is a normal, adaptive part of the process of disengagement from an incentive.

While the preceding account is clearly speculative, it attempts to illustrate the relationship between biological, cognitive, and interpersonal events and depressions. The review of current treatment procedures suggests that both behavioral and cognitive interventions are similar in their effectiveness. In a recent paper that reports equally effective treatments that focused either on interpersonal skills, cognition, or pleasant events, Zeiss et al. (1979) suggest that all treatments in their experiment may have been effective because they provided training in self-help skills "thus increasing the patient's expectations of mastery and encouraging the perception of greater positive reinforcement as a function of the patient's greater skillfullness [p. 438]."

On the basis of our current formulation, we would slightly alter these conclusions to suggest that effectiveness is related to the persons' increased confidence in their ability to regulate their own behaviors to achieve the behavioral criteria they have set for themselves and in their ability to do so with their own resources. This formulation suggests that for each patient the particular skill deficits, be they interpersonal or cognitive, have to be assessed carefully so that a program can be devised to remedy these specific deficits. The practical question facing the therapist is to what specific deficit or external event does the client attribute hopelessness. The development of a treatment program requires a series of clinical decisions, based on assessment data, situational demands and resources, and continuing treatment response, similar to the intervention strategy described by McLean (1976). We have assumed that multiple and individually different antecedents have resulted in a similar pattern of negative self-reactions (and this pattern is the current cause of the complaint). Therefore, specific skill training must be linked with training to utilize feedback from increased success experiences in the formulation of self-statements that can serve as cues for an increased range of positive behaviors, the development of new incentives, and the utilization of coping mechanisms to handle future failures and unexpected setbacks more effectively. It is obvious that both biochemical intervention and the provision of a social environment that is differentially responsive only to the patient's constructive behaviors should contribute to successful treatment outcome.

Most treatment programs presume that depressed clients are motivated to change. We have speculated that an increase of aversiveness in the depressive cycle, if suicide does not intervene, might eventually provide such motivation and activate the patient toward reconstructive activities. Considering our emphasis on the person's perception that improvement is attributable to his or her own efforts and not to external manipulations, it would seem particularly important with depressed clients to use various techniques for remotivation (Kanfer, 1980) that help the person develop a conceptualization of a desirable state of affairs toward which he or she can strive.

In a sense, it is not externally provided reinforcement for increased activity and tolerance of normally pleasurable experiences that is seen as the effective treatment strategy but the patient's self-generated involvement and enthusiasm that must be created to activate him or her to pursue normal constructive activities. While increased activities, physical exercise to reduce disturbing body feedback, social skill training, or verbal interaction with the therapist can provide the necessary skills and create the conditions for client motivation, it is not treatment compliance but the client's self-generated concern for attaining a different life pattern that must serve as the motivational prerequisite for effective treatment. A therapeutic alliance (Cameron, 1978) can serve as the bridge between them. Both cognitive and behavioral treatment approaches appear to create such favorable conditions indirectly. Rehm and Kornblith's (1979) review of over 50 studies of depression therapy suggests that patients can be motivated in a variety of ways to terminate self-defeating self-regulatory behaviors. What appears to be common in different treatments is that patients learn to rely on self-generated feedback about their competence rather than to remain dependent on uncertain and fortuitous success experiences or environmentally generated evaluations for setting their goals and maintaining their activities.

## Research Implications

The model presented here is still very speculative. Research is required to strengthen and test its descriptive, predictive, and explanatory utility, especially in the following four areas: the advantages in predictive power gained by the expansion of the model, its utility as a model of depressive processes, its value as a base for the development of therapy methods, and its relevance to the understanding of unaided recovery from depression, especially in relation to biochemical and genetic correlates. Some examples of the research implications in each area are presented, although they are not exhaustive.

1. The first area of research needed to increase the validity of the model involves an investigation of variables affecting central points of the model itself. For example, prior success or failure experiences, reinforcement history, and environmental conditions need to be experimentally varied in order to explore their relative effects upon the categorization of the situation to be monitored as either alpha, beta, or gamma controlled. Similarly, these variables might be evaluated in relation to changes in the levels of behavioral standards. Changes in the expectation that one can alter either one's behavior or the situation in which failure to meet one's standards occurred may also be influenced by past success or failure experience, reinforcement history, and environmental variables. Additionally, skills in defining and solving problem situations should affect the perception that one can alter one's behavior or situation. Experimental manipulation of such experience would provide support for our prediction that the probability that restitutive efforts will occur depends upon the perception that a change can be effected. Data available from the studies on relieving helplessness (from experiments conducted within Seligman's framework) can serve as a point of departure for this work.

Of central importance to the viability of our model is the development of means of assessing the content of a current concern. Klinger (1979a, 1979b) has developed and utilized a series of self-report methods to assess it. In addition, behavioral measures and physiological recording techniques are needed for the identification of current concerns.

While causal attribution is theoretically postulated to affect the value of success and failure and the subject's subsequent self-reinforcement (Bandura,

1977; Nelson & Craighead, 1977), little direct evidence for this hypothesis exists. For example, experimental manipulation of instructional sets and feedback regarding performance are needed to explore their respective effects on the levels of standards and the probability that a shift from ST to LT standards will occur. Some relevant research on the change in content of behavioral criteria is available in the literature on achievement and level of aspiration. Further research is required to specify the various conditions that affect the establishment and change in standard content and level, especially in the development of depression. Variables potentially implicated in standard development include exposure to models, instructions, demands from the social environment via the normative perofrmance of peer subjects, and the client's reinforcement history. These variables, introduced after standards have been assessed, are also expected to affect conditions under which a shift in ST–LT standards occurs.

2. The postulated sequences in the development of depressive reactions requires further study. It is important to ascertain whether depressives do change the content of their current concerns over time. While inducing a depressive reaction to investigate the developmental sequence is ethically not permissible, continuous assessment of the content of current concerns during the course of therapy would be an appropriate method to study changes in current concerns. The cues to which depressives attend in self-monitoring also need to be studied over the course of therapy. This assessment would help to answer the question of whether depressives are prone to overattend to gamma input variables in later stages of a depressive cycle. Depressed subjects should be compared with nondepressed psychiatric and normal control subjects on the level of standards they set for themselves in simple tasks. The conditions under which standard levels change or shift from ST to LT concerns (or conversely) in each of the three groups may then be explored. Finally, investigating the ease with which each of the groups gives up in attempting to reach a preestablished goal, and the conditions under which this occurs, is also essential in testing the applicability of our model to depression.

Possible personality and life history variables may be correlated with standard levels set by individuals. Whether depressives are predisposed to setting criterion levels that are more likely to produce discrepancies when behavioral outcomes are compared against them should be examined. This sort of research would presume that previous explorations of the relationship between failure situations and criterion levels had already established discrepancies as central to the depressive cycle. Finally, the respective individual contribution of and the interactions between experience with the failure situation, causal attribution, criterion levels, expectation of the ability to change the situation, and cues selected for self-monitoring need to be explored in relation to the susceptibility of depressives to cease restitutive efforts in the face of (repeated) failure to reach a goal. These variables should also be systematically varied to examine their effect upon the depressive's ability to perceive, label accurately, and monitor success experiences. The latter is especially important for the development of therapeutic techniques.

3. Rehm and his coworkers (Fuchs & Rehm, 1977; Rehm, 1977; Rehm, et al., 1979) have conducted research on therapeutic interventions based upon our earlier model as a whole (Kanfer, 1970, 1971). But the current modifications regarding its applicability to the development of depressive cycles need to be explored further in relation to the particular processes proposed in the model for which preventive or remedial action can be taken. Specifically, techniques need to be developed and tested for shifting the value of incentives from the depressive current concern to other life sectors. Setting up and reinforcing success experiences in small, seemingly unimportant tasks has often been used as a therapeutic technique. It remains to be established whether and how such exercises contribute to an enduring shift reestablishing the incentive values of a broader range of reinforcers. If it can be clearly demonstrated that depressives overattend to interoceptive stimuli and their dysphoric mood, already available methods for altering the cue value or "meaning" of somatic and self-monitored cognitive inputs could be adopted for specific use with depressives.

4. Finally, the factors that affect the phenomenon of unaided recovery (i.e., recovery not specifically associated with a known therapeutic intervention) in some depressed patients need to be studied. As in other areas that deal with resolution of personal problems, understanding the "natural" course of depression may point the way to effective treatment.

Although not of central concern to this model, the contributions of biochemical and genetic factors in the development of the depressive cycle will eventually need to be integrated into a behavioral framework. The question of the incremental efficacy of behaviorally oriented therapy over biochemical interventions can be raised for study. At this time, our model suggests a framework for research at various stages of the depressive cycle that recognizes but does not yet include the role of biochemical and genetic factors in depression.


## Summary

In this chapter, we have indicated some issues that require further attention in the current behavioral models of depression. We have then presented a revised version of our self-regulation model and indicated its potential utility for describing the development of depressive reactions. The tentative formulation postulates that feedback effects between self-regulatory processes, affective arousal, and interpersonal behaviors mutually strengthen a spiraling pattern that is characteristically observed in depressed patients. The main self-regulatory dysfunctions in depression can be summarized by the following features:

1. Various skill deficits, losses of critical life supports, decrements in skill repertoires, or biological dysfunctions result in severe or cummulative failure experiences.
2. Attempts to remedy the situation fail because of personal deficiencies or unalterable external changes. The results are twofold: (a) eventually the patient resigns and gives up attempts to change; and (b) a critical shift occurs in attribution of responsibility for failures to personal shortcomings that are incompatible with previous long-term norms and generalized expectancies for one's ability to cope with life.
3. Increased self-preoccupation and concurrent emotional stress follow, leading to a focus on negative events and thoughts. A spiral effect is started, in which interpersonal and environment-relevant behaviors deteriorate and affective and cognitive events become increasingly negative, confirming the self-perception and shifting the person's dominant and pervasive motivational state (current concern) to a continuing evaluation of personal adequacy. The central theme becomes an attempt to resolve the insufficiency of the self-regulatory system to initiate and sustain goal-directed activity.
4. Intervention in the "downward spiral" by drugs or psychological treatment or by a self-limiting aversiveness of the state gradually restores or supplements efforts to establish future-oriented goals, increases positive self-evaluations in some areas, and decreases self-preoccupation, thus reversing the spiral effect.

Two critical shifts occur: First, a shift of attribution of responsibility for failures to oneself, resulting in generalization of the relevance of failures to long-term criteria. Second, an increasing imbalance toward control of self-generated (alpha) stimuli over external (beta) stimuli and focus on self-adequacy alters motivational priorities and their associated instrumental behaviors. The first shift also increases emotional arousal and thus supplies further cues for self-preoccupation that facilitates the second shift.

## Acknowledgments

The authors would like to express their appreciation to Carol Kulik and Jim Smith for their assistance in preparing this chapter.

## References

Akiskal, H. S., & McKinney, W. T., Jr. Depressive disorders: Toward a unified hypothesis. *Science,* 1973, *182,* 20–29.
Akiskal, H. S., & McKinney, W. T., Jr. Overview of recent research in depression. *Archives of General Psychiatry,* 1975, *32,* 285–305.

Arieti, S. (Ed.). *American Handbook of Psychiatry.* New York: Basic Books, Inc., 1959.

Bandura, A. Self-reinforcement—Theoretical and methodological considerations. *Behaviorism,* 1976, *4,* 135–155.

Bandura, A. Self-efficacy: Toward a unifying theory of behavior change. *Psychological Review,* 1977, *84,* 191–215.

Baron, R. M. Social reinforcement effects as a function of social reinforcement history. *Psychological Review,* 1966, *73,* 527–539.

Beck, A. T. *Depression: Causes and treatment.* Philadelphia: University of Pennsylvania Press, 1967.

Beck, A. T. The core problem in depression: The cognitive triad. *Science and Psychoanalysis,* 1970, *17,* 47–55. (a)

Beck, A. T. Role of fantasies in psychotherapy and psychopathology. *The Journal of Nervous and Mental Disease,* 1970, *150,* 3–17. (b)

Beck, A. T. *Cognitive therapy and the emotional disorders.* New York: International Universities Press, Inc., 1976.

Bem, D. J. Self-perception theory. *Advances in Experimental Social Psychology,* 1972, *6,* 1–62.

Blaney, P. H. Contemporary theories of depression: Critique and comparison. *Journal of Abnormal Psychology,* 1977, *86,* 203–223.

Cadoret, R. J., & Tanna, V. L. Genetics of affective disorders. In G. Usdin (Ed.), *Depression: Clinical, biological and psychological perspectives.* New York: Brunner/Mazel, 1977.

Cameron, R. The clinical implementation of behavior change techniques. In J. P. Foreyt & D. P. Rathjen (Eds.), *Cognitive behavior therapy: Research and application.* New York: Plenum, 1978.

Ciminero, A. R., & Steingarten, K. A. The effects of performance standards on self-evaluation and self-reinforcement in depressed and nondepressed individuals. *Cognitive Therapy and Research,* 1978, *2,* 179–182.

Costello, C. G. Depression: Loss of reinforcers or loss of reinforcer effectiveness? *Behavior Therapy,* 1972, *3,* 240–247. (a)

Costello, C. G. Reply to Lazarus. *Behavior Therapy,* 1972, *3,* 251–252. (b)

Costello, C. G. A critical review of Seligman's laboratory experiments on learned helplessness and depression in humans. *Journal of Abnormal Psychology,* 1978, *87,* 21–31.

Crosby, F. A model of egotistical relative deprivation. *Psychological Review,* 1976, *83,* 85–113.

Coyne, J. C. Toward an interactional description of depression. *Psychiatry,* 1976, *39,* 28–40.

Davidson, P. Therapeutic compliance. *Canadian Psychological Review,* 1976, *17,* 247–259.

Davison, G. C. Counter-control in behavior modification. In L. A. Hamerlynck, L. Handy, & E. J. Mash (Eds.), *Critical issues in behavior modification.* Champaign, Ill.: Research Press, 1973.

Depue, R. A., & Monroe, S. M. The unipolar–bipolar distinction in depressive disorders. *Psychological Bulletin,* 1978, *85,* 1001–1029.

Deutsch, A. M. Self-control and depression: An appraisal. *Behavior Therapy,* 1978, *9,* 410–414.

Eastman, C. Behavioral formulations of depression. *Psychological Review,* 1976, *83,* 277–291.

Ericsson, K. A., & Simon, H. A. *Retrospective verbal reports as data* (CIP Working Paper 388). Unpublished manuscript, Carnegie-Mellon University, 1978.

Ferster, C. B. Classification of behavioral pathology. In L. Krasner & L. P. Ullmann (Eds.), *Research in behavior modification: New developments and implications.* New York: Holt, Rinehart and Winston, Inc., 1965.

Ferster, C. B. Animal behavior and mental illness. *The Psychological Record,* 1966, *16,* 345–356.

Ferster, C. B. The use of learning principles in clinical practice and training. *The Psychological Record,* 1971, *21,* 353–361.

Ferster, C. B. An experimental analysis of clinical phenomena. *The Psychological Record,* 1972, *22,* 1–16.

Ferster, C. B. A functional analysis of depression. *American Psychologist,* 1973, *28,* 857–870.

Ferster, C. B. The difference between behavioral and conventional psychology. *The Journal of Nervous and Mental Disease,* 1974, *159,* 153–157.

Friedman, R., & Katz, M. (Eds.). *The psychology of depression: Contemporary theory and research.* Washington, D.C.: U.S. Government Printing Office, 1974.

Fuchs, C. Z., & Rehm, L. P. A self-control behavior therapy program for depression. *Journal of Consulting and Clinical Psychology,* 1977, *45,* 206–215.

Goldstein, A. P., & Kanfer, F. H. *Maximizing treatment gains: Transfer enhancement in psychotherapy.* New York: Academic Press, 1979.

Graham, D. Psychophysiology and medicine. *Psychophysiology,* 1971, *8,* 121–131.

Hammen, C. L., & Krantz, S. Effect of success and failure on depressive cognitions. *Journal of Abnormal Psychology,* 1976, *85,* 577–586.

Hammen, C. L., & Peters, S. D. Interpersonal consequences of depression: Responses to men and women enacting a depressed role. *Journal of Abnormal Psychology,* 1978, *87,* 322–332.

Hoffmann, N. *Depressives Verhalten: Psychologische Modelle der Atiologie und der therapie.* Salzburg: Otto Muller Verlag, 1976.

Holroyd, K. A., & Appel, M. A. Test anxiety and physiological responding. In I. Sarason (Ed.), *Test anxiety: Theory, research and applications.* Hillsdale, N. J.: Laurence Erlbaum Pub., 1979.

Jackson, B. Treatment of depression by self-reinforcement. *Behavior Therapy,* 1972, *3,* 298–307.

Kanfer, F. H. Verbal conditioning: A review of its current status. In T. R. Dixon & D. L. Horton (Eds.), *Verbal behavior and general behavior theory.* Englewood Cliffs, N. J.: Prentice-Hall, 1968.

Kanfer, F. H. Self-regulation: Research, issues and speculations. In C. Neuringer and J. L. Michael (Eds.), *Behavior modification in clinical psychology.* New York: Appleton-Century-Crofts, 1970, 178–220.

Kanfer, F. H. The maintenance of behavior by self-generated stimuli and reinforcement. In A. Jacobs & L. B. Sachs (Eds.), *Psychology of private events.* New York: Academic Press, 1971.

Kanfer, F. H. The many faces of self control, or behavior modification changes its focus. In R. B. Stuart (Ed.), *Behavioral self-management.* New York: Brunner/Mazel, 1977. (a)

Kanfer, F. H. Self-regulation and self-control. In H. Zeier (Ed.), *The psychology of the 20th century (Vol. 4): From classical conditioning to behavioral therapy.* Zurich: Kindler Verlag, 1977. (b)

Kanfer, F. H. Self-management: Strategies and tactics. In A. P. Goldstein & F. H. Kanfer (Eds.), *Maximizing treatment gains: Transfer-enhancement in psychotherapy.* New York: Academic Press, 1979.

Kanfer, F. H. Self-management methods. In F. H. Kanfer & A. P. Goldstein (Eds.), *Helping people change* (2nd ed.). New York: Pergamon Press, 1980.

Kanfer, F. H., & Grimm, L. G. Freedom of choice and behavioral change. Journal of Consulting and Clinical Psychology, 1978, *46,* 873–878.

Kanfer, F. H., & Karoly, P. Self-control: A behavioristic excursion into the lion's den *Behavior Therapy,* 1972, *3,* 398–416.

Kanfer, F. H., & Phillips, J. S. *Learning foundations of behavior therapy.* New York: Wiley, 1970.

Kanfer, F. H., & Saslow, G. Behavioral analysis: An alternative to diagnostic classification. *Archives of General Psychiatry,* 1965, *12,* 529–538.

Kanfer, F. H., & Saslow, G. Behavioral diagnosis. In C. M. Franks (Ed.), *Behavior therapy: Appraisal and status.* New York: McGraw Hill, Inc., 1969.

Kantor, J. R. *Principles of psychology.* Bloomington, Ind.: Principia Press, 1924.

Kerber, K. W., & Coles, M. G. H. The role of perceived physiological activity in affective judgment. *Journal of Experimental Social Psychology,* 1978, *14,* 419–433.

Kielholz, P. *Diagnose und therapie der depressionen fur den praktiker.* München: Lehmann, 1971.

Klein, D. F. Endogenomorphic depression: A conceptual and terminological revision. *Archives of General Psychiatry,* 1974, *31,* 447–454.

Klinger, E. *Structure and functions of fantasy.* New York: Wiley, 1971.

Klinger, E. Consequences of commitment to and disengagement from incentives. *Psychological Review,* 1975, *82,* 1–25.

Klinger, E. *Meaning and void: Inner experience and the incentives in people's lives.* Minneapolis: University of Minnesota Press, 1977.

Klinger, E., Barta, S. G., & Maxeiner, M. E. Current concerns: Assessing therapeutically relevant motivation. In P. C. Kendall & S. D. Hollon (Eds.), *Cognitive–behavioral interventions: Assessment.* New York: Academic Press, 1979. (a)

Klinger, E., Barta, S. G., & Maxeiner, M. E. *Motivational correlates of thought content frequency.* Unpublished manuscript, University of Minnesota, 1979. (b)

Koller, P. S., & Kaplan, R. M. A two-process theory of learned helplessness. *Journal of Personality and Social Psychology,* 1978, *36,* 1177–1184.

Kovacs, M., & Beck, A. T. Maladaptive cognitive structures in depression. *American Journal of Psychiatry,* 1978, *135,* 525–533.

Langer, E. *The facilitation of mindlessness and its consequences.* Paper presented at meetings of the American Psychological Association, Toronto, 1978. (a)

Langer, E. The illusion of incompetence. In L. Perlmutter & R. Monty (Eds.), *Choice and perceived control.* Hillsdale, N. J.: Erlbaum, 1978. (b)

Langer, E., & Benevento, A. Self-induced dependence. *Journal of Personality and Social Psychology,* 1978, *36,* 886–893.

Langer, E., Blank, A., & Chanowitz, B. The mindlessness of ostensibly thoughtful action: The role of "placebic" information in interpersonal interaction. *Journal of Personality and Social Psychology,* 1978, *36,* 635–642.

Lazarus, A. Learning theory and treatment of depression. *Behavior Research and Therapy,* 1968, *6,* 83–89.

Lazarus, A. Some reactions to Costello's paper on depression. *Behavior Therapy,* 1972, *3,* 248–250.

Lazarus, R. S. Psychological stress and coping in adaptation and illness. *International Journal of Psychiatry in Medicine,* 1974, *5,* 321–333.

Lehmann, H. E. Depression: Somatic treatment methods, complications, failures. In G. Usdin (Ed.), *Depression: Clinical, biological and psychological perspectives.* New York: Brunner/Mazel, 1977.

Lewinsohn, P. M. Clinical and theoretical aspects of depression. In K. Calhoun, H. Adams, & K. Mitchell (Eds.), *Innovative treatment methods in psychopathology.* New York: Wiley, 1974.

Lewinsohn, P. M. The behavioral study and treatment of depression. In M. Hersen, R. M. Eisler, & P. M. Miller (Eds.), *Progress in behavior modification* (Vol. 1). New York: Academic Press, 1975.

Lewinsohn, P. M., & Amenson, C. S. Some relations between pleasant and unpleasant mood-related events and depression. *Journal of Abnormal Psychology,* 1978, *87,* 644–654.

Lewinsohn, P. M., & Atwood, G. E. Depression: A clinical–research approach. *Psychotherapy: Theory, Research and Practice,* 1969, *6,* 166–171.

Lewinsohn, P. M., Mischel, W., Chaplin, W., & Barton, R. *Social competence and depression: The role of illusory self perceptions?* Unpublished manuscript, University of Oregon, 1979.

Lewinsohn, P. M., & Shaffer, M. Use of home observations as an integral part of the treatment of depression: Preliminary report and case studies. *Journal of Consulting and Clinical Psychology,* 1971, *37,* 87–94.

Lewinsohn, P. M., Shaffer, M., & Libet, J. *A behavioral approach to depression.* Paper presented at meetings of the American Psychological Association, Miami Beach, 1969.

Lewinsohn, P. M., Weinstein, M. S., & Alper, T. A behavioral approach to the group treatment of depressed persons: A methodological contribution. *Journal of Clinical Psychology,* 1970, *26,* 525–532.

McLean, P. Therapeutic decision-making in the behavioral treatment of depression. In P. O. Davidson (Ed.), *The behavioral management of anxiety, depression and pain.* New York: Brunner/Mazel, 1976.

Miller, I. W., III, & Norman, W. H. Learned helplessness in humans: A review and attribution-theory model. *Psychological Bulletin,* 1979, *86,* 93–118.

Mischel, W. Toward a cognitive social learning reconceptualization of personality. *Psychological Review,* 1973, *80,* 252–283.

Natsoulas, T. What are perceptual reports about? *Psychological Bulletin,* 1967, *67,* 249–272.

Nelson, R. E., & Craighead, W. E. Selective recall of positive and negative feedback, self-control behaviors, and depression. *Journal of Abnormal Psychology,* 1977, *36,* 379–388.

Nisbett, R. E., & Wilson, T. D. Telling more than we can know: Verbal reports on mental processes. *Psychological Review,* 1977, *84,* 231–259.

Paykel, E. Classification of depressed patients: A cluster analysis derived grouping. *British Journal of Psychiatry,* 1971, *118,* 275–288.

Paykel, E. Life events and acute depressions. In J. P. Scott & E. C. Senay (Eds.), *Separation and depression.* Washington, D.C.: American Association for the Advancement of Science, 1973.

Pennebaker, J. W., Burnam, M. A., Schaeffer, M. A., & Harper, D. C. Lack of control as a determinant of perceived physical symptoms. *Journal of Personality and Social Psychology,* 1977, *35,* 167–174.

Pennebaker, J. W., & Skelton, J. A. Psychological parameters of physical symptoms. *Personality and Social Psychology Bulletin* 1978, *4,* 524–530.

Pennebaker, J. W., Skelton, J. A., Wogalter, M., & Rodgers, R. J. Effects of attention on the experience of physical symptoms. Paper presented at meetings of the American Psychological Association, Toronto, 1978.

Pribram, K. H. Reinforcement revisited: A structural view. In M. Jones (Ed.), *Nebraska Symposium on Motivation* (Vol. 1). Lincoln, Neb.: University of Nebraska Press, 1963.

Pribram, K. H., & McGuinness, D. Arousal, activation, and effort in the control of attention. *Psychological Review,* 1975, *82,* 116–149.

Prkachin, K. M., Craig, K. D., Papageorgis, D., & Reith, G. Nonverbal communication deficits and response to performance feedback in depression. *Journal of Abnormal Psychology,* 1977, *86,* 224–234.

Rahe, R. H., Meyer, M., Smith, M., Kjaer, G., & Holmes, T. H. Social stress and illness onset. *Journal of Psychosomatic Research,* 1964, *8,* 35–44.

Rehm, L. P. A self-control model of depression. *Behavior Therapy,* 1977, *8,* 787–804.

Rehm, L. P. Self-control and depression: A reply to Deutsch. *Behavior Therapy,* 1978, *9,* 415–418.

Rehm, L. P., Fuchs, C. Z., Roth, D. M., Kornblith, S. J., & Romano, J. M. A comparison of self-control and assertion skills treatments of depression. *Behavior Therapy,* 1979, *10,* 429–442.

Rehm, L. P., & Kornblith, S. J. Behavior therapy for depression: A review of recent developments. In M. Hersen, R. M. Eisler, & P. M. Miller (Eds.), *Progress in behavior modification* (Vol. 7). New York: Academic Press, 1979.

Rodin, J. Somatopsychics and attribution. *Personality and Social Psychology Bulletin,* 1978, *4,* 531–540.

Rotter, J. B. *Social learning and clinical psychology.* New York: Prentice-Hall, 1954.

Rotter, J. B. Generalized expectancies for problem solving and psychotherapy. *Cognitive Therapy and Research,* 1978, *2,* 1–10.

Rush, A. J., Beck, A. T., Kovacs, M., & Hollon, S. Comparative efficacy of cognitive therapy and pharmacotherapy in the treatment of depressed outpatients. *Cognitive Therapy and Research,* 1977, *1,* 17–38.

Schildkraut, J. J. Biochemical research in affective disorders. In G. Usdin (Ed.), *Depression: Clinical, biological and psychological perspectives.* New York: Brunner/Mazel, 1977.

Schrader, S. L., Craighead, W. E., & Schrader, R. M. Reinforcement patterns in depression. *Behavior Therapy,* 1978, *9,* 1–14.

Seligman, M. E. P. *Helplessness: On depression, development, and death.* San Francisco: W. H. Freeman & Co., 1975.

Spitzer, R. L., Endicott, J., Woodruff, R. A., & Andreason, N. Classification of mood disorders. In G. Usdin (Ed.), *Depression: Clinical, biological, and psychological perspectives.* New York: Brunner/Mazel, 1977.

Usdin, G. (Ed.). *Depression: Clinical, biological, and psychological perspectives.* New York: Brunner/Mazel, 1977.

Weiner, B., Heckhausen, H., Meyer, W., & Cook, R. E. Causal ascriptions and achievement behavior: A conceptual analysis of effort and reanalysis of locus of control. *Journal of Personality and Social Psychology,* 1972, *21,* 239–248.

Zeiss, A. M., Lewinsohn, P. M., & Muñoz, R. F. Nonspecific improvement effects in depression using interpersonal skills training, pleasant activity schedules, or cognitive training. *Journal of Consulting and Clinical Psychology,* 1979, *47,* 427–439.

# 7

# A Functional Analysis of Behavior Therapy

CHARLES B. FERSTER

Despite the separate history of applications of behavioral psychology to therapy from traditional clinical approaches and despite the apparent close connection, heretofore, between behavioral analysis and specific techniques of behavior therapy, it is not clear that the main contribution of behavioral analysis is to the design of specific therapies. An alternative is to use practical information discovered by clinicians, from whatever clinical perspective, and to make heretofore esoteric, mentalistic, or rule-of-thumb knowledge communicable by a descriptive language that encourages detailed, objective observation. The clinical, intuitive enterprise discovers the phenomenon, and a behavioral description of the actual items of conduct, if they can be uncovered, makes the therapy procedures communicable and subject to refinement and correction.

The relevance of a behavioral analysis to the clinical phenomenon of depression falls into three main areas of diagnosis, etiology, and therapy. The diagnosis of depression needs to be considered first, since it concerns the delineation and specification of the behavioral events that pose the problem for which therapy is sought. What, indeed, is the specimen to put under the microscope?

## Diagnosis

### The Phenomenon of Depression

The most serious difficulty facing the experimentalist, eager to put the science of behavior to work for new treatments of depression, is to say what depression is. Willy–nilly, we are forced to common experience, the novelist, the

181

BEHAVIOR THERAPY FOR DEPRESSION

Copyright © 1981 by Academic Press, Inc.
All rights of reproduction in any form reserved.
ISBN 0-12-585880-9

practicing clinician, and other such perceptive commentators and observers of the human condition to ascertain the pathology for which a solution is sought. The traditional clinical (usually psychodynamic) formulations of depression are deficient, not because they are wrong, but because they are the practitioner's judgment and reaction to data, rather than an account of the data themselves. It is a remarkable paradox of clinical skill that experts who are such keen observers of the most delicate nuances of human behavior provide so little of the raw data in their published accounts. Clinical accounts often skip over the details of human interactions by describing its larger significance. Not only is such data not reported, but its significance is disparaged as a rote recitation.

As an example, consider the clinical descriptions of patients as compulsive, alluding generally to "an irresistible impulse to carry out an act." Such descriptions detract us from observing the actual conduct, because they attend to the broad characteristics of a person (usually phrased as an inner event, homunculus, or force) instead of to the actions and events from which the judgment is made. When we observe the actual instances of performance at such high frequency, they are prepotent over what is usually expected. As a result they are described as irrational. Both descriptions are essentially correct, except that the clinical one is phrased as an explanation of the conduct, while the behavioral exposes the items separately from their functional connection to the environment. Given the intention to make a detailed description, trained clinicians do, in fact, observe the constituent items of conduct, and in considerable detail.

Four manuscripts, published between 1972 and 1977, constitute an evolution of the overall concept of depression presented here. Many of the analyses of the present chapter are developed in greater detail in these earlier papers. The first paper, "The Experimental Analysis of Clinical Phenomena" (Ferster, 1972b), an expansion of the ideas of arbitrary and natural reinforcement (Ferster, 1972a, 1977), details how verbal interactions in therapy can influence behavior elsewhere. The second, "A Functional Analysis of Depression" (Ferster, 1973), is an overall conception of depression as changes in the frequency of broad classes of operant behavior. "A Functional Analysis of the Verbal Aspects of Depression" (Ferster, 1975) extends the functional analysis of depression to areas of verbal conduct that are so fundamental to its diagnosis, etiology, and therapy. The fourth paper, "A Laboratory Model of Psychotherapy" (Ferster, 1979a), clarifies the concepts of arbitrary and natural reinforcement (Ferster, 1972a, 1967) by applying the theoretical definition of the operant as performance and reinforcer combined in an integral unit, particularly in respect to a refined definition of verbal reinforcement.

## Distinction between Testing and Description

Tests such as the Minnesota Multiphasic Personality Inventory (MMPI) or the Rorschach are another way to diagnose depression. Unfortunately, these tend to be tests rather than descriptions of the phenomenon. The psychological test is to the underlying phenomenon of depression as litmus paper is to hydrogen ion concentration. They do not help us define what depession is, because their purpose is to provide a simple indicator that is correlated with clinical judgment. The tests therefore contain minimal descriptions of the actual behaviors that are the core of the phenomenon, despite their objectivity. Descriptive inventories come closer to the mark, because they talk about details of the actual conduct.

## Analyzing Depression Functionally

What then is the actual phenomenon that clinicians and their clinical theories expose? Previous publications by this writer (Ferster, 1973, 1974) present a view of depression in which the frequency of the main categories of an individual's operant repertoire and its relation to the basic behavioral processes provide an outline for a behavioral diagnosis. That analysis noted that the most prominent characteristic of depressed persons is reduced frequency of their overall activity. This, in turn, limited the range of reinforcers that could potentially maintain the individual's activity.

Because depression is a condition of the entire repertoire, a single profile of behavioral deficits or a single causal factor cannot be expected to characterize all instances of it. Every process that increases or decreases the frequency of a person's actions may contribute to a distinctively different profile of depressed behavior. Some of these factors will be discussed in the next section on the etiology of depression. Some causes of depression need to be anticipated here, however, because the different ways in which depression comes about surely have counterparts in the descriptions of the primary, underlying items of conduct.

Some depressions appear as cessations of all but the simplest activities. Often the lost behaviors have been stable features of the person's life, so the critical issue is their dramatically reduced frequency. Such depressions, often described as reactive (as opposed to endogenous) may come from sudden changes in the life cycle, such as aging, a loss of employment, the death of a spouse, or an upheaval of the larger social environment supporting the individual's life. Bettleheim (1960), for example, has described the depressive impact of the dislocations produced by incarceration in concentration camps in Germany during the period of Nazi rule. The enormous impact of aging and the dislocation of elderly people from their accustomed lives when they are placed in institutions has been described by Butler (1975). While it is certainly true that predisposing characteristics from early development may contribute to the impact of such cataclysms as the sudden loss of an important relationship or life-style, the important distinction from other depressions is that without the extraordinary stress there would be no depression.

A schedule of reinforcement in which a relatively fixed and large amount of activity is required for reinforcement may be a cause of depression, similar in its result to that caused by sudden changes like those just described (Ferster,

1974, p. 36). They are similar because the activities that decrease frequency have been and still . are potentially effective parts of the person's repertoire. At issue is their reduced frequency because of a sudden change in the reinforcing environment or their current schedule of reinforcement. In contrast are those kinds of deficits, to be discussed later, where new modes of conduct are needed if the person is to engage reinforcers supported by potentially available environments. The depressive impact of schedules of reinforcement are suggested by the week-by-week experience of the salesperson who needs to call on a large number of people before consummating a sale; the homemaker's routine activity, requiring a fixed and relatively large amount of work; and the work of the novelist who writes many months with little indication of success before actually completing a book. The process is exemplified by the classic episode of the highly successful author who, upon reaching the pinnacle of achievement, undergoes a profound depression.

Many depressions are autocatalytic beyond the specific items of behavior whose frequencies have been reduced. A hiatus in behavior, for whatever cause, during the adolescent years or before will retard normal development because a person's environment makes progressively complex demands paced with the person's chronological age. Such a negative autocatalysis is seen in its most stark form in the way that preverbal deficits in simple kinds of motor activity leave a child without the basic discriminative repertoire and interactional patterns from which verbal behavior develops. If there is no repertoire by which a child influences an adult preverbally, then there is no reinforcer for maintaining verbal interactions (Ferster, 1972b, p. 106). In general, the discriminative control by the environment grows out of a large repertoire of activities whose reinforcement is differential, depending on the circumstances under which they are emitted. It is in this sense that clinical writers assert that the infant's activity of taking objects into his or her mouth or spitting them out is the basis for all the infant's perceptions. Consider, for example, the complexity and depth of performance differentiation and discriminative control that arises from such a seemingly simple interaction as an infant and mother adjusting to each other while the child is being held during feeding. Such an interaction has been described by this author (Ferster, 1976) as complex one in which the actions of each of the parties is shaped by the actions of the other. The situation that occurs when a parent is insensitive to the child is the kind of social restriction that is characteristic of those restraints that Seligman (1975) has described as learned helplessness and will be discussed in the next section, etiology.

Even in adulthood, where the cumulative development of a repertoire is not at issue, we would expect reduced frequencies of a depressed repertoire to have compound impact. Many reinforcing events, such as sex or eating, have collateral components that are essential for their reinforcement. Thus a reduction in interpersonal activity could even reduce the frequency and reinforcement of eating, which usually occurs socially and often depends on the secondary support of large amounts of interpersonal activity.

The significance, for diagnoses, of the developmental retardation described earlier is the possibility that various kinds of depression may leave the individual with a repertoire that is, in fact, not capable of a full sustaining interaction with environments with which the individual has potential access. Such deficiencies would arise even though, in the formative stages of the depression, the only pathology involved was a reduced frequency of items that might otherwise reappear in the person's repertoires.

## Depression Is a Verbal Phenomenon

Even though depression involves broad changes in repertoire, the actual behaviors that are observed are mostly verbal. The main diagnostic techniques used clinically are generally interviews or tests in which patients talk, read, or write about the events in their lives. Therapies, behavioral or psychodynamic, involve a patient and therapist talking about the events in the patient's life, and the developmental events clinical theories implicate refer to the patient's thoughts, speech, and perception. The main diagnostic characterization—grief, mourning, self-debasement, and impaired thought—refer to verbal behaviors that are tacts under the discriminative control of private events (Skinner, 1957). A large proportion of the total verbal repertoire might consist of complaints, criticism, demands for relief, or assertions of distress, all functionally avoidance and escape behaviors. Frequently the complaints are in the form of self-blame and criticism. The function of these verbal behaviors and their place in the etiology of depression will be discussed in the next section.

The strength and persistence of these aversively maintained verbal behaviors take on special prominence in comparison to the weakness of the rest of the repertoire; or they may have a basis in the inertial aspects of depression, which will be discussed in the next section, as one of the factors in the etiology of depression. Even though such behaviors are topographically avoidance and escape mechanisms, and even though they may be offshoots of such mechanisms, they nonetheless do not actually terminate or avoid current aversive situations or alleviate current distress. Their characteristics appear functionally of the same process as the "extended mand" described by Skinner (1957). The major characteristic of the mand is that it is controlled more by the person's level of deprivation or distress than by the presence of a listener or audience who could realistically minister to the distress.

High frequencies of hand wringing, sighing, crying, and agitated pacing appear to be functionally parallel to other instances of magic mands (Skinner, 1957, Chap. 3). They are significant not only of themselves but for the other verbal performances that they preempt. A verbal repertoire depressed by preemption, disruption, or incomplete development will cause much extinction and punishment, because the missing intraverbal behavior is the means for observing when performances can or cannot be reinforced, like pointing to small features of a pattern or text to enhance its discriminative control in the manner of an observing response.

When patients can accurately describe their own conduct, the conduct of those who influence them, and the connection between the two, the remaining remedies that might be required can occur naturally or by simple educational supports. We would expect that when a patient is capable of utilizing specific suggestions and instructions, there will be a change in the kinds of verbal activities that are occurring. Until the high frequency of complaints and demands gives way to tacts and intraverbal behaviors that correspond to and amplify the patient's current conduct, it can be predicted that little use could be made of instructions or prompts.

## Summary

Everyday talk about depression as a substance like a toxin or tumor rather than as an aspect of a person's overall conduct obscures its most important dimension: frequency. Virtually every behavioral process, as well as physiological and somatic–pathological factor, that can influence the frequency of an operant performance acts together in depression—but in a great variety of combinations and emphases. Depression is, therefore, not homogeneous except topographically. It cannot be expected, therefore, that a theoretical account can have the status of an all-inclusive theory in a simple, abstract form, except at the risk of preempting aspects of depression that are now recognized as significant.

# Etiology

Of concern here is the step from the basic processes, such as intermittent reinforcement and discriminative and aversive control, to a complex of life circumstances that produce the massive deficits of depression. There is, of course, a large literature of studies exploring the various contributions of genetic and physiological factors, epidemiology, family structure, and early childhood experiences. The purpose of this section is to explore the same factors from the perspective of the basic behavioral processes of which the frequency of behavior is a function. That early childhood experiences are an important etiological factor in depression is by now a well-established conclusion accepted by most clinicians and theorists. It is still useful in the detail of a functional analysis to talk about how parental and other environments produce the behavioral influences that cumulate in depression. The omission of biological factors in this discussion is not a statement that they are unimportant. Rather it reflects the view that the biological substrate is a parameter of behavior and that its expression comes from the interaction with the environment.

## Inertial Aspects of Depression

The heart of the impediments to the normal development of a full repertoire is the inertial quality of behavior that insulates the repertoire from effective shaping by the environment. This is the paradox of operant conditioning's claim that any person's repertoire can be shaped by approximation or collateral support so that it can produce the reinforcers of an environment. Instead of an autocatalytic strengthening that progressively seeks out positive reinforcement, there often appears to be an inertial perversity, best described by the characters of a Dostoevsky novel. A behavioral analysis of this inertia, based on a previous publication of this author (Ferster, 1976), is presented in the following paragraphs.

The control of behavior by its level of deprivation, more than by the audience or occasion that governs where and when it can be reinforced, is the important aspect of this inertia. The process appears in its purest form in the infant's early feeding patterns, controlled mostly by how long it has been since the child last ate. The counterpart of the child's demand is the social and biological patterns of a parental environment, totally dedicated to satisfying the child's needs. As the child grows, however, the occasions when the child is fed become more complex, cued by person, mood, time, and place. With normal development, the child's level of deprivation is balanced with the parent's inclination to feed the child. The reinforcement of the parent by the child occurs when the aversive demands of the child end and the child becomes satiated from eating. The child's crying is reinforced by the food and attention given by the parent. When the repertoires of parent and child are in dynamic balance, the experience of satisfying the child is the reinforcer for feeding the child and the food prevents levels of deprivation in the child that evoke behaviors that are aversive to the parent. The process is constantly in tension, because the parent weans the child as the child grows older and because changes in the parent's mood alter the threshold of the parent's response to the child's aversiveness.

The childhood pattern suggests a strong parallel to that of adult depressed persons, who often emit behaviors controlled more by the level of deprivation than by the characteristics of the audience and have interpersonal styles that typically evoke reactions in others by negative reinforcement. A corollary of such a repertoire is the failure to observe, in full detail and at some distance from personal deprivations, the characteristics of other persons in whose repertoires there are potential reinforcers.

Just as feeding, closely controlled by food deprivation, anchors one end of the child's development, verbal repertoires, where the adult speaker has the burden of tapping the reactivity of the listener, anchor the other. Speech, even complex forms, may be functionally equivalent to the infant feeding if it is maintained because of reinforcement closely controlled by the speaker's level of deprivation rather than because of the more deferred, broad social effect from generalized reinforcement. The unique character of the fully developed verbal repertoire is its relative independence of immediate levels of deprivation. A composition, a novel, or an invention, however, could function as a complaint or demand, despite its complex topography.

Feeding delays in infancy have the potential for creating the inertial elements seen in the repertoires of depressed persons. If a parent is depressed, occupied, or otherwise unreactive to the hungry infant, there is a powerful differential effect on the infant, which may prolong the intense, reciprocal way the parent and infant influence each other. Given the extreme persistence of feeding activity, a depression in the parental feeding pattern is a natural reinforcer that will differentially and almost automatically reinforce that activity on the part of the child, to overcome the parent's lassitude, usually through aversive control. So long as the child persists, the child's performance will have enough variability to uncover the ways that the parent is sensitive to disruption. Thus, the parent's vulnerability to disruption is a negative reinforcer that determines the form of the child's actions. The most likely mode of influence is an escalation of the aversive effect on the parent, who feeds the child to escape the aversive stimulation.

The struggle between parent and child over feeding can preempt playful and varied behavior—particularly those kinds of verbal behaviors that allow sensitive observation of each other's conduct. Such observation, to be descriptive enough to be useful, needs to be relatively independent of current deprivations. Children playing with the variations in the sounds they make, sustaining a parent's tickling and handling by gurgling pleasurably, or watching the range of their own hands or feet from different perspectives are all examples of activities through which the features of the environment come to control children's attention discriminatively. Such activities are the bases for expanding the child's view of the environment. The parallel in adult life is social and physical play not connected to the pressures of daily living. If feeding or relief from an irritating diaper requires high-frequency, persistent interpersonal control, largely based on negative reinforcement, the more playful, less compelling activities are preempted. The emphasis on strongly reinforced primitive behavior is likely, in the long term, to produce a cumulative deficit in the variety and amount of the natural interactions.

The deficiencies in sensitive control by the environment have some of the qualities of a "chicken and egg" riddle. The lack of a discriminative repertoire leads to extinction and intermittent reinforcement because performances are emitted on occasions when they are not reinforced or even punished. Punishment and the low level of positive reinforcement makes it unlikely that the intraverbal capacity can be strengthened. Some aspects of these phenomena may be alluded to in the psychodynamic formulations of "orality," "the differentiation of self from others," and "primary and secondary process."

*Focal Incidents*

An allusion has already been made to focal incidents, disruptive of a child's repertoire, that may produce a hiatus in development, in turn leading to cumulative deficits. Such would be the case with a child experiencing general difficulties in feeding that prevent the give-and-take that normally makes eating a natural part of a continuous interaction with the mother. The mother may not be aware of the flow of milk from the bottle, so that it passively pours down the child's throat, or the flow might be so slow and require so much sucking that the movements are reinforced on a fixed-number schedule that strains the behavior seriously. A clinical account is on record where a mother, believing that it was imperative for the child to finish each bottle completely, held it in the child's mouth however long it took or how great a struggle was necessary to resist the child's attempts to push the nipple out of his mouth or turn his head to escape it or struggle from the parent's grasp. The shift of the feeding interaction from one in which the behavior of each party is shaped by the reactivity of the other one to a struggle controlled by strong deprivation and aversive stimulation is likely to preempt other important components of the child's development. The natural reinforcement of operants occur when mother and child "talk" to each other, when the child moves his or her hand playfully over the texture of the blanket while feeding, or when mother and child adjust to each other's posture when the child is held by the mother. The absence of these naturally reinforced performances, because of the prepotency of the power struggle over feeding, detracts from the child's normal development because the discriminative control that is part of the function of these playful activities is also missing.

The results of such feeding restraints and restrictions as those just described have many of the properties that Seligman (1975) described as learned help-lessness. This can be inferred from a comparison with the behavioral processes involved when a dog, restrained by a harness, is shocked severely. There, the behaviors weakened are those of avoidance and escape, normally triggered by electric shock. The infant, held by an inept parent, struggles in vain to escape body tension. The child, choking on a too rapid or an unwanted flow from the bottle, thrashes about helplessly without escaping the engulfing milk. A slow milk flow results in high levels of food deprivation coupled with severely weakened performances due to the fixed-ratio strain that is inherent in the large amount of sucking required to produce a given volume of milk.

## By-Products of Aversive Control

The high frequency of self-punishment so common in depression is a clue to how rejection, isolation, and interpersonal loss become aversive events of such a magnitude that they cause a severe disruption of the depressed person's repertoire. Self-criticism and -punitiveness may be considered a blend of two strong operants, neither of which can be emitted successfully alone. One source of strength is the aggressive (angry) activity toward the person whom the patient experiences as causing isolation or loss. The other source is the counter control the patient engenders as a result of his or her aggressive acts. When complaints reach the magnitude of rage and anger, their impact on those it is directed at is large and disruptive. Not only is such anger noticed, but it may be punished by reciprocal aggression or by loss of the relationship, isolation, and ostracism, which in turn evoke further anger and rage. The blend occurs when the counter control shapes the aggressive behavior, by negative reinforcement, into a covert form. The person mutters the angry statement under his or her breath. In a more extreme form, the counter control drives the performance into such covertness that the person may be totally unaware of it. Pathological magnitudes of the process occur because the more isolation and loss the patient experiences, the more aggressive are his or her inclinations. The process is autocatalytic, increasing the isolation and loss. Such behavior exists in a dynamic balance between emission and suppression, even though it is not being emitted at any particular time. The existence of a large, strongly maintained repertoire that is constantly in high frequency will cause further counter control despite its covert form and will preempt other potentially positive modes of action, particularly those highly differentiated verbal activities that are based on generalized reinforcement rather than primary deprivations.

## Summary

The preceding discussion has developed some of the ways that the failure to develop a full range of verbal behavior, supported by generalized reinforcement rather than by close control by immediate deprivations, contributes to processes underlying depression. The difference between pathological depression and short-term mood swings is continuous rather than abrupt when one looks at overall changes in the frequency of behavior. In other respects, however, depressions that come from different histories have very different properties. One kind of depressive phenomenon that appears to have a generic unity has as a prominent causal factor large changes in the environment, such as aging, disability, natural catastrophies, ecomomic dislocation, and prolonged stressful situations, such as those that occur in military combat. All of these weaken behavior through the basic behavioral processes by reduction in positive reinforcement, sudden changes in stimulus control, extremes of intermittent reinforcement, and aversively evoked performance that preempt naturally maintained behaviors of daily life. Such depressions are generally described clinically as "reactive." The other generic category comprises the depressive phenomena caused by inertial properties of the repertoire carried from childhood. The first category involves a catastrophic dislocation of an essentially normal repertoire; the second involves the failure of a repertoire that can sustain normal commerce to emerge. Despite the large differences in causal factors and conceivable modes of treatment, the two depressive phenomena occur through the same behavioral mechanisms. With developmental arrests, the lack of connection to the environment emerges as the prominent variable, just as with sudden changes in the environment. It occurs slowly, however, because the temporary supports and special treatment of childhood are withdrawn, paced with the child's chronological age and physical growth rather than with the development of the increasingly complex kinds of conduct that the community requires.

Despite the heuristic advantages of classifying reactive depressions separately from those caused by inertial factors from childhood, the two, in practice, would inevitably interact with each other. Sudden changes in the environment will have more impact on those individuals sensitive to short-term deprivations, and individuals with few means of interacting with complex environments may sustain relatively stable lives if their environments are sheltered from change.

## Psychotherapy

The actual events of psychotherapy are mostly interactions between two people talking to each other, even though the eventual objective is the ameliora-tion of the pateint's life outside the therapeutic relationship. The behavior that occurs in therapy is a verbal operant, determined by the patient's history and the reinforcement by the listener with (to) whom the patient is talking. The rein-forcer is the influence, whether emotional, verbal, or practical, on the other person. Thus all of the performances and their generically related reinforcers are available for observation by both the patient and the therapist.

There is a danger of confusing the patient's speech about the events of his or her life that are causing difficulty and the events themselves. Even behavioral therapies for depression deal predominately with a verbal interaction between patient and therapist, despite the emphasis in theory on the actual behaviors in the patient's daily life. Desensitization therapy turns out to be, with few excep-tions, verbal behavior "about" troublesome events in daily life. Even behavior modification procedures (perhaps with the exception of token economies) are by and large verbal interactions in which the product of therapy is speech intended to influence the patient elsewhere, instructionally. The concept, rel-evant to the nature of the reinforcers that can operate in therapy, is that of the generic nature of the operant, combining performance and reinforcement as an integral unit. (See Ferster, 1976 for a theoretical account of the concept and its application to psychotherapy.) Many of the cognitive and self-control approaches to therapy exemplified by the work of Rehm and his colleagues, as well as the recent work in the mode of cognitive behavior therapy (Rehm & Kornblith, 1979), show how verbal repertoires developed in interaction with the therapist provide the patient with behaviors that can decrease the amount of nonreinforcement and aversive control elsewhere. These verbal behaviors serve as discriminative stimuli that enhance observation of the conditions of rein-forcement and punishment.

### Influence of Psychotherapy on the Patient's Life

The difficult technical question about therapy, whether behavior or conven-tional, is the exact manner by which conversation about the events in the patient's life elsewhere can influence those events. There are three aspects to the process. The first is the behavioral changes that occur in the immediate context of the therapy situation as patient and therapist gain the capacity to influence each other. The second is a verbal repertoire objectively descriptive about the behavioral control in the immediate interactions between patient and therapist. The third is the way in which the verbal repertoire about the immediate events of the therapeutic interaction enhance observation elsewhere, thereby increasing the frequency of positive reinforcement and decreasing the frequency of aversive stimulation.

The discomfort and stress that brings the patient to therapy comes predominately from verbal and nonverbal transactions in daily life, maintained by the generically related reinforcers there. But the therapist and patient have a limited and frequently distorted view of those events. In psychodynamic parlance, the patient's report is described as a mental representation of the observed events, and psychologists use the term *perception* to describe the slippage between the objective fact of the environment and the way it is processed by the observer. Behaviorally, we speak of the objective environment as a discriminative stimulus that controls specific, usually verbal, performances. What all these ways of conceptualizing the control by the environment have in common is the recognition that there can be wide discrepancies between the person's experience and his or her description of it. The problem is exaggerated in depression, where patients are usually described as having impaired thought processes, a limited view of the world, and other evidence that their level of deprivation has a disproportionate influence on the accuracy of their observations. The limits of the patient's ability to observe the external environment, and particularly his or her relation to it, fail to provide objective data about the patient's life other than the adequacy of the observation. The events talked about, those of the patient's life outside the therapeutic relationship, are subject to distortion and incomplete description, no matter how behavioral or objective the terminology or conceptual system that is used. As was discussed in the section on diagnosis, one of the objectives of therapy is to enable patients to develop a clear, undistorted view of their own behavior and the events in their lives. Lewinsohn's home observational technique provides another source of data for evaluating the clarity of the patient's view of life (Lewinsohn & Shaffer, 1971).

It is in the immediate interaction between patient and therapist that there is objective data about the patient's repertoire, and the therapist, as a trained observer, is in a position to differentially reinforce accurate observation. In therapy, even though they may be talking *about* events, the patient can learn to observe his or her own behavior, the therapist's, and the way they influence each other. The events of the therapy itself, therefore, are as crucial determinants of the patient's behavior as the events talked about. All the ways that the therapist, as a unique kind of audience, controls the patient's activities in the therapy situation cannot be described here. It is sufficient, for the present purposes, to note that without such control little influence over the patient would be possible and that the interpersonal control that results is a partial model that has characteristics shared by other personal interactions. Furthermore, as a trained observer, the therapist is in a position to teach the patient to objectively observe the elements and various dimensions of their transactions.

### The Difference between Psychotherapy and Education

Because patient and therapist reinforce each other's behavior directly, psychotherapy, in its essential form, is a way of producing new behavior. The shaping of the behavior of the two parties by their immediate reactions to each other is different from instruction, which assumes that there is a repertoire currently reinforced in the daily environment and occurring at high enough frequency. Therapy creates behavior which did not exist; instruction uses discriminative stimuli as collateral supports to bring existing repertoires into new relations with existing reinforcers. Supportive therapy or education illustrates an educational mode that is usually seen as helping the patient find an environment in which his present character is compatible. Psychotherapy may be seen as changing character structure. Clearly there are instructional elements in psychotherapy and therapeutic issues in education. Important therapeutic changes have occurred when a patient can utilize instruction or observe the difficulties of doing so. However, no amount of instruction can benefit a student who does not have strong behavior reinforced by increments toward increased competence in the subject matters being learned.

### Summary

The essentially verbal nature of psychotherapy defines it as an interactive process in which new behaviors are reinforced and shaped by their influence on the therapist. The generic definition of verbal behavior clarifies psychotherapy as an objective behavioral event in which the behaviors are the interactions between patient and therapist, potentially observable by both. It is the shaping of new forms of personal interaction that distinguishes therapy from instructional methods.

## Summary and Implications for Research

The preceding analysis has described three parallel systems of behavior, each maintained and defined by its system of reinforcement. These are (a) the reciprocal influences that occur in therapy between patient and therapist; (b) the events in the patient's daily life and their generic reinforcers; and (c) alterations of the stream of interactions in the patient's daily life by the repertoires emerging from therapy.

*Reciprocal Influences of Therapy*

The therapeutic interview is an important jumping off point for a research effort because it is one of the major methods for defining dysfunction and for obtaining data. The risk is that the coin will be searched for "under the lamp post because the light is better there." The relevance of data from clinical interviews for studying depression rests on the interpersonal control between patient and therapist that has elements in common with other portions of the patient's life, the objectivity of the therapist as a trained observer who can describe the events of therapy at the same time he or she is being controlled by them, and the complex view that the patient's verbal reports are determined as much by the person to whom they are told and by the patient's history as they are by the events being described.

POTENTIAL OBJECTIVITY OF THE THERAPEUTIC INTERACTION

The events of therapy can, at least potentially, be observed as objectively as any other data in psychology. At issue is the mass of the observations that need to be focused and the need for a framework that describes the events functionally, systematically, and factually in a manner other than a tedious enumeration of the events. The major difficulties occur when the events talked about are inferred from the reports rather than the reports viewed as being controlled simultaneously by the events talked about, the patient's history, and the effect on the listener to whom they are directed. Clearly, actual events and the patient's history cannot be controlled in a therapeutic interaction. But, to the extent that the patient's speech is controlled by the influence on the therapist–listener, the nature of the listener's reaction is an important differential reinforcer. It is for this reason that the concept of transference seems to be given so much emphasis clinically. It represents the process that sustains the interaction until the patient's activity is functionally controlled by its effect on the therapist–listener rather than by its historical or other inertial characteristics. Of course, what the patient is talking about has importance aside from its function in the immediate reactivity of the therapist. The content of life's experiences that the patient relates is of intrinsic interest to the therapist, who, remembering the details, is organizing the data into a coherent pattern by trial hypotheses, questions, and tentative formulations. This attempt of the therapist to understand, as a specially trained audience, is another dimension of the therapist's reinforcing properties as a listener. Not only is the therapist reactive to understanding the events of the patient's life outside of therapy, he or she is also especially reactive to understanding the events that occur in therapy—the patient's lateness, an avoidance of certain topics, a temporary depression in the interaction, an outburst of pique or anger or sudden increments of anxiousness, and so on. These current events, as well as the patient's account of outside and historical events, are data that are directly observable by both parties. As a result, the therapist is in a position to reinforce verbal behaviors descriptive of these events and hence to bring the patient's attention under the control of them. One direction of a research program would be to use video recordings of therapy sessions or of selected segments of sessions supplemented by interviews with the therapist. The data so gained could then be compared with independent observations of the patient in daily life or in structured environments such as those used in group work. Of course, videotapes of therapy have been extensively used in research on psychotherapy, but the new feature that could be productively added is the functional analysis along the lines of the conceptual scheme described, which would sift the masses of observation into a more manageable number of categories.

PRIVATE EVENTS

Part of the functional analysis of the therapist's interaction with the patient comes from the therapist's skill in describing the private reaction that occurs in his or her own repertoire when interacting with the patient. Often, for example, an aggressive remark cannot be identified by the topography of the patient's speech. The nature of aversive pressure is such that it takes a subtle form, determined jointly by the uneasiness it produces and the avoidance of counter control. Thus, frequently, the patient's aggressiveness may be hidden topographically (often described clinically as covert) and identifiable only by the annoyance that it generates. The objective description of such private events, although intrinsically difficult, rests on the availability of collateral data, much as it is possible to estimate the significance of verbal reports of tooth pain by tapping or X–raying the tooth or exposing the pulp. The therapist's private response to the patient would serve, in an empirical investigation, as an indication to look for collateral data in observable behavior. If the therapist's annoyance, as in the example, is a functional counterpart (in the sense of a generically related reinforcer) of the patient's aggressive acts, it should be possible to observe the collateral signs in the component behaviors of the preceding interaction. The distinction is between "symptom," as the report of an internal state, and "sign," as objective evidence of dysfunction.

## Events in the Patient's Life

Obviously the significance of therapy is in the corresponding changes that occur in the patient's daily life. As with the study of the patient–therapist interaction, there is a tension between the necessity of detailed direct observation by a passive observer and a problem posed by the mass of observations that is too large to be digested. One way to limit the scope of data collected to manageable proportions would be to use natural observations to confirm the kinds of repertoires exposed in therapy or to generate hypotheses about aspects of the patient's repertoire that were not apparent in therapy because of its limited context. As with the therapeutic interview, a functional analysis of the patient's overall repertoire (Ferster, 1973) can be used as a framework and guide by providing broad, functional categories of behavior in place of a huge number of observational details.

Curiously, observations in the natural environment are needed to uncover the mechanism by which the repertoires developed in therapy influence the patient's daily conduct. Several hypotheses have been proposed in earlier papers (Ferster, 1972b, 1979b) for how the interaction might occur. These involved mostly the operation of a verbal repertoire that clarifies contingencies of reinforcement and aversive control along with a parallel development of generalized reinforcement as it pertains to behaviors that are predominately under the control of large levels of deprivation and aversive stimulation.

# References

Bettleheim, B. *The informed heart.* Glencoe, Ill.: Free Press, 1960.

Butler, R. *Why survive: Being old in America.* New York: Harper & Row, 1975.

Ferster, C. B. Arbitrary and natural reinforcement. *Psychological Record,* 1967, *17,* 341–347.

Ferster, C. B. The experimental analysis of clinical phenomena. *The Psychological Record,* 1972, *22,* 1–16. (a)

Ferster, C. B. Clinical reinforcement. *Seminars in psychiatry, 4,* No. 2, 1972. (b)

Ferster, C. B. A functional analysis of depression. *American Psychologist,* 1973, *28,* 857–870.

Ferster, C. B. Behavioral approaches to depression. In R. J. Friedman & M. M. Katz (Eds.), *The psychology of depression: Contemporary theory and research.* New York: Wiley, 1974.

Ferster, C. B. A functional analysis of the verbal aspects of depression. Paper presented at the Loyola University Conference on Depression, 1976.

Ferster, C. B. A laboratory model of depression: The boundary between clinical practice and experimental psychology. In P. O. Joden, & Bates (Eds.), *Trends in behavior therapy.* New York: Academic Press, 1979. (a)

Ferster, C. B. Psychotherapy from the standpoint of a behaviorist. In J. D. Keehn (Ed.), *Psychopathology in Animals.* New York: Academic Press, 1979. (b)

Ferster, C. B., Culbertson, S. A., & Perrott-Boren, M. C. *Behavior principles.* Englewood Cliffs, N. J.: Prentice Hall, Inc.

Lewinsohn, P. M., & Shaffer, M. The use of home observation as an integral part of the treatment of depression: Preliminary report and case studies. *Journal of Consulting and Clinical psychology,* 1971, *37,* 87–94.

Rehm, L. P., & Kornblith, S. J. Behavior therapy for depression: A review of recent developments. In Hersen, M., Eisler, R. M., & Miller, P. M. (Eds.), *Progress in behavior modification* (Vol. 7). New York: Academic Press, 1979.

Seligman, M. E. P. *Helplessness: On depression, development and death.* San Francisco: Freeman, 1975.

Skinner, B. F. *Verbal behavior.* New York: Appleton-Century-Crofts, 1957.

# 8

# Matching Treatment to Patient Characteristics in an Outpatient Setting

PETER D. McLEAN

Surprisingly little can be stated without qualification when talking about clinical depression, despite increased activity in the areas of theory construction, innovative treatment, and outcome research since the mid-1960s. There seems to be little reason to alter Becker's 1974 conclusion that "no findings specific to depression have been firmly validated yet [p. 197]." On the other hand, the nature of the major variables in the depression-treatment sequence are now better understood, as are the research design steps necessary to calibrate their influence. This appears to apply particularly in the case of matching treatment to subject characteristics.

Ideally, and as is often stated, the right client would be assigned to the right therapist offering the right treatment at the right time for the client, in order to produce the best outcome. This is to say nothing of the influence of a whole host of nonspecific variables, such as treatment setting, client expectations, client's attributional process in perceiving improvements, and rationale afforded to account for the etiology, maintenance, and reversal of the client's depression, all of which influence the outcome of the treatment endeavor. In practice, both in research and in the delivery of clinical services, it has not been possible to closely approximate this ideal, for very understandable and predictable reasons.

Given that there are a variety of competing schools of thought to account for the occurrence of clinical depression and since there are no definitive findings to date, a logical first step in the development of theory performance (e.g., treatment efficacy) is to pit a theory-derived treatment against either a treatment comparison, a control group, or both. The aim here is to see whether there is a main treatment effect across the individual differences of subjects. To maximize this possibility, investigators attempt to reduce subject heterogeneity at the time

197

BEHAVIOR THERAPY FOR DEPRESSION

of selection and then randomly assign subjects to a treatment or control group. Virtually all of the clinical research studies to date are of this type.

Since other factors, such as therapist differences, treatment differences within the same school of thought, lack of standardized outcome measures, subject differences (i.e., characteristics and expectations), and nonspecific factors, combine and interact to determine outcome variance with this design, it is necessary to replicate clinical research findings to produce stable findings across settings that can be attributed to procedures. Generally speaking, replication studies have been the exception rather than the rule. Nevertheless, the recent number of treatment comparison studies that show behavior and cognitive therapy[1] procedures to be efficacious indicate a positive trend. These studies have all used random assignment[2] to allocate clients to treatment, thereby making any relationship between client characteristics and treatment difficult to identify with the relatively small number of clients that are typically assigned to each group.

There are at least three ways in which the relationship between client characteristic and treatment outcome can be investigated:

1. By looking for relationships between client characteristics and outcome variables after clients have been assigned on either a random or matched basis—correlations between client and outcome variables, multivariate techniques to predict treatment response based on client characteristics (e.g., discriminant function analysis of high and low treatment response based on client characteristics), etc.
2. By assigning different client cluster types to the same treatment.
3. By assigning different client cluster types to specific treatment components within the same treatment approach based upon the apparent need of the client (e.g., socially withdrawn, unemployed, single depressed men may receive a behavioral treatment program consisting of the development of social and job-finding skills).

A fourth way to determine the nature of the relationship between client characteristics and treatment outcome is to assign the same clients or client cluster types to serial treatments in a repeated measures design. The problems of controlling for the potential interactive effects resulting from serial exposure as well as for the fluctuations in the course of clinical depression over extended periods of time outweigh the obvious advantages of this design format.

A research design in which matched pairs of clients were split into two groups—one in which exposure to treatment components was random and the other in which exposure to treatment components was determined on the basis of client variables (i.e., apparent need of the client)—would, all else being equal,

---

[1] Because of the increasing overlap in the treatment delivery of these two theoretical approaches, they are being considered as one for the purposes of this review.
[2] Most, but not all, studies demonstrate comparability in group assignment in before-treatment comparisons on critical outcome measures.

indicate the amount of improvement during treatment that could be attributed to the client–treatment matching process.

It may be, of course, that the search for the ideal client–treatment match is a misguided one. The nonspecific factors involved in treatment may bring about therapeutic effects of a magnitude equivalent to the assumed effects of treatment. This possibility is easier to appreciate when statistical and clinical significance is contrasted. A comparative study may show that Treatment A is statistically superior to Treatment B, for example, while from either a clinical or cost–benefit point of view, this advantage is relatively immaterial since both treatment groups improved dramatically from their pretreatment baselines. Luborsky, Singer, and Luborsky's (1975, p. 995) review of the treatment literature, which found only "insignificant differences in the proportion of patients who improved" in a variety of controlled, comparative treatment studies, supports this point of view. Alternatively, clients may do equally well, or poorly, regardless of their individual characteristics (assuming reasonable sample homogeneity), as a function of the treatment they received (e.g., Hollon, Beck, Kovacs, & Rush, 1977; McLean & Hakstian, 1979). In this case, treatment effects outweigh the effects of client characteristics.

## Drawbacks in the Collection of Information

### Small Number of Clinical Subjects

Outpatient treatment scheduled at no more than one or two visits a week represents an artifact in the lives of most clients. The range of influences that interact with client characteristics in the hour-by-hour, day-by-day lives of clinical research subjects must be enormous. Competing with all of this for life-style influence is the hour or two of treatment plus any homework assignments the client may have. Given the range of individual differences in client characteristics, even in "homogeneous" samples, as well as ongoing environmental influences, very large sample sizes are required in research programs in order to identify client characteristic–treatment interactions. This requirement places studies that could investigate these interactions beyond the scope of typical Ph.D. thesis work and beyond the capability of investigators who do not have access to large numbers of clinically depressed clients (i.e., minimum of 200+ per year).

### Lack of Replication in Research Studies

Generally, the investigation of client–treatment interactions is a second-order event, the first being the demonstration of a main treatment effect.[3] Rarely are

---

[3] The practice of collecting pretreatment data on salient client characteristics, in order to group

treatment comparison studies replicated, and this reviewer could find no replicated verbal treatment study in the area of clinical depression in which client–treatment interactions were investigated. One can speculate about the reasons why investigators find replication of research studies in this area less attractive than the generation of unique studies, but the end result is that our information field in this area is unstable.

*Sample Heterogeneity*

Investigators typically use exclusion criteria to increase the homogeneity of clinically depressed subject populations (e.g., age limitations, nonalcoholic, unipolar, absence of psychotic symptoms). Disagreement as to the value of descriptive psychiatric diagnostic categories to classify client subgroups within depression has not promoted a sharper focus on the question of sample homogeneity. For example, Thompson and Hendrie (1972) were unable to distinguish endogenous from reactively depressed clients on the basis of frequency of life change events. Klein (1974), on the other hand, advocates a descriptive division of depression into three types: reactive, chronic neurotic, and endogenomorphic. Further, the distinction between student and nonstudent clinical populations may produce a qualitative as well as a quantitative subject difference (Mathews, 1978) in research findings.

*Dissimilar Dependent Variables*

There are over 30 psychometric depression inventories in use in the psychological and psychiatric literature of the 1970s. There are also a host of role functioning, personality, and specific skill questionnaires, as well as a number of individualized measures and event inventories that are often used to calibrate change in depression status. Investigators tend to choose those dependent variables that they consider to be sensitive to the treatment goals valued by their school of thought, with the result that direct comparisons between studies are hampered. Furthermore, considerable reliance has been vested in individual depression questionnaires that primarily measure self-evaluation of mood, to the relative neglect of more comprehensive measurement strategies. The result is that the investigator achieves only a single-dimension view (typically a symptom inventory) of the client's status, goals, and capabilities. And this view is only as accurate as the measure itself is valid and reliable.

*Dissimilar Client Description Variables*

Large-scale studies of client characteristic–treatment interaction that use a narrow, rather than a comprehensive, range of client descriptors frustrate

---

clients and cross with treatment effects in a two-way classification design to identify client–treatment interactions, is inconsistent in the literature.

between-study comparisons. For example, both the Paykel, Prusoff, Klerman, Haskell, and DiMascio (1973) and the McLean and Hakstian (1979) studies utilized client descriptors as the basis by which clients were grouped into typological clusters. These client cluster types were then related to treatment response. The problem here is that the two studies measured different dimensions (e.g., pathology versus adaptive functioning), with the result that quite different client clusters emerged, thereby precluding direct comparisons.

## Incomplete Treatment Description

It is difficult to interpret any client–treatment interactions that may have been identified in a study if the treatment description is incomplete. At the very least, a description of the intended therapeutic principles, followed by a description of treatment procedures and their sequence, is necessary in order to understand what client–treatment interactions can be attributed to. Some investigators now make available unpublished treatment manuals that contain treatment scripts and explain how high-frequency treatment problems (e.g., noncompliance, preoccupation with somatic complaints) are handled.

## The Role of Nonspecific Factors

The therapeutic effect of nonspecific factors can be as powerful as that of many of the treatments that have been used routinely for depression. This is evident from the relative success of many placebo or contrived treatment comparison groups in the treatment of depression. These factors are possibly more powerful than client characteristics in the determination of treatment response and need to be better understood and exploited. Many of the control-group treatments offered to clients in treatment comparison studies lack credibility (e.g., placebo antidepressant medication that does not produce cholinergic-like side effects). The questions here are, how much of treatment outcome is the result of client-perceived credibility, regardless of the actual merits of the program, and what client characteristics interact with this perception? Is, for example, a client with a history of treatment failure likely to respond poorly to treatment on the basis of his or her pretreatment expectation? Other nonspecific factors presumably interact with client characteristics and treatment in unknown ways. For example, Hart (1978) has demonstrated that self-monitoring enhanced goal attainment. Kanfer and Grimm (1978) report that subjects who are given a choice in speed-reading training procedures do significantly better than those who have no choice in the matter. Would these considerations apply to depressed clients? Zeiss, Lewinsohn, and Munoz (1978) conclude that Bandura's (1977) self-efficacy model explains a similar improvement found in their depressed clients who received either interpersonal skill training, pleasant-activity schedules, or cognitive training. In summary, nonspecific improvement effects need to be more fully accounted for and their interaction with client characteristics investigated, particularly in the case of obvious factors (e.g., treatment rationale and setting and therapist credibility).

There are many other factors that are thought to contribute to the understanding of client–treatment interactions that need not be detailed here (e.g., therapist factors, follow-up of treatment dropouts). The point is that the drawbacks discussed in the preceding paragraphs represent many of the main reasons why so little is known about the degree of interaction between client characteristics and treatment methods. Put differently, if there are major client–treatment interactions, it is most unlikely that they will be identified if the present style of research persists. Garfield (1978) stated it succinctly, ". . . the task of attempting to interpret the current array of diverse procedures and findings is overwhelming. While each investigator has been free to pursue his own hypotheses with his own procedures, a tribute to our free society, the result is frequently chaotic [p. 225]."

## Client-Treatment Interaction Findings

*Nonbehavioral Treatment Comparisons*

A number of studies have attempted to relate client characteristics to antidepressant treatment response in the psychiatric literature. A review by Bielski and Friedel (1976) found social class directly related to tricyclic treatment response, number of previous episodes inversely related to positive treatment response, and endogenous depression more responsive than reactive depression to tricyclic medication. In contrast, Wittenborn and Kiremitci (1975) found no evidence that treatment response interacted with the diagnostic classification in depressive disorders. Similarly, Covi, Lipman, Derogatis, Smith, and Pattison (1974) found no relationship between a tricyclic (imipramine) and client subclassification (anxious, hostile, agitated, or retarded). Klerman and Paykel (1970) have shown that social background is associated with hospital assignment: Higher social class patients were admitted to a general hospital, lower social class patients were admitted to the state mental hospital, and middle-class patients were seen primarily in a mental health center.

Three studies report modality-specific responses (i.e., specific treatments influence only specific measurement variables), using treatment comparison designs. Friedman's (1975) study showed antidepressant medication to be more effective than marital treatment in symptom relief and clinical improvement but marital treatment to be superior in fostering family role task performance and promotion of the marital relationship. Klerman, DiMascio, Weissman, Prusoff, and Paykel (1974) found no difference between antidepressant drug therapy and psychotherapy, either alone or in combination, in terms of treatment response. However, psychotherapy facilitated the social adjustment and interpersonal relations of clients. Similarly, Weissman, Klerman, Paykel, Prusoff, and Hanson (1974) report that psychotherapy improved personal and social adjustment in a large-sized outpatient treatment study, that tricyclic medication did not affect clients' social adjustment, and that there were no interaction effects between drug and psychotherapy. These studies suggest that depressed clients should be matched to treatment according to the nature of their complaints—antidepressant medication for somatic symptoms and psychotherapy for personal and social adjustment problems.

The most sophisticated client–treatment interaction study in this area is that of Paykel *et al.* (1973). Based on previous work, in which depressed patients had been classified by multivariate cluster analysis (Paykel, 1971), four groups of clients (psychotic depressives, anxious depressives, hostile depressives, and young depressives with personality disorders) were found to predict outcome to tricyclic medication. The same 29 predictor variables that were used to assign clients to these four groups were again used to successfully predict outcome using linear multiple regression analyses.

### Behavioral Treatment Comparisons

All of the treatment comparison studies employing behavioral treatment have utilized reasonably similar client exclusion criteria in order to reduce subject heterogeneity. Even Lewinsohn, Munoz, Youngren, and Zeiss (1978) are careful to spell out exclusion criteria (e.g., suicidal tendency). The effect of these exclusion criteria is to increase sample homogeneity and, therefore, reduce any potential client–treatment interactions.

The Zeiss *et al.* (1979) study detected no treatment differences between interpersonal skills training, cognitive training, and pleasant-activities schedule groups. The authors suggest that nonspecific effects (e.g., self-efficacy) have promoted the improvement and provide an interesting description of the conditions under which these effects can be expected to emerge. Similarly, Staples, Sloane, Whipple, Cristol, and Yorkston (1976), in a treatment comparison study, were unable to detect a significant difference between behavior and psychotherapy groups in treatment efficacy and concluded that patient (i.e., nonspecific) rather than treatment characteristics had prevailed. Neither of these studies investigated potential client–treatment interactions. Three other interesting treatment comparison studies have been completed, but their sample sizes are too small to permit a client–treatment outcome prediction to be made.

By correlating 3- and 6-month follow-up data with treatment response, Hollon *et al.* (1977) found that chronicity of disorder and initial expectations of improvement were not associated with outcome, whereas ego strength and low treatment history were associated with improvement in the case of antidepressant medication.

In a relatively large comparative treatment study, McLean and Hakstian (1979) compared the relative efficacy of psychotherapy, behavior therapy, relaxation therapy (control group), and amitriptyline. By means of cluster analysis, 196 clients were classified into four subject clusters. These subject clusters did not produce a main effect across treatment groups, nor did they interact with treatment either at end of treatment or at follow-up (treatments effects were significant). In an effort to pursue the prediction of outcome based on client characteristics, clients were rank-ordered according to treatment response (treatment conditions collapsed), and the top and bottom thirds were compared. A Hotelling's $T^2$ analysis, followed by discriminant analysis, was performed on 24 client characteristics. Discriminant function analysis was used to classify clients into predicted high and low response categories. The proportion of correct classifications by discriminant function scores (i.e., the "hit rate") was 68%. This represents an improvement upon chance classification of only 18%.

Subsequent analysis, again using the high and low treatment responder distinction—except this time the distinction was maintained over a 15-month follow-up—has improved upon this hit rate by correctly identifying 81% of high and low responders based on nine pretreatment client characteristic variables (cell sizes here are too low to permit double cross-validation). The nine client variables were sex, marital status, number of suicide attempts, a life events score, the psychoticism score from Eysenck's Eysenck Personality Questionnaire (EPQ), number of depressed persons in family, average satisfaction, cognitive functioning, and personal activity (the last three variables represent composite variables). Further, there was no difference in the client cluster distribution between high and low treatment response groups, and the highest correlation between outcome and 32 pretreatment client characteristics within the behavior therapy group was .29.

In clinical practice, and in the absence of the type of information outlined in the preceding discussion, clinicians develop their own criteria for assigning clients to treatments (e.g., McLean, 1976), based entirely upon pragmatic considerations and clinical experience. For example, clients are evaluated before treatment in terms of skill deficits in specific areas, such as communication, social interaction, assertiveness, and behavioral productivity. A modular treatment program can then be developed on the basis of the salient skill deficits of the individual client (e.g., Liberman, Chapter 10, this volume).

## Summary

Within the past 2 decades, there has been an increase in the number of published controlled treatment studies in the area of depression, the volume of which has no historical precedent. These studies include a variety of psychological and psychotropic treatment interventions, used alone or in combinations, and are usually designed in a treatment comparison format. It is appropriate to ask what new information has been yielded by these studies on the issue of optimal matching between client characteristics and treatment.

Almost all studies published to date are relatively small-sized treatment comparison studies that employ nonstandardized design features in the pursuit of unique information. Replication studies, unfortunately, are not in vogue. Their sample size precludes the use of multivariate methodologies to identify relationships between client variables and treatment group outcome.

At a clinical level, many client variables are thought to be related to treatment outcome. At an empirical level, there is at this time no consistent evidence to suggest that treatment response can be improved by nonrandom treatment assignment in the case of the verbal therapies.

This review located only two studies (McLean & Hakstian, 1979; Paykel et al. 1973) that have used multivariate methodologies to predict treatment response on the basis of pretreatment client information. Both of these studies started from relatively large sample sizes (165 and 196 clients, respectively). In the larger of these two studies, based on end-of-treatment outcome data and 29 pretreatment predictor variables, discriminant function analysis scores permitted the correct classification of 68% of "high" and "low" treatment responders. With treatment response data collected over a 15-month follow-up period and using nine pretreatment client predictor variables, the correct classification hit rate of high and low responders increased to 81%.

It may well be that the effect of nonspecific treatment factors (e.g., the persuasive power of the rationale offered by the therapist) simply overwhelms any therapeutic gains made by optimal client–treatment matching. Information relevant to this empirical question can best be gained from a number of controlled, large-scale clinical studies that incorporate standardized design features.

All of us who have labored in clinical practice with depressed clients believe, with some certainty, that we know which client requires what treatment and in what sequence. The empirical evidence to date indicates that such matching between client and treatment characteristics is more personally than scientifically persuasive. Does this mean that the available empirical means of investigating client–treatment characteristic interaction are insensitive, or is it that there is really little interaction in the first place? This question cannot readily be answered with the evidence at hand and requires a commitment to future quality research wherein these characteristics and interactions are accounted for. Clinical experience suggests that certain clients, for one reason or another, will respond better to one treatment than another. We have seen that there has been little controlled research of sufficient magnitude to really illuminate the client–treatment interaction question. What research there is on this topic indicates that matching client and treatment characteristics, while providing a convincing and palliative rationale for the client, may affect treatment outcome less than has been anticipated. Investigators who increase their group sample size to permit the use of multivariate statistical techniques and who carefully describe their treatment, setting, recruitment, client, and therapist characteristics will greatly increase the information now available on whether matching client and treatment characteristics has merit in terms of treatment results or whether it is simply another clinical myth best laid to rest.

## References

Bandura, A. Self-efficacy: toward a unifying theory of behavioral change. *Psychological Review,* 1977, *84,* 191–215.

Becker, J. *Depression: Theory and research.* New York: Wiley & Sons, 1974.

Bielski, R., & Friedel, R. O. Prediction of tricyclic response. *Archives of General Psychiatry,* 1976, *33,* 1479–1489.

Covi, L., Lipman, R. S., Derogatis, L. R., Smith, J. E., & Pattison, J. H. Drugs and group psychotherapy in neurotic depression. *American Journal of Psychiatry,* 1974, *131,* 191–198.

Friedman, F. S. Interaction of drug therapy with marital therapy in depressive patients. *Archives of General Psychiatry,* 1975, *32,* 619–637.

Garfield, S. L. Research on client variables in psychotherapy. In S. L. Garfield & A. E. Bergin (Eds.), *Handbook of psychotherapy and behavior change* (2nd ed.). New York: Wiley & Sons, 1978.

Hart, R. R. Therapeutic effectiveness on setting and monitoring goals. *Journal of Consulting and Clinical Psychology,* 1978, *4,* 1242–1245.

Hollon, S. D., Beck, A. T., Kovacs, M., & Rush, A. J. Cognitive therapy of depression: An outcome study with six-month follow-up, Paper presented at Society for Psychotherapy Research, Madison, Wisconsin, 1977.

Kanfer, F. H., & Grimm, L. C. Freedom of choice and behavioral change. *Journal of Consulting and Clinical Psychology,* 1978, *46,* 873–878.

Klein, D. F. Endogenomorphic depression: A conceptual and terminological revision. *Archives of General Psychiatry,* 1974, *31,* 447–454.

Klerman, G. L., DiMascio, A., Weissman, M., Prusoff, B., & Paykel, E. S. Treatment of depression by drugs and psychotherapy. *American Journal of Psychiatry,* 1974, *131,* 186–191.

Klerman, G. L., & Paykel, E. S. Depressive pattern, social background and hospitalization. *The Journal of Nervous and Mental Disease,* 1970, *150,* 466–478.

Lewinsohn, P. M., Munoz, R. F., Youngren, M. A., & Zeiss, A. M. *Control your depression.* Englewood Cliffs, N. J.: Prentice-Hall, 1978.

Luborsky, L., Singer, J. B., & Luborsky, L. Comparative studies of psychotherapies. *Archives of General Psychiatry,* 1975, *32,* 995–1008.

Mathews, A. Fear reduction research and clinical phobias. *Psychological Bulletin,* 1978, *85,* 390–404.

McLean, P. D. Therapeutic decision-making in the behavioral treatment of depression. In P. O. Davidson (Ed.), *Behavioral management of anxiety, depression and pain.* New York: Brunner/Mazel, 1976.

McLean, P. D., & Hakstian, A. R. Clinical depression: Comparative efficacy of outpatient treatments. *Journal of Consulting and Clinical Psychology,* 1979, *47,* 818–836.

Paykel, E. S. Classification of depressed patients: A cluster analysis derived grouping. *British Journal of Psychiatry,* 1971, *118,* 275–288.

Paykel, E. S., Prusoff, B. A., Klerman, G. L., Haskell, D. & DiMascio, A. Clinical response to amitriptyline among depressed women. *Journal of Nervous and Mental Disease,* 1973, *156,* 149–165.

Staples, F. R., Sloane, R. B., Whipple, K., Cristol, A. H., & Yorkston, N. Process and outcome in psychotherapy and behavior therapy. *Journal of Consulting and Clinical Psychology,* 1976, *44,* 340–350.

Thompson, K. C., & Hendrie, H. C. Environmental stress in primary depressive illness. *Archives of General Psychiatry,* 1972, *26,* 130–136.

Weissman, M. M., Klerman, G. L., Paykel, E. S., Prusoff, B., & Hanson, B. Treatment effects on the social adjustment of depressed patients. *Archives of General Psychiatry,* 1974, *30,* 771–778.

Wittenborn, R. J., & Kiremitci, N. A comparison of anti-depressant medications in neurotic and psychotic patients. *Archives of General Psychiatry,* 1975, *32,* 1172–1176.

Zeiss, A. M., Lewinsohn, P. M., & Munoz, R. F. Nonspecific improvement effects in depression using interpersonal skills training, pleasant activity schedules, or cognitive training. *Journal of Consulting and Clinical Psychology,* 1979, *47,* 427–439.

# 9

# Matching Treatment to Patient Characteristics in an Inpatient Setting

BRIAN F. SHAW

The focus of this chapter is on the interaction between cognitive–behavioral therapies and patient variables in the inpatient treatment of depression. The content of the chapter includes: (*a*) a comparative description of six components of treatment for depression; (*b*) a discussion of relevant patient characteristics; (*c*) a review of the problem-oriented system to determine clinical outcome; (*d*) the presentation of results of a preliminary investigation examining the interaction of the aforementioned three variables (treatment, patient, and outcome); and (*e*) recommendation for future clinical research to examine changes in depressed patients as a function of various treatments.

The term *depression*, as used in this chapter, is defined as an interrelated group of symptoms (a syndrome) according to the criteria of Feighner, Robins, Guze, Woodruff, Winokur, and Munoz (1972). In the approach to the current work as well as in past efforts (Shaw, 1977), depression is measured with self-report and objective clinical ratings to determine the severity and symptom patterns. It should be noted that the inclusion criteria used in these studies are substantially different from the criteria for depression as a mood. The specific subject characteristics used to describe the depressed patients (e.g., severity, type of depression) will be detailed later.

## Cognitive–Behavioral Treatment Components

Other chapters will describe various cognitive–behavioral approaches currently employed in the treatment of depression. The task of selecting certain

209

patients for particular treatments is difficult, given the need to demonstrate that any form of psychotherapy is effective in depression. There are too few well-controlled outcome studies in the literature to propose ideal patient–therapy combinations. The present analysis will be initially restricted to the treatments employed in the inpatient unit, Department of Psychiatry, University Hospital, London, Canada. The components utilized in the treatment of depression on the unit were not empirically selected but rather are a function of the staffing patterns and interests. Other inpatient units will of course differ in the treatments used and will require detailed investigations of their own. The reader of this volume should be well aware that it is simply not possible to determine generally efficacious behavioral treatments, much less inpatient treatments.

The unit has 20 beds, 65% of which are occupied by depressed patients. The treatment approach is multidisciplinary (psychologists, psychiatrists, occupational therapists, social workers, nurses, and students), with interventions having a decidedly behavioral character. The decision-making process for treatment occurs at triweekly rounds and follows a problem-oriented system (Weed, 1968). The specific therapeutic program is comprised of treatment components designed to alter specific problems. The methods employed tend to emphasize the learning of new coping skills and/or the alteration of CNS function via psychopharmacological agents.

### Stress Reduction

Stress reduction concerns the nonspecific aspects of the inpatient therapy. The milieu of the unit includes regular ward activities, communal housekeeping duties, and above all, a reduction of environmental stressors. For the purpose of the present analyses, counseling that did not involve broadly defined interventions designed to train new skills (such as financial planning, job assessment, and the assessment of activities of daily living) was subsumed in this component. The stress reduction component is based on a staff attitude that a period of hospitalization where learning can occur under relatively minimal external stress conditions is useful. This component is not simply "a rest from the world," as some patients expect. Nevertheless, short-term benefits for many patients accrue from a radical change in environment (i.e., a change from home to hospital). In the consideration of effective components of inpatient treatment, the stress reduction component is ubiquitous. The effects of stress reduction on the patients' depression are inevitably introduced. Thus, when reference is made to, for example, a cognitive therapy component, this component occurs in interaction with the stress reduction component. The nonspecific effects of hospitalizations must be borne in mind throughout the chapter.

### Social Skill Training

Social skill training was greatly influenced by the work of Lewinsohn (1974) and the work on assertiveness training. It has a primary goal of teaching patients how to deal effectively with others. The interpersonal skills include assertiveness, accurate empathy, and other skills designed to obtain a maximal amount of response-contingent positive reinforcement from the social environment. Three therapeutic methods serve as the foundation of the component: (a) modeling of the desired behavior; (b) behavior rehearsal; and (c) feedback from the group. Patients typically read *When I Say No I Feel Guilty* (Smith, 1975) as an introduction to this component. The therapists provide feedback about the patient's behavior, including latency of response, infrequent positive statements, and nonverbal cues (e.g., eye contact, posture). The goal of this feedback is to improve the patient's knowledge of his or her stimulus value to others. Appropriate social skills, particularly those useful in solving current interpersonal problems, are role played in the group. Assertiveness situations are given a priority.

## Marital Counseling

Marital counseling concerns conjoint interventions whereby the patient and his or her spouse are trained to clarify their communication patterns. This component follows many of the detailed suggestions of McLean (1976). Patients are encouraged to have daily conversations (on the ward or on the telephone) with their spouses. In the conjoint sessions, an agreement to adopt a positive control position (e.g., accepting responsibility, showing appreciation, being affectionate) is required. A contract for six to eight sessions with specific behavioral goals (e.g., to spend 2 hours Saturday working together on a household project versus the more general goal of "feeling happier together") is used. The focus then is on improved communication and positive control. One observation about the communication skills component is that the patient and his or her spouse are often able to alter their criticisms of each other in such a way that concrete problem solving can occur. For example, one patient constantly complained of a lack of attention from her spouse. When careful records were kept, however, they showed that the husband was spending 3.5–5 hours per day with his wife, but he attended to her complaints and self-criticism not to her attempts to improve her self-esteem. This discovery led to a change in their interactions such that only positive behavior was discussed. The self-critical ideas were left for evaluation using a cognitive therapy approach.

## Cognitive Therapy

The cognitive therapy component directly follows the individual therapy approach described by Beck, Rush, Shaw, and Emery (1979). Two phases of inpatient treatment can be distinguished: attempts to alter specific cognitions and attempts to alter assumptive systems. The first phase concerns discrete cognitive and behavioral change, and such techniques as the collection of cognitions, cognitive restructuring, mastery and pleasure recording, and the triple-column technique are employed. The focus is on the symptoms of depression, such as apathy, hopelessness, intense negative affect, and self-criticism, and on the patient's interpretation of environmental events. The second phase concerns the major postulate systems or the predisposing cognitive schema (Beck, 1967) of the patient. The therapist attends to the patient's self-concept (see Epstein, 1973) and his or her rules for living that are assumed to be connected with the onset or maintenance of the depression. For example, one patient placed a high value on business success but also found himself to be "inadequate" in interpersonal confrontation situations. After reviewing many situations and the associated cognitions, the patient detected one of his major assumptions, namely, "I'm a failure unless everybody likes me." The goal of therapy was to examine the effects of this assumption on his life and, in particular, to relate the assumption to the onset of his depressions. He found that even "successful" business deals in which he had to drive a hard bargain were personally unsatisfying. Instead of crediting himself for a sound business dealing, he experienced anxiety that he would be seen as a "tyrant." In time, most patients receiving cognitive therapy learn to assess, analyze, and, if necessary, modify dysfunctional assumptions.

In general, patients are first trained to observe and if necessary modify their cognitions (or automatic thoughts) and thinking styles. Typically, the second phase of therapy (challenging assumptions) is conducted on an outpatient basis. The present analysis is almost exclusively concerned with matching patients to the first phase of cognitive therapy.

## Psychopharmacology and Electroconvulsive Treatment

The use of antidepressants in the treatment of depression cannot be underestimated. Marks (1978) submitted the following challenge to behaviorally oriented therapists: "To be more useful than drugs, behavioral approaches have either (1) to be cheaper than drugs for the same amount of improvement, or (2) to produce greater improvement alone or in combination with drugs, or (3) to help sufferers who do not respond to drugs or do not take them because of side effects [p. 532]." Another favorable outcome that should be considered is to decrease the relapse rate in a generally recurring disorder. Psychopharmacological or electroconvulsive treatment (ECT) presumably alters CNS biochemistry (e.g., norepinephrine, serotonin, dopamine) hypothesized to maintain the depression. Despite hundreds of studies, it remains unclear how antidepressants or ECT effect change. One of the major difficulties is that the hypothesized CNS changes are difficult to measure. Nevertheless, there is an impressive literature showing that many antidepressants are effective in the treatment of depression (see Morris & Beck, 1974).

Since many depressed patients receive antidepressants and/or ECT to treat their depression, this chemical–physiological component was included in the analysis as a standard for comparison. The literature on the combination of drug therapy and psychotherapy has been reviewed with specific reference to depression by Hollon and Beck (1978). The literature on the matching of patients to specific drug treatments or ECT will not be reviewed in the present chapter.

### Problem Solving and Activity Scheduling

Problem solving and activity scheduling focus on specific activity programs that follow a practical series of guidelines. The guidelines include such rules as "beds are for sleeping only" and "activity is better than inactivity." This component also includes therapeutic attempts to help patients identify problems by discussing stressful areas in their lives. This component is not unique to cognitive–behavioral therapies. The encouragement of the patient to increase his or her activity and to solve problems in a constructive manner is the basis of many commonsense approaches to treatment. Nevertheless, the monitoring of activity and the assignment of graded tasks are well within the behavioral perspective. The identification of problems and therapeutic attempts to alter the patient's symptoms of inactivity and withdrawal are also described as part of cognitive–behavior therapy (see Beck et al., 1979).

## Patient Characteristics

Traditionally, psychotherapy researchers have not singled out specific groups, such as depressed patients, when studying the influence of patient characteristics on the course and outcome of therapy. Garfield (1978), in his excellent review, listed most of the relevant findings on subject characteristics. For example, he concluded that social class is positively related to acceptance for psychotherapy treatment. Different socioeconomic status (SES) groups receive different types of treatment, and social class is positively related to premature termination from treatment. In general, significant relationships between premature termination and such variables as age, sex, or diagnosis have not emerged. Interestingly, Weissman, Geanakoplos, and Prusoff (1973) found a low attrition rate across a range of depressed women from different SES groups. There were no differences between SES groups on the rate of attrition during psychotherapy.

Concerning the outcome of psychotherapy, it appears that SES and education level are important factors. It is generally agreed that psychotherapy with the higher functioning person (i.e., higher coping abilities, more integrated, less psychopathology) holds a better outcome probability. Frank (1974) noted that patients with anxiety or depression symptoms as opposed to somatic symptoms were more likely to improve with psychotherapy. Sloane, Staples, Cristol, Yorkston, and Whipple (1975), in their comparative study of behavior therapy and psychoanalysis, found that behavior therapy was successful regardless of the initial level of psychopathology (as measured by the Minnesota Multiphasic Personality Inventory).

The match between the patient's expectations and the nature of the therapy also appears to be important. Heine and Trosman (1960) studied people who terminated and those who remained in psychotherapy. The "remainers" were characterized by expectations of active collaboration and advice or help in changing behavior. The nature of the presenting complaint was unrelated to continuation in treatment. Friedman (1963) found a direct relationship between expectancy and symptom reduction. Symptoms associated with anxiety and depression were the most affected by the expectancies (the higher the patient's expectation for change in anxiety or depression, the greater the probability of symptom reduction).

Based on the general review of the literature and my own theoretical biases (see Shaw, in press), six areas of subject classification have been identified.

## Demographic

The commonly studied variables include age, sex, race, education, intelligence, religion, and socioeconomic status. Depression is not reliably related to these demographic variables, with the exception of sex and perhaps age. The ratio between men and women who seek help for depression in mental health settings is generally considered to be one to two (Rehm & Kornblith, 1979). There is also some evidence that age is related to varying manifestations of depression (Ripley, 1977). With some of the cognitive therapies, the initial reactions of many clinicians is that education or intelligence is likely implicated, but there have been no reports of this nature to date.

## Psychopathological

The severity and chronicity of the depression are potentially relevant, predictive characteristics. The severity of the depression can be measured by such instruments as the Hamilton Rating Scale (Hamilton, 1969) and the Beck Depression Inventory (Beck, Ward, Mendelson, Mock, & Erbaugh, 1961). The chronicity of depression includes the duration of the present episode (self-reported and, hopefully, corroborated by reports of significant others) and the frequency of past depressive episodes. Hollon and Beck (1979) have made initial attempts to develop a severity–chronicity scale.

Other psychopathological characteristics include the unipolar–bipolar dimension (see Dupue & Monroe, 1978, for a review) and the endogenous–exogenous (reactive) dimension. The latter dimension appears to have fallen into general disfavor because of the extreme difficulty in determining the etiological factors (e.g., Leff, Roatch, & Bunney, 1970) assumed by the dichotomy. The unipolar–bipolar dimension, on the other hand, can be differentiated reliably with respect to symptoms, clinical signs, genetics, and drug treatment. Thus, it would appear to be a useful categorization of psychopathology.

*Personality*

While there are no reliable personality correlates predictive of depression (Becker, 1974), one study (Klerman & Weissman, 1976) reported the predictive value of the Eysenck Personality Inventory (EPI) (Eysenck & Eysenck, 1964) neuroticism (N) scale. The N scale proved to be the single most important predictor of outcome (i.e., reduction in depressive symptoms) with drug treatment and/or psychotherapy. The combination of no active treatment after the acute phase of depression and a high EPI-N score predicted the poorest outcome 20 months after the acute phase. The subjects in this study were women aged 25–60 who had responded to treatment with amitriptyline, and thus, the results must be restricted to this sample. Of perhaps greater interest, Klerman and Weissman (1976) detailed the variables that did not differentiate outcome group in their study. These included age, race, social class, marital status, religion, number of previous depressions, number of suicide attempts, early deaths or separations as a child, neurotic traits as a child, amount and type of stress during 6 months prior to onset, severity of pretreatment symptoms, and severity of pretreatment social role functioning.

Dobson (1980) has completed work on an interactional (situation x traits) scale that is a potentially valuable predictor in depression. He noted that detailed knowledge of the idiosyncratic "stressful" situations and the coping styles (traits) of the person may distinguish subtypes of depressed individuals. One finding was that males reported depression in response to achievement-oriented situations, whereas females reported interpersonal situations as the most depressogenic. The interactional model moves away from traditional personality assessment. While individuals who have high needs for achievement or affiliation may not be more susceptible to depression, individuals who are depression prone may be more reactive to achievement or affiliation situations.

Another notable personality characteristic concerns the expectations of the patient. It has been found that for both psychotherapy and systematic desensitization the match between the patient's expectancies about therapy and the type of therapy is important (cf. Garfield, 1978; Lick & Bootzin, 1975). It may be that, with depressed patients, therapy expectations are simply one class of their general expectations about the world (i.e., depressed patients have minimal expectations for successful therapy, but, in general, they predict personal failure in skilled tasks). Nevertheless, expectations for drug therapy or psychotherapy require investigation as potentially important predictive variables of outcome.

*External Demands*

It may be useful to adopt Lazarus and Launier's (1978) definition of stress in our considerations of patient characteristics. Stress is defined as "any event in which environmental or internal demands (or both) tax or exceed the adaptive resources of the individual [p. 16]."

External, or environmental, demands may be objectified using a scale such as the Social Readjustment Rating Scale (Holmes & Rahe, 1967). Ilfeld (1977) reported a correlational study of 2299 adults, aged 18–65, showed that such social stressors as marriage and parenting were closely related to depression. Schless, Schwartz, Goetz, and Mendels (1974) examined the significance with which depressed inpatients view life events. Depressed subjects viewed a wide variety of events as more stressful than did nondepressed subjects, and these judgments were independent of severity and level of recovery.

It may be important to delineate the actual social stressors by rating the natural environment on a number of characteristics. In essence, this type of measurement is not a patient characteristic. Yet, Coyne (1976) has described the changing environment that faces the increasingly depressed person. Significant others may react with unrealistic reassurance, possibly because of their own feelings of anger thereby altering the demands on the patient.

At present, many clinicians make use of information about the patient's social environment to determine salient stress factors. A person whose family and friends are realistically supportive is more likely to make the necessary adjustments in his or her interactions with others. It may be useful to develop and validate a measure of the environmental demands (or, conversely, supports) placed on an individual.

## Internal Demands

The second aspect of Lazarus and Launier's (1978) definition of stress concerns the demands patients make of themselves. There are few objective ways of measuring these internal demands. One specific approach may be to obtain ratings of the level of aspiration endorsed by an individual prior to his or her attempt at some task. In this way, information about the individual's goal-setting standards (i.e., internal demands) may be obtained. A second method of quantifying these internal demands would be to administer a test that assesses attitudes relevant to stress or depression. The Dysfunctional Attitude Scale (Weissman, 1979) was developed to identify persons who may be prone to depression as a function of their attitudes. This research follows Beck's (1976) proposals that the depression-prone person views the self, world, and future in a negative way. Another possible method of measuring the internal demands of the patient would be Jones's (1968) Irrational Beliefs Scale (IBS). Nelson (1977) found a moderate correlation ($r = .53$) between the IBS and the Beck Depression Inventory (BDI) (Beck et al., 1961) in a group of college students.

## Cognitive Assessment

The adaptive resources used by individuals to cope with internal or external demands has received relatively little attention. Rippere (1977) studied commonsense beliefs about depression and the coping strategies employed by individuals who were depressed. She proposed that knowledge of the person's coping strategies was integral information and necessary to understand the development of depression.

There are, of course, many different ways of assessing cognitions related to depression (see Shaw & Dobson, in press, for a review). Cognitive assessment has been approached by self-report paper and pencil methods and more recently by experimental methodologies (e.g., Paivio, 1976). One of the major motivations of assessment in this area has been to evaluate cognitive change as a function of treatment. No consistent results have emerged to date.

Gioe (1975), in his study of cognitively oriented therapy for depression, found no change in self-concept as a result of treatment. One possible explanation is that his measure of self-concept was not sensitive to change. Only future studies will determine the usefulness of such measures, but we are following an alternative research strategy.

One early attempt to study cognitive change involved the experimental self-concept measures used by Diggory (1966). Loeb, Beck, and Diggory (1971) employed similar methods in their study of the differential effects of success and failure on the expectations of depressed patients. Shaw (1980) essentially replicated the Loeb et al. (1971) methodology in an attempt to measure cognitive change as a result of psychotherapy.

Briefly, the methodology involves presenting subjects with a task of sorting cards with various symbols onto a master board within a specified time limit. Prior to the task, the subject's estimates of probability of success and level of aspiration are obtained. The outcome of the task is experimenter controlled, and patients receive either success or failure feedback. A measure of their actual task performance and ratings of their estimated achievement level (e.g., How well did you do?) are also obtained.

In one pilot study (Shaw, 1980), subjects were tested before and after psychotherapy (cognitive, behavior, or nondirective therapy). Two groups (successfully and unsuccessfully treated depressed subjects) were compared to a normal untreated control group matched for age. The cognitive measures of interest were (a) probability of success (the subjects' probability estimates of whether they would reach an experimenter-defined goal within five trials); (b) level of aspiration (the subjects' personal goals for each trial); (c) actual performance (the number of seconds to sort a predetermined number of cards); and (d) performance evaluation (the rating of personal performance compared to the performance of others who had completed the task).

The results and a comparison to Loeb et al.'s (1971) study are summarized in Table 9.1. The result of greatest interest is the significant ($p < .05$) difference between the successfully treated and the unsuccessfully treated depressed groups on the probability of success estimates. The estimate was referred to by Loeb et al. (1971) as a measure of the self-concept. The pilot study must be interpreted with caution. The subjects were college students (aged 18–26) with clinical depressions of moderate severity (BDI mean = 27.2). The successfully treated depressed group (defined as BDI < 10) received either cognitive therapy

**TABLE 9.1**

Means of Probability of Success, Level of Aspiration, Performance Evaluation, and Actual Performance in Remitted and Nonremitted Depressed Subjects and Normal Controls

| | Shaw, 1980 | | | Loeb, Beck & Diggory, 1971 | |
|---|---|---|---|---|---|
| | Normals N = 10 | Remitted depressed N = 9 | Nonremitted depressed N = 23 | High depressed | Low depressed |
| Pre[a] | | | | | |
| Probability of success (100) | 64.5 | 66.9 | 51.8 | 56.3 | 70.0 |
| Level of aspiration (20) | 16.2 | 17.0 | 15.5 | 18.1 | 18.0 |
| Performance evaluation (100) | 65.5 | 62.2 | 58.3 | — | — |
| Actual performance (sec/cards) | 1.19 | 1.22 | 1.23 | 1.30 | 1.27 |
| Post[a] | | | | | |
| Probability of success | 59.0 | 72.6 | 48.3 | — | — |
| Level of aspiration | 16.4 | 16.4 | 15.6 | — | — |
| Performance evaluation | 67.5 | 58.0 | 54.0 | — | — |
| Actual performance (sec/cards) | 1.29 | 1.16 | 1.20 | — | — |
| Number of subjects who received failure at pre | 5 | 5 | 11 | — | — |

[a] Combined success and failure feedback mean scores.

($N = 5$), behavior therapy ($N = 2$), or nondirective therapy ($N = 2$). We are currently collecting data to investigate the predictive validity of the probability of success measure with an inpatient population.

Although not particularly relevant to the current discussion, the reader may be interested to note that at the post testing the normal control subjects who received failure feedback at first testing ($N = 5$) were significantly more pessimistic and actually performed more poorly than did the normal subjects who were "successful" in the first test. The results indicate that normals tend to react to failure with greater cognitive and behavior changes than do depressed subjects.

The cognitive assessment illustrated by this study has been extended by Giles (1980), who employed tasks other than card sorting and more behaviorally oriented measures. She used a methodology similar to Loeb et al. (1971) but also employed interpersonal problem-solving tasks (from Platt & Spivack, 1972). Some preliminary results using the Giles (1980) variables as predictors are presented later. In general, the aim has been to develop experimentally based measures of cognitive change that can be correlated with cognitive–behavioral treatment outcome. In time, we will be able to compare the validity and discriminability of the experimental methods versus psychometric measures of cognition.

To summarize, most studies that have looked specifically at subtypes of depressed patients have concerned diagnostic or psychopathological typologies. It is proposed that, in addition to these methods, serious attention be given to the cognitive or behavioral characteristics of the depressed sample. For illustrative purposes, subdivisions based on cognitive variables were introduced. A better understanding of changes that depressed patients undergo as a function of therapy is needed.

## Outcome Measures Used in the Inpatient Setting

Now that a subset of treatments have been defined and some patient characteristics identified, it is necessary to choose outcome variables—variables that can be used to assess the patient's progress. It is not as easy a task as it may seem to define the outcome measures of inpatient treatment.

Within an inpatient setting, continuation in treatment (i.e., the dropout problem) is rarely a significant issue. For this reason, the number of days in the hospital may be a useful indication of "successful" outcome. Of course, the discharge data are influenced by a variety of factors, ranging from the decision criteria of the psychiatrist to the goals of patients to the practical socioeconomic concerns of inpatient hospitalization. The follow-up plans for the individual are also key factors.

A behavioral measure that was relatively independent of the inferential judgments of clinicians and the self-reports of patients was viewed as the most desirable. As a result, the inpatient unit uses a scale, known as the Nurses' Observation Behavior-Scale (NOBS) (Brawley, Lancee, Allon, & Brown, in press), to measure the presence or absence of relevant patient behaviors. The scale is a 172-item behavioral checklist completed daily on the basis of an observation period of at least 20 minutes. Scales of acceptable reliability have been generated to distinguish improvement and nonimprovement for a number of clinical conditions, including depression. The NOBS was specifically designed for use as a change measure in general psychiatric inpatient units. It is particularly useful because the raters make note of discrete depressive behaviors (e.g., crying, isolated in room).

In addition to the NOBS and days in the hospital, we often employ the Beck Depression Inventory and the Hamilton Rating Scale as aids to the clinical judgments of improvement. These scales are important data sources, since a number of studies have demonstrated the problems with global, subjective estimates of improvement by clinicians and patients (e.g., Fontana & Dowds, 1975).

It would be very desirable, if not necessary, to generate outcome measures specific to the cognitive–behavioral components (e.g., Does the patient assert himself or herself after social skill training? Do cognitions change after cognitive therapy?), but these measures have not been developed or introduced on the unit to date. McLean (1976) provides an excellent model of goal attainment scaling in depression that begins to address the problem.

## The Problem-Oriented System

One of the important goals preceding any treatment phase is the development of a specific plan for treatment. One general framework for treatment is the problem-oriented system (Weed, 1968). This system was initially developed as an effective method of record keeping in medical units but has been adapted for psychiatry (McLean & Miles, 1974). A problem is not equivalent to a patient complaint. Problems also include tasks that the treatment team needs to complete (e.g., problem—incomplete data on assertiveness). Clinical syndromes (e.g., problem—depression) may be subdivided into more specific problems (e.g., inactivity). Therapy may focus on one problem while a second (and third, etc.) is under assessment. Treatment, therefore, consists of a series of assessments and therapeutic interventions with resultant feedback and changes in the plan as necessary. It may be possible eventually to consider the number of problems resolved as an outcome measure. At present, the system simply provides a relatively good method of structuring and recording the introduction, termination, and sequencing of various treatment components.

## Preliminary Investigation

When initially faced with the task of discussing the predictors of successful cognitive–behavioral treatment, it was quite apparent that, without specific reference to a well-controlled outcome study with inpatients or outpatients, the task would be difficult. The next best option (albeit a weak one) was to complete a correlational study examining the relationship between various treatment, patient, and outcome variables in the unit at University Hospital. The idea was that by completing the study recommendations for further work might develop.

The research strategy was as follows:

1. Delineate the treatment components to be studied. The treatment components have been presented, and it must be recognized that they are limited in scope. Obviously, for any one patient, many factors lead to the implementation of a specific treatment. All patients by the very nature of their inpatient status received the stress reduction component, and thus, it was excluded from further study. For the other treatment components, such variables as the availability of

trained staff, the expectations of patients (and significant others), and the result of the staff's assessments influenced the decision to introduce a treatment component at a particular point in time.

2. Detail the patient characteristics under consideration. These include some demographic (age, sex), psychopathological (severity of depression), and cognitive variables in the present analysis. Personality variables and measures of the patient's internal and external demands as previously discussed were not included. Only patients who were hospitalized for more than 1 week were included in the data analysis.

3. Review and record outcome data. These data include the length of hospitalization and four bits of NOBS data (the pre score, the post score, and the mean scores from the first and second halves of the hospitalization).

4. Compute the intercorrelation matrix between variables, followed by the appropriate tests of significance. All correlations were based on 37 subjects. In the case of the cognitive variables, only nine female subjects were studied. Obviously, with these small numbers the results must be interpreted with caution and cannot be generalized beyond the University Hospital unit.

5. Conduct a stepwise multiple regression analysis to determine predictors of days of hospitalization and NOBS-post scores (the two outcome measures of interest).

Demographically, the sample was characteristic of many unipolar depressed inpatient groups. Briefly, 25 females and 12 males with average age of 41.8 years and 12.3 years of education were treated as inpatients for a mean of 30 days. The patients were in general, severely depressed as evidenced by a mean MMPI-D scale ($T$) score of 83. Thirteen (35%) of the patients were hospitalized following a suicide attempt.

The NOBS data, which had been collected daily, were reduced to four data points. The reduction was accomplished by using the first day (NOBS-pre) and last day (NOBS-post) scores and the mean scores of the first half and second half of hospitalization (NOBS-1 and NOBS-2). Because the NOBS is a relatively new instrument, the correlations between NOBS and the two measures of the severity of depression (BDI and MMPI-D) were calculated. The relationship between the MMPI-D score and the NOBS-1 (i.e., the mean of the first half of observations minus the pre score) was significant ($N = 26, r = .35, p < .05$), as was the BDI-NOBS-1 correlation ($N = 31, r = .60, p < .01$). There was a significant relationship between NOBS-1 and sex; males manifested fewer depressed behaviors in the first phase of hospitalization than did females.

Concerning treatment outcome, the NOBS-pre was significantly higher (i.e., patients more depressed) than the NOBS-post ($N = 37, t[\text{correlated}] = 3.29, p < .01$). Only consecutive NOBS scores were significantly correlated (e.g., NOBS-pre with NOBS-1; NOBS-1 with NOBS-2), while all other correlations were nonsignificant. This suggested that a linear function best describes the data, as would be expected with gradual improvement.

An examination was then made of the correlations between the NOBS data and the use of different treatment components. Those patients who had longer hospitalizations and were more depressed (according to NOBS-pre, NOBS-1, and NOBS-2) were more likely to receive ECT. The relationship between cognitive therapy and problem solving–activity scheduling, social skills training, and ECT was interesting. Two types of patients tended to receive cognitive therapy. The first type of patient responded to social skills training or the problem solving–activity scheduling component with increased activity and social interactions and then received cognitive therapy ($r = .55, p < .01$). These patients tended to continue in cognitive therapy as outpatients, with the goal of changing assumptions as well as specific depressive cognitions. The second type of patient was characterized by severe social withdrawal and noncommunication (e.g., a 64-year-old man bedridden with depression for 8 months; a 49-year-old woman hospitalized with delusions that her "bowels were rotting" because she had failed her family). These patients often received both cognitive therapy (at least the first phase) and psychopharmacology or ECT ($r = .37, p < .01$).

Interestingly, the more education the patient had, the longer the hospitalization ($r = .37, p < .01$). Recall that past research found low-SES and low-educated persons tend to drop out of treatment earlier than those with a higher SES and more education (Garfield, 1978). Importantly, the more education the patient had, the more likely it was that he or she would receive cognitive therapy ($r = .45, p < .01$). This decision seems to reflect an assessment that the patient was "psychologically minded"; this will be discussed later. Finally, the older the patient, the more likely it was that he or she would receive psychotropic medication, almost always an antidepressant preparation ($r = .30, p < .05$).

How can we understand these results in the context of the inpatient unit? First, the data reflect a willingness to utilize both cognitive and behavioral techniques with severely depressed inpatients. Psychological treatments are almost always used concomitantly with physiological treatments. Readers are reminded that different types of cognitive–behavioral interventions were used.

The next step was to use the patient, treatment component, and outcome variables to predict the length of hospitalization (in days) and NOBS-post score. The stepwise multiple regression with days in hospital as the dependent measure was significant ($F = 6.86, p < .001$). The best predictors (with the amount of variance accounted for given in parentheses) were: (a) cognitive therapy (18.8%); (b) problem solving–activity scheduling (14.6%); (c) education (8.1%); and (d) NOBS-post (8.0%). The four variables accounted for 49.5% of the overall variance. The other eight variables accounted for only 11% of variance. The stepwise multiple regression with NOBS-post as the dependent measure was significant ($F = 4.33, p < .01$). The best predictors (with the amount of variance accounted for given in parentheses) were: (a) NOBS-2 (14.7%); (b) days in hospital (10%); (c) education (8.7%); and (d) sex (4.5%). These four variables accounted for 37.9% of the overall variance.

The fact that both cognitive therapy and problem solving–activity scheduling were useful predictors of the days in hospital is interesting. A detailed examination of the weightings of the predictors revealed that the problem solving–activity scheduling was negatively weighted, whereas cognitive therapy was positively weighted. The problem solving–activity scheduling component is introduced early in treatment, whereas cognitive therapy is employed later. This result reflects decisions to use cognitive therapy with patients who have problems of hopelessness, suicidal ideation, or extreme apathy. Using the NOBS-post as the criterion, we find that the best predictors (NOBS-2 and days in hospital) are simply other outcome variables. Education (which was also a predictor of days in hospital) and sex are useful demographic predictors. Males and better educated patients were likely to be discharged with higher NOBS-post scores. These results suggest that our treatment is less successful with patients with these characteristics.

Clearly, these results are preliminary as very few cases ($N = 37$) were studied. A simple review of the frequency of different treatment components revealed a biased emphasis toward problem solving–activity scheduling (35 of 37) and drugs–ECT (32 of 37). The study was undertaken to provide preliminary leads and most of all to provide an example of a research strategy in the absence of a controlled outcome study.

Now let us turn to the sample of nine female patients who received experimental cognitive tasks (i.e., the problem-solving tasks). These measures were employed for two reasons. The main reason was to test Beck's (1976) cognitive model of depression (Giles, 1980). The second reason was to develop a battery of psychological procedures that may be useful in predicting outcome of treatment for depression.

Before examining the cognitive assessment variables, correlations were calculated on the outcome measures. A significant relationship between the NOBS-post and the days in hospital ($N = 9$, $r = .79$, $p < .01$) was detected. A significant correlation was also found in the larger sample ($N = 37$, $r = .29$, $p < .05$). This finding indicates the more severe the depression, the longer the patient had remained in hospital. Despite the longer treatment, these patients were less successfully treated (i.e., had poorer outcomes).

The reason for this outcome is unknown. Patients who were poor responders to treatment were not purposefully selected. These nine patients were compared with 15 others (who were tested at a different general hospital or who had missing NOBS data). We examined the experimental, demographic, and psychopathological data and found the nine subjects to be representative of the larger sample of 24 subjects (i.e., there were no group differences). Perhaps the criteria for acceptance, including clinical and self-report severity measures, into this pilot study were such that the more severely depressed patients were inadvertently selected.

The main dependent measures of interest were: (a) probability of success estimate (P(s)), subject's estimate of achieving her goals on each trial; (b) level of perceived personal achievement (LPA), a judgment of how well the subject performed compared to personal standards; and (c) level of achievement relative to others (LAO), a judgment of how well the subject fared relative to others who had taken the test. One of the measures, LPA, from the problem-solving tasks was significantly related to the NOBS-post ($r = -.54, p < .05$) and the days in hospital ($r = -.60, p < .01$). This level of aspiration measure was proposed earlier in the chapter as a possible measure of the patient's cognitions.

The subjects who judged their own performances to be poor relative to what they expected of themselves did not respond well to treatment in hospital. The LPA measure is potentially important because it is not dependent on the type of task (interpersonal or impersonal) nor is it dependent on the type of feedback (success or failure) given to the patients (see Giles, 1980). One is tempted to speculate that the LPA measure quantifies the relationship between a person's aspirations and her perceived achievement, a measure that may be related to self-esteem. For now, however, it is notable that this measure may be a useful predictor of a poor response to inpatient treatments in University Hospital. Hopefully, this work illustrates that the cognitive variables as measured by experimental methods are potentially valuable for future outcome studies.

## Recommendations for Future Research

Rehm and Kornblith (1979) point to a number of elements common to diverse cognitive–behavioral strategies. Despite the use of the term *components*, it is recognized that these modules are not independent units. Patients who received social skills training and marital communications training probably heard similar therapist comments about their behavior. Similarly, the problem solving–activity scheduling and the cognitive therapy components are related (see Beck *et al.*, 1979). Some features shared by all of the cognitive–behavioral components include a high level of structure with specific treatment goals and a focus on developing new skills to cope with depression. An interesting question is: what therapeutic changes can be produced by a number of the treatment components and what changes are unique to specific components? Of course, in order to answer a question like this, much more developmental work must be completed on the relevant measures of change (e.g., what cognitive or behavioral changes correlate with depressive improvement?).

When studying inpatients, one is faced with the seemingly inevitable confounding of different modalities of treatment. Within this type of setting, controlled outcome studies are difficult to accomplish. For example, we considered comparing cognitive–behavior therapy with drug therapy in the treatment of depression. Unfortunately, it was difficult to isolate the drug therapy because the staff, despite cautions, tended to use cognitive or behavioral methods in their interactions with the patients. For this and similar reasons, it will probably be more advantageous to consider multiple baseline designs or to study treatment components with specific hypotheses (e.g., social skills training is more effective in improving social skills behavior than other components) than continue the component analysis. It should be noted that the component type of study will take much longer to complete (more subjects are needed because of the confounding of independent variables).

Rehm and Kornblith (1979) also propose that subjects be classified according to the specific deficits they manifest and then treatment should be matched to those deficits. This goal would appear to be a distant one at present. The preliminary analysis suggests that with depressed inpatients, such demographic predictors as education and intelligence could be examined initially. Recall the concept of "psychological mindedness" introduced by Brill and Storrow (1960). Initially, they found that acceptance for psychotherapy was positively related to social class status. They attempted to evaluate the related factors to low social class and found that the following variables were related: (a) low estimated intelligence; (b) a tendency to view the problem as physical rather than emotional; (c) a desire for symptomatic relief; (d) a lack of understanding of the psychotherapeutic process; and (e) a lack of desire for psychotherapy. Perhaps the concept of "psychological mindedness" is relevant to cognitive–behavior therapy, particularly the cognitive components. Some patients who are unresponsive to cognitive–behavior therapy may maintain a medical model to understand their problems. A skill training or learning approach would conflict directly with their expectations for treatment.

A review of the records for patients who were the most resistant to any type of inpatient treatment showed some of the important clinical characteristics to be sex, education, and delusional thinking. According to the experimental measures those individuals who have generally negative expectations for their own abilities and those who evaluate their performance as inferior relative to their own standards seem to have the poorest treatment response.

Males, particularly well-educated males who have overgeneralized and magnified their weaknesses, leave the unit after a long hospitalization with relatively high depression scores. Paradoxically, these individuals do well with cognitive–behavior therapy as outpatients. One possible explanation is that, in order to change their cognitions, these individuals appear to need concrete feedback from the environment. Clearly, more research is needed on the subject and treatment interactions.

The present chapter was concerned with inpatient treatment. One would expect that there are significant differences between inpatients and outpatients, but this expectation may vary depending on the setting and clinicians. Controlled outpatient studies will likely have a higher probability of completion, but, of course, one would not want to be dogmatic in this assertion.

This chapter was limited in the treatment, subject, and outcome variables that were discussed. The field needs more outcome studies to provide an empirical base from which to test hypotheses about potential predictors of treatment. Before these outcome studies are started, however, sensitive measures need to be developed to determine the deficits in depression (if, indeed, there are deficits and not just differences). With observable behaviors (e.g., social skills as defined by Lewinsohn, 1974), we seem to have a relatively good start. However, it is strongly recommended that more behavioral measures and measures of the content and process of cognition in depressed persons be developed and validated.

Obviously, some well-defined treatment modalities were omitted in the present analysis, specifically the self-control treatment of Rehm and his colleagues (Fuchs & Rehm, 1977; Rehm, Fuchs, Roth, Kornblith, & Romano, 1979) and the contingency management of depressive behaviors (e.g., Liberman & Raskin, 1971). The exclusion of these procedures was based solely on the practical limitations of the inpatient unit.

The psychological study of depression expanded rapidly in the 1970s. From a therapeutic viewpoint, it is time that we determine the types of changes that occur with successful treatment of depression. This means that longitudinal studies will be necessary. Many more studies will have to be conducted before we can determine the relative efficacy (hopefully, measured by depression outcome and specific theoretically relevant target variables) of the cognitive and behavioral treatments of depression.

## Summary

This chapter dealt with the matching of depressed inpatients to treatment. In the absence of controlled outcome studies in the literature, it was clear that any comments would be speculative. For this reason, a preliminary investigation was undertaken that was specific to one hospital inpatient unit. The results indicated that the usual inpatient treatment involved a smorgasbord of treatment components, but some patterns in the selection of certain components emerged. Patients tended to be treated with drugs–ECT and with problem solving–activity scheduling. Cognitive therapy was employed in two different ways: (a) after successful attempts to increase the patients' activity level and/or social interaction; and (b) during ECT treatment in an attempt to alter specific cognitions. The variables age, education, and "psychological mindedness" were seen as important variables for future consideration. More attention to the actual changes in the behaviors and cognitions of depressed patients is warranted.

# References

Beck, A. T. *Depression: Clinical, experimental and therapeutic aspects.* New York: Harper & Row, 1967.

Beck, A. T. *Cognitive therapy and the emotional disorders.* New York: International Universities Press, 1976.

Beck, A. T., Rush, A. J., Shaw, B. F., & Emery, G. *Cognitive therapy of depression.* New York: Guilford, 1979.

Beck, A. T., Ward, C. H., Mendelson, M., Mock, J., & Erbaugh, J. An inventory for measuring depression. *Archives of General Psychiatry,* 1961, *4,* 561–571.

Becker, J. *Depression: Theory and research.* Washington, D. C.: V. H. Winston and Sons, 1974.

Brawley, P., Lancee, W., Allon, R., & Brown, P. A simple method of monitoring behavior change in the ward. *Research Communications in Psychology, Psychiatry, and Behavior,* in press.

Brill, N. Q., & Storrow, H. A. Social class and psychiatric treatment. *Archives of General Psychiatry,* 1960, *3,* 340–344.

Coyne, J. C. Toward an interactional description of depression. *Psychiatry,* 1976, *39,* 28–40.

Diggory, J. *Self-evaluation: Concepts and studies.* New York: Wiley, 1966.

Dobson, K. D. *Assessing the interface between stress and depression:* A proposal. Unpublished Ph.D. dissertation, University of Western Ontario, 1980.

Dupue, R. A., & Monroe, S. M. The unipolar–bipolar distinction in the depressive disorders. *Psychological Bulletin,* 1978, *85,* 1001–1029.

Epstein, S. The self-concept revisited. *American Psychologist,* 1973, *28,* 404–416.

Eysenck, H. J., & Eysenck, S. B. G. *Eysenck Personality Inventory.* London: University of London Press, 1964.

Feighner, J. P., Robins, E., Guze, S. B., Woodruff, R. A., Winokur, G., & Munoz, R. Diagnostic criteria for use in psychiatric research. *Archives of General Psychiatry,* 1972, *26,* 57–63.

Fontana, A. F., & Dowds, B. N. Assessing treatment outcome: 1: Adjustment in the community. *Journal of Nervous and Mental Disease,* 1975, *161,* 221–230.

Frank, J. D. Therapeutic components of psychotherapy: A 25-year progress report of research. *The Journal of Nervous and Mental Disease,* 1974, *159,* 325–342.

Friedman, H. J. Patient-expectancy and symptom reduction. *Archives of General Psychiatry,* 1963, *8,* 61–67.

Fuchs, C. Z., & Rehm, L. P. A self-control behavior therapy program for depression. *Journal of Consulting and Clinical Psychology,* 1977, *45,* 206–215.

Garfield, S. L. Research on client variables in psychotherapy. In S. L. Garfield & A. E. Bergin (Eds.), *Handbook of psychotherapy and behavior change: An empirical analysis* (2nd ed.). New York: Wiley, 1978.

Giles, D. E. The cognitive triad: A test of the major assumption in Beck's cognitive theory of depression. Unpublished Ph.D. dissertation, University of Western Ontario, 1980.

Gioe, V. J. Cognitive modification and positive group experience as a treatment for depression. Unpublished Ph.D. dissertation, Temple University, 1975.

Hamilton, M. Standardized assessment and recording of depressive symptoms. *Psychiatric Neurologia, Neurochirurgic,* 1969, *72,* 201–205.

Heine, R. W., & Trosman, H. Initial expectations of the doctor–patient interaction as a factor in the continuance of psychotherapy. *Psychiatry,* 1960, *23,* 275–278.

Hollon, S. D., & Beck, A. T. Psychotherapy and drug therapy: Comparison and combinations. In S. L. Garfield & A. E. Bergin (Eds.), *Handbook of psychotherapy and behavior change: An empirical analysis* (2nd ed.). New York: Wiley, 1978.

Hollon, S. D., & Beck, A. T. The severity–chronicity scale. Unpublished manuscript, University of Pennsylvania, 1979.

Holmes, T. H., & Rahe, R. H. The social readjustment rating scale. *Journal of Psychosomatic Research,* 1967, *11,* 213–218.

Ilfeld, F. W. Current social stressors and symptoms of depression. *American Journal of Psychiatry,* 1977, *134,* 161–166.

Jones, R. A factored measure of Ellis' irrational belief systems with personality and maladjustment correlated. Unpublished Ph.D. dissertation, Texas Technological College, 1968.

Klerman, G. L., & Weissman, M. M. Personality as a predictor of outcome and treatment of depression. Paper presented at the meeting of the Eastern Psychological Association, New York, April 1976.

Lazarus, R. S., & Laurier, R. Stress-related transactions between person and environment. In L. A. Pervin & M. Lewis (Eds.), *Internal and external determinants of behavior.* New York: Plenum, 1978.

Leff, M. J., Roatch, J. F., & Bunney, W. E. Environmental factors preceding the onset of severe depression. *Psychiatry,* 1970, *33,* 293–311.

Lewinsohn, P. M. A behavior approach to depression. In R. J. Friedman & M. M. Katz (Eds.), *The psychology of depression: Contemporary theory and research.* New York: John Wiley and Sons, 1974.

Liberman, R. P., & Raskin, D. E. Depression: A behavioral formulation. *Archives of General Psychiatry,* 1971, *24,* 515–523.

Lick, J., & Bootzin, R. Expectancy factors in the treatment of fear: Methodological and theoretical issues. *Psychological Bulletin,* 1975, *82,* 917–931.

Loeb, A., Beck, A. T., & Diggory, J. Differential effects of success and failure on depressive and nondepressive patients. *Journal of Nervous and Mental Disease,* 1971, *152*(2), 106–114.

Marks, I. M. Behavioral psychotherapy of adult neurosis. In S. L. Garfield & A. E. Bergin (Eds.), *Handbook of psychotherapy and behavior change: An empirical analysis* (2nd ed.). New York: Wiley, 1978.

McLean, P. Therapeutic decision-making in the behavioral treatment of depression. In P. O. Davidson (Ed.), *The behavioral management of anxiety, depression and pain.* New York: Brunner/Mazel, 1976.

McLean, P., & Miles, J. E. Evaluation and the problem-oriented record in psychiatry. *Archives of General Psychiatry,* 1974, *31,* 622–625.

Morris, J. B., & Beck, A. T. The efficacy of antidepressant drugs: A review of research (1958 to 1972). *Archives of General Psychiatry,* 1974, *30,* 667–674.

Nelson, R. E. Irrational beliefs in depression. *Journal of Consulting and Clinical Psychology,* 1977, *45,* 1190–1197.

Paivio, A. Neomentalism. *Canadian Journal of Psychology,* 1976, *29,* 263–291.

Platt, J., & Spivack, G. Problem-solving thinking of psychiatric patients. *Journal of Consulting and Clinical Psychology,* 1972, *39,* 148–151.

Rehm, L. P., Fuchs, C. Z., Roth, D. M., Kornblith, S. J., & Romano, J. A comparison of self-control and social skills treatments of depression. *Behavior Therapy,* 1979, *10,* 429–442.

Rehm, L. P., & Kornblith, S. J. Behavior therapy for depression: A review of recent developments. In M. Hersen, R. M. Eisler, & P. M. Miller (Eds.), *Progress in behavior modification.* New York: Academic Press, 1979.

Ripley, H. S. Depression and the life span—epidemiology. In G. Usdin (Ed.), *Depression: Clinical, biological and psychological perspectives.* New York: Brunner/Mazel, 1977.

Rippere, V. Commonsense beliefs about depression and antidepressive behavior: A study of social consensus. *Behavior Research and Therapy,* 1977, *15,* 465–473.

Schless, A. O., Schwartz, L., Goetz, G., & Mendels, J. How depressives view the significance of their life events. *British Journal of Psychiatry,* 1974, *125,* 406–410.

Shaw, B. F. Comparison of cognitive therapy and behavior therapy in the treatment of depression. *Journal of Consulting and Clinical Psychology,* 1977, *45,* 543–551.

Shaw, B. F. Depression and stress: A cognitive perspective. In R. W. J. Neufeld (Ed.), *Psychological stress and psychopathology*. New York: McGraw-Hill, in press.

Shaw, B. F. The prediction of successful psychological treatment of depression: A pilot study. Manuscript in preparation, 1980.

Shaw, B. F., & Dobson, K. S. Cognitive assessment of depression. In T. V. Merluzzi, C. R. Glass, & M. Genest (Eds.), *Cognitive assessment*. New York: Guilford Press, in press.

Smith, M. J. *When I say no, I feel guilty*. New York: Dial Press, 1975.

Sloane, R. B., Staples, F. R., Cristol, A. H., Yorkston, N. J., & Whipple, K. *Psychotherapy versus behavior therapy*. Cambridge, Mass.: University Press, 1975.

Weed, L. L. Medical records that guide and teach. *New England Journal of Medicine*, 1968, *278*, 593–600.

Weissman, A. *The dysfunctional attitude scale*. Unpublished Ph.D. dissertation, University of Pennsylvania, 1978.

Weissman, M. M., Geanakoplos, E., & Prusoff, B. Social class and attrition in depressed outpatients. *Social Casework*, 1973, *54*, 162–170.

# 10

## A Model for Individualizing Treatment

ROBERT PAUL LIBERMAN

Clinical researchers in psychiatry and psychology are frequently urged to strive toward that happy day when their expanded data base will permit conclusions about which type of treatment is best for specific diagnostic groups of patients. With a variety of effective therapies now available for depression, it is understandable that behavior therapists have a strong desire to progress toward fitting the right behavioral techniques to the right depressed persons, using research evidence for rational clinical decision making. In my view, this ideal end point of clinical practice may be fatuous and unlikely to come to pass, because it overlooks the overarching importance of individual differences in depression. Contributing to these differences are varied causes of depression; sources maintaining symptoms and malfunctioning; patients' deficits, excesses, assets, and interpersonal resources; and patients' environments. These manifold differences between depressed persons override their commonalities and may require tailored and somewhat unique treatment approaches for each patient.

Indeed, therapeutics has been guided in most of medicine by an appreciation of and adherence to the special needs and responses of the individual patient. A brief inspection of the records of patients on a medical ward, all of whom may be suffering from congestive heart failure, will reveal various types and doses of digitalis preparations, a variety of diets, different levels and rates of ambulation and exercise, and different medications, including antihypertensive and anti-arrhythmia drugs and coronary vasodilators. Furthermore, even in patients who have similar regimens, the patterns by which the discrete components of the regimen were introduced over time will vary immensely across individuals. Another medical analogy is in the use of antibiotics in the treatment of infectious disease. While we know from *in vitro* studies that penicillin is bacteriocidal

231

for pneumococci, variations in bacterial sensitivities and resistances, host factors, immune responses, and allergic reactions require the clinician to determine empirically the best antibiotic, and the proper dose level and route of administration, with needed ancillary treatments for his individual patient.

Given the complexity of brain neurochemistry and neurophysiology—which easily matches the variability in individuals' life experiences—it is not surprising that the pharmacological approach to the treatment of patients with depression is likewise highly individualized. A search for a single common biochemical pathway linked with depression will be as illusory as the search for a single psychosocial cause or mechanism explaining depression. Certainly, some parameters, such as family history and symptom criteria, lead to the rational use of lithium, tricyclics, and monoamine oxidase inhibitors with targeted subgroups of depressives. However, drug treatment by an enlightened clinician will be guided more by empirical results—by changes noted in the patient's level of functioning, verbal and nonverbal behavior, and self-rating of depressive symptoms—than by the characteristics of the patient. Excerpts from a highly regarded text on psychopharmacology (Barchas, Berger, Cigramello, & Elliot, 1977) illustrate the empirical and individualized approach to the pharmacotherapy of depressed persons.

> If the depressed person has symptoms of psychosis, the patient should probably be treated with an antipsychotic. If the patient is extremely anxious, hostile, irritable, or agitated, an antipsychotic–tricyclic combination may be helpful. Prescribing both drugs separately allows for a flexible dosage ratio. The pattern of symptoms can help the physician choose among the available tricyclics. . . .
> It is difficult to judge the proper dose of tricyclics since the antidepressant effect takes about two weeks to appear in severe depression. Empirically, the dose should be increased gradually to near the maximal range or until the presence of unwanted side effects makes further increase in dose intolerable.

The authors go on to describe further interindividual variability and special conditions requiring a trial-and-error strategy in determining, for any one patient, the acute dosage, schedule of administration, maintenance dosage, and withdrawal of antidepressant medication. Thus, even when a generic type of antidepressant drug is found to be effective, the enormous interindividual variability in absorption, transport, binding, metabolism, excretion, and compliance make it necessary to individually tailor the drug regimen.

## Variability in Behavioral and Environmental Determinants of Depression

A person's experience and phenomenology of depression and responsiveness to treatment techniques will depend upon a multiplicity of past and present life events, reinforcement contingencies, behavioral repertoires, biological diathesis, and social networks. Lest we reify depression with our enthusiasm for a singular theoretical or therapeutic orientation, a brief excursion through current speculations on the "learning of depression" may sober us to the varied pathways and manifestations of what we refer to, in short-hand fashion, as depression.

The first step in understanding depressive phenomena from a behavioral or learning framework requires the therapist to specify those actions, verbal and nonverbal expressions, and behavioral deficits and excesses that are the criteria used to determine the presence of depression. The importance of this first step of charting the behavioral boundaries and dimensions of depression cannot be underestimated. Without a clear understanding and reliable agreement on what constitutes depression in observable terms, there cannot be a scientific analysis of causes and treatment effects. A multilevel or multidimensional evaluation of depressed persons includes their:

1. *Verbal statements* of dysphoria, self-depreciation, guilt, somatic complaints, and anhedonia.
2. *Nonverbal expressions*, such as lowered rates of smiling, vocal monotone, slouched posture, frowning, and whining.
3. *Distorted attitudes* and consistently negative and critical views of themselves, the future, and the world.
4. *Reduced rate of engaging in constructive, instrumental, and interpersonal behaviors*—grooming and self-care deficits, social withdrawal, lowered rates of talking, and diminution or cessation of work and tasks, household duties, and recreation.
5. *Increased rate of nonproductive activities*, such as pacing, rubbing of hands and face, and lying down.
6. Problems with *vegetative symptoms*—anorexia, constipation, insomnia (including changes in the sleep EEG), and loss of libido.
7. *Failure to respond to events, people, and items* that were previously reinforcing and pleasurable.
8. *Dream content and fantasy life* that contains masochistic and self-depreciative themes.

The individual's experiences at multiple levels of behavior, affect, cognition, physiology, and fantasy that operationally define depression are only the most obvious layers of complexity and variability in this syndrome. Another layer of variability between individuals with depression is the degree to which the multiple levels of experience coexist in a given case, thereby giving rise to different syndromes. Some depressed patients will have only cognitive and affective changes, while maintaining their premorbid level of overt behavioral function. Others will have a reduction in productive activity but will not verbally complain about their symptoms. Some, but not all, patients will experience vegetative symptoms. The patterns of symptom fluctuations will also vary from person to person, with some depressives finding little change in symptom intensity, while others swing from one extreme to the other. Even within the same depressed individual, one is not likely to note a constant affective level 24 hours a day, 7 days a week.

To further complicate depressive phenomena, each level of behavior, affect, physiology, and cognition may change with treatment at differing rates. Just as many phobics show diminution in behavioral avoidance of feared situations before diminution in felt anxiety, the same can be seen in some depressed individuals who show changes in productive and interpersonal behavior before experiencing much improvement in affective state. These phasic lags or inter-level latencies are important to observe in constructing individualized and changeable treatment programs. It is thus vital to have multiple measures and sources for the evaluation of change in depressed persons if we are to be prepared for treating the exigencies and evolving nature of their disorders.

While multilevel assessment and monitoring of depressives is vital to the therapeutic enterprise, reliable and valid specification of depressive phenomena are limited by our measurement tools and tactics, which are still in an early stage of development. Naturalistic observation, confederate tests, time-sampling behavioral codes, and standardized role-played test situations are infusions from behavior therapy that are adding new approaches to the still important, but older, methods of self-report inventories and structured inter-views. Assessment of an individual's environment through such recently de-veloped instruments as the Ward Atmosphere Scale, the Behavior Observation Instrument, the Reinforcement Survey Schedule, and the Pleasant Events Schedule adds another important dimension to behavioral analysis of depres-sion and to the development of individualized treatment programs.

Individual variability clearly exists for the panoply of behaviors, cognitions, affects, physiological symptoms, and fantasies experienced by a person labeled depressed; however, even greater individual differences—requiring specially formulated treatments—can be seen to arise from the multifarious ways that people "learn" to become depressed. Starting with the onset or acquisition of depression, environmental factors that can help to explain depressive reactions include a lowered rate of positive reinforcement for adaptive behaviors; model-ing of depressive behaviors; aversive or punishing experiences; and stimuli and symbolic events that have been associated in the past with unhappiness, sadness, or a reduction in activity level.

An important causative factor is thought to be a lowered rate of positive reinforcement from the environment. This can impinge on an individual through fewer potentially reinforcing events (e.g., when a person moves to a new locale or work situation where there are fewer potential interactions with friends, neighbors, coworkers, and supervisors) as well as a reduction in the real availability of reinforcement (e.g., when a person experiences loss of interper-sonal contacts through separation, divorce, death, or forced isolation). The most important type of reinforcer deficiency for the onset of depression is a decrease in social or interpersonal interaction. This is illustrated in the case of depressions precipitated by job promotions where status, prestige, and financial rewards increase but where, at the same time, there are fewer opportunities to gain supportive and positive reactions from those higher in the organization and there are greater demands to give support and help to those below in the organization. The ratio of social reinforcement received to that given can decrease with job promotions. A similar situation can occur with the motherhood role, where the ratio of attention received from others to attention given to others may shift downward. Since life changes such as job promotions and motherhood are accompanied by variable response-reinforcement contingencies, even susceptible individuals may not encounter potential or actual decrements in social reinforcement. Lewinsohn and his colleagues (Lewinsohn, 1975), marshaling evidence to support the role of response-contingent positive reinforcement in the genesis of depression, suggest that low rates of reinforcement result in low rates of constructive behavior and concomitant symptoms and negative feelings about oneself and one's environment.

Modeling of depressive behaviors by others also is likely to produce aspects of depression in relevant observers. The factors that combine to facilitate observational learning include similarity and interpersonal closeness between model and observer, status and reinforcement given to the model, possession by the observer of the requisite component behaviors being modeled, attentional mechanisms, and reinforcement provided to the observer when imitation does occur. The occasional reports of suicide epidemics in institutions are examples of imitative learning. In a study of repeated suicide attempters, it was found that each patient had a close relative or friend who had made a suicide attempt prior to the initial attempt by the patient (Liberman & Eckman, 1980).

Aversive and traumatic events can evoke depressive reactions, such as in the "learned helplessness" model (Seligman, Klein, & Miller, 1976). However, it should be noted that threats, bodily assaults, or physical illness must be persistent or prolonged, and not isolated incidents, to produce depressive behaviors. Punishing experiences are also characteristically accompanied by a loss or lowered rate of positive social reinforcement.

Depressive reactions can come under stimulus control whereby an event or locale symbolizes and reminds the individual of a past period of grief, helplessness, sadness, or depression. The anniversary of the death of a loved one or a return to the site of unhappy experiences can evoke mood changes that, given other factors of susceptibility and reinforcement loss, can escalate into a full-blown clinical episode of depression.

In the temporal sequence of events, it may be assumed that the types of environmental antecedents described in the preceding paragraphs can evoke or elicit depressive symptoms, such as sadness, insomnia, anxiety, anorexia, and reduced activity levels (Liberman & Raskin, 1971; Lewinsohn, 1975). These elicited behaviors are then likely to lead to cognitively mediated self-statements, such as "I am weak, sick, depressed, unhappy, helpless, or bad";

"The world is bleak, threatening, and rejecting"; and "The future is hopeless, grim, and not worth living for." Through self-attribution with distorted negative views of the evoked affective changes, individuals tend to exaggerate their faults and the obstacles in their path. This verbal labeling of affect magnifies the dysphoria and instigates further decrements in feelings and performance (Beck, 1976).

Beck and his colleagues, who have amassed data bearing on the role of cognitions in depression, posit that the negative thinking patterns by which depressed persons view themselves, the future, and the world are developed throughout childhood and adolescence when the maturing individual is exposed to frequent critical evaluation by significant others. The individuals adopt these highly critical standards as their own through the normal social learning processes, with the result being persons who get little reward in life because they are constantly debasing their performances.

Continuing our speculative odyssey from the acquisition to the maintenance of depression, the vicious cycle of dysphoria, negative self-statements, and greater dysphoria may be fueled by the attention, concern, sympathy, and nurturance provided to depressed persons by their relatives, friends, physicians, and other "helpers." The positive social reinforcement of depressive affect and verbal and nonverbal expressiveness can put the depression into a maintenance phase that can become a chronic, persistent problem. Iatrogenic factors may contribute to the chronicity of depression when medical personnel focus on the depressive symptoms or persistently investigate physical explanations for the symptoms. Another element in the maintenance of depression is the social withdrawal and isolation that occurs, principally as a result of anhedonia, social anxiety, and self-attribution of worthlessness, hopelessness, and negative world views. Isolation and alienation from others produce even greater obstacles to reconstituting interpersonal sources of reinforcement for adaptive behaviors and positive verbalizations. Social alienation also moves into a vicious cycle, because the depressed individual fails to provide reinforcement to friends and relatives and thus gradually tends to be avoided. As the isolation from others becomes greater, the individual becomes more unpleasant as a companion, which in turn leads to mutual avoidance and further isolation.

Figure 10.1 is a diagram of the environmental process that, given our current understanding of the disorder, might be considered as relevant to the evocation and maintenance of depressive behaviors. This diagram, while seemingly complex, actually oversimplifies the dynamic flux among premorbid and current behavior, coping style, and environmental factors that account for the considerable inter- and intraindividual variation found in depression. Even the most elaborate behavioral and interactional observation codes are not likely to capture the subtle nuances in the behavioral–environmental interchanges that serve as modifiers of depressive phenomena. The content of any one person's depressive feelings and behavior is also an outcome of the individual's idiosyncratic familial, cultural, and personal premorbid experiences. For example,

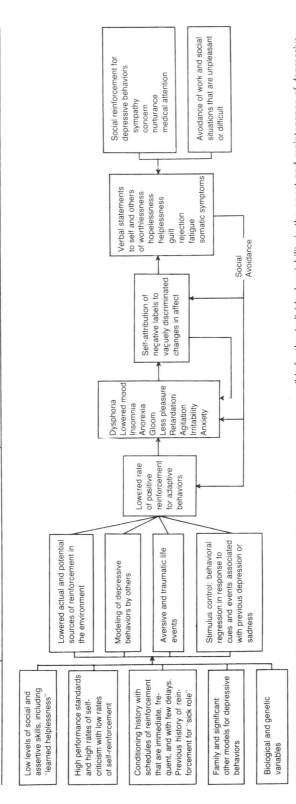

**FIGURE 10.1.** Diagram of the environmental antecedents and consequences responsible for the individual variability in the onset and maintenance of depressive behaviors. (Adapted from P. M. Lewinsohn, The behavioral study and treatment of depression. In M. Hersen, R. Eisler, & P. Miller (Eds.). *Progress in Behavior Modification* (Vol. 1). New York: Academic Press, 1975. )

individuals tend to fall back to anachronistic responses that successfully pro-
cured reinforcement in the past during childhood or at the times of real physical
illnesses.

## Formulating Treatment Strategies to Meet Diversity in Depression

Interindividual diversity among depressed persons has important implications for the design of treatment programs. To review, diversity stems from
variations in the multilevel phenomenology of depressive components; from variations in the acquisition and maintenance of depressive components; from
differences in history, personal assets, and resources that serve as sources of
vulnerability to depression; and from variations in the depressed person's
environmental dynamics and social support network. These sources for diversity are outlined in Table 10.1, together with their implications for treatment. Full
appreciation of the diverse potentialities for the development, manifestation,
and course of depressive phenomena—including interactions among biological, behavioral, and environmental influences—suggests that therapeutic interventions must be flexibly responsive to the varied needs of the individual
depressed person. In the many forms of depression with differential antecedents and courses, most experienced clinicians would agree that some combination of underlying organic disorder, social skills deficits, lack of engagement in constructive and rewarding activities, and cognitive distortion may be
implicated. But the balance or the amount of the variance in each clinical case

**TABLE 10.1**
Sources of Diversity in Depression That Have Functional Ties
to the Choice of Treatment Intervention

| Level or dimension | Example | Treatment implication |
| --- | --- | --- |
| Biological–genetic | Bipolar manic–depres-sive phenomena | Use of lithium |
| Subjective affect | Presence of anxiety | Use of anxiety management or desensi-tization |
| Motor behavior | Anergic apathy and idle-ness | Graded assignments with positive feed-back |
| Cognitive | Negative self–evalua-tions | Cognitive therapy |
| Social compe-tence | Unable to ask others to help or assist self | Social skills or assertion training |
| Social network | Presence of concerned spouse | Involvement of spouse in couple therapy |
| Vocational | Depression precipitated by job promotion | Target changes in work setting |
| Social system | Pension for disability due to depression | Changing social security regulations to provide incentives for rehabilitation |

that is accounted for by each of the implicated factors may be different for every case and next to impossible to determine at the start of treatment.

One option for designing treatment that takes into account individual differences is to construct a comprehensive therapeutic package that incorporates key interventions aimed at remediating most problem areas. For example, a broad-spectrum approach that might be suitable for the needs of a majority of depressed patients could emphasize (a) reengagement of the depressed individual in constructive and rewarding activities in order to increase the level of response-contingent positive reinforcement; (b) specific training in skills in which the client is deficient, focusing specifically on social skills, because social interaction has been shown to be a powerfully reinforcing activity and depressives have been shown to be generally deficient in this area; and (c) changes in the way the depressive thinks about and construes his or her own performance and standards of self-reward.

One might postulate that different components of this broad-spectrum treatment approach will satisfy the needs of depressives having different developmental histories. For example, the social skills training portion of the package may be the active ingredient for depressives who have a history of social inadequacy predating their first depressive episodes. On the other hand, reengagement in constructive and rewarding activities, or cognitive restructuring, may be the crucial component of the treatment strategy for those depressives who, having previously made adequate social adjustments, now are at an impasse born of apathy or irrational attitudes.

The comprehensive, broad-spectrum approach to treating depressed patients has wide appeal. It satisfies the proponents of each of the major theoretical schools within the behavioral camp, since it draws component techniques from each of them. In fact, most of the published reports of behavioral treatment of depression, both controlled and case studies, utilize a comprehensive, multicomponent approach, despite the highlighting of one or another of the techniques by the authors (Biglan & Dow, chapter 4, this volume). An example of a systematic and purposeful effort to formulate and evaluate a comprehensive, broad-spectrum approach was carried out by Harpin (1978) with chronic depressives who had been unresponsive to drugs and psychotherapy. By way of illustration, Harpin's multicomponent treatment program is described in Table 10.2. Since so many techniques are brought to bear on the varied needs of depressed patients, it is not surprising that most of the published accounts of broad-spectrum behavior therapy proffer favorable outcomes.

While the broad-spectrum treatment approach is attractive because of its potentially wide applicability and likely efficacy, it is costly in terms of time, training of personnel, and multidimensional evaluation of ongoing progress. For example, the package used by Harpin requires a psychologist or other well-trained professional who has wide experience in behavior therapy and who can offer two treatment sessions a week for at least 2 months. At that, given the successful outcomes in only half of his chronic depressives, Harpin thought that

**TABLE 10.2**
Outline of the Components in a Broad-Spectrum Behavioral Treatment Procedure for
Chronically Depressed Psychiatric Outpatients[a]

A. *Self-Monitoring of Pleasant Events and Constructive Activities*
  1. Use of structured diary with limited response requirements
  2. Diary developed from patient's responses to assessment battery, premorbid functioning, and desired goals of therapy
  3. Regular prompts for keeping diary and completing graded assignments
  4. Positive feedback for responses in diary
    a. From significant other
    b. From therapist at sessions

B. *Improving Contingencies of Social Attention*
  1. Reach consensus between patient and significant other after giving rationale
  2. Instruct on ignoring depressive verbal and nonverbal behaviors
  3. Instruct on attending to constructive and positive verbal and motor behaviors
  4. Use behavior rehearsal (role playing) and modeling by therapist to demonstrate appropriate ignoring and attending contingencies
  5. Prestructured treatment sessions so that depressive and sick-role talk is permitted during the final 10 minutes only

C. *Self-Control and Cognitive Behavior Change*
  1. Contingency self-management. Use symptomatic and depressive behaviors to contingently reinforce adaptive, lower frequency behaviors (during initial period when depressive behaviors are occurring at a high rate). A diary is constructed to provide monitoring of these self-instigated contingencies
  2. *Cognitive therapy*
    a. Teach self-instructional procedures in areas of Beck's cognitive triad (views of self, world, and future) via Meichenbaum technique
    Overt modeling by therapist
    Overt practice by patient (loud then soft)
    Covert practice by patient
    Homework assignments to practice positive self-statements
    b. Use of logical argumentative and confrontational techniques to convince patient that negative thinking patterns are incorrect
    c. Thought-stopping or massed practice for persistent negative thoughts and suicide thoughts

D. *Training in Social Skills*
  1. Involve relative or significant other where possible
  2. Give homework assignments and consequate with positive feedback
  3. Goals of training to include: assertion, giving affection and acknowledgment to others, requests for assistance (delegating responsibility), expressing anger and requesting changes in the behavior of others, and handling situations where the social attention contingencies are for depressive talk and behavior.

E. *Anxiety Management Training* (when necessary)

[a]From R. E. Harpin, A psychosocial treatment for depression. Unpublished doctoral dissertation, Department of psychology, State University of New York at Stony Brook, 1978.

many more treatment sessions were needed for difficult cases. The broad-spectrum approach also is intrusive and encumbers the patient with many interventions and assignments, some of which may not be necessary or applicable. An alternative to the broad-spectrum approach, but one that still meets the varied needs of individuals who are depressed, is a modular strategy in which the therapist uses flexible levels of intervention depending upon the response of the patient.

## Modular Strategy for Treatment of Depression

The modular approach starts with the assumption that "less is better than more treatment." Interventions and sessions are limited to only those required to bring about improvement satisfactory to the patient and possibly his or her relatives. The full array of problem-specific treatment techniques are available to the clinician in the modular approach; however, they are selected and implemented only when the patient's specific problems or lack of response to previous interventions calls for them. The cognitive, contingency, self-control, pleasurable activities, anxiety management, and social skills training methods are tailored to the individual case. The preliminary assessment as well as ongoing feedback provided by the patient's response to treatment guide the therapist in deciding which components of the broad-spectrum approach to utilize with the individual case and how much time and emphasis to place on each of the chosen components.

This modular approach to treatment is congruent with the process of most clinical endeavors in medicine, psychiatry, and psychology. It follows the Hippocratic imperative to do no harm to the patient. It gives maximum influence to the patient in the therapy process because, each time a choice point is reached regarding the utilization of an additional module, the patient participates fully in the decision making. Thus, there are many more opportunities for active involvement by the patient in deciding the type, duration, and outcomes of therapy. With such a strategy, advantages also accrue to the therapist who self-consciously and regularly must evaluate and review clinical progress; consider treatment alternatives for goals and methods; and question whether or not he or she has something of value to offer the patient. This empirical approach to therapy is depicted in Figure 10.2.

### Initial Modules

How might this modular approach be adapted and used with depressed patients? The flowchart in Figure 10.3 outlines the first few decision points facing the therapist who begins to evaluate and treat a depressed person. The initial visit or contact, whether it be in a clinic, mental health center, or private

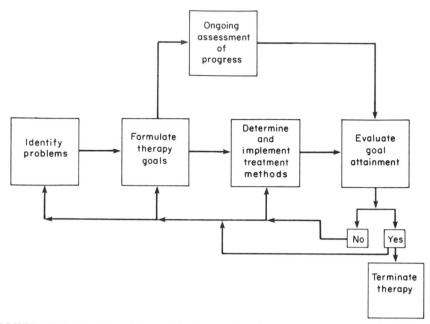

**FIGURE 10.2.** Flowchart of the empirical approach to the treatment of clinical problems. When clinical goals are attained, therapist and patient consider termination or working on additional problems and goals.

office, is consumed with a variety of tasks. Regardless of one's theoretical and clinical orientation, the first session usually includes history taking, relationship building, ventilation of feelings and symptoms, and evaluation of the extent and severity of the problem.

Many times, especially in cases of mild disorders where depressive symptoms are precipitated by transient situational events, the first visit may suffice as an intervention in itself. We know from research done on the process of psychotherapy that significant symptomatic relief occurs between the time a patient enters a waiting room and the time he or she leaves after being interviewed by a clinic secretary; thus, it should not be surprising that some patients with mild depressions can be sufficiently helped through the clarification, catharsis, and hopefulness of an evaluation interview.

If the clinician, at the time of the initial session, deems the depression severe or life threatening, a choice point is reached for the utilization of hospitalization and antidepressant medication. While hospitalization is not included as a choice point in Figure 10.3, it is an important consideration at the time of the screening evaluation. Drug therapy may be avoided if the patient has previously received drugs and experienced severe side effects or has a medical condition such as cardiac or renal disease for which the use of tricyclic drugs is contraindicated. If the decision to use antidepressant drugs is made, another question arises of whether the drug therapy should be given alone, with perhaps only supportive

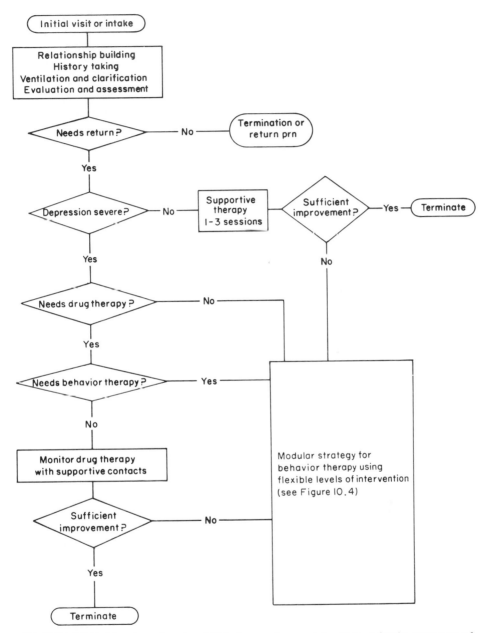

**FIGURE 10.3.** Flowchart depicting initial phases of a modular strategy for the treatment of depression.

contacts, or be accompanied by systematic behavior therapy. The best criterion for making the decision comes from the work of Weissman and Paykel (1974), who found suggestive evidence that patients with social skill deficits prior to becoming depressed might require some form of psychosocial therapy beyond drug therapy for satisfactory clinical outcomes.

In the case where a patient needs more than one visit but is not thought to be severely enough depressed to warrant the use of medication, two alternatives exist. One is to begin a modular course of behavior therapy; the other is to continue with another one to three supportive therapy sessions with opportunities for the patient to abreact, complain about symptoms, and receive esteem, warmth, and concern from the therapist. From an economical point of view, and without evidence on the differential effectiveness of behavior therapy in preventing or forestalling relapses, the choice probably would be to offer supportive therapy for another few sessions. That is all that might be necessary to help a person through a brief and mild depression occasioned by some life event or loss. If behavior therapy is chosen with or without concomitant drug therapy, the clinician can draw treatment modules from the techniques developed in the past 10 years and described as promising in a literature still marked more by clinical enthusiasm than by hard, controlled data.

## Initial and Ongoing Assessment

Whether drug therapy, supportive therapy, or behavior therapy is offered to a depressed person, a basic requirement for the empirically based, modular strategy outlined in this chapter is a thorough initial assessment and ongoing evaluation of the patient's progress. An initial assessment can help the clinician in the stepwise decision-making process from minimum to maximum levels of intervention. For example, if a patient presents with a severe depression and a family history of depression, a decision might be made to offer drug therapy with the speculation that genetic–biological influences are involved. If the initial assessment uncovers a marked paucity of recreational and leisure time activities, the clinician might set goals and give graded assignments to develop such outlets. If the patient shows social withdrawal, scores low on assertiveness questionnaires, and has progressed through earlier modules without satisfactory clinical benefit, a decision might be made to offer social skills training.

The initial assessment, in addition to the conventional social and psychiatric history, should include measures of the extent and intensity of the depression— measures that can be used repeatedly throughout therapy as a way of gauging progress. A patient may complain of subjective symptoms of depression (e.g., hopelessness, loss of confidence, anxiety, sadness) with or without concurrent vegetative symptoms (e.g., sleep interruptions, loss of appetite and weight, loss of libido) and behavioral changes (e.g., psychomotor retardation, social withdrawal). Before developing priorities for treatment intervention, the clinician must first survey the patient's presenting deficits, excesses, and assets. This initial step in a behavioral analysis can lead to guidelines for where and how to institute treatment. Depressive behaviors include a variety of overt motor, cognitive–verbal, and physiological–biological events. The measurement of components in each of these behavioral classes will help to guide the therapist in prioritizing treatment procedures and monitoring their effects.

There are a number of psychometrically sound measures that are convenient and easy to use by clinicians: Beck Depression Inventory, Zung Self-Rating Depression Scale, Hopkins Symptom Checklist, Raskin Rating Scale for Depression, and Hamilton Rating Scale. The clinician can use one or more of these scales to monitor the patient's symptomatic changes as time passes, thereby obtaining information necessary for deciding, with the patient, when treatment should be continued, altered, tapered, or terminated. The crucial importance of initial and ongoing assessment of the symptomatic status of the patient cannot be overemphasized. Without a firm and reliable data base—even one based solely on the self-report of the patient—we become too easily captives of our theories and soon forget that what we perceive happening in therapy may be full-blown projections of our minds.

Besides an ongoing measure of symptomatic status, the clinician utilizing the modular treatment strategy will want to have other measures, at the time of initial evaluation and for repeated monitoring, that tap such dimensions as available reinforcers (e.g., a reinforcement survey), the family's emotional climate (e.g., the Camberwell Family Interview), the patient's range and amount of activity (e.g., behavioral diaries or logs), social adjustment (e.g., ratings from the patient and significant others), and assertiveness (e.g., the Rathus Assertiveness Scale).

### Behavior Therapy Modules

A flowchart depicting the decision points of a stepwise, minimum-to-maximum use of behavioral modules in the treatment of depression is shown in Figure 10.4. The discussion that follows would be equally applicable to patients who are being treated with behavior therapy alone or in combination with drugs. At each choice point in the progress of the patient through the behavior therapy modules, the therapist and patient should review the amount of improvement gained and decide whether additional therapy is needed. The informational resources the therapist can use in making decisions include (a) the changes occurring in the patient's symptoms and other behavioral and social measures, and (b) the available techniques that have been reported to be helpful to depressed patients.

PROBLEM FORMULATION AND GOAL SETTING

Before introducing more complex and time-consuming techniques, the therapist should begin with one to three sessions using a problem-solving focus. The patient is helped to view his or her problems, including symptoms, not as hopeless burdens but rather as challenges to cope with and overcome. The first step in this process is to identify the problems—the symptoms, functional

**Figure 10.4.** Flowchart depicting the modular use of behavioral techniques in the treatment of depression. Sufficient improvement can be determined by multiple methods and sources of assessment. The sequence of modules in the large box does not necessarily reflect priorities of temporal ordering of treatment.

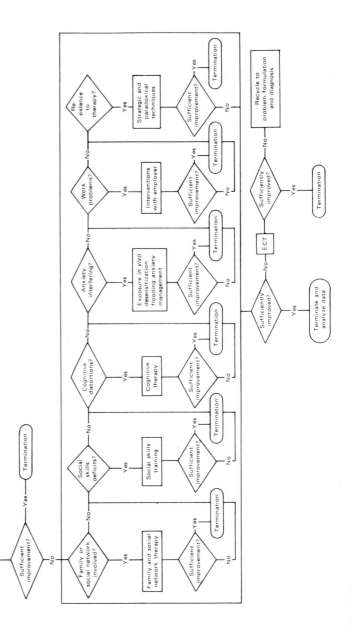

impairments, and their antecedents and consequences. It is important for the therapist to help the patient to describe the problems in the patient's terms and then, afterward, to translate feelings and concerns into behavioral terms. The focus is on pinpointing what the patient is doing and saying and the environmental context. In a collaborative fashion and a spirit of inquiry, the patient and therapist together ask the following questions:

- Which problems are interfering most with the patient's functioning? (E.g., if the person is self-destructive, the immediate priority may be hospitalization and close supervision; if the person is about to lose a cherished job, then the immediate intervention may be intercession with employer or behavioral rehearsal of a scene with job supervisor aimed at obtaining sick leave.)
- Which problems are most responsible for the patient's being maintained in a state of depression? (E.g., a patient with chronic depression whose symptoms are being reinforced by a sympathetic relative may have immediate need for intervention with the relative to change the reinforcement contingencies.)
- Which assets, if strengthened, can serve as a wedge toward breaking the depressive cycle? (E.g., if a person has had good social relationships that have been recently dormant, the therapist may initially aim at social skills training that reconstitutes these relationships.)
- What are the most practical means that can produce the desired changes in this individual? (E.g., manipulation of the environment or the self-attitudes of the client.)

Once some problem definition has occurred, the therapist helps the patient set goals for the therapy. The therapist asks the patient for possible alternative behaviors to those currently producing an impasse. The therapist also suggests alternatives for the patient's evaluation. Questions are asked, such as "What would you like to do that you're not now doing?"; "How would you like your everyday life to be different from the way it is now?"; "What changes would you like to make in your routines and relationships?"; "How might you cope with the problems confronting you?" In the problem-solving approach, generating alternatives is accompanied by evaluating their probable consequences or outcomes. Once the pros and cons of the various alternatives for dealing with the problem are evaluated, the therapist assists the patient to choose one that seems reasonable.

Problem formulation and goal setting can provide the necessary impetus for the patient to cope better and get symptomatic improvement sufficient for termination. The problem-solving approach can be carried out in a total of three to seven sessions, including the initial visits. It should be noted that the median number of visits made by outpatients to community mental health centers around the country is six. An open-ended problem-solving group was run for 5 years in a community mental health center as a front-line, first-step clinical service for a wide variety of patients presenting with crises, anxieties, depression, and family problems. Most patients achieved their goals and experienced significant symptomatic improvement within six weekly sessions. A brief therapy course such as the one just described is obviously cost effective and will often be sufficient with patients who come to therapy with many assets and a good premorbid adjustment.

CONTINGENCY MANAGEMENT AND SELF-CONTROL

For those patients who need additional therapy beyond the problem-solving phase, the therapist can use attention and praise as contingent reinforcers for adaptive verbalizations during the therapy session and for reports of attempting homework assignments between therapy sessions. The therapist will be able to use the already established positive therapeutic alliance in a contingent manner to strengthen assets and to help the patient accomplish goals that were selected during the earlier problem-formulating module. Thus, the contingency management and problem-formulating modules interlock in a natural way. If the patient is hospitalized because of functional incapacity or suicidal risk, contingencies can be used that stem from hospital privileges and from social reinforcement by the entire interdisciplinary staff. By using graded assignments for adaptive behavior coupled with positive feedback, the therapist ensures that instructions are given clearly, specifically, affirmatively, and with the structuring of positive expectations for success. At times, this must be accomplished in subtle ways, including the use of paradoxical instructions. Shaping is also kept in mind as this module progresses.

While the therapist is using his therapeutic relationship as a contingent reinforcer for the reestablishment of positive speech and activities as alternatives to depressive behaviors, the patient can also be taught to use self-control methods to increase desired behaviors and interactions. One such method is to make the patient's performance of highly probable behavior (e.g., withdrawal to bed, smoking, being alone) contingent upon the patient's first engaging in positive, desirable, but less likely self-statements or activities. Another method is self-monitoring, self-evaluation, and self-reinforcement with an emphasis on monitoring positive events and setting realistic attainable behavioral goals that would be expected to reduce depressive affect. These self-control procedures are described more fully in a review article by Rehm and Kornblith (1979). This module might continue as long as good progress is being made, with termination for satisfactory improvement occurring after perhaps 2–10 sessions.

BEHAVIORAL FAMILY THERAPY

Family therapy would be appropriate for patients who have not made progress after a few sessions of contingency management and self-control and whose family interactions might conceivably be maintaining the depressive behaviors. In a heuristic study, Vaughn and Leff (1976) found that depressed patients relapsed much more often when they were living with a key relative who made two or more critical remarks about them during a 90-minute Camberwell

Family Interview. The susceptibility of depressed patients to criticism appears to be greater than that of schizophrenics. Thus, in cases where a Camberwell Family Interview is conducted at the time of intake, patients at high risk for relapse can be identified and their relatives encouraged to engage in family therapy.

The family or marital therapy itself can proceed along several flexible levels of intervention, ranging from simple instructions to relatives to provide differential attention for adaptive and depressive behaviors to such instructions plus social and recreational activities, communication skills training, and contingency contracting. The use of minimum to maximum levels of intervention in behavioral marital therapy is illustrated in three publications (Liberman & Roberts, 1976; Liberman, Wheeler, DeVisser, Kuehnel, & Kuehnel, 1980; Liberman, Wheeler, & Sanders, 1976), one of which (Liberman & Roberts, 1976) details a case study with a depressed woman.

OTHER MODULES

A variety of other behavioral methods—cognitive therapy, anxiety management techniques, social skills training, and paradoxical or strategic methods—have been well described in the literature, and varying amounts of evidence support their efficacy. The decision to utilize any one of these techniques would be made on the basis of insufficient progress from previous modules and information regarding specific deficits of the patient that could be remediated by the technique.

The decision points for these modules are shown in Figure 10.4 as having equal significance; however, only the accumulation of empirical experience with large numbers of depressed patients can indicate how often and how valuable any one of these techniques might be. For example, while it appears that a sizable majority of depressed patients demonstrate the cognitive distortions described by Beck (1970), it does not necessarily follow that all such patients would require a full course of specific cognitive therapy for relieving their depression. Some of these patients might improve sufficiently with five sessions of ventilation, catharsis, and problem formulating and goal setting. Others might improve sufficiently with the addition of a few sessions of contingency management. When a patient continues to show cognitive distortions and to remain depressed and in need of further therapy, then the use of the cognitive therapy approach would be more strongly indicated. Similarly, the use of the other techniques currently in vogue for depression might not be required unless the patient does not respond well to initial treatment. It should be clear that a modular approach to behavior therapy for depression offers a more stringent test of the efficacy of any one technique than does the use of a variety of these techniques from the very start of a patient's professional contact. As time passes and experience with a modular strategy accumulates, both individual clinicians and the research community can "shake down" the various modules and adapt and evolve new techniques that can be expected to have greater impact on depressive behaviors.

Strategic or paradoxical therapy techniques deserve a special note because they can be employed together with other more straightforward behavior therapies to enhance cooperation and commitment and increase compliance with instructions and assignments. As we develop a wider body of techniques for depression, we learn that the discovery of what people need to do to overcome their problems is not the most difficult clinical task. Getting people to do what they need to do is the most difficult task. We now possess a group of prescriptive methods that, if followed properly by the patient, can yield meaningful improvement. But, as any experienced behavior therapist will admit, it is getting patients to do what is prescribed that usually provides the challenges to therapeutic acumen. These techniques have been described in a number of publications (Haley, 1967, 1973; Johnson & Alevizos, 1975; Minuchin, 1974).

CHOOSING APPROPRIATE MODULES

The depiction of the various behavior therapy modules in Figure 10.4 in the horizontal sequence does not denote a preferential ordering of each module's utility or priority of presentation. Figure 10.4 is presented as a hypothetical starting point for empirical testing. Even the suggestion that a contingency management and self-control module be used prior to other modules is offered as a speculative leap into the proposed modular approach. It is conceivable that a different module—say, cognitive therapy—may be more useful than the contingency management and self-control module. The use of a module with a patient and its temporal priority in the therapeutic sequence would be determined by (a) the specific needs of each patient as elucidated by the initial behavioral assessment and ongoing monitoring of progress; (b) the empirically documented efficacy of any one module in the hands of the service provider as well as in the literature; and (c) the cost and intrusiveness of any one module. It is also important to keep in mind that, within each module, considerable individualization will be necessary to fit the interventions to each case.

As clinical and research experience accumulates with the use of a modular approach to the behavioral treatment of depression, the utility of each module for remediating the specific deficits of an individual as well as for improving symptoms and mood will become more evident. For example, it may be found that social skills training is effective in helping depressed persons establish social relationships but not much good for improving symptomatic state. The number of patients exposed to each module should clarify the types of deficits that depressed persons have; furthermore, the modular approach should make clearer the need for additional treatment modules addressing deficits and problems that our current behavioral technology does not cover. By weeding out the less seriously depressed patients and those who would respond favorably to nonspecific factors in therapy, the modular strategy provides a more stringent test of the efficacy of each of the constituent treatment interventions.

## Summary

The behavioral formulation of depression derives from the intensive study of an individual's depressive behaviors as they interact with socioenvironmental antecedents and consequences. Emphasis is placed on the empirical and reliable measurement of multiple levels of depressive phenomena from methods including clinical interviews, rating scales, self-reports, and objective observation in natural settings. A lowered rate, range, or amount of social reinforcement for adaptive behavior and aversive experiences are the antecedent conditions that may evoke depressive affect and behaviors. Self-attribution of negative labels, social withdrawal, and reinforcement for depressive speech and actions may be responsible for the maintenance of depression. Differential susceptibility of individuals in developing depressive reactions to reinforcement loss and traumatic or aversive experiences may be accounted for by deficits in premorbid social and assertion skills, a history of high rate schedules of social reinforcement, and learned helplessness. Behavioral analysis involves accepting and capitalizing upon the fact of individual differences by studying the depressed person's symptom picture in its functional relationship to its environmental antecedents and consequences. With manifold behavioral–learning principles potentially affecting an individual's susceptibility to and development and continuance of depression, it is to be expected that a range of necessary but not sufficient factors will explain the onset and remission of depressive behaviors from person to person.

While biological factors undoubtedly play a part in the onset and maintenance of depression, there are interactions among biological–behavioral–environmental variables that are complex and governed by as yet unknown homeostatic feedback systems. The behavioral approach can help us avoid the pitfall of searching for unitary concepts in understanding and treating depression, because the social learning paradigm points to the tremendous importance of individual differences and an open-ended, inductive orientation toward treatment. Depressions are likely to be constituted differently for each person. That is, some combination of social skills deficits, lack of engagement in constructive and rewarding activities, and cognitive distortion may be implicated in all or most cases of chronic depression; however, the balance, amount, interactions, and etiological significance contributed by each of these factors may be different for every case.

We may never be able to specify to clinicians which behavioral technique to use with which cases showing which prognostic indicators and subject characteristics. Rather, the clinician may have to enter upon each case with a comprehensive, multidimensional, and modular treatment strategy in hand and adjust the timing and amount of emphasis given to each module in response to the preliminary assessment of the patient's problems and deficits and the ongoing feedback gleaned from the patient's cumulative response to treatment. We should aim to generate a variety of interventions, pharmacological as well as psychosocial, that we can apply sequentially with continuing monitoring of the responses of the depressed patient on multiple levels of behavioral expression and experience. A modular strategy for the treatment of depressed persons, using flexible levels of intervention to meet the specific needs of each individual, is presented in this chapter. The strategy is built upon the importance of individual differences in how depression is acquired and maintained and in responsiveness to treatment. Modular treatment proceeds with clinical decisions being made on the basis of assessing each patient's assets, symptoms, and deficits and measuring relevant ongoing symptoms and behaviors while various therapeutic interventions are sequentially applied and withdrawn.

It is unlikely that any one set of general principles will ever satisfactorily explain the onset, duration, and remission of depression. We may have to accept the overriding fact of individual differences and learn to tolerate the likelihood that, for the range of individuals presenting with depression, many different biological and environmental factors are responsible and many different biological and environmental treatment interventions will be necessary.

# References

Barchas, J. D., Berger, P. A., Ciaramello, R. D., & Elliot, G. R. (Eds.), *Psychopharmacology: From theory to practice*. New York: Oxford University Press, 1977.

Beck, A. T. *Cognitive therapy and the emotional disorders*. New York: International University Press, 1976.

Beck, A. T. Cognitive therapy: Nature and relation to behavior therapy. *Behavior Therapy*, 1970, *1*, 184–200.

Haley, J. *Strategies of psychotherapy*. New York: Grune & Stratton, 1967.

Haley, J. *Uncommon therapy: The psychiatric techniques of Milton H. Erickson*. New York: Norton, 1973.

Harpin, R. E. A psychosocial treatment for depression. Unpublished doctoral dissertation, Department of Psychology, State University of New York at Stony Brook, 1978.

Johnson, S. M., & Alevizos, P. N. Strategic therapy: A systematic outline of procedures. Paper presented at the Ninth Annual Conference of the Association for the Advancement of Behavior Therapy, San Francisco, 1975.

Lewinsohn, P. M. The behavioral study and treatment of depression. In Hersen, M., Eisler, R., & Miller, P. (Eds.), *Progress in Behavior Modification* (Vol. 1). New York: Academic Press, 1975.

Liberman, R. P., & Eckman, T. Behavior therapy vs. insight-oriented therapy for repeated suicide attempters. Manuscript under editorial review, 1980.

Liberman, R. P., & Raskin, D. E. Depression: A behavioral formulation. *Archives of General Psychiatry*, 1971, *24*, 515–523.

Liberman, R. P., & Roberts, J. Contingency management of neurotic depression and marital disharmony. In H. Eysenck (Ed.), *Case studies in behavior therapy*. London: Routledge and Kegan Paul, 1976.

Liberman, R. P., Wheeler, E., DeVisser, L., Kuehnel, J., & Kuehnel, T. *Handbook of marital therapy*. New York: Plenum, 1980.

Liberman, R. P., Wheeler, E., & Sanders, N. Behavioral therapy for marital disharmony. *Journal of Marriage and Family Counseling*, 1976, *2*, 383–390.

Minuchin, S. *Families and family therapy*. Cambridge, Mass.: Harvard University Press, 1974.

Rehm, L. P., & Kornblith, S. J. Behavior therapy for depression: A review of recent developments. In M. Hersen, R. M. Eisler, & P. M. Miller (Eds.), *Progress in behavior modification* (Vol. 7), New York: Academic Press, 1979.

Seligman, M. E. P., Klein, D. C., & Miller, W. R. Depression. In H. Leitenberg (Ed.), *Handbook of behavior modification and behavior therapy.* Englewood Cliffs, N. J.: Prentice Hall, 1976.

Vaughn, C. E., & Leff, J. P. The measurement of expressed emotion in the families of psychiatric patients. *British Journal of Social and Clinical Psychology,* 1976, *15,* 157–165.

Weissman, M. W., & Paykel, E. S. *The depressed woman: A study of social relationships.* Chicago: University of Chicago Press, 1974.

# 11

# Assessment: A Clinical and Cognitive Emphasis

CONSTANCE L. HAMMEN

The impetus for this book arose partially in response to enormous changes in both the apparent frequency of and interest in depressive phenomena and partially in response to important developments in conceptions and methods of behavioral treatments to include complex and often covert phenomena. Both of these themes warrant more than passing mention and bear directly on strategies of assessment and evaluation that will be the focus of this chapter.

The high incidence of depressive symptomatology has been amply documented (Ilfeld, 1977; Levitt & Lubin, 1975; National Institute of Mental Health, 1973). Blum (1978) reported that the rate of diagnosis of depressive disorders has increased sharply over the past two decades; while hospitals in all parts of the country need to be studied as well, common impressions confirm the increased usage of diagnoses of affective disorders. Concurrently, scores of studies of depression have appeared in psychology journals within just a decade, including studies of mechanisms of depressive symptomatology as well as of depressive features in every age group—from children to the elderly.

This massive outpouring of interest certainly reflects the recognition of the sheer magnitude of the problem in terms of human suffering, with its attendant demands for cost-effective and readily available treatment. Perhaps equally problematic, however, is the scientific challenge of systematizing knowledge about depressive behaviors, their interrelations, distinctions between symptoms and syndromes, possible subtypes of depressions, and a host of related matters. The wildly proliferating body of research data cannot possibly raise our level of knowledge (or ability to help people) without simultaneous efforts to improve the communicability and establish the basic properties of the phenomena we are so eager to study. Fundamental definitional questions remain unanswered: What are the differences between "normal" mood depression and "clinical"

255

BEHAVIOR THERAPY FOR DEPRESSION

depression? What is the nature of the relationship between cognitive, affective, somatic, and behavioral symptomatology? Do changes in one sphere affect other spheres, and what is their effect? Do different situations affect response specificity, and how? From such basic issues may arise useful classification systems for matching individual characteristics to particular treatments and improvement of methods for teaching prevention of or coping with depressive behaviors.

Thus, concerted and sophisticated efforts to treat the widespread incidence of depression have the opportunity, if not the responsibility, to extend the realm of basic knowledge through fine-grained analyses of subject characteristics and depressive behaviors in a variety of spheres. Our nonpsychologist colleagues have made a strong beginning in these realms, but behavioral psychologists have yet to take full advantage of much of this background.

The second aspect of the present volume that affects this chapter's approach to assessment and evaluation concerns the development and status of behavioral interventions. We can all be justifiably pleased with the progress and accomplishments of behavioral approaches over the past two decades. However, we might also take this opportunity to cast a critical eye upon the legacy of research on behavioral conceptions and treatments. The history of behavioral interventions includes a plethora of apparently successful procedures. Yet many of us are aware that the published reports (a) made procedures and applications seem simpler than they were when we tried to apply them; (b) did not typically shed much light on the behavioral deficits or dysfunctions themselves; (c) commonly turned out to involve more complex mechanisms of change than originally conceived; and (d) on closer examination, frequently showed an absence of generalization or maintenance of effects.

Alas, simple paradigms for simple response deficits must give way to the recognition of enormously complex and interactive processes (e.g., Bandura, 1978) and the need for assessing process and mechanisms of change in a variety of modalities, including covert behaviors. Moreover, applications of behavioral techniques to increasingly complex forms of behavior, along with the need for generalized and enduring changes, have occasioned an increased emphasis on problem-solving or coping skills (Bandura, 1977; Mahoney & Arnkoff, 1978; Thoresen & Mahoney, 1974). While we can take advantage of accumulated knowledge in classification and clinical features of depression, behavioral psychologists may be especially able to contribute to the conceptualization and assessment of such coping skills and the maintenance of treatment gains.

## Strategies of Assessment

These introductory remarks apply very directly to proposals for the selection and use of assessment and outcome-evaluation procedures. Two superordinate themes and several specific strategy principles can be used to summarize. The themes are communicability and complexity. Communicability requires adoption of assessment procedures that yield clients and behaviors whose characteristics can be comprehended by all researchers. This is a basic requirement of clinical research, of course, but for a variety of reasons, both theoretical and practical, they have heretofore been applied by behaviorists in very limited ways. Complexity requires the assumption that no simple procedure will be best for all persons or all depressive behaviors. It also requires the application of measuring instruments sufficiently sensitive to help answer questions pertaining not only to treatment-outcome interactions but also to processes of change. In combination, these themes should help direct us not only to the development of cost-effective means but also to the concurrent pursuit of some very basic information about the phenomena of depression.

At the risk of oversimplification, let me briefly note the specific principles that are offered as criteria for helping to plan assessment and outcome methodologies. A fuller discussion of these will constitute the remainder of the chapter.

1. *Population description principle.* This principle requires movement away from overly simple descriptive data about target groups, such as mere reports of scores of self-administered depression inventories. As a minimum, currently accepted criteria for diagnosing affective disorders, such as the Feighner diagnostic criteria (Feighner, Robins, Guze, Woodruff, & Munoz, 1972), should be employed. Dozens of other person variables, either empirically or conceptually significant, many have predictive or descriptive utility. While behaviorists have commonly eschewed psychiatric diagnosis, with its implication that dysfunctional behaviors are merely symptoms of the process requiring treatment, such avoidance seems unwise if not unfounded for depression. Classification seems a minimum requirement for meeting the population description principle, and extensive descriptive information should also be obtained for predictive purposes, based both on theory and on the extensive psychiatric literature.

2. *Response specificity principle.* Closely related to the population principle is the need to assess different spheres of functioning in which dysfunctions or deficits occur. At present, the most universally understood meaning of clinical depression (by professionals) entails various behaviors that comprise a syndrome. Much of the intervention research reported by behaviorists appears to have been conducted on individuals with depressed *mood* only. As yet, we have inadequate knowledge (cf. Depue & Monroe, 1978a) of the link between mood depression and the syndrome of depression, and differences in symptomatology may have considerable implications for applications of treatments and their outcomes. While it is commonly noted that self-reported, behavioral and physiological concomitants of dysfunctional behavior change at different rates and in different degrees, the implications of such patterning are unknown but potentially significant. Is it true, for example, as is commonly reported, that somatic and behavioral changes in clinical depression precede affective

changes? If true, what are the implications? Assessment of response specificity also requires a multimethod approach, so that different sets of data are not open to the same sources of error variance.

3. *Process principle.* It is insufficient to assess symptomatology in various spheres. It is theoretically as well as practically important to assess particular modes of functioning that have been hypothesized to covary with the depression, such as social skills, self-regulatory behaviors, and certain kinds of cognition. While therapeutic changes in depression through alteration of a particular response deficit do not of course validate etiological hypotheses, they can shed light on possible mechanisms of therapeutic improvement. Following Bandura's (1977) distinction between procedures and processes of change, it is important not only to evaluate whether specific interventions succeed but also to assess how they may have had their effects.

4. *Maintenance principle.* In some ways, this is a specific case of the process principle, in that it refers to the goal of assessing a realm of functioning that may be central to depression. However, the maintenance principle goes far beyond that in invoking a strategy aimed at evaluating individuals' ways of preserving their gains—specifically, the problem-solving or coping behaviors they engage in to try to prevent new stresses and losses from causing new depression. This principle places a premium not only on follow-up evaluation but also on assessment of the ability to cope with real-life problems.

## Goals of Assessment

The four principles briefly outlined implicitly acknowledge the multiple purposes or goals of assessment in outcome research. For example, the suitability of individuals for the intended treatment must be evaluated, and group characteristics must be described so that communicability is assured and the realm of generalizability of results is known. Particular subject characteristics may dictate assignment to treatment, or the topography of problematic behaviors for an individual may dictate the type or order of interventions. Severity of the problematic behavior must be assessed so that change can be evaluated in both targeted and nontargeted spheres of behavior. Processes of assessing maintenance and generalization of changes are also highly important. In each of these realms, there are dozens of choices of processes and procedures. Some answer questions of *what* works; some, questions of what works for *whom*; and some answer *how.*

No two intervention projects will give the same priority to the various assessment goals and questions. Moreover, the different goals probably entail somewhat different psychometric qualities for the instruments to be employed, although the basic requirements for established reliability and validity remain. Because of the diversity of goals and means for assessment, it is impossible to discuss adequately all the relevant procedures for assessing depressive phenomena and therapy outcomes. The four principles outlined, on the other hand, are presented as minimal goals. Therefore, in the discussion to follow, I have chosen to address these four basic assessment principles in a consideration of (a) classification, symptom description, and assessment of severity of depressive behaviors; (b) evaluation of depressive cognition; and (c) assessment of maintenance via coping and problem-solving skills.

## Classification, Symptomatology, and Severity

Behavior therapists have traditionally disavowed alliance with the medical model in general and the practice of diagnosis in particular. Pursuing the goal of empirical precision and eschewing any hints of "underlying pathology," they have assessed and treated behavioral deficits. The relatively poor track record for diagnostic reliability and predictive validity are among the factors that contributed to the popularity and apparent utility of the behavioral strategy. Unfortunately, however, it has become increasingly apparent that such a strategy applied to the phenomena of depression constitutes dysfunctional behavior. Amidst a virtual deluge of research demonstrating the predictive utility in terms of possible etiology, course, prognosis, and treatment of certain diagnostic subtypes of affective disorder (e.g., Depue & Monroe, 1978b), investigators have commonly persisted in merely "diagnosing" "depressed" and "nondepressed" research subjects on the basis of scores on a self-administered depression inventory neither intended nor appropriate for such use (Depue & Monroe, 1978a). Research on behavioral interventions for depression have employed a variety of techniques for "diagnosing" depression, only some of which have validity for those purposes, and relatively few have employed the Research Diagnostic Criteria. The sheer frequency of mood depression as a primary or secondary component of distressed and dysfunctional behavior demands that we be more precise in our investigations. Not only is there some apparent predictive utility in differential diagnoses of the affective disorders, but it is also no longer true that diagnostic categories are applied so unreliably as to be misleading or a waste of time. The Research Diagnostic Criteria, for example, show kappa coefficients of agreement for present episodes of major depressive disorder of .88–.90 (Spitzer, Endicott, & Robins, 1977).

While communicability is the chief aim of careful diagnostic evaluation in behavioral interventions for depression, there are additional goals as well. Diagnosis in this realm clearly implies that depression is a syndrome, and such a notion forces us to ask fundamental questions about differences between "normal" and "clinical" depression, the appropriateness of matching clients to treatments, and the possible interaction between affective, cognitive, somatic, and behavioral modes of functioning within individuals.

Although it may be relatively easy and certainly worthwhile to apply the Research Diagnostic Criteria in our outcome studies, such a process does not solve two very challenging issues: the heterogeneity of unipolar depression (or major depressive disorders) and the matter of measuring severity or current status for evaluation of outcome. The heterogeneity problem is fundamentally an empirical one: Do different individual and situation characteristics predict different courses of behavior, prognosis, and response to treatment? There is no shortage of empirically or theoretically based methodologies to pursue such questions. For example, Paykel (1971) used cluster analysis techniques on various symptom, personality, and life event factors in depressed patients and isolated four reasonably homogeneous groups. Classifying a different group of patients using the typology, he found (Paykel, 1972) that response to amitriptyline was significantly predictable. As a minimum, careful collection and presentation of diagnostic (symptom and subtype) and client (demographic, psychiatric history, and selected personal and situational) data could help to sharpen the indistinct boundaries of generalizability of outcome studies. Paykel's work is only one of many approaches to the heterogeneity issue. Complex and sophisticated studies built into the framework of behavioral outcome research not only could address generalizability issues but also might contribute to basic research in the etiology and psychopathology of depressive phenomena.

Related to the problem of heterogeneity of the depressions is the issue of assessing severity, particularly with the eventual goal of evaluating therapy outcome. All other outcome measures are secondary to evaluation of depression, and indeed most additional supplementary measures of outcome, such as interpersonal behaviors, activity levels, cognitive functioning, and self-regulation, have been validated against some criterion of depression. Thus, the choice of procedures that lead to reliable, valid, and useful results, when assessing severity of depression, is crucial. At the heart of the difficulty is the issue of what comprises depression and the question of depression as mood, symptom, or syndrome.

## Self-Reported Severity of Depression

Depression is frequently (although by no means always) characterized by subjective states of dysphoria. Although it is possible to obtain overt behavioral ratings of such correlates of depressed mood as facial expression, posture, and activity level (e.g., Williams, Barlow, & Agras, 1972), self-report measures are far more sensitive and economical. However, behaviorists have not been kind, for the most part, to self-report measures, partly because of the excess in the claims for validity and utility of traditional instruments and partly because of the trait assumptions that caused the instruments to have poor predictive utility. Cautions regarding the validity and utility of self-report measures of depression are still applicable today, but in a strict sense, as Bellack and Hersen (1977) have noted, "when the target of assessment is the subjective experience of the actual subject, self-report responses are *ipso facto* valid [p. 58]." Of course, the obtained scores are affected by individuals' interpretations of constructs, rating scale response choices, and self-presentational goals.

There is certainly no paucity of self-administered depression rating scales that yield a severity score. Many of these have been listed by Levitt and Lubin (1975), who attempted to distinguish trait and state instruments in terms of the temporal instructional set of the scales. Although an important distinction, trait–state categories are not as critical as differentiating between scales aimed at mood only and those that attempt to assess additional realms of functioning in the depressive syndrome. Additional reviews by Bellack and Hersen (1977) and Rehm and Kornblith (1979) also fail to note the latter distinction but generally identify four scales that are the best validated and most widely used in depression outcome research by psychologists: the depression scale of the Minnesota Multiphasic Personality Inventory (MMPI-D), the Depression Adjective Check List (Lubin, 1965), the Zung Self-Rating Depression Scale (Zung, 1965), and the Beck Depression Inventory (Beck, Ward, Mendelson, Mock, & Erbaugh, 1961).

The MMPI-D was originally developed to identify severely depressed patients. The group contrast, or criterion keying, method of test construction employed in the MMPI typically yields heterogeneous items that may be difficult to inter- pret and may capitalize by chance on extraneous factors that distinguish one group from another. The 60 items of the MMPI-D are indeed heterogeneous; several studies have identified complex factor substructures (e.g., Comrey, 1957; Harris & Lingoes, 1955). Dempsey (1964) investigated coefficients of dimensionality of the MMPI-D and determined that there was considerable systematic error variance in both normal and patient samples. Subsequent psychometric analyses of items and cross-validation showed that a subscale of 30 items yielded a more nearly unidimensional depression scale that permitted distinctions within as well as between groups. Although perhaps psychometri- cally improved and made more sensitive to true variations in depression level than the original, the MMPI-D-30 nonetheless does not sample from the entire realm of depressive symptomatology (especially lacking are somatic re- sponses), and the items nearly all require highly subjective interpretation. Moreover, as Dempsey (1964) notes, the items "[call] for the admission of what the subject undoubtedly considers a limitation or weakness. Few of them refer directly to feelings of unhappiness or depression [p. 368]." While neither Dempsey (1964) nor Padesky and Hammen (in press) found sex differences in total scores, in both studies individual items were differentially likely to be endorsed by men and women.

The Depression Adjective Check List (Lubin, 1965), especially Form E, has been favorably reviewed (Bellack & Hersen, 1977; Levitt & Lubin, 1975) as an adequately validated and psychometrically sound brief measure of depressed mood state. It appears to distinguish between normals, nondepressed persons, and depressed patients and to correlate significantly although modestly with the MMPI-D, the Beck Depression Inventory (Lubin, 1966), and the Zung Self-

Rating Depression Scale (Levitt & Lubin, 1975). It appears that there are sex differences in total scores for patient samples, especially at higher levels of scores. The greatest obstacle to the instrument as an outcome measure of interventions for depression is that it is a measure of depressed mood only, which of course is only one of the response dysfunctions that comprise the syndrome of depression.

The Zung Self-Rating Depression Scale (SDS) (Zung, 1965) was based on the author's efforts to incorporate the symptoms of the syndrome of depression into a self-rating format. Previous research on factor analytically derived symptom clusters led to the selection of 20 items covering "pervasive affect," "physiological equivalents or concomitants," and "psychological concomitants." Although Zung reports generally adequate validation data (e.g., Zung, 1965, 1973) and generally high correlations with the Beck Depression Inventory (Brown & Zung, 1972) and other self-ratings of depression (Zung, 1973), others have been skeptical. For example, Carroll, Fielding, and Blashki (1973) assessed patient samples known to have different degrees of depressive psychopathology (severely ill mostly psychotically depressed inpatients, moderately depressed day hospital patients, and mildly depressed general-physician-treated patients). Although interview-based ratings of depression distinguished the groups, the Zung SDS did not. The overall correlation of .41 between the interview-based ratings and the self-rated depression was statistically significant, suggesting that such correlations give a misleading picture of the sensitivity of the self-rating instruments for distinguishing between mild and severe depression. Carroll et al. (1973) attribute the problem to the self-report method in general, which requires information access to a clinical perspective that patients do not possess, and to the Zung methodology in particular. The Zung scale requires patients to evaluate frequency of occurrence of symptoms, in such terms as "a good part of the time" or "some of the time." Like most self-rating methods, it also emphasizes subjective responses more than behavioral and somatic manifestations of depression.

The Beck Depression Inventory (BDI) (Beck et al., 1961) is probably the most satisfactory of the multisymptom self-rating scales, in part because the response choices for the 21 items are somewhat more precise in their meaning than those of such scales as the MMPI-D, the MMPI-D-30, and the Zung. Originally developed as an interviewer-assisted procedure, the BDI is widely used today as a self-report measure. Validation studies have shown that scores correlate well with clinician ratings of severity of depression (Beck et al., 1961; Metcalfe & Goldman, 1965), with behavioral ratings of depression (Williams, et al., 1972), and with other self-report measures of depression. Critical evaluations have begun to appear, however. Carroll et al. (1973) argue strongly that moderate correlations between BDI scores and scores on the Hamilton Rating Scale for Depression obscure the fact that there is little congruence at severe levels of depression, suggesting that the figures are inflated by high concordance in the low range of scores. Bech, Gram, Dein, Jacobsen, Vitger, and

Bolwig (1975) are critical of the psychometric properties of the BDI (e.g., cali-bration, ascending monotonicity, and dispersion), suggesting that its proper-ties contribute to the inadequacy of the scale for distinguishing moderate and severe depression as assessed by global clinician ratings. Depue and Mon-roe (1978a) have pointed out that two-thirds of the BDI items pertain to sub-jective feelings in contrast to behavioral and somatic features, which may over-weigh factors that are more pronounced in mild depressions than in severe depressions. This point will be considered further in the following section. Hammen and Padesky (1977) have shown that in college samples there are systematic sex differences in response to items for both relatively depressed and nondepressed groups. Although men and women did not differ in total depression scores, the suggestion of differential symptom expression may have implications for both diagnosis and evaluation of outcome for men and women.

Despite the limitations in the Beck Depression Inventory, it remains the most satisfactory self-rating instrument for severity of depression. It must be reiter-ated that neither it nor any of the self-rating scales is a diagnostic instrument. The separate symptoms of the depressive syndrome are typically not unique to depression, and individuals may obtain relatively high scores on the instrument for depressive symptoms secondary to certain other psychiatric or health prob-lems or as reflections of a transient mood state. (It is worth noting, however, that Beck [1972] specifically claims greater discriminability of depression and anxi-ety with his instrument than for the other self-report measures cited here.) Therefore, the use of severity of depression scores as outcome measures for treatment of depression is appropriate only in the context of effective diagnostic evaluation.

An additional suggestion concerns symptom response specificity. In his review of behavioral self-report measures, Tasto (1977) strongly urged the use of factor scores as supplements to overall scores, since total scores have traitlike implications and may be very misleading if different proportions of subscales accounted for the score. Similarly, Bellack and Hersen (1977) urged analysis of situation- and response-specific scores in order to increase predicta-bility and to avoid trait conceptions. An additional reason for collecting and reporting factor scores or symptom profile scores is to study the possibility that different symptom patterns respond to different interventions and that different causal mechanisms differentially affect response modalities (e.g., Abramson, Seligman, & Teasdale, 1978).

Weckowitz, Muir, and Cropley (1967) factor analyzed the Beck Depression Inventory, on the basis of results from 254 psychiatric inpatients who scored 17 or above, corresponding to Beck's designation of a "clinically significant degree of depression." The authors reported three interpretable factors, accounting for 24% of the total variance and 69% of the common variance. The factors were labeled "guilty depression" from loadings on subjective experiences and self-concept; "retardation," or perhaps more precisely, "loss of vital energy"; and "somatic concerns" that loaded on appetite and sleep disturbances. The psychometric adequacy of such factor subscores of the BDI requires evaluation through additional studies, including those with more homogeneous patient groups. The related but even more complex matter of different subtypes of affective disorder based on symptomatology has been extensively researched (see review by MacFadyen, 1975) and, of course, could profit from data obtained in behavioral intervention studies.

### Interviewer-Based Ratings of Severity of Depression

The themes of communicability and complexity are addressed through applications of the population description and response specificity principles, employing procedures with demonstrated reliability and validity for the purposes intended. The related "multimethod principle" is also vital, and there are at least two aspects of this principle to consider: (a) maximization of the validity of conclusions by avoiding systematic error variance due to reliance on single forms of data; and (b) enhancement of understanding and predictability by assessment of outcomes in various spheres of functioning. The latter issue will be addressed in a later section.

Some intriguing although problematic results emerge when interview-based severity ratings are compared with self-report ratings of depression. More seriously impaired individuals (as evidenced by disruptions in physiological and behavioral functioning) typically do not rate themselves as more depressed than do less seriously impaired individuals. For example, Carroll et al. (1973) found no differences on the Zung Self-Rating Depression Scale between psychotically depressed inpatients and mildly depressed outpatients. They found, however, that the Hamilton Rating Scale for Depression (Hamilton, 1960) did significantly distinguish groups and argued that self-report scales overweight subjective scores. This is particularly a problem since "normal depressions" may include the mood disturbance but not the other symptom patterns of depression. For example Weissman, Prusoff, and Pincus (1975) found that women who were unhappy and seeking career guidance but not psychiatric help were rated significantly higher for depressed mood by clinical interviewers than were women seeking therapy for acute depressive episodes. The latter group rated higher, however, in other symptoms of depression.

Paykel, Prusoff, Klerman, and DiMascio (1973) compared patient self-report and clinical interview data in two samples of depressed patients. Their complex study yielded several important observations: There is only moderate concordance at best between self- and interviewer-rated symptoms; self-reports may be most adequate for evaluating presence but not severity of symptoms; the discrepancies between clinician and self-ratings are greatest at the initial evaluation; and psychotic depressives underestimated their disturbance compared to interviewers' assessment, whereas neurotic depressives overestimated it. The results are discussed in terms of response sets and possible biases arising from both sources of ratings. The authors strongly recommend use of several kinds of measures, analyzed separately, to describe patients and responses to treatment.

Taken together, these studies strongly indicate the necessity of both interviewer- and self-reported ratings of the symptoms of depression. Clinician ratings may be relatively more adequate for distinguishing severity of disturbance as based on less subjective components of depression. Procedures of any kind that especially emphasize the mood component may provide misleading information (Depue & Monroe, 1978a).

Of the instruments available for clinical interview assessment of severity of depression, the most widely used is Hamilton's Rating Scale for Depression (Hamilton, 1960, 1967). Ratings on the 21 items covering mood, cognitive, behavioral, and somatic symptoms are based on a psychiatric interview. The scale has been extensively employed as an outcome measure in pharmacological treatment of depression because of its established concurrent validity and high rates of interrater reliability (Hamilton, 1976). Hamilton (1967) reports several sex differences in responses to items among depressed men and women. The scale of course requires training to attain high reliability of scoring and assumes skill in clinical interviewing.

The Raskin Global Severity of Depression Scale (Raskin, Schulterbrandt, Reatig, Crook, & Odle, 1974) has also been used in many pharmacological treatment studies. As its title implies, it is a much more global, less response-specific scale, requiring three ratings on 5-point scales for (a) verbal reports of the subjective symptoms of depression; (b) observed depressive behaviors (sad facial expression, low energy, sadness in voice); and (c) secondary symptoms (primarily reports of somatic symptoms). The Raskin scale requires clinicians with considerable training to standardize the judgments, and although it has the advantage of simplicity, it also has the disadvantage of lack of specificity.

It is suggested that the diagnostic information (Research Diagnostic Criteria), patient history, and interviewer ratings of severity be obtained in the context of the semistructured Schedule for Affective Disorders and Schizophrenia (SADS) (Endicott & Spitzer, 1977). Although it requires training and practice to administer reliably, the gains in communicability justify the effort.

*Suggestions for Behavioral Clinicians*

This lengthy section has presented little that is new to most clinical researchers. It is the emphasis on classification and communicability that may be new for some behavioral clinicians. While behavioral outcome research would do well to ponder if not employ the accumulated diagnostic and assessment information reviewed, this discussion in no way implies that there are no improvements that can be made in the traditional assessment procedures. Indeed, there is considerable need for improved methods of evaluating specific depressive responses. For example, more precise evaluations of behavioral, somatic, and cognitive functioning are needed to supplement the judgments of clinicians and patients themselves. Reliable and useful behavioral observations, overt responses in structured tasks, and other procedures may be highly appropriate to the evaluations of outcomes of certain treatments. Indeed, both the process and maintenance principles of assessment outlined earlier provide tasks that are especially suited to the interests and skills of behavioral psychologists and are addressed in the following sections.

## Assessing Specific Problems in Depression

Relatively few of the major pharmacological outcome studies of depression have gone beyond assessment of depression as described in the previous section. Psychotherapy outcome studies of depression, however, and particularly behavioral procedures, have targeted specific behaviors as a focus of therapy hypothesized to directly or indirectly affect the depressive syndrome. Although the choice of targeted behaviors, and therefore outcome measures, is largely theory determined, it would be desirable to evaluate not only the specific deficit hypothesized to be crucial but also additional realms of functioning. For example, while one might hypothesize that skill building in the interpersonal realm is necessary to reduce depressive symptoms, it is possible that such training has its most important effects on altering social beliefs and attitudes rather than on response acquisition directly. The multiplicity of theories of intervention in depression makes interpretations of results difficult unless there is some commonality in use of activity-reinforcement, interpersonal behaviors and attitudes, cognitive distortion, self-regulatory, or similar response-specific measures. Use of reliable and well-validated measures across several realms of functioning might help not only to evaluate the efficacy of procedures aimed at specific changes but also to elucidate the change process in depression interventions. Space does not permit review of available measures in each sphere of functioning, so that only procedures of assessing aspects of depressive cognition will be discussed in this chapter. Discussions of behavioral responses appear elsewhere in this volume, and an article by Lewinsohn and Lee (1979) reviews procedures for various areas of functioning.

### Norm-Referenced versus Criterion-Referenced Assessment

Before turning to a brief discussion of assessment of depressive cognition, one general dilemma requires mention. As behavioral outcome research has moved increasingly toward sophisticated group comparison designs, the highly idiographic, individually tailored single-case methodologies have been foregone (although depression treatments vary considerably in individualized application). It seems desirable to find methods for evaluating groups of individuals on standardized measures while also attempting to assess clients' individual progress toward achieving personal goals. Perhaps some modification of a behavior-analytic methodology (Freedman, Rosenthal, Donahoe, Schlundt, & McFall, 1978; Goldfried & D'Zurilla, 1969; Goldsmith & McFall, 1975) for specifying the kinds of problems and goals commonly reported by depressed patients could yield an appropriate scale. Topics that might be evaluated would cover such realms of functioning as occupational satisfaction and relations with an intimate partner. Behaviorally specific steps on the scale could indicate current (initial) functioning and ratings of the importance of specific goals, as well as the level at the end and follow-up points of therapy. Behavioral "profiles" could be used to describe each client's circumstances, as well as to evaluate individual outcome, perhaps in a manner somewhat similar to goal attainment scales (Kiresuk & Sherman, 1968). This approximation to criterion-referenced assessment would thus supplement norm-referenced group outcome assessment but would not supplant it.

## Assessment of Cognitive Distortion in Depression

Beck's (1972, 1976) theory of depression as a cognitive dysfunction argues that the tendency to exaggerate negative and pessimistic perceptions and interpretations constitutes the major problem of depression. Although there have been a number of experimental tests of this hypothesis (e.g., Beck & Rush, 1979; Hammen & Krantz, 1976; Nelson & Craighead, 1977; Rizley, 1978), few attempts have been made to develop an assessment procedure to test individual differences and help evaluate therapy outcome. One obvious reason for the delay is the difficulty of valid assessment of internal processes (cf. Nisbett & Wilson, 1977; Smith & Miller, 1978). While it is obvious that depressed individuals truly do have access to pessimistic, hopeless, and helpless thoughts, clients commonly have to be taught to "catch" these thoughts (e.g., Beck, Rush, Shaw, & Emery, 1979), and the assessment of such thoughts is open to response bias of various forms.

Another assessment difficulty has been lack of precision in the term *cognition* (Mahoney, 1977), with the word used to mean both process and content; different levels, temporal segments, and types of internal process are commonly lumped together. Rush (1978) makes a useful distinction between cognitions as immediate responses to stimuli versus beliefs as rules inferred from cognitions. Clearly, psychometric advances in this realm can proceed only with advances in conceptual rigor. Three groups of measures of depressive cognitions can be drawn from Rush's general distinction: measures of general beliefs, measures of situation-specific cognitions (with either fixed or free-response formats), and procedures that are mixtures of both. (This is of course an artificial distinction for convenience, since general beliefs affect situation-specific thoughts.)

The Irrational Beliefs Test devised by Jones (1968) from Albert Ellis's (1962) list of maladaptive thoughts was shown to correlate on several subfactors with self-reported depression in mildly depressed college students (Nelson, 1977).

Drawing heavily upon Ellis's views as well as those of Beck relevant to depression, Weissman and Beck (1978) reported development of a Dysfunctional Attitude Scale (DAS) that attempts to evaluate adherence to certain themes and assumptions thought to underlie depressive thinking. Two 40-item parallel forms were developed and tested on college students. The instrument has high internal consistency and high test–retest stability over 8 weeks. In terms of validity, the DAS correlated .36 with the Beck Depression Inventory and .52 with the Hammen and Krantz (1976; Krantz & Hammen, 1979) cognitive distortion test. Since the test–retest correlations for the DAS were higher than those for the Beck Depression Inventory, the authors conclude that theirs is a measure of a trait of cognitive distortions. There have not yet been studies of the instrument with clinically depressed populations, either as a screening or outcome measure. Also, factor analyses of the heterogeneous items have not been reported but might prove to be more useful than overall scores.

Lewinsohn, Munoz, and Larson (1978) have reported results of their Personal Beliefs Inventory, whose content is rather similar to that of Weissman and Beck's DAS in its inclusion of beliefs about success, failure, fatalism, and control. Lewinsohn et al. (1978) also reported a Subjective Probability Questionnaire (SPQ), requiring expectation ratings of positive and negative present and future events concerning the self and the world. The SPQ discriminated between depressed patients, nondepressed psychiatric controls, and normals in the predicted directions and identified the area of self-relevant cognitions as most negative for depressed persons. The SPQ seems to fit the category of instrument assessing a mixture of general beliefs and specific cognitions. Another such instrument is the authors' Cognitive Events Schedule (CES), which indicated that depressed individuals think specific negative thoughts about themselves more frequently than do nondepressed controls. Extensive psychometric analyses of these measuring instruments are not yet available, although the preliminary work is promising. Factor analyses on both the SPQ and the CES have helped identify specific types of dysfunctional thoughts but remain to be cross-validated. The instruments have the additional advantage of having been employed as outcome measures in a behavioral outcome study (Zeiss, Lewinsohn, & Munoz, 1979). All of the measures reflected improvement by the end of treatment, although there were no differences between treatment modalities or between immediate- and delayed-treatment groups.

Several additional instruments have appeared that assess both general beliefs and specific cognitions in depressed individuals. Seligman, Abramson, Semmel, and von Baeyer (1979) have reported an Attributional Style Scale, which assesses individuals' beliefs about the causes of 12 standardized events, half of which have positive and half negative outcomes; half have affiliation themes and half have interpersonal themes. Although psychometric data are lacking on the scale properties, the authors report support for their hypothesis that mildly depressed students are more likely than nondepressed students to construe causes of negative outcomes as internal, stable, and global. Hammen, Krantz, and Cochran (in press) have also assessed the causal attributions of depressed and nondepressed individuals, but they used the individuals' own personal stressful life events rather than contrived stories as in Seligman et al. (1979). Ratings across a variety of attributional dimensions were relatively stable over an 8-week period. In contrast to Seligman et al. (1979), Hammen et al. (1979) observed that the most depression-related attributional pattern involved perception of low control with external locus of casuality, stability, and globality. A cross-validation study is under way, and an additional study of the causal attributions of depressed and nondepressed clinic outpatients will be completed shortly. Assessment of causal attributions about specific personal events has the dual advantage of naturalism and limited focus in that only a subset of cognitions is measured—those pertaining to causal ascriptions.

Another questionnaire that evaluates specific aspects of depressive thinking related to self-control has been reported by Rehm and his colleagues (Fuchs & Rehm, 1977; Rehm, Fuchs, Roth, Kornblith, & Romano, 1979; Rehm, Kornblith, O'Hara, Lamparski, Romano, & Volkin, 1978). The three aspects of the questionnaire are self-evaluation, self-reward or punishment, and self-control attitudes and beliefs. The latter appeared to be most sensitive to change in a self-control treatment program. Psychometric details of the instrument are not known at this point.

Finally, two relatively situation-specific cognitive tasks have been reported by Hammen and Krantz (1976; Krantz & Hammen, 1979) and Watkins and Rush (1978). The Hammen and Krantz procedure consists of six stories with problematic themes, followed by multiple-choice questions pertaining to the central character's thoughts and feelings. For each question, the response choices include one of each of the following: depressed and distorted, depressed and not distorted, nondepressed and distorted, or nondepressed and nondistorted. A "distortion" is an interpretation or conclusion that is logically not warranted by the information provided. Krantz and Hammen (1979) report extensive psychometric and validation work on the Cognitive Distortion Task. Most importantly, it is sensitive to differences in levels of depression, and significant differences in depressive distortions have been found between depressed and nondepressed students and depressed and nondepressed clinic outpatients and inpatients. The measure has also been successfully used as an outcome measure in one small investigation of a behavioral intervention for depression (Glass, 1978). Although, like all the instruments reported, the Cognitive Distortion Task is susceptible to the influences of response bias, it is not as transparent as most of the others.

Another instrument that avoids some of the transparency problem is the Watkins and Rush (1978) Cognitive Response Test (CRT), which aims at assessing "the instantaneous 'automatic thoughts' occurring in conjunction with specific situations rather than beliefs [p. 3]." The CRT presents 50 sentence-completion vignettes based on major areas of social interaction. A scoring manual for evaluating whether a response is rational or irrational and depressed or not has been developed, and the investigators report fairly high interrater agreement following training. Outpatients diagnosed as having a major depressive disorder had significantly higher scores for irrational–depressed responses than did nondepressed psychiatric outpatients, nondepressed medical patients, and nondepressed nonpatients. Additional work is currently under way to evaluate test–retest reliability and to identify the most discriminating of the items.

Only two behavioral, as opposed to some form of questionnaire, measures of depressive cognition are known. Zeiss *et al.* (1979) reported observer and peer assessment of "cognitive style." Depressed patients and controls were rated on six characteristics (such as "reasonable," "has a positive outlook on life"), following small group interactions. Both observer and peer ratings showed significant positive changes associated with treatment, but there were no differences in treatment modalities or between immediate- and delayed-treatment groups. Interrater reliabilities for the observer and peer ratings were not reported specifically, so that the psychometric properties of the scales are not known at this time. Glass (1978) had an interviewer ask a standard question, "How does the future look to you at this point?" to clients before and after brief behavioral treatment for depression. Independent judges evaluated "pessimism of verbal content" as well as depressive voice tone on 7-point scales. Interrater reliability for pessimism averaged .75. The treatment group that achieved the most reduction of depression on self-rating (Beck Depression Inventory) also showed the most improvement on the behavioral measurement of cognition, although differences between treatment groups were not significant. Although the question posed to the clients represents only a limited sphere of potential depressive cognition, such a behavioral analysis of verbal responses may be used to supplement self-reports.

## Assessment of Maintenance Skills

While only a subset of behavioral clinicians might believe that alteration of characteristically negativistic and pessimistic cognitions is the key to depressive symptom reduction, nearly all would agree that long-term maintenance of treatment gains is an important therapy goal. Toward this end, virtually all orientations attempt to teach behaviors that either permanently alter the immediate environment of the depressed person, hopefully causing enduring mood change, or attempt to alter the coping and problem-solving responses of individuals so that they can minimize or avoid depressive reactions to stressful events. Both strategies of course require long-term follow-up assessment of severity of symptomatology and functioning in specific target areas. The self-regulatory or coping skills treatment strategy requries assessment of acquired problem-solving skills, both at the end of treatment and at follow-up periods. In this section material is presented that overlaps with the previous section on assessing specific targets, especially cognitive behaviors, but that also has implications for monitoring the follow-up process in any behavioral intervention.

### Assessment of Coping and Problem-Solving Deficits

Several projects have been reported that link depressed mood to real or perceived difficulties in coping with problematic life events. Like most behavioral approaches to depression, complex issues are raised, such as whether there is a true deficit (ability) or merely a problem in current performance (cf. Mischel, 1973). Other issues concern the effects of multiple stresses and the possible problem of coping with only "minor" difficulties or covert, internal difficulties whose effects may be obscured by the assessment instruments. While highly problematic to investigators of the role of stress in depression, these issues also represent challenges that might profit from the development and use of effective instruments for assessing stress and coping.

One study using a behavioral–analytic technique (Funabiki & Calhoun, 1979) suggests that relatively depressed students perceived that they would have more difficulty than nondepressed students in coping with problematic situations. Several investigations of depressed individuals' coping construction competency (cf. Mischel, 1973) have suggested that, indeed, relatively depressed persons do have more difficulties compared with nondepressed persons in generating coping responses to standardized situations. For example, Padesky and Hammen (1978) asked students to generate specific types of coping options in response to mild or severe academic and interpersonal problems previously assessed as frequent and problematic for students. They were asked, for example, to suggest ways of coping with feelings and with the situation, using solitary and social, overt and covert means. Results showed that there were no general deficits across all categories of coping processes for depressed students, but these students had significantly fewer overt coping strategies, especially overt strategies aimed at coping with the problem situation itself, compared with nondepressed students.

Glass (1977, 1978) developed an Alternative Solutions Measure (ASM), requiring subjects to list as many solutions as possible to each of six problems (such as difficulty with one's employer, being lonely and wanting to meet people). A judges manual was developed for rating the quality of each response, although interrater reliability data are not presented. The number of solutions correlated $-.37$ ($p < .05$) with Beck Depression Inventory scores, while mean ratings of quality of solutions correlated $-.48$ ($p < .01$). Unfortunately, however, the ASM did not appear to be sensitive to changes in depression level in a brief treatment program aimed at helplessness reduction, and Glass (1977) noted that the open-ended response format is very susceptible to differences in subject motivation and instructional set.

A procedure that is somewhat less open ended, although still possibly affected by motivational level, is the Means–Ends Problem-Solving (MEPS) task (Platt & Spivack, 1975). Individuals are presented with 10 stories, each of which has a problematic theme but a happy ending. The subjects' task is to make up a story that explains how the ending is achieved. An extensive scoring manual provides procedures for assessing steps in problem solving, or "relevant means," "irrelevant means," "no means," and various subcategories. The authors report high interrater reliabilities on scoring, and, in terms of construct validity, several studies have shown significant differences between patient and nonpatient groups. Additional psychometric data have been reported and suggest that the instrument is a reliable and valid test of problem-solving cognitions. Gotlib and Asarnow (1979) employed the social situation items of the MEPS to test hypotheses about interpersonal problem solving in mildly depressed students and students seeking psychological help at the university counseling center. The relatively more depressed students in both groups gave significantly fewer relevant-means and more irrelevant-means and no-means responses; overall Beck Depression Inventory scores correlated significantly negatively with number of relevant means. On the whole, the MEPS has promise as a problem-solving measure, although additional studies with clinically depressed persons and as an outcome measure with adults are needed.

Apart from instruments for assessing problem-solving ability in depressed persons, Dubin and Hammen (1979) have employed both questionnaire and interview formats to assess procedures depressed persons actually employ to cope with depressing events and feelings. The psychometric properties and the implications of the data for teaching specific coping skills were not reported.

All of the preceding measures of problem-solving or coping depend on self-report in questionnaire or interview form. The advantages of having supplementary behavioral assessment are obvious. For example, role-playing procedures might be developed for certain types of problem-solving assessment. Assertion situations are a common type of problematic situation typically requiring instantaneous problem solving, and, of course, suitable reliable and validated procedures are available for such behavioral assessment (e.g., Eisler, Hersen, Miller, & Blanchard, 1975). While not precisely a behavioral assessment, information from friends, relatives, and coworkers could also be sought regarding certain more extended problem-solving or coping behaviors of depressed individuals.

## Suggestions for Further Research on Maintenance Processes

To summarize briefly, it appears that depressed individuals have difficulty in generating problem-solving or coping responses in certain situations. Therefore, intervention procedures might directly attempt to teach such skills or at least to evaluate them as potential indirect outcomes of alternative treatments. However, to a large extent, the procedures reviewed present hypothetical situations in which responses may be affected by a variety of extraneous factors. What is needed is a method of assessing problematic situations that arise in the client's life and the actual processes he or she employs to cope with the situations and the unpleasant feelings associated with them. A method is needed that enables the evaluation of responses to common and frequent, as well as more major and infrequent, problematic events. Such a procedure could involve a behavioral diary format or a more standardized checklist format. The former has the advantage of being idiographic, with the disadvantages of difficulty of scoring and comparison across individuals. The checklist format may be more standardized but has the additional shortcoming of potential response bias, leading to invalid results. Nonetheless, it might be fruitful to pursue such possibilities. The checklist approach implies a behavioral–analytic type of methodology for situational analysis, response enumeration, and response evaluation (Goldfried & D'Zurilla, 1969). It seems appropriate and highly congruent with the aims and methods of behaviorists to end with a call for assessment of situations as well as of behaviors that are relevant to depression. Both treatment and assessment goals for behavioral approaches to depression would be served by careful analyses of situational requirements, individual response capabilities, and the dysfunctional reactions that are obstacles to successful coping or adaptive functioning.

## Summary

The assessment procedures employed in any therapy research play a much larger role than merely marking the outcomes of the treatments. They may also function to communicate the generalizability of outcomes by identifying the characteristics of persons selected for treatment and, potentially, which kinds of individuals were most responsive to which treatments. Moreover, careful selection of assessment procedures can help elucidate the particular kinds of dysfunctional responses that change and the processes that induce change. The complex phenomena of depression and the multiplicity of theories about its origin and treatment demand outcome research programs that go beyond the simple question of whether a treatment is effective or relatively more effective than another. Thus, outcome research on depression places stringent demands on the assessment process, but the potential reward is new knowledge about depression as well as about effective treatment.

This chapter reviewed a number of fairly traditional diagnostic and level-of-severity measures in terms of their ability to communicate useful and valid information. Suggestions were offered for future research in developing criterion-referenced assessment and profiles of dysfunctional behavior and symptoms. The relatively new area of assessing cognitive bias in depression was discussed as a specific example of a dysfunctional behavior that may be targeted for intervention or serve as a measure of a process by which other behaviors change. There is considerable room for additional research in this realm. Finally, the importance of long-term maintenance of therapy improve-- ment was discussed. One mechanism for the maintenance of gains is change in coping and problem-solving skills. Pertinent assessment procedures were reviewed, although this is an area especially in need of new research.

## References

Abramson, L. Y., Seligman, M. E. P., & Teasdale, J. D. Learned helplessness in humans: Critique and reformulation. *Journal of Abnormal Psychology*, 1978, *87*, 49–74.

Bandura, A. Self-efficacy: Toward a unifying theory of behavioral change. *Psychological Review*, 1977, *84*, 191–215.

Bandura, A. The self-system in reciprocal determinism. *American Psychologist*, 1978, *33*, 344–358.

Bech, P., Gram, L. F., Dein, E., Jacobsen, O., Vitger, J., & Bolwig, T. G. Quantitative rating of depressive states: Correlations between clinical assessment, Beck's Self-Rating scale, and Hamilton's objective rating scale. *Acta Psychiatria Scandinavia*, 1975, *51*, 161–170.

Beck, A. T. *Depression: Causes and treatments.* Philadelphia: University of Pennsylvania Press, 1972.

Beck, A. T. *Cognitive therapy and the emotional disorders.* New York: International Universities Press, 1976.

Beck, A. T., & Rush, A. M. Cognitive approaches to depression and suicide. In G. Servan (Ed.), *Cognitive defects in the development of mental illness.* New York: Brunner/Mazel, 1979.

Beck, A. T., Rush, A. J., Shaw, B. F., & Emery, G. *Cognitive therapy of depression.* New York: Guilford Press, 1979.

Beck, A. T., Ward, C. H., Mendelson, M., Mock, J., & Erbaugh, J. An Inventory for measuring depression. *Archives of General Psychiatry*, 1961, *4*, 53–63.

Bellack, A. S., & Hersen, M. Self-report inventories in behavioral assessment. In J. Cone & R. Hawkins (Eds.), *Behavioral assessment: New directions in clinical psychology.* New York: Brunner/Mazel, 1977.

Blum, J. D. On changes in psychiatric diagnosis over time. *American Psychologist*, 1978, *33*, 1017–1031.

Brown, G., & Zung, W. Depression scales: Self or physician-ratings? *Comprehensive Psychiatry*, 1972, *13*, 361–367.

Carroll, B. J., Fielding, J. M., & Blashki, T. G. Depression rating scales: A critical review. *Archives of General Psychiatry*, 1973, *28*, 361–366.

Comrey, A. A factor analysis of items on the MMPI depression scale. *Educational Psychology Measurement*, 1957, *17*, 578–585.

Dempsey, P. A. A unidimensional depression scale for the MMPI. *Journal of Consulting Psychology*, 1964, *28*, 364–370.

Depue, R. A., & Monroe, S. M. Learned helplessness in the perspective of the depressive disorders: Conceptual and definitional issues. *Journal of Abnormal Psychology*, 1978, *87*, 3–20. (a)

Depue, R., & Monroe, S. The unipolar–bipolar distinction in the depressive disorders. *Psychological Bulletin*, 1978, *85*, 1001–1029. (b)

Dubin, L. A., & Hammen, C. Coping behaviors reported by depressed and nondepressed students. Unpublished manuscript, 1979.

Eisler, R., Hersen, M., Miller, P., & Blanchard, E. Situational determinants of assertive behaviors. *Journal of Consulting and Clinical Psychology*, 1975, *43*, 330–340.

Ellis, A. *Reason and emotion in psychotherapy.* New York: Stuart, 1962.

Endicott, J., & Spitzer, R. A diagnostic interview: The schedule for affective disorders and schizophrenia. Paper presented at the meetings of the American Psychiatric Association, Toronto, May 1977.

Feighner, J. P., Robins, E., Guze, S. B., Woodruff, R. A., Winokur, G., & Munoz, R. Diagnostic criteria for use in psychiatric research. *Archives of General Psychiatry*, 1972, *26*, 57–63.

Freedman, B., Rosenthal, L., Donahoe, C., Schlundt, D., & McFall, R. A social–behavioral analysis of skill deficits in delinquent and nondelinquent boys. *Journal of Consulting and Clinical Psychology*, 1978, *46*, 1448–1462.

Fuchs, C. Z., & Rehm, L. P. A self-control behavior therapy program for depression. *Journal of Consulting and Clinical Psychology*, 1977, *45*, 206–215.

Funabiki, D., & Calhoun, J. Use of a behavioral–analytic procedure in evaluating two models of depression. *Journal of Consulting and Clinical Psychology*, 1979, *47*, 183–185.

Glass, D. R. Measures of helplessness in research on depression. Paper presented at the meetings of the Western Psychological Association, Seattle, April 1977.

Glass, D. R., Jr. An evaluation of a brief treatment for depression based on the learned helplessness model. Unpublished doctoral dissertation, University of California, Los Angeles, 1978.

Goldfried, M., & D'Zurilla, T. A behavioral–analytic model for assessing competence. In C. Spielberger (Ed.), *Current topics in clinical and community psychology*, (Vol. 1). New York: Academic Press, 1969.

Goldsmith, G. B., & McFall, R. M. Development and evaluation of an interpersonal skill-training program for psychiatric inpatients. *Journal of Abnormal Psychology*, 1975, *84*, 51–58.

Gotlib, I. H., & Asarnow, R. F. Interpersonal and impersonal problem-solving skills in mildly and clinically depressed university students. *Journal of Consulting and Clinical Psychology*, 1979, *47*, 86–95.

Hamilton, M. A rating scale for depression. *Journal of Neurology, Neurosurgery and Psychiatry*, 1960, *23*, 56–62.

Hamilton, M. Development of a rating scale for primary depressive illness. *British Journal of Social and Clinical Psychology*, 1967, *6*, 276–296.

Hamilton, M. Clinical evaluation of depression: Clinical criteria and rating scales, including a Guttman Scale. In D. M. Gallant & G. M. Simpson (Eds.), *Depression: Behavioral, biochemical, diagnostic and treatment concepts*. New York: Spectrum Publications, 1976.

Hammen, C., Krantz, S., & Cochran, S. Relationships between depression and causal attributions about stressful life events. *Cognitive Therapy and Research*, in press.

Hammen, C. L., & Padesky, C. A. Sex differences in the expression of depressive responses on the Beck Depression Inventory. *Journal of Abnormal Psychology*, 1977, *86*, 609–614.

Harris, R., & Lingoes, J. Subscales for the MMPI: An aid to profile interpretation. Unpublished manuscript, University of California, San Francisco, Department of Psychiatry, 1955.

Ilfeld, F. W., Jr. Current social stressors and symptoms of depression. *American Journal of Psychiatry*, 1977, *134*, 161–166.

Jones, R. G. *A factored measure of Ellis' irrational belief systems*. Wichita, Kansas: Test Systems, Inc., 1968.

Kiresuk, T. J., & Sherman, R. E. Goal Attainment Scaling: A general method for evaluating comprehensive community mental health programs. *Community Mental Health Journal*, 1968, *4*, 443–453.

Krantz, S., & Hammen, C. The assessment of cognitive bias in depression. *Journal of Abnormal Psychology*, 1979, *88*, 611–619.

Levitt, E. E., & Lubin, B. *Depression: Concepts, controversies and some new facts*. New York: Springer, 1975.

Lewinsohn, P., & Lee, W. Assessment of affective disorders. In D. H. Barlow (Ed.), *Behavioral assessment of adult disorders*. New York: Guilford Press, 1979.

Lewinsohn, P., Munoz, R., & Larson, D. Measurement of expectations and cognitions in depressed patients. Paper presented at the 12th Annual Meetings of the Association for the Advancement of Behavior Therapy, Chicago, November 1978.

Lubin, B. Adjective checklists for the measurement of depression. *Archives of General Psychiatry*, 1965, *17*, 183–186.

Lubin, B. Fourteen brief depression adjective checklists. *Archives of General Psychiatry,* 1966, *15,* 205–208.

MacFadyen, H. W. The classification of depressive disorders: 1. A review of statistically based classification studies. *Journal of Clinical Psychology,* 1975, *31,* 380–401.

Mahoney, M. J. Reflections on the cognitive-learning trend in psychotherapy. *American Psychologist,* 1977, *32,* 5–13.

Mahoney, M., & Arnkoff, D. Cognitive and self-control therapies. In S. Garfield & A. Bergin (Eds.), *Handbook of psychotherapy and behavior change.* New York: Wiley, 1978.

Metcalfe, M., & Goldman, E. Validation of an inventory for measuring depression. *British Journal of Psychiatry,* 1965, *111,* 240–242.

Mischel, W. Toward a cognitive social-learning reconceptualization of personality. *Psychological Review,* 1973, *80,* 252–283.

National Institute of Mental Health. *The depressive disorders.* Special report: prepared by S. K. Secunda. Rockville, Maryland: U.S. Department of Health, Education, and Welfare, 1973.

Nelson, R. E. Irrational beliefs in depression. *Journal of Consulting and Clinical Psychology,* 1977, *45,* 1190–1191.

Nelson, R. E., & Craighead, W. E. Perception of reinforcement, self-reinforcement, and depression. *Journal of Abnormal Psychology,* 1977, *86,* 379–388.

Nisbett, R. E., & Wilson, T. D. Telling more than we can know: Verbal reports on mental processes. *Psychological Review,* 1977, *84,* 231–259.

Padesky, C., & Hammen, C. Knowing and doing: Coping response patterns in depressed and nondepressed college students. Paper presented at the meetings of the Western Psychological Association, San Francisco, April 1978.

Padesky, C., & Hammen, C. Sex differences in depressive symptom expression and help-seeking among college students. *Sex Roles,* in press.

Paykel, E. S. Classification of depressed patients: A cluster analysis derived grouping. *British Journal of Psychiatry,* 1971, *118,* 275–288.

Paykel, E. S. Depressive typologies and response to amitriptyline. *British Journal of Psychiatry,* 1972, *120,* 147–156.

Paykel, E. S., Prusoff, B. A., Klerman, G. L., & DiMascio, A. Self-report and clinical interview ratings in depression. *Journal of Nervous and Mental Disease,* 1973, *156,* 166–182.

Platt, J., & Spivack, G. *The MEPS procedure manual.* Community Mental Health/Mental Retardation Center, Hahnemann Medical College and Hospital, Philadelphia, Pa., 1975.

Raskin, A., Schulterbrandt, J., Reatig, N., Crook, T. & Odle, D. Depression subtypes and response to phenelzine, diazepam, and a placebo. *Archives of General Psychiatry,* 1974, *30,* 66–75.

Rehm, L., Fuchs, C., Roth, D., Kornblith, S., & Romano, J. A comparison of self-control and assertion skills treatments of depression. *Behavior Therapy,* 1979, *10,* 429–442.

Rehm, L., & Kornblith, S. Behavior therapy for depression: A review of recent developments. In M. Hersen, R. Eisler, & P. Miller (Eds.), *Progress in behavior modification* (Vol. 7). New York: Academic Press, 1979.

Rehm, L., Kornblith, S., O'Hara, M., Lamparski, D., Romano, J., & Volkin, J. An evaluation of major elements in a self-control therapy program for depression. Paper presented at the 12th Annual Meetings of the Association for the Advancement of Behavior Therapy, Chicago, November 1978.

Rush, A. J. Symposium: Measurement of cognitions, beliefs, and thought patterns in depressed persons. Paper presented at the 12th Annual Meetings of the Association for the Advancement of Behavior Therapy, Chicago, November 1978.

Rizley, R. Depression and distortion in the attribution of causality. *Journal of Abnormal Psychology,* 1978, *87,* 32–48.

Seligman, M., Abramson, L., Semmel, A., & von Baeyer, C. Depressive attributional styles. *Journal of Abnormal Psychology,* 1979, *88,* 242–247.

Smith, E., & Miller, F. Limits on perception of cognitive processes: A reply to Nisbett and Wilson. *Psychological Review,* 1978, *85,* 355–362.

Spitzer, R., Endicott, J., & Robins, E. Research Diagnostic Criteria: Rationale and review. Paper presented at the meetings of the American Psychiatric Association, Toronto, May 1977.

Tasto, D. Self-report schedules and inventories. In A. Ciminero, K. Calhoun, & H. Adams (Eds.), *Handbook of behavioral assessment.* New York: John Wiley, 1977.

Thoresen, C. E., & Mahoney, M. J. *Behavioral self-control.* New York: Holt, Rinehart, & Winston, 1974.

Watkins, J. T., & Rush, A. J. The Cognitive Response Test. Paper presented at the 12th Annual Meetings of the Association for the Advancement of Behavior Therapy, Chicago, November 1978.

Weckowitz, T., Muir, W., & Cropley, A. A factor analysis of the Beck inventory of depression. *Journal of Consulting Psychology,* 1967, *31,* 23–38.

Weissman, A. N., & Beck, A. T. Development and validation of the Dysfunctional Attitude Scale. Paper presented at the 12th Annual Meetings of the Association for the Advancement of Behavior Therapy, Chicago, November 1978.

Weissman, M., Prusoff, B., & Pincus, C. Symptom patterns in depressed patients and depressed normals. *Journal of Nervous and Mental Disease,* 1975, *160,* 15–23.

Williams, J. G., Barlow, D. H., & Agras, W. S. Behavioral measurement of severe depression. *Archives of General Psychiatry,* 1972, *27,* 330–333.

Zeiss, A., Lewinsohn, P., & Munoz, R. Nonspecific improvement effects in depression using interpersonal skills training, pleasant activity schedules, or cognitive training. *Journal of Consulting and Clinical Psychology,* 1979, *47,* 427–439.

Zung, W. A self-rating depression scale. *Archives of General Psychiatry,* 1965, *12,* 63–70.

Zung, W. W. K. From art to science: The diagnosis and treatment of depression. *Archives of General Psychiatry,* 1973, *29,* 328–337.

# 12

# The Assessment of Overt Behavior

NEIL S. JACOBSON

Depression is an affective disorder. Although the most influential definitions include multiple criteria, the sine qua non of clinical depression is a severe disturbance in mood (American Psychiatric Association, 1968; Beck, 1967; Grinker, Miller, Sabshin, Nunn, & Nunnally, 1961; Mendels, 1970). The fact that depression is not fundamentally a disorder of overt behavior has probably delayed its entry into the arena of behavior therapy research. To be sure, there have been theories attempting to redefine depression as a behavioral syndrome (e.g., Lewinsohn, Biglan, & Zeiss, 1976), as well as operant models focusing on the function of depressive behavior (Ferster, 1973); but only in the past few years, as the definition of behavior therapy has broadened to include the analysis and treatment of internal events, have widespread applications of a behavioral model to the study of depression occurred (Eastman, 1976; Rehm & Kornblith, 1979).

The behavioral assessment of depression is in an indeterminate state. There is no clear consensus on the role of behavioral assessment for an affective disorder. Traditional assessment has been criticized for treating behavior as merely a sign of more fundamental, underlying processes that account for most of the consistency and variability in behavior (Goldfried & Kent, 1972; Mischel, 1968). Behavioral assessment is based on the assumption that the measurement of overt behavior, and its environmental correlates, is a more efficient and direct assessment strategy, whether the goal is discovering the causes of behavior or designing treatment strategies for modifying behavior. What can the role of behavioral assessment be for a disorder such as depression, which is defined as a dysfunctional internal state?

Traditional assessment has also been criticized for ignoring the content of test items, a practice that follows from the view that behavior is primarily a

279

function of underlying personality traits, independent of its situational context (Goldfried & Kent, 1972). Behavioral assessment emphasizes an adequate sampling of the gamut of situations in which behavior occurs, and hence, content validity has become a central concern. Yet, as Rehm (1976) cogently argued, a comprehensive situational analysis may carry little utility in the study of depression:

> While mood varies as a function of various environmental events and contingencies . . . specific eliciting stimuli are not so easily identifiable. This fact has implications for assessment. Severity of depression is not measureable in terms of the number of situations in which it occurs, nor is it feasible to assess overt-motor or physiological responsivity to some set of depression-eliciting stimuli. Depression is usually thought of as a pervasive "mood," which affects many kinds of responses in all situations. It is usually assumed to have a general effect on responding in one time period in contrast to a previous time period [p. 234].

Thus, depression is usually thought of as a pervasive state. When a person is depressed, a situational analysis may not be particularly useful. This raises some questions regarding the appropriateness of the standard, functional analytic procedures for the understanding of depression.

A basic tenet of this chapter is that it is unclear whether or not the measurement of overt behavior will prove fruitful in studying depression. Any attempt to explore the utility of behavioral assessment must come to terms with a number of important issues. First, which behaviors should be measured? This is an empirical question, but an investigator must begin with a somewhat truncated universe in order to render the domain of inquiry manageable. Second, in what settings and under what conditions should these behaviors be measured? Third, what analytic techniques should be used to make sense of the data that are collected from the behavioral observations? Fourth, what questions are being addressed in the measurement of the behavior of depressed people, and by what criterion can we determine whether or not these questions are being adequately answered?

This chapter is organized around an attempt to consider the various options for answering those four questions. In the process, a critical review of current attempts to construct a behavioral assessment technology will be provided. Since Lewinsohn and his associates have been responsible for most of the innovations in this area, their seminal contributions will receive particular emphasis.

In order to limit the subject matter to manageable proportions, some decisions have been made regarding material to be included or excluded. For one thing the assessment of "cognitions" will not be discussed. Although it has become commonplace to include a cognitive framework within perspectives on depression labeled as behavioral (e.g., Rehm & Kornblith, 1979), our interest here is on the utility of measuring overt behavior. A second limitation on the subject matter for the present chapter is that only unipolar depression will be considered, and in particular the discussion will be focused on an outpatient, moderately depressed population. This decision is somewhat arbitrary, but it reflects a growing body of evidence that a subpopulation of diagnosed depressives suffer from disorders that are biochemically based, genetically transmitted, and probably not best understood by means of a behavioral analysis (Fowles & Gersh, in press; Kiloh, Andrews, Neilson, & Bianchi, 1972; Winokur, Clayton, & Reich, 1969).

## What Behaviors Should Be Measured?

What are the overt, observable behaviors that lead to the diagnosis of depression? Traditionally, the vast majority of cues leading to the diagnosis of depression have been inferred on the basis of client self-reports (Beck, 1967; Levitt & Lubin, 1975; Mendels, 1971). The verbal statements that lead to the diagnosis of depression include sadness, hopelessness, guilt, worthlessness, irritability, and suicidal intent (cf. Beck, Ward, Mendelson, Mock, & Erbaugh, 1961; Grinker et al., 1962; Hamilton, 1967; Levitt & Lubin, 1975; Zung, 1965).

In the typical diagnostic procedures utilized both in clinical settings and in traditional psychiatric research on depression, even the so-called behavioral concomitants of depression are inferred largely on the basis of client self-reports. On self-report questionnaires (Beck et al., 1961) and on interview rating scales (Hamilton, 1967), patients are asked about their activity level, degree of sleep disturbance, loss of appetite, and the like. Most of the research attempting to discriminate between depressed people and other psychiatric patients on the basis of these behaviors has used rating scales and self-report questionnaires; seldom are such discriminations based on observable differences in behavior.

Thus, one basic strategy for developing behavioral assessment techniques is to find more objective, precise ways of measuring those behaviors that are typically used as criteria for the diagnosis of depression. However, there are other possible strategies. One could begin with a theoretical model of depression and deduce from that model the appropriate behavior to measure. In this case, the utility of the theoretical model would be validated, at least in part, by its identification of a set of behaviors that are unique to depression. Still another strategy would be an empirical approach that begins with exploratory research devoid of theoretical presuppositions. Each of these strategies will be examined.

### Measuring Behaviors Commonly Associated with Depression

Although many of the descriptive terms commonly associated with depression refer to internal states (sadness, low self-esteem, guilt, pessimism, etc.), many others refer either to observable or potentially observable behaviors. Motor retardation, reduced activity level, loss of appetite, and sleep disturbance are all examples of complaints often voiced by depressed people (Beck, 1967;

Becker, 1974; Grinker *et al.*, 1961; Levitt & Lubin, 1975; Mendels, 1976; Paykel, 1972). Yet, in both clinical settings and research investigations, the diagnosis of depression is usually made on the basis of clients' self-reports regarding these behaviors rather than by direct observation of the behaviors in question. For example, there have been no systematic attempts to use self-monitoring techniques to assess the degree and nature of sleep disturbance, loss of appetite, or sexual activity in depressed people. As incredible as it may seem, this author knows of no direct evidence that, in the natural environment, depressed people sleep more poorly, eat less, or have sexual intercourse less often than anyone else. Virtually all of the evidence relevant to these dysfunctions is supplied indirectly, from clients' self-reports of their naturalistic behavior.

There is evidence relevant to the behavior of depressives, collected either in hospital or laboratory settings. Hawkins (1978), for example, summarizes sleep research conducted in such settings. Although findings confirm a variety of unusual and dysfunctional sleep patterns in depressed people, relative to others, they also suggest substantial discontinuity between observed sleep patterns of depressed people and their subjective reports of their sleep patterns. Thus, there is some evidence that sleep patterns may be a relevant set of behaviors in the behavioral assessment of depression.

Williams, Barlow, and Agras (1972) used a checklist to measure the activity level of depressed inpatients. The checklist was completed each ½ hour by nursing staff in a hospital setting. The response classes that were tracked included talking, smiling, motor activity, and time out of room. Combining the daily ratings into a single index of severity, the authors found substantial correlations between the behavioral observations and self-report and interview ratings. They also reported that the behavioral measure was a better predictor of posthospital adjustment than either of the other measures (Beck Depression Inventory, Hamilton Rating Scale). This checklist represents a promising first step in the development of a behavioral measure of depressed behavior in an inpatient setting. Although the focus of this chapter is on less severely depressed populations, this research is significant, because it suggests that when the opportunity for continuous observation exists, useful data can be collected.

Since continuous observation of outpatient depressives is not feasible, self-monitoring of activity level may be the only recourse for those interested in collecting an ongoing sample of day-to-day behavior. The most sophisticated example of such a measure is the Pleasant Events Schedule (PES), developed by Lewinsohn and his associates (Lewinsohn *et al.*, 1976; MacPhillamy & Lewinsohn, 1971). Lewinsohn has argued that depression is associated with a reduction in the rate of behaviors that are effective in producing rewarding consequences. With the PES, subjects track the daily frequency of events that they themselves have defined as rewarding. The PES has been used as a retrospective questionnaire where subjects are asked to estimate the frequency of pleasant events occurring over the previous month. These events are rated not only according to their frequency but also according to their pleasantness. The amount of reinforcement obtained during the 30-day period is estimated by summing the products of the frequency and pleasantness ratings for each item.

As a retrospective instrument, the PES seems to discriminate depressed people from both psychiatric controls and normal controls (MacPhillamy & Lewinsohn, 1971). Depressed subjects report a reduced frequency of events, lower pleasantness ratings, and less obtained reinforcement than both control groups. However, MacPhillamy and Lewinsohn provide no evidence regarding the accuracy of the subject's retrospective estimates. Thus, the criterion-related validity of the PES, when used as a retrospective instrument, is questionable. Any observed differences between depressed subjects and others could be a function of differential accuracy; that is, depressed people may tend to under-estimate the frequency of pleasant events relative to other subjects. Such a tendency would be consistent with research on cognitive distortions in depres-sion; this research suggests that depressed people construe their experiences in such a way as to reinforce a negative, pessimistic view of themselves and their environment (Lewinsohn, Mischel, Ebbesen & Zeiss, 1980; Nelson & Craighead, 1977; Wener & Rehm, 1975). Although there is some controversy in the literature regarding whether or not this tendency to attend to negative aspects of situations reflects a distortion (Alloy & Abramson, 1979; Lewinsohn, Mischel, Chaplin, & Barton, 1980), the retrospective PES may measure nothing more than the tendency to recall positive and negative events, apart from the actual occurrence of those events. In addition, the pleasantness ratings may be an artifact of the subjects' current mood, rather than an accurate assessment of pleasantness at the time those events occurred. Since pleasantness ratings figure directly into the calculation of obtained reinforcement, the latter may be biased by the tendency on the part of depressed people to negatively alter the valence of past experiences because of their current depressed mood. In sum, this retrospective PES is of limited utility as a measure of activity level per se and is probably best regarded as another self-report measure.

More compelling as a vehicle for measuring the behavior of depressives is the daily tracking of events in the natural environment. The risk of retrospective bias is greatly reduced when subjects record the frequency of pleasant events each day. Lewinsohn and Libet (1972) and Lewinsohn and Graf (1973) had subjects track the daily frequency of pleasant events for 30 days. Both studies found a significant correlation between the frequency of pleasant events reported on a particular day and subjective mood ratings for that day. More importantly for the present discussion, depressed people reported a reduced daily frequency of pleasant events, relative to the control groups.

This latter finding brings us a step closer to identifying a difference in overt behavior between depressed and nondepressed people. However, once again the accuracy of this self-recorded behavior must be questioned. Whether such findings reflect differences in activity level, perception of activity level, or record-ing behavior cannot be determined from present research.

More recently, Lewinsohn and Amenson (1978) have evaluated the construct validity of the PES and a corresponding checklist of unpleasant events, the Unpleasant Events Schedule (UES). After identifying those items from both the PES and UES that were predictive of daily mood ratings, a new sample of depressed, nondepressed psychiatric, and normal subjects completed the ret-rospective forms of the PES and UES. The first noteworthy finding was that the proportion of the population for whom a PES item correlated with mood was strongly related to the item's mean enjoyability rating ($r = .65$). This was viewed by the authors as providing justification for using the percentage of the popula-tion for whom a pleasant event is correlated with mood as a measure of the reinforcing potential of the event. The relationship between mean aversiveness rating of each UES item and the percentage of the population for whom the item significantly correlated with mood was less strong ($r = .25$). Although this relationship may have been attentuated by the fact that the most aversive items tended to occur rarely, it is not clear whether the percentage of population from whom an aversive event is correlated with mood will be a useful measure of the punishing impact of aversive events.

The most significant finding in the Lewinsohn and Amenson (1978) study was that mood-related items had greater discriminant validity than non-mood-related items. This suggests the possibility that activities of high positive or negative valence are particularly associated with depression and that general activity level may be less discriminating of depression than participation in pleasant or unpleasant activities.

The direct assessment of overt behaviors commonly associated with de-pression has been a rare occurrence. Virtually all of this work has been in hospital or laboratory settings, mostly with severely depressed inpatient popula-tions. The closest approximation to such research with outpatients has been Lewinsohn's attempt to assess the frequency of engaging in pleasant and unpleasant events. There does seem to be considerable value in collecting this information, since depressed people do manifest unique responses. But whether or not the information provided by these self-recording instruments tells us anything about depressed behavior, or simply reflects the idiosyncratic perceptions and recording biases of depressed people, remains an open ques-tion.

*Measuring Behaviors Predicted by a Theory of Depression*

In the previous section, attempts to measure those behaviors typically associ-ated with the diagnosis of depression were described. In this section, a very different strategy is delineated. Here, the behaviors targeted for measurement are derived from a theoretical model that predicts that the targeted behaviors will discriminate between depressed people and others.

Behavioral investigators have hypothesized that depressed people possess social skills deficits (Coyne, 1976a; Lewinsohn et al., 1978; Libet & Lewinsohn, 1973; McLean, Ogston, & Grauer, 1973; Wells, Hersen, Bellack, & Himmelhoch, 1980). In attempting to develop observational techniques for assessing the behavior of depressed people, these investigators have relied on their own operationalized version of the social skill construct. Thus, the behaviors targeted for observation depend not only on the theory espoused by the investigator but also on the way that theory is translated into particular predictions about behavior.

There are many different ways to operationalize social skill. Since the concept is vague and poorly defined, the investigator's choices are largely based on intuition. The characterization of depressed people as lacking in social skills can be traced back to some early psychodynamic treatises on depression (Abraham, 1971; Adler, 1959; Cohen, Baker, Cohen, Fromm-Reichmann, & Weigert, 1954; Freud, 1917/1957; Jacobson, 1971). In one form or another, the psychodynamic perspective draws attention to the dependent, passive, self-defeating interpersonal behavior of the predepressive, although its fundamental emphasis remains on the intrapsychic precursors to these immature interpersonal responses. More recently, Weissman and Paykel (1974) reported social adjustment ratings of depressed and nondepressed women, based on interviews. During periods of depression, depressed women were rated as less socially adjusted than normals. Although clinical improvement was associated with higher social adjustment ratings, the ratings remained lower than those of normal women. These data are widely cited as supporting the social skills deficit hypothesis, despite the fact that the ratings were based entirely on client self-reports, and the raters were not blind to the diagnostic classifications of their subjects. Moreover, Weissman and Paykel provide a much broader definition of social skill, in their concept of social adjustment, than the interpersonal behaviors typically investigated by behavioral researchers.

Once an investigator has decided to study the importance of social skill in depression, a decision has to be made regarding whether to define social skill functionally, topographically, or empirically. The functional approach is attempted by Lewinsohn and his associates when they define social skills deficiencies as "the ability both to emit behaviors which are punished or extinguished by others [Libet & Lewinsohn, 1973, p. 304]." A topographical approach is exemplified by standardized behavioral coding systems that define social skill on the basis of speech content or the topography of motor behavior. It will be argued below that Lewinsohn's approach ends up as a topographical one, despite the functional definition of a social skill deficit. Finally, the empirical approach, which will be described in the following section, starts with no theoretical assumptions about what behaviors will be important and evolves an observational coding system out of the differences that emerge between depressed and nondepressed subjects.

Libet and Lewinsohn (1973) attempted to test the general hypothesis that depressed persons are less socially skillful than nondepressed individuals. They defined social skill as the ability to emit a relatively high rate of behaviors that are positively reinforced by others and a relatively low rate of behaviors that are punished by others. Subjects participated in a series of group discussions during which their behaviors were coded by trained observers. Positive and negative "actions" and "reactions" were defined a priori. Although nondepressed psychiatric control subjects were included in the group discussions, the analysis is reported only for depressed and normal control subjects.

Depressed subjects emitted significantly fewer actions than did nondepressed subjects. However, this was true only for the early group sessions, and even then only for one of the two groups studied. A second observed difference was that depressed males restricted the range of their interpersonal behavior, relative to nondepressed males; that is, they interacted with fewer group members. No differences were discovered between depressed and nondepressed females on this measure of interpersonal range.

Although other findings are reported in the Libet and Lewinsohn (1973) study, the only additional measures that discriminated between depressed and nondepressed subjects (positive reactions and action latency) can be considered artifacts of the differences in activity level. No attempts were made to partial out the activity level differences before examining residual discriminability in other measures. Other hypotheses were either not supported or only partially supported. Thus, the only noteworthy finding is that in a group situation depressed subjects participate less than others. Since psychiatric controls were not included in the analysis, it is impossible to rule out the possibility that this difference in participation may be a general characteristic of distressed people rather than a phenomenon unique to depression. Overall, this study provides only meager evidence for the existence of interpersonal behaviors that are unique to depression but confirms the prevailing belief that depression corresponds to a reduction in the rate of interpersonal activity (Beck, 1967; Levitt & Lubin, 1975).

Libet, Lewinsohn, and Javorek (1973), in an expanded version of Libet and Lewinsohn (1973), compared depressed and nondepressed subjects in small-group situations and in their homes as they interacted with their families. The behaviors that characterized the depressed people varied from one situation to another. There were also sex differences in the behaviors that best discriminated depressed from nondepressed people. In general, differences between depressed and nondepressed subjects emerged more strikingly for males; the differences found in the group setting generally paralleled those of the Libet and Lewinsohn study. Significant differences did not emerge for female subjects. At home, both depressed males and females emitted fewer actions, had longer latencies before responding to others, and received less positive reinforcement from others than did their nondepressed counterparts.

Youngren and Lewinsohn (1980) compared 75 depressed subjects, 69 psychiatric controls, and 80 normals on a variety of verbal and nonverbal behaviors emitted both in group and dyadic settings. In addition, all subjects completed the Interpersonal Events Schedule (IES), an inventory patterned after the PES, comprising a list of interpersonal events. Subjects were asked to estimate the frequency and pleasantness of each event listed on the inventory over the past 30 days. Comparisons were based on the frequency (summed over all items), the pleasantness ratings (summed over all items), and an estimate of the total amount of reinforcement from interpersonal events (obtained by summing the cross-products of frequency and pleasantness ratings over all items). The IES is divided into a number of factors, and on most of them, depressed subjects could be discriminated from nondepressed subjects: On all three of the measures derived from the IES (mean frequency, mean pleasantness, mean cross-product), depressed subjects reported lower ratings on the factors of social activity, assertion, cognition, give positive, and receive positive. Thus, on a variety of interpersonal behavior dimensions, depressed people reported both lower frequencies and a less positive impact resulting from the interpersonal events than did psychiatric control subjects or normal subjects.

Turning to the behavioral measures, none of the categories of verbal behavior differentiated between depressed subjects and others. The measures included those used in Lewinsohn's previous research (activity level, positive and negative reactions elicited), as well as a variety of others. Thus, Youngren and Lewinsohn failed to replicate Libet and Lewinsohn (1973). Nonverbal measures were equally unproductive in discriminating among the diagnostic groups in the dyadic interaction situations. In the small groups, depressed subjects spoke more slowly and softly, maintained less eye contact, and showed less pleasant and less animated facial expressions than did normals. However, these findings were not unique to depression, since depressed subjects could not be distinguished from psychiatric controls on any of the measures.

Additional analyses included ratings of interpersonal style taken in the group setting by the subjects themselves, their peers, and observers. Dyadic interactions were rated for interpersonal style by observers only. In the group setting, depressed subjects rated themselves more negatively and were evaluated more negatively by peers, as well as by observers, than were subjects in either control group. There were no significant differences between the diagnostic groups on observer ratings based on the dyadic interaction. Finally, on measures of interpersonal attraction and friendship attraction, there were no differences between diagnostic groups.

It is difficult to summarize and interpret the findings of Lewinsohn's research. Ultimately, little support is provided for the proposition that depressed people enact unique, discriminating interpersonal behaviors (cf. Coyne, 1976b for similar findings). Most of the positive findings from the initial studies were not replicated in the subsequent study by Youngren and Lewinsohn. In the latter study, there was not a single response category—either verbal or nonverbal—that was uniquely associated with depression. Yet, it would be premature to accept the null hypothesis that depressed people cannot be differentiated from others on the basis of interpersonal characteristics. For one thing, on the measures derived from the small-group interactions, both observers and peers rated depressed subjects as less socially skillful than others. It seems that the depressed subjects were responding in a way that lead others to downgrade their performance; yet, these behavioral differences were not captured by any of the categories in Lewinsohn's coding system. This is not particularly surprising, since the behavioral categories in Lewinsohn's coding system were derived intuitively.

Even if reliable differences between depressed and nondepressed people had been uncovered, the temporal relationship between interpersonal skill and depression would need to be unraveled. For interpersonal skills to be identified as antecedents of depression, they must at least be shown to precede the onset of a depressive episode. Without such a demonstration, the logical alternative interpretation of social skill differences cannot be ruled out—namely, that the differences are consequences or concomitants of, rather than antecedents to, depression.

If depressed people have impoverished interpersonal repertoires, the deficits should be revealed even during the nondepressed state. Lewinsohn's own research suggests that this is not the case. Lewinsohn et al. (1979) and Youngren and Lewinsohn (1980) found that observer and peer ratings of social skill improved as the episode of depression subsided. Moreover, Tanner, Weissman, and Prusoff (1975) conducted a longitudinal study that fails to support the social skill deficit hypothesis. Social adjustment was measured in people who were found to be either depressed or not depressed 2 months following the assessment. This measure of social adjustment did not discriminate between the two groups.

In attempting to study the relationship between social skill and depression, more attention needs to be directed at the definition of the construct "social skill." Lewinsohn's functional definition is only tangentially related to the very broad concept "social adjustment" used by Weissman and Paykel (1974). A functional definition, given our collective ignorance regarding the topography of socially skillful behavior, seems to beg the question. The difficulty lies in moving from a functional defintion to a functional analysis: If social skill is defined as an inability to emit reinforcing behaviors, it is necessary to establish the reinforcing impact of depressed versus nondepressed social behavior. In addition, the topography of these behaviors must be described in detail so that a taxonomy of behaviors that are indicative of various degrees of interpersonal skill can be delineated. In the research conducted by Lewinsohn and his associates, despite a functional definition of social skill, operationalization of social skill is done a priori; the categories in the coding system were derived independent of their functional significance. For example, positive reactions include affection, approval, agreement, laughter, interest, etc. Negative reactions include criticism, disapproval, ignoring, changing topics, etc. There is no way to move from a coding system such as this to the assessment of one subject's reinforcing impact on another. Such a functional analysis would require a priori determination of what is actually reinforcing for each individual subject. No a priori assumptions should be brought forth. The insurmountable difficulties in this endeavor are underscored by the consideration that, no matter how we punctuate and code interactional behavior, we have no way of knowing whether or not our divisions are occurring along the relevant dimensions. Should our codes classify behavior in terms of topic choice, affability, amount of self-disclosure, use of praise? Or are all of these dimensions irrelevant?

The conclusion of this writer is that a functional definition of social skill deficits in depression is premature and probably inhibits progress in identifying those interpersonal behaviors that are unique to depression. Before it becomes possible to decide whether or not depression can be explained, even in part, by social skill deficits, it is important to know what socially skillful behaviors are.

## Identifying Discriminating Behaviors through Empirical Analysis

A critical analysis of Lewinsohn's research implies that an empirical approach may be more worthwhile at present. Such an approach starts with few or no a priori assumptions about the differences between depressed people and others but simply collects a massive amount of data on a variety of behaviors in a variety of situations and looks for the behavioral differences that emerge. In this exploratory endeavor, a great deal of cross-validation would be essential before we could be confident of the reliability of any observed differences. But at least in principle, this type of research would be more consistent with the current state of our knowledge.

Although a purely empirical approach to the development of behavioral assessment techniques has been absent from the literature on depression, it has proven to be a fruitful approach in other areas of observational research (cf. Duncan & Fiske, 1977). One type of empirical analysis that has yet to be applied to depression, but that has helped develop sophisticated behavioral assessment techniques in other areas, is the behavior–analytic method (Goldfried & D'Zurilla, 1969). A systematic behavioral analysis, devoid of theoretical constraints, would attempt to sample the behavior of depressed people across a variety of situations, instead of choosing tasks on an intuitive or a priori basis.

In regard to the assessment of social skills and depression, behavioral research has been hampered by uncertainty regarding the nature of social skill. An empirical analysis of social skill, designed to uncover the behavioral components of this poorly understood construct, must precede a definitive evaluation of the social skill deficit hypothesis in regard to depression. Such research is under way, although it is still in its early stages (cf. Conger, Wallander, Mariotto, & Ward, 1980). As a first step, an empirical analysis of social skill attempts to identify the interpersonal behaviors corresponding to high ratings of skill and attractiveness on the part of peers and to distinguish such behaviors from those corresponding to low ratings of skill and attractiveness.

The outcome of such an analysis, which would systematically sample interpersonal behavior across a variety of tasks, situations, and subject populations, would be a taxonomy of socially skillful and unskillful behaviors. With the establishment of an empirical base, the relationship between interpersonal skill and depression could be systematically examined.

Although an empirical approach to the construction of behavioral assessment techniques has much to recommend it, it is not without its pitfalls. For one thing, it is virtually impossible to sample behavior without making some assumptions about what should be coded and what should be ignored. In order for observational data to be reducible, some punctuation must occur, and the decision as to how and where to divide the stream of behavior into discrete units requires some presuppositions regarding what aspects of behavior are important. In a related vein, the absence of a theoretical model to oversee the task of data reduction can make the latter an overwhelming task. The essential point is that even in so-called atheoretical research some a priori decisions must be made: Not all behaviors can be assessed; nor can all situations be sampled. Clearly, the differences between an empirical analysis and one based on a theoretical model are a matter of degree. Finally, the less specific our predictions are, or the less theoretically based our research is, the greater the danger is of capitalizing on chance. Thus, psychometric considerations, such as the criteria for labeling a difference reliable, become even more critical.

This concludes the discussion of how to identify the appropriate behaviors in the behavioral assessment of depression. Since few overt behaviors have been reliably associated with depression, it is premature to put forth any set of behaviors and argue that they should be assessed. In the following section, the focus shifts from the consideration of the behaviors themselves to a consideration of the situational context in which these behaviors are measured.

## In What Situations Should the Behaviors Be Measured?

Research reviewed in the previous section reported findings based on behavior measured in specific situational contexts. For example, it will be recalled that in Lewinsohn's research on the relationship between social skill and depression, subjects were observed in either small groups, dyads, or at home while engaged in interaction with other family members (Libet & Lewinsohn, 1973; Libet et al., 1973; Youngren & Lewinsohn, 1980). One consistent finding was the inconsistent results across various situations. There were few examples of behaviors that discriminated between depressed and nondepressed subjects in more than one setting. Given the absence of correspondence across situations, no single setting can be assumed to elicit behavior that is representative of depressed behavior across a variety of situations.

Whether or not laboratory-based samples of behavior, taken either in small groups or in a dyadic setting, can be generalized to behavior in the natural environment is an empirical question. An additional problem relates to the nature of the task instructions themselves. In the procedures utilized by Lewinsohn and his associates, subjects interacted with one another, either in small groups or in dyads. Since each subject interacted with a different partner or group of partners, in effect each subject was exposed to a different set of interactional stimuli. Although each subject's behavior was measured during conversation, each was reacting to different conversational cues. Given the constraints on one subject's interpersonal behavior by the partner's behavior, individual differences between partners must have accounted for a substantial portion of the variance in subjects' behavior. Since partner characteristics were free to vary, the variance due to partners became just another component of the "error variance." This source of uncontrolled task variability could easily override or obscure interpersonal differences between depressed and nondepressed subjects.

An alternative procedure that minimizes this error variance due to partners involves the use of a standardized procedure where all subjects are exposed to identical or at least very similar situational cues. One example of such a task would be the behavioral role-playing task typically employed in assertiveness training and other social skill research (Nay, 1977). Another example would involve the use of confederates as interaction partners for the subjects. In our investigations of the interpersonal characteristics of depression, we have made use of actors who are trained to respond to subjects in a standardized manner (Jacobson, Anderson, Anderson, Rathe-Vail, & Watley, 1978). The subjects enter a room where they await the experimenter's instructions. Seated across from them is a confederate who is introduced as another subject. The 10-minute period of interaction between subject and confederate is observed, taped, and later analyzed. In this procedure, the actor is following a script that is flexible enough to be adjusted to subject differences but also produces a performance that is relatively standardized from one subject to another.

Rather than confining the assessment to one or two arbitrarily designated situations and assuming that such situations are representative of the relevant social encounters in the real world, either representative tasks need to be determined empirically or systematic sampling from a variety of situations must occur. What are the situations in which depressed people are expected to behave differently? Encounters with strangers? Casual conversations with a family member? Behavior—analytic techniques would be most appropriate for identifying the kinds of social situations, as well as the types of social relationships, in which the behavior of depressed subjects can be distinguished from the behavior of nondepressed subjects.

## How Should the Data Be Analyzed?

The typical investigation of behavioral differences between a target group and a control group involves comparing mean differences between the groups on the behavior of interest. Libet and Lewinsohn (1973) and Youngren and Lewinsohn (1980) followed this tradition in their analysis of behavioral differences between depressed and nondepressed subjects.

A comparison of depressed and nondepressed subjects based exclusively on mean differences in the overall frequencies of various behaviors is problematic, because it ignores the important question of timing—that is, when in the interaction sequence do specific behaviors occur? It is quite conceivable that the interpersonal skill deficits in depressed people consist of either the emission of certain behaviors at inappropriate times within an interaction sequence or the inability to emit certain behaviors at appropriate times. All such information is lost in an examination confined to overall frequencies.

Statistical techniques have been described for analyzing sequential dependencies among various forms of interactional data (Bakeman, 1978; Gottman & Notarius, 1978). One type of sequential analysis, using Markov matrixes, has been widely adopted in some fields that study dyadic interactions. Let us consider an example from our research program. Our procedure involves studying dyadic interactions between subjects and actors. Included among these subjects are depressed people. If the behavior of the subject is considered to be a series of discrete units, and each unit is given a behavioral code, Table 12.1 identifies the unconditional probability of a particular behavior ($x$). This has been the unit of analysis for most studies of interpersonal skill. In our research, one of the behaviors of interest has been labeled "self-reference" (SR). Thus, the unconditional probability of a self-reference is the frequency of SRs divided by the total number of coded behaviors during the interaction sequence. Our prediction is that, while depressed and nondepressed subjects will not differ in their overall frequency of SRs, depressed people are more likely than nondepressed people to emit SRs immediately following an SR on the part of the actor. Thus, the probability of a SR given an immediately prior SR by the actor is expected to reduce uncertainty regarding when SRs will occur.

The behavioral coding system includes 10 categories. It is an exhaustive coding system. Based on this 10-category system, it is possible to construct a $10 \times 10$ matrix based on the transitional probabilities at lag one. For example, one depressed subject emitted 20 SRs during a 10-minute conversation, $P(SR) = 0.149$. Four of these SRs were delivered immediately following an SR on the part of the actor: Thus, the $P(SR_s/SR_a) = 0.20$.

The next step in the analysis asks the following question: Is uncertainty in our ability to predict $SR_s$ significantly reduced by knowledge that $SR_a$ has just occurred? This question can be answered by a z-score based on $P(SR_s)$, $P(SR_a)$, and $P(SR_s/SR_a)$.

$$Unconditional\ probability = P(x) = \frac{\#x}{Total\ number\ of\ coded\ behaviors}$$

$$Conditional\ probability = P(x/y) = \frac{Frequency\ of\ x\ following\ y}{Total\ frequency\ of\ x}$$

$z = (x - NP/\sqrt{NPQ})$ where $x$ = observed joint frequency of $x$ and $y$
$NP$ = predicted joint frequency
$NPQ$ = variance of the difference between predicted and observed joint frequency

if $z > 1.96$, then $P(x/y) > P(x)$

If $SR_s$ is significantly more likely to follow $SR_a$ than to follow other actor codes, then $z \geq 1.96$. A z-score less than 1.96 argues against a sequence effect (assuming $\alpha = .05$).

The type of sequential analysis that we have used in our laboratories is offered here as simply one possible approach. Summary statistics that completely ignore sequential dependencies are bound to result in considerable information loss. Although there may be times when it is desirable to simplify observational data and look for central tendencies, at the present time, given that the research area under discussion is in an exploratory stage, the loss of information comes at great cost.

## Utility of Measuring Overt Behavior

This section presents a summary and overview of the criteria for evaluating the utility of measuring the overt behavior of depressives. In addition to reviewing the contribution of research cited in previous sections, new findings will be presented when appropriate.

### Criterion-Related Validity

To what extent do the measures of depressive behavior accurately reflect the occurrence of that behavior in the natural environment? Currently, there are no data that can be brought to bear on this issue. Lewinsohn's self-monitoring questionnaires (PES, UES, IES) may or may not measure actual activity level. The measurement of interpersonal behavior in the laboratory may or may not be predictive of interpersonal behavior in the natural environment.

One problem in evaluating the criterion-related validity of laboratory measures of depressive behavior is that it is not clear what real-life social situations the laboratory measures are trying to predict. It is doubtful, for example, that Lewinsohn and his associates are ultimately interested in the behavior of depressives in small groups per se. Since the social skill deficit hypothesis is generally stated in nonspecific terms, devoid of situational referents, it is difficult to derive from current theoretical formulations a set of naturalistic criteria.

Coyne (1976a) has described a deficiency in interpersonal skill attributed to depressed people that is much more specific than previous descriptions, particularly in regard to the conditions under which the dysfunctional behaviors are expected to emerge. Coyne's formulation describes depressive behavior as a manipulative attempt to receive support and validation from others. The monotonous, repetitive complaints and self-accusations contribute to rejection at the hands of others, which serves to strengthen the depressive behavior in a continually escalating attempt to attain reassurance and support from the environment. Although Coyne is not particularly specific about the topography of these provocative behaviors, his formulation does suggest that the dysfunctional behavior would more likely emerge in interactions with those people involved in ongoing relationships with the depressed person. Perhaps conversations with strangers do not reflect this dysfunctional behavior. The point is that, in attempting to develop laboratory analogues that reflect interpersonal deficits in the natural environment, more thought needs to be given to the situations in the environment that the laboratory interactions are attempting to approximate.

As Goldfried and Linehan (1977) have argued, "estimates of criterion-related validity are directly related to cross-situational behavioral consistency [p. 22]." The little evidence that currently exists does suggest that the behavior of depressed people is highly situation specific (Libet et al., 1973). Unfortunately, these data are difficult to interpret, since they reflect differences between subjects, each one having been observed in only one situation, rather than differences within subjects.

When the behavioral observations occur in the natural environment, one circumvents the problem of criterion-related validity. In this regard, Lewinsohn and his associates are to be applauded for their efforts to observe depressed people in their homes (Lewinsohn et al., 1976; Libet et al., 1973). At the present time, however, data from home observations remain preliminary and unreplicated. Moreover, the methodological problems that must be surmounted before naturalistic observations can be trusted have yet to be addressed in depression research (Johnson & Bolstad, 1973; Kent & Foster, 1977); in particular, the extent to which reactivity and observer bias play a role in the naturalistic observations of depressive behavior remains to be determined.

### Content Validity

To the extent that a depressive episode is defined as a pervasive mood state, with a set of concomitant behaviors that are equally pervasive across situations during the depressive episode, the issue of content validity may be irrelevant to behavioral assessment techniques attempting merely to measure those behaviors that are commonly associated with the diagnosis of depression. However, content validity is a relevant consideration for those behavioral assessment techniques derived from a theoretical model that predicts deficits in certain situations but not in others. To their credit, MacPhillamy and Lewinsohn (1971) did generate their items for the PES from a situational analysis of a college population. A careful sampling of interpersonal situations has not been conducted, however, in the assessment of interpersonal skills and depression. This point has been reiterated throughout the chapter. Content validity is also a relevant consideration in developing adequate home observation techniques. It is doubtful whether a representative sample of family interactions can be accomplished by a few brief periods of home observation.

## Construct Validity

A substantial portion of the present discussion has been devoted to the construct validity of particular behavioral assessment techniques used with depressive subjects. At issue here is not the construct "depression," but rather the constructs that are hypothesized to be associated with depression. Thus, the establishment of construct validity for these measures is tied to the establishment of their theoretical validity. Nevertheless, as was mentioned previously, before the validity of a construct put forth to account for depression can be adequately assessed, the construct validity of the instrument measuring the construct must be established. Lewinsohn and Amenson (1978) have provided evidence that the PES does measure "pleasant events." Thus, the instrument seems suitable to investigate the association between depression and pleasant events, as long as it is remembered that the PES may measure nothing more than subjects' recollection or perception of their engagement in pleasant events. In contrast, there are no behavioral coding systems designed to measure interpersonal skills whose construct validity has been established. Therefore, no adequate criteria are currently available for an evaluation of the relationship between depression and interpersonal skill.

The establishment of construct validity is unnecessary if an instrument is being used simply to measure "depression." To evaluate behavioral assessment techniques simply as measures of depression, construct validity can be inferred from either the establishment of convergent or discriminant validity. Convergent validity is established to the extent that an instrument is highly correlated with another measure whose validity as a measure of depression is well established. The Williams, Barlow, and Agras (1972) checklist, developed to measure depressive behavior in a hospital setting, is one example of an instrument whose convergent validity has been established. However, convergent validity would in most cases be insufficient to justify a behavioral assessment instrument, since there are usually more efficient, less costly ways to obtain the same information. The Williams *et al.* checklist is impressive primarily because of its predictive validity; its daily index of severity was a better predictor of posthospital adjustment than the more traditional measures with which it was highly correlated.

The establishment of discriminant validity has been the primary focus of the research by Lewinsohn and his associates on the measurement of depressives' interpersonal behavior in small-group, dyadic, and home settings. As we have seen, observers, peers, and the subjects themselves rate the behavior of depressives as significantly less skilled than that of normals (Youngren & Lewinsohn, 1980). However, the behavioral differences that account for these discriminating ratings are unclear. Other research, heretofore unmentioned, has successfully discriminated between depressed people and others on behavioral measures. Hinchliffe, Lancashire, and Roberts (1971), for example, found that depressed patients spoke more slowly than normals did. Ekman and Friesen (1974) found that depressed patients engaged in fewer "illustrators" and a greater frequency of "adaptors" than did normals. Illustrators are hand motions that facilitate communication, whereas adaptors are hand motions that are gratuitous, such as ear scratching and nose picking. Other differences between depressed people and normals have been reported on such measures as eye contact and facial expression (Waxer, 1974). However, these findings have not been replicated, and they were based on very small samples of hospitalized depressives who were interacting at the time with a staff member or an interviewer. Thus, one could question their reliability, generality, and criterion-related validity. Youngren and Lewinsohn were unable to find nonverbal behaviors that differentiated depressed from normal subjects. Thus, although the lower global ratings given to depressed people on measures of interpersonal skill suggest that interpersonal skills may be a promising way to characterize depression, the promise has not yet been fulfilled.

*Clinical Utility*

The specific, objective data garnered from a careful assessment of overt behavior have often been related to the selection of an appropriate intervention strategy. One of the major purposes of behavioral assessment, since its inception, has been the delineation of a treatment plan (Goldfried & Sprafkin, 1974). Its utility in this regard can be established only by demonstrating that response to treatment on the part of depressed clients is significantly enhanced as a result of this idiographic assessment process. There is an abundance of anecdotal accounts and systematic case studies that illustrate how a behavioral assessment of depression can generate an effective treatment plan (Rehm & Kornblith, 1979). Much of this evidence stems from the contributions of Lewinsohn and his associates (e.g., Lewinsohn *et al.*, 1976). But, although these case studies paint a sanguine picture of the clinical utility of assessing depressive behaviors, systematic research remains to be conducted.

## Social Validity

The interpersonal environment of depressed people has been neglected as a source of relevant assessment data. Yet, some theoretical formulations have suggested that the response of significant others to the depressed person may play a significant role in maintaining the latter's dysfunctional behavior (e.g., Coyne, 1976a). Moreover, Coyne (1976b) has provided evidence that depressed people produce negative emotional reactions in others. Peer ratings may prove to be a valuable source of assessment data; the collection of peer ratings and other measures to provide social validation for observational measures has already been recommended by some (Kazdin, 1977).

## Diagnostic Considerations

Finally, an apology is in order. For ease of discourse, and because of space limitations, this chapter has been written as if its subject matter consisted of a monolithic entity. Yet most would agree that an unusually heterogeneous group of individuals receive the diagnosis of depression. Although it has become commonplace to distinguish between two types of depression (endogenous–reactive, bipolar–unipolar, psychotic–neurotic, etc.), there is also a growing body of evidence that the population normally referred to as "neurotic" or "reactive" consists of a number of subgroups (e.g., Paykel, 1971). The implications of this heterogeneity include a pressing need to specify carefully the subject population used in a particular study. Moreover, the competing accounts of depression may be reconciled, and the appropriate assessment instruments more easily constructed, once systematic data are obtained regarding the similarities and differences between subtypes. It may make little sense to speak of the task of assessing depression. Instead, it may ultimately prove more useful to simply specify the behaviors that would lead to such a diagnosis. The entire process of assessment depends on, and in turn will contribute to, unraveling the diversity within the generic construct "depression."

## Summary

This chapter has critically evaluated attempts to apply behavioral assessment techniques to the study of depression. It began with a consideration of what behaviors should be assessed. A number of different strategies for identifying such behaviors were considered, including measuring behaviors commonly associated with depressions, measuring behaviors whose importance is suggested by particular theoretical models of depression, and conducting an empirical analysis. A second major section considered the situations in which the behavior of depressed people should be measured. A third section considered the important question of data analysis. The chapter concluded with a consideration of factors that must be satisfied before the utility of a behavioral assessment of depression can be confirmed. Criterion-related validity, content validity, construct validity, clinical utility, social validity, and diagnostic considerations were all discussed.

# References

Abraham, K. Notes on the psycho-analytical investigation and treatment of manic–depressive insanity and allied conditions. In K. Abraham (Ed.), *Selected papers of Karl Abraham.* London: Hogarth, 1949.

Adler, A. *The practice and theory of individual psychology.* Patterson, NJ: Littlefield, 1959.

Alloy, L. B., & Abramson, L. Y. Judgment of contingency in depressed and nondepressed students: Sadder but wiser? *Journal of Experimental Psychology: General,* 1979, *108,* 441–485.

American Psychiatric Association. *Diagnostic and statistical manual of mental disorders* (2nd ed.). Washington, D.C.: American Psychiatric Association, 1968.

Bakeman, R. Untangling streams of behavior: Sequential analyses of observation data. In G. P. Sackett (Ed.), *Observing behavior.* Baltimore: University Park Press, 1978.

Beck, A. T. *Depression: Clinical, experimental, and theoretical aspects.* New York: Harper & Row, 1967.

Beck, A. T., Ward, C. H., Mendelson, M., Mock, J., & Erbaugh, J. An inventory for measuring depression. *Archives of General Psychiatry,* 1961, *4,* 561–571.

Becker, J. *Depression: Theory and Research.* Washington: Winston, 1974.

Cohen, M. B., Baker, G., Cohen, R. A., Fromm-Reichmann, F., & Weigert, E. B. An intensive study of twelve cases of manic–depressive psychosis. *Psychiatry,* 1954, *17,* 103–137.

Conger, A. J., Wallander, J. L., Mariotto, M. J., & Ward, D. Peer judgments of heterosexual anxiety and skill: What do they pay attention to anyhow? *Behavioral Assessment,* 1980, *2,* 243–260.

Coyne, J. C. Toward an interactional description of depression. *Psychiatry,* 1976, *39,* 14–27. (a)

Coyne, J. C. Depression and the response of others. *Journal of Abnormal Psychology,* 1976, *25,* 186–193. (b)

Duncan, S., Jr., & Fiske, D. W. *Face-to-face interaction.* Hillsdale, N.J.: Erlbaum, 1977.

Eastman, C. Behavioral formulations of depression. *Psychological Review,* 1976, *83,* 277–291.

Ekman, P., & Friesen. W. V. Non-verbal behavior in psychopathology. In R. J. Friedman & M. M. Katz (Eds.), *The psychology of depression.* New York: Wiley, 1974.

Ferster, C. B. A functional analysis of depression. *American Psychologist,* 1973, *28,* 857–870.

Fowles, D. C., & Gersh, F. Neurotic depression: I. The endogenous–neurotic distinction. In R. A. Depue (Ed.), *The psychobiology of the depressive disorders: Implications for the effects of stress.* New York: Academic Press, in press.

Freud, S. Mourning and melancholia. In J. Strachey (Ed. and trans.), *The standard edition* (Vol. 14). London: Hogarth Press, 1957. (Originally published, 1917.)

Goldfried, M. R., & D'Zurilla, T. J. A behavioral–analytic model for assessing competence. In C. D. Speilberger (Ed.), *Current topics in clinical and community psychology.* New York: Academic Press, 1969.

Goldfried, M. R., & Kent, R. N. Traditional versus behavioral personality assessment: A comparison of methodological and theoretical assumptions. *Psychological Bulletin,* 1972, *77,* 409–420.

Goldfried, M. R., & Linehan, M. M. Basic issues in behavioral assessment. In A. R. Ciminero, K. S. Calhoun, & H. E. Adams (Eds.), *Handbook of behavioral assessment.* New York: John Wiley & Sons, 1977.

Goldfried, M. R., & Sprafkin, J. N. *Behavioral personality assessment.* Morristown, N.J.: General Learning Press, 1974.

Gottman, J., & Notarius, C. Sequential analysis of observational data using Markov chains. In T. Kratochwill (Ed.), *Strategies to evaluate change in single subject research.* New York: Academic Press, 1978.

Grinker, R. R., Miller, J. B., Sabshin, M., Nunn, R., & Nunnally, J. C. *The phenomena of depressions.* New York: Harper & Row, 1961.

Hamilton, D. M. Development of a rating scale for primary depressive illness. *Journal of Clinical and Social Psychology,* 1967, *6,* 278–296.

Hawkins, D. R. Depression and sleep research. In G. Usdin (Ed.), *Depression.* New York: Brunner/Mazel, 1977.

Hinchliffe, M. K., Lancashire, M., & Roberts, F. J. A study of eye contact in depressed and recovered psychiatric patients. *British Journal of Psychiatry,* 1971, *119,* 213–215.

Jacobson, E. *Depression: Comparative studies of normal, neurotic, and psychotic conditions.* New York: International Universities Press, 1971.

Jacobson, N. S., Anderson, D. J., Anderson, E. A., Rathe-Vail, B., & Watley, G. The relationship between interpersonal skills and depression. Paper presented at the annual meeting of the Association for the Advancement of Behavior Therapy, Chicago, November 1978.

Johnson, S. M., & Bolstad, O. D. Methodological issues in naturalistic observation. In L. A. Hamerlynck, L. C. Handy, & E. J. Mash (Eds.), *Behavior change: Methodology, concepts, and practice.* Champaign, Ill.: Research Press, 1973.

Kazdin, A. E. Assessing the clinical or applied importance of behavior change through social validation. *Behavior Modification,* 1977, *1,* 427–452.

Kent, R. N., & Foster, S. L. Direct observational procedures. In A. R. Ciminero, K. S. Calhoun, & H. E. Adams (Eds.), *Handbook of behavioral assessment.* New York: John Wiley & Sons, 1977.

Kiloh, L. G., Andrews, G., Neilson, M., & Bianchi, G. N. The relationship of the syndromes called endogenous and neurotic depression. *British Journal of Psychiatry,* 1972, *121,* 183–196.

Levitt, E. E., & Lubin, B. *Depression.* New York: Springer, 1975.

Lewinsohn, P. M., & Amenson, C. S. Some relations between pleasant and unpleasant mood-related events and depression. *Journal of Abnormal Psychology,* 1978, *87,* 644–654.

Lewinsohn, P. M., Biglan, A., & Zeiss, A. M. Behavioral treatment of depression. In P. O. Davidson, (Ed.), *The behavioral management of anxiety, depression and pain.* New York: Brunner/Mazel, 1976.

Lewinsohn, P. M., & Graf, M. Pleasant activities and depression. *Journal of Consulting and Clinical Psychology,* 1973, *41,* 261–268.

Lewinsohn, P. M., & Libet, J. Pleasant events, activity schedules, and depression. *Journal of Abnormal Psychology,* 1972, *79,* 291–295.

Lewinsohn, P. M., Mischel, W., Chaplin, W., & Barton, R. Social competence and depression: The role of illusory self-perceptions. *Journal of Abnormal Psychology,* 1980, *89,* 194–202.

Libet, J., & Lewinsohn, P. M. The concept of social skill with special references to the behavior of depressed persons. *Journal of Consulting and Clinical Psychology,* 1973, *40,* 304–312.

Libet, J., Lewinsohn, P. M., & Javorek, F. The construct of social skill. Unpublished manuscript, 1973.

Lishman, W. A. Selective factors in memory: II. Affective disorder. *Psychological Medicine,* 1972, *2,* 248–253.

Lloyd, G. G., & Lishman, W. A. Effect of depression on the speed of recall of pleasant and unpleasant experiences. *Psychological Medicine,* 1975, *5,* 173–180.

MacPhillamy, D. J., & Lewinsohn, P. M. The Pleasant Events Schedule. Unpublished manuscript, 1971.

McLean, P. D., Ogston, K., & Grauer, L. A behavioral approach to the treatment of depression. *Journal of Behavior Therapy and Experimental Psychiatry,* 1973, *4,* 323–330.

Mendels, J. *Concepts of depression.* New York: John Wiley & Sons, 1970.

Mischel, W. *Personality and assessment.* New York: Wiley, 1968.

Nay, W. R. Analogue measures. In A. R. Ciminero, K. S. Calhoun, & H. E. Adams (Eds.), *Handbook of behavioral assessment.* New York: John Wiley & Sons, 1977.

Nelson, R. E., & Craighead, W. E. Selective recall of positive and negative feedback, self-control behaviors, and depression. *Journal of Abnormal Psychology,* 1977, *86,* 379–388.

Paykel, E. S. Classification of depressed patients: A cluster analysis derived grouping. *British Journal of Psychiatry,* 1971, *118,* 275–288.

Paykel, E. S. Correlates of a depressive typology. *Archives of General Psychiatry,* 1972, *27,* 203–210.

Rehm, L. P. Assessment of depression. In M. Hersen & A. S. Bellack (Eds.), *Behavioral assessment.* London: Pergamon, 1976.

Rehm, L. P., & Kornblith, S. J. Behavior therapy for depression. In M. Hersen, R. M. Eisler, & P. M. Miller (Eds.), *Progress in behavior modification.* New York: Academic Press, 1979.

Tanner, J., Weissman, M., & Prusoff, B. Social adjustment and clinical relapse in depressed outpatients. *Comprehensive Psychiatry,* 1975, *16,* 547–556.

Waxer, P. Nonverbal cues for depression. *Journal of Abnormal Psychology,* 1974, *53,* 319–322.

Weissman, M. M., & Paykel, E. S. *The depressed woman.* Chicago: University of Chicago Press, 1974.

Wells, K. C., Hersen, M., Bellack, A. S., Himmelhoch, J. Social skills training in unipolar nonpsychotic depression. *American Journal of Psychiatry,* 1979, *136,* 1331–1332.

Wener, A. E., & Rehm, L. P. Depressive affect: A test of behavioral hypotheses. *Journal of Abnormal Psychology,* 1975, *84,* 221–227.

Williams, J. G., Barlow, D. H., & Agras, W. S. Behavioral measurement of severe depression. *Archives of General Psychiatry,* 1972, *27,* 330–333.

Winokur, G., Clayton, P. J., & Reich, T. *Manic–depressive illness.* St. Louis, Mo.: C. V. Mosby, 1969.

Youngren, M. A., & Lewinsohn, P. M. The functional relationship between depression and problematic interpersonal behavior. *Journal of Abnormal Psychology,* 1980, *89,* 333–341.

Zung, W. W. K. A self-rating depression scale. *Archives of General Psychiatry,* 1965, *12,* 63–70.

# 13

## The Assessment of Deficits and Outcomes[1]

MICHEL HERSEN

Before going on to a discussion of the assessment of deficits and outcomes in the behavioral treatment of depression, it first would be of use to review some of the unique contributions of behavioral assessment in general. In so doing, it should prove of heuristic value to consider the unique differences in how behavioral assessment strategies are applied in clinical and research contexts (cf. Bellack & Hersen, 1980, Chapter 5; Hersen & Bellack, 1976). Although this issue has previously been discussed in the literature (e.g., Hersen, 1976; Hersen, 1979b), further discussion is warranted. Indeed, there is concern that some of our more esoteric strategies can only be employed by those individuals who are fortunate enough to have squadrons of trained observers at their disposal as a result of research funding through grants. If there is an expectation (and the hope is that there would be) that those in clinical practice (who obviously do not have such amenities) eventually will use our behavioral observation methods, then perhaps we might develop somewhat less complex and less cumbersome methods. From a research standpoint, use of more complicated assessment strategies is the standard procedure and acceptable. But it would appear that the objective of research should not be research for the sake of research. Much to the contrary, one would think that the fruits of research should be passed on to clinicians practicing in the community to be used effectively with clients and patients.

Further, it seems that some of the problems of behavioral assessment as currently applied need to be squarely faced and repeatedly addressed. These include the overall questions of psychometric reliability and validity. The unresolved issue as to which response system should be designated as a criterion

[1] Preparation of this chapter was facilitated by grant MH 28279-01A1 from the National Institute of Mental Health.

301

(e.g., Hersen, 1973, 1978) also needs further commentary. This becomes of considerable statistical import in research when many strategies (motoric, self-report, and physiological) are employed and only a few show clinically meaningful and significant pre–post differences as a function of treatment.

A brief comment is in order on what is perceived as the major contribution of behavioral assessment. Although a complete behavioral assessment certainly involves a tripartite evaluation of motoric, self-report, and physiological channels (e.g., Van Hasselt, Hersen, Bellack, Rosenblum, & Lamparski, 1979), there can be no doubt that the precise measurement of motoric behaviors (be they verbal or nonverbal) clearly is the major legacy of the behaviorists. Of course, when possible, this measurement is done in a natural situation (e.g., in the home of the depressed client). When not feasible, measures under laboratory or analogue conditions have been taken. The question here is whether measures in the analogue situation truly mirror (i.e., correlate highly with) those same measures obtained in the natural environment. (This currently is the subject of considerable controversy in the assessment of social skill deficits in a variety of populations: see Bellack, 1979).

In many instances, behaviorists have been quick on their feet and have developed on-the-spot schemes for measuring overt behavior. The same behaviors so measured are then targeted for direct modification. In short, this is the essence of the experimental analysis of the behavior model (cf. Hersen & Barlow, 1976), wherein the controlling effects of treatment variables over clearly designated dependent measures (most of which are motoric) are examined. This, then, makes for an excellent demonstration of cause-and-effect relationships. However, very often the generality and validity of the rapidly developed measurement system is not established in formal psychometric fashion. Nonetheless, there is some internal validity to this strategy, in that presumably the targeted measure is one that needs to be increased or decreased.

It is necessary to expand the discussion of the differences in how behavioral assessment is conducted clinically, for purposes of single-case research, and in large-scale group comparison research designs. Because of the limitations inherent in clinical practice (e.g., no physiological recording equipment or availability of independent observers), the behavioral assessment is largely based on the clinician's observations (often uncoded), self-assessment tests (e.g., the Beck Depression Inventory [Beck, Ward, Mendelson, Mock, & Erbaugh, 1961]), and the reports of significant others when a family member or friend is sought for additional information. More complicated behavioral coding schemes of overt behavior, such as those developed by Lewinsohn and his research colleagues (e.g., Lewinsohn & Shaffer, 1971) for assessing depression, are rarely used. Even the simpler coding techniques (e.g., Williams, Barlow, & Agras, 1972) do not find their way into the average clinical setting. Also, the more formal methods for obtaining information from the significant other about the social and community functioning of the client (e.g., Katz & Lyerly, 1963) are not employed. Surprisingly, the vast majority of behavioral clinicians obtain such information more informally.

By contrast, when conducting single-case research, considerable care is directed at measuring the client's overt behavior (see Hersen, Eisler, Alford, & Agras, 1973). Here, much attention is devoted to obtaining interrater agreement or reliability of observation in at least two independent observers. Innovative observation techniques frequently are devised during the course of repeated assessment in the single-case strategy, but very often these assessment methods are not tested for their reliability, validity, or factorial structure if relevant. Of course, in the single-case approach, long baselines prior to treatment intervention are obtained. In addition, multiple measurement is taken during treatment itself, thus permitting a visual trend analysis of the intervention's efficacy and vicissitudes.

In the large-scale group comparison studies, many assessment devices are used concurrently at pretreatment, midtreatment, posttreatment, and follow-up points. By contrast to the single-case approach, very few measurement points are obtained in baseline and during treatment. Often, baseline measurement is represented by only one assessment prior to the clinical intervention. The typical study funded by the NIMH or the VA includes self-report, motoric, significant other reports, clinical rating scales, and physiological assessments. Moreover, to impress review panels, several such measures in each of the aforementioned categories usually are employed. Frequently, measures within a given category may be highly correlated, thus yielding obvious and needless duplication of measurement. Generally, those measures selected for study have relatively well-documented reliability, validity, and other important psychometric characteristics. As for the total number of such measures included, it is not uncommon in a large-scale outcome study to have one to two dozen major dependent variables, which can be broken down still further into additional subcategories.

This, then, brings us to the issue of which scale or which category of measurement is to be selected as the primary criterion for improvement. For example, consider a group comparison study in which there are 20 dependent measures, but only two or three show significant improvement on a pre–post basis when experimental and control conditions are contrasted. Although this number of significant differences is greater than what one would expect on the basis of chance (i.e., 1 out of 20), the increment over chance levels is not at all impressive. However, as consumers of research and as journal editors, we have seen investigators make important inferences from such scanty confirmatory data. As already noted, inclusion of a plethora of measures is a political decision (to impress grant reviewers of the investigator's breadth of knowledge), but unfortunately not one based on sound knowledge of statistical requirements. However, parenthetically, it should be stated that most investigators are compelled to play this political game. Caveat emptor!

With the impetus of behavioral assessment, the question of which response system is to be used as a criterion has caused researchers further problems. In the old days it was simpler; mainly self-report and observational scales were employed. Now, with the introduction and proliferation of motoric and physio-logical assessment techniques, the issues have become much more compli-cated. For example, what if a client says he or she feels better (i.e., self-report) as a function of treatment, but motoric observation and physiological evaluations do not confirm self-reported improvements? Conversely, what if motoric im-provement is considerable and self-reported (i.e., subjective) feelings lag be-hind? Although elsewhere (Hersen, 1973) this phenomenon has been termed *attitudinal lag,* use of this rubric obviously does not answer the question: Which criterion does one use to evaluate improvement? Ideally, of course, each of the three response systems (self-report, motoric, and physiological) should evince maximum change (Hersen, 1973, 1978).

As recommended elsewhere (Hersen, 1973, 1978), each of the response systems should be directly modified, thus enhancing the probability that all three will change proportionally in concert. Certainly, application of cognitive strategies should lead to improvements in the cognitive dimension, application of biofeedback to improvements in the physiological dimension, and applica-tion of an operantly based technique to improvements in the motoric dimen-sion. Also, spillover from one system to another definitely does occur at times. However, in practice, specific attention as just outlined is more the exception than the rule. Let us illustrate by describing a study where this was the case (Van Hasselt *et al.,* 1979). In this study, the effects of relaxation training and system-atic desensitization therapy were evaluated in multiple baseline fashion for three distinct phobias (height, blood, test taking) in an 11-year-old boy. Responses in motoric, cognitive, and physiological channels were repeatedly assessed in baseline and treatment phases. As a function of treatment, there was improve-ment for two of the three phobias at the motoric level (batting average = .667), on all three phobias at the cognitive level (batting average = 1.000), and on only one of the three phobias at the physiological level (batting average = .333).

Given the aforementioned data, what conclusive statements can one legiti-mately make about the extent of improvement? Unfortunately, one is unable to satisfactorily answer this question. Perhaps if experimenters were to set specific criteria for improvement on a strictly a priori basis, then subsequent data analyses would or would not confirm the excellence of treatment. Otherwise, at this point in time, it very much remains an audience variable rather than an experimental or statistical one. Kazdin's (1977) motion of assessing the clinical or applied importance of behavior change through social validation undoubt-edly represents the ideal that all clinicians are striving to achieve. Thus, an attempt to change in the direction of social norms (to the extent possible) is the goal in modifying deviant behavior.

Let us now turn to the issue of self-report in behavioral assessment. Although initially behavior therapists may have eschewed the use of self-reports as major criteria for assessing change (see Hersen, 1976), this no longer seems to be the case (Cautela & Upper, 1976; Hersen, 1978), particularly in the area of depression (Rehm, 1976). Indeed, judging from the large number of self-report devices developed by our behavioral colleagues (see Cautela & Upper, 1976), the self-report seems to be very much alive and well in today's research endeavor. Undoubtedly, the upsurge in interest in cognitive variables and treatment have enhanced its well-being. Certainly, as noted elsewhere (Bellack & Hersen, 1977; Hersen, 1973, 1978), no matter how well the patient looks (i.e., the motor assessment) and how improved his or her physiology, how he or she actually feels can never be discounted as an important consideration. In the area of depression, where one's cognitions are so important (Rush & Beck, 1978), the client's self-report must always be given central status. Presumably, the correlation between how a given patient looks and how he or she feels should be quite high when evaluating the extent of depression. This was the case in a study conducted by Williams *et al.* (1972), whereby a correlation of $r = 0.67$ was obtained between behavioral measures of depression (whether the patient was talking, smiling, or physically active when periodically observed on the ward) and the Beck Depression Inventory (BDI).

Before considering the assessment of depression in particular, it is necessary briefly to tackle the issue of psychometrics and behavioral assessment. Presumably, in their zeal to be different and change the nature of assessment from an indirect to direct strategy, many behavioral assessors initially totally discarded the importance of the psychometric characteristics of their assessment devices. Although, as earlier indicated, there probably is some internal validity for the on-the-spot measures developed for assessment in single-case research, evidence for their external validity generally is not indicated. In that sense, behavioral assessors essentially "threw out the baby with the bath water" when they innovated.

Not only has this now made it difficult to draw conclusions about the efficacy of some of our treatments (cf. Rehm, 1978a), but it has often led our nonbehavioral colleagues to label us as "naive," at least in the psychometric sense. In reviewing assessment instruments in order to recommend a standard battery for use in depression research, Rehm (1978a) argues:

> For many of the instruments the psychometric development is incomplete. Data on such important issues as internal consistency, characteristics of reliability over time, and discriminant validity from other psychopathological constructs is often missing. Those instruments which have been evaluated more thoroughly have usually been evaluated under very different circumstances which makes comparability difficult. By and large one must compare ranges of statistics which are generally overlapping, albeit adequate in an absolute sense [p. 100].

It is necessary to be more specific on these issues of considerable importance. Very few of the scores of self-assessment tools described by Cautela and Upper (1976) have been evaluated psychometrically. For example, the Wolpe-Lazarus Assertiveness Scale (Wolpe & Lazarus, 1966), a 30-item true–false inventory assessing level of assertiveness, has been used for many years in social skill research. Only recently, however, have item analyses, split-half and test–retest reliabilities, and factor analyses been performed and reported in the literature (e.g., Hersen, Bellack, Turner, Williams, Harper, & Watts, 1979). Similarly, even though the Behavioral Assertiveness Test (Eisler, Hersen, Miller, & Blanchard, 1975; Eisler, Miller, & Hersen, 1973; Hersen, Bellack, & Turner, 1978), a behavioral role-play test for evaluating the verbal and nonverbal components of assertiveness, has been used extensively in social skill research for about 10 years, only recently have there been attempts to establish its external validity (cf. Bellack, Hersen, & Turner, 1978; Bellack, Hersen, & Turner, 1979).

## Behavioral and Psychiatric Assessment of Depression

Let us turn to a more specific evaluation of the behavioral assessment of depression. Since Rehm (1976, 1978a) already has carefully and comprehensively evaluated the specific behavioral and psychometric issues, it is not necessary to duplicate the many aspects of his two excellent review papers. Rather, comment will be directed to some concerns that have not received considerable articulation in behavioral publications.

Generally, behavioral assessors (mainly clinical psychologists) and psychiatric researchers (usually physicians) have followed somewhat parallel (but certainly not intertwined) paths in their respective studies of depressive psychopathology and symptomatology. This has been articulated elsewhere in a different format (e.g., Hersen, 1979a); however, many of our behavioral colleagues do not keep abreast of the important developments in the psychiatric arena. Conversely, psychiatric researchers tend not to keep abreast of developments in behavioral assessment. This rather severe and chronic case of "double parochialism" is most unfortunate inasmuch as the needed cross-fertilization between these two sets of researchers in assessing depression is, at least to us, highly apparent. Perhaps the recent invitation by the American Psychiatric Association to the Association for Advancement of Behavior Therapy to comment on DSM-III represents the needed first step to achieve some semblance of integration of thinking.

It will be useful to make a few general statements about the behavioral assessment of depression and then examine each of the issues in greater detail. First, on the whole, behavioral researchers have looked at depression as a unitary phenomenon and have not spent much time evaluating the many subcategories of the disorder. Second, behaviorists have not devoted too much attention to the very specific precipitants of depression (i.e., stressors and life events). Third, the genetic features of and bases for some depressions have been virtually ignored by behavioral researchers. Fourth, sleep studies of depressed patients have not been carried out by most behavioral assessors. Fifth, different familial characteristics as they relate to subtypes of depression also have received almost no space in the behavioral literature. Sixth, social competencies of patients receiving a variety of sublabels of depression have not been investigated in behavioral fashion.

In examining work of behaviorists in the assessment and modification of depression, we found that most of the studies have been concerned with unipolar (nonpsychotic) depression (cf. Lewinsohn, 1975; Rehm & Kornblith, 1979). However, precisely similar diagnostic criteria do not seem to be used from one study to the next (see Rehm, 1978a). Indeed, very often behavioral studies have been carried out with subclinical volunteer populations. Thus, of course, conclusions reached on the basis of studies with these subjects may not necessarily hold for the more severely disabled (cf. Hersen, 1979a).

The subvarieties of depression are rarely alluded to in the behavioral literature. For example, generally a distinction has not been made between different categories of unipolar depression (e.g., Akiskal, Bitar, Puzantian, Rosenthal, & Walker, 1978; Kupfer, Pickar, Himmelhoch, & Detre, 1975). The studies of Winokur (1979) separating unipolar depression in terms of family history of depression, alcoholism, or antisocial personality have not affected the thinking of behavior therapists. Nor have behavior therapists paid much attention to the important distinction found between primary and secondary depression (see Akiskal & McKinney, 1975; Andreasan & Winokur, 1979) and the critical unipolar–bipolar differences in etiology, course, and personality characteristics (e.g., Beigel & Murphy, 1971; Kupfer, Foster, Detre, & Himmelhoch, 1975).

Considering the fact that the subtypes of depression do have vastly different genetic bases, etiologies, prognoses, and responsivity to behavioral and pharmacological treatments, it seems that our disregard of these finer diagnostic distinctions is regrettable from both scientific and clinical perspectives. Aside from the high probability of the genetic factor in depressive disorder, given vastly different family milieus for various subtypes of depression, greater attention to these important diagnostic distinctions would lead to improved therapy because of the behavior therapist's penchant for carefully tailoring treatment to the needs of the individual patient. In brief, to view depression as a unitary phenomenon under a singular label is not at all consistent with the facts available to researchers. Unfortunately, this would have to be labeled as a case of naive behaviorism (cf. Hersen & Bellack, 1977b).

Further, in the study of depression by nonbehaviorists and behaviorists alike, there is the almost tacit assumption that the daily life of the depressed client is a unitary phenomenon (i.e., that level of depression is relatively consistent irrespective of the stimulus situation). This probably is not the case inasmuch as different stimulus situations elicit different amounts of depression. Indeed, the work of Lewinsohn and Rehm and their colleagues (e.g., Lewinsohn & Libet, 1972; Rehm, 1978b) on pleasant and unpleasant events touches on this issue to some extent.

We currently are examining this issue from a different perspective in our own laboratory by having depressed patients interact with a significant other (family member, friend) under different instructional sets—discussion of problem areas versus discussion of nonproblem areas. The two areas are discussed in alternating 6-minute sequences. The model described is based on our prior work (Hersen, Miller, & Eisler, 1973) with male alcoholics and their nonalcoholic spouses, in which the couples were videotaped while interacting under instructions to talk about the alcoholic problem and then about anything but the alcoholic problem in an ABAB fashion. The results of this study showed that as a function of the nature of the discussion (alcohol versus nonalcohol), the verbal and nonverbal behavior (e.g., eye contact) was radically different. Thus, at least with male alcoholics and their wives, there appears to be pronounced behavioral differences as a result of differing stimulus pulls. If this is replicated in some measure with our depressed unipolar female patients, such findings, of course, would have considerable implications for the subsequent treatment of these patients.

The next point to discuss is the issue of precipitants and life stressors that may lead to depression in relation to behavioral assessment practices. Although the initial notion of behavioral assessment (e.g., Kanfer & Saslow, 1969) seemed to be based in terms of the client's presentation of overt symptoms (e.g., phobia, obsessive–compulsive habits, tics, crying spells), it appears that, in clinical practice, behavior therapists have not rigidly adhered to this model (cf. Swan & MacDonald, 1978). Indeed, on the basis of their survey of 353 active behavior therapists who are members of the Association for Advancement of Behavior Therapy, Swan and MacDonald (1978) stated:

> Respondents reported having neither a strong inclination nor a strong disinclination to deal exclusively with client presented problems as they are stated. This finding is somewhat discrepant from the frequently stated dictum that client problems should be conceptualized in accord with the client's initial point of view . . . and suggests that some sort of clinical judgment process is characteristic of behavior therapy as it is of more traditional diagnostic systems; the nature of this process warrants further study. Therapists are moderately to slightly likely to include past history information in their assessment phases; in contrast to assessment in research, then, assessment in practice is not ahistorical [p. 804].

What colors the behavior therapist's judgment in clinical work is not only the symptomatic presentation by the client but certainly the history and, in particular, those very specific life stimuli that immediately preceded symptomatic expression (see Thomson & Hendrie, 1972). Thus, in the case of depression, it would be fruitless to evaluate vegetative, verbal, nonverbal, and physiological symptoms in a vacuum that does not consider the life milieu that undoubtedly produced them in the first place. For example, if a patient's unassertiveness and passive style in dealing with the environment were to result in depression (cf. Wells, Hersen, Bellack, & Himmelhoch, 1979), a more reasonable behavioral target for treatment than the symptoms of depression themselves would be the unassertive behaviors evinced in interpersonal situations. That is not to say, however, that the Beck Depression Inventory (BDI) or the Hamilton scale would not be employed during the course of a comprehensive assessment. Rather, it is argued that response to the BDI and Hamilton would reflect changes in depression, but only as a function of whether the patient's ability to deal with life stresses (i.e., situations requiring assertive responding) were to be modified. Thus, in depression, how the patient deals with loss, conflict, anxiety, ambiguity, death, illness, separation, divorce, and other life events would be the primary target for behavioral intervention. Measurement of depressive symptoms in this scheme simply would be a barometer of the patient's interpersonal coping ability. One might also note that when an incomplete behavioral assessment leads to an incomplete behavioral treatment, then the possibility for symptomatic return or substitution looms large (cf. Blanchard & Hersen, 1976; Hersen, 1979a).

Consider the issues of genetic influences on behavior, a topic that has received but the scantest attention by behavioral assessors, therapists, and researchers. With two notable exceptions (Eysenck, 1952; Wolpe, 1970), most behaviorists have, at best, only given lip service to the possible genetic influences and family predispositions to psychologic disturbance. Given the behavior therapists' penchant for using learning theory to explain diverse behavioral phenomena (cf. Bandura, 1969; Kanfer & Phillips, 1970), this certainly is a very understandable omission. Of course, we are trying to redigest the old nature–nurture controversy here. As we all know, that is an argument that has not and probably never will be resolved. However, it should be brought to the attention of behavioral assessors that there are some important and interesting data adduced by psychiatric researchers showing the genetic influence on the elicitation of depressive behaviors.

As there is a very large literature on the genetic factor in psychiatric disorder in general, and now more recently on genetic–familial factors in depression, we will not belabor the point and review it all. However, two studies conducted by Winokur and his group (Winokur, Behar, VanValkenburg, & Lowry, 1978; Winokur, Cadoret, Dorzab, & Baker, 1971) that are illustrative of genetic and familial classification in depression will be described.

In the first study, Winokur et al. (1971) evaluated 100 depressed probands. Of the 100 probands, family histories and studies were accomplished with 129 primary relatives. From the resulting analysis of the genetic data, two types of depressive illnesses (i.e., disorders) were identified: "depression spectrum disease" and "pure depressive disease." Depression spectrum disease is characterized by "a female with an onset prior to age 40 in whose family more depression is seen in female relatives than male relatives and the deficit in males is made up by alcoholism and sociopathy [p. 135]." Pure depressive disease involves a male proband whose depressive disorder begins after age 40. In his family background, there is an equal proportion of depression in both male and female relatives. However, alcoholism and sociopathy in male relatives is rather low.

In a second study, Winokur et al. (1978) were able to separate most unipolar depressives into three groups based on family constellation: patients with depression spectrum disease, those with pure depressive disease, and those with sporadic depressive disease. Sporadic depressive disease patients tend to be older than those in the other two groups at the onset of the depression. The pure depressive disease group tends to have more episodes of depression than the depression spectrum disease group. On the basis of their work, Winokur et al. (1978) state: "It is reasonable to conclude that a familial definition of depression may be a useful heuristic device for further research. It is quite conceivable that specific family backgrounds may indeed define different autonomous illnesses [p. 768]." Thus, it would seem warranted for the behavioral assessor to evaluate the depressive client carefully, not only in terms of ongoing symptomatology, but also in terms of family history for depressive, alcoholic, and personality disorders.

A major omission that has characterized the research of behavioral assessors in the area of depression involves the physiological aspects of the disorder(s). This lack has been most pronounced in the area of sleep research. Although behavior therapists have been concerned with the assessment and treatment of insomnia (cf. Bootzin & Nicassio, 1978), they surprisingly have based almost all of their conclusions on their clients' self-reports. Naturally, in this area, where there are more objective means for making accurate assessments, we think that it behooves behaviorists to revamp their current methodologies.

Exceptions, of course, are to be found in the behavioral literature. For example, Rosekind, Thomas, Coates, and Thoresen (1978) obtained all-night sleep recordings (EEG) that were carried out in the clients' homes but transmitted over telephone lines to a polygraph in a distant laboratory. Again, however, it should be underscored that this is one of few such exceptions where sleep recordings have been examined by behavioral assessors studying insomnia. Moreover, in studying insomnia (often one of the cardinal symptoms of depression), behavioral assessors have not refined diagnostic assessments by separating their patients into carefully delineated subcategories of depression or other diagnostic groupings.

The importance of carefully measuring the sleep of depressed individuals (polygraphically) has received increasing attention in the psychiatric literature (e.g., Hauri, Chernik, Hawkins, & Mendels, 1974; Kupfer et al., 1975; Mendels & Hawkins, 1967). A study by Hauri et al. (1974) merits the careful scrutiny of all researchers concerned with depression, irrespective of theoretical persuasion. Hauri et al. evaluated a group of 14 "recovered" patients who previously had been hospitalized with unipolar depression. This group of patients was matched with a control group of "normals." Patients in each of the groups were asked to sleep five consecutive nights in the laboratory while being monitored polygraphically for a number of physiological indicators. The results of the study indicated that both the "recovered" depressed patients and the controls slept approximately the same total amount of time (i.e., 6.5 hours). However, there were several significant differences between the two groups. Recovered patients showed (a) a delayed sleep onset; (b) less delta sleep and more Stage 1 sleep; (c) a slower sleep cycle; and (d) significantly greater variability on a night-by-night basis for just about all of the indicators.

From this study, it is clear that simple remission of overt depressive symptomatology may not be sufficient. Indeed, the underlying physiological (and/or biological) mechanisms also need to be evlauated. Hauri *et al.* (1974), on the basis of these data, conclude:

> Sleep was clearly disturbed in our remitted patients more than six months after substantial clinical improvement, discharge from the hospital, and return to their accustomed life style. This finding is especially noteworthy because our sample is probably biased toward remitted patients who sleep well.
>
> The findings of this study contribute to the growing evidence that in some depressed patients, behavioral, physiological, and biochemical abnormalities persist even during remission. It is unknown, however, how much genetic factors contribute to such chronic disturbances and how much is contributed by early experiences, such as loss and bereavement, at crucial developmental stages [p. 390].

Next, let us turn to the issue of evaluating the social competence and social skill of depressed patients. Lewinsohn (1974, 1975; Libet & Lewinsohn, 1973), as is well known, has implicated deficient social skills as an etiologic factor in depression. His experimental data certainly suggest that the depressed individual is significantly less socially skillful than his or her nondepressed counterpart. In the Lewinsohn scheme, five operational definitions concerned with social skill have been proposed. Each is assumed to be related to the amount of positive reinforcement a person receives from others:

1. The most basic measure is the rate of behavior emitted.
2. Interpersonal efficiency focuses on the relationship between number of behaviors emitted and number of behaviors elicited from others.
3. interpersonal range concerns the number of persons one interacts with in a given period of time.
4. The rate of positive reactions indicates the number of behaviors directed toward the patient to which he or she responds in a positively reinforcing way.
5. Action latency or time consists of the reaction by another person to the patient's next verbal interaction.

As pointed out earlier, there is some question as to whether Lewinsohn's subjects may be described as truly clinically depressed (at least in the sense that they sought out treatment at their own initiative). Thus, generality of his findings to more seriously disturbed populations remains in question. Moreover, relatively few investigations compare the social skill responses of clinically depressed patients with those of other psychiatric groupings. Perhaps more important, however, is the fact that social skills as defined by Lewinsohn (1975) and Hersen and Bellack (1977a) have not been evaluated in terms of .the subcategories of depression. Although it is alleged (cf. Detre & Jarecki, 1971) that the premorbid personalities of unipolar depressives are characterized by anxiety and interpersonal disturbance and that most bipolar depressives evidence healthy premorbid interpersonal functioning, no published study has examined this factor using Lewinsohn's coding scheme or the Behavioral Assertiveness Test-Revised (Hersen et al., 1978). Also, Winokur's three categories of depression (depression spectrum disease, pure depressive disease, and sporadic depressive disease) definitely have not been contrasted in behavioral fashion with regard to social skill functioning.

Again and again, it needs to be pointed out that the paths of behavioral and psychiatric researchers in depression do not seem to converge. One would think that the time would be ripe for such a convergence of ideas and methodologies.

Before summarizing the points that have been made, a number of additional issues related to the assessment of depression need to be considered. First, in light of some of the data he has adduced, Lewinsohn (1975) posits that the unipolar depressive's inadequate social skills result in depression. If indeed social ineptness is causative for depression, then the mere pharmacologic treatment of the disorder will not lead to a lasting remission of symptoms nor will it change the patient's skill level. The work of Klerman, DiMascio, Weissman, Prusoff, and Paykel (1974) certainly suggests that drugs and psychotherapy have a synergistic effect, with drugs altering mood and vegetative symptoms and psychotherapy affecting social competence. Thus, in a comprehensive assessment, mood, vegetative symptoms, and social skill all need to be carefully evaluated.

Second, in studies of depression, such scales as the Hamilton Rating Scale for Depression tend to be filled out by psychiatric personnel on the basis of an interview with the patient (Hamilton, 1960). Although the scale does have acceptable reliability (cf. Rehm, 1978), it cannot be assumed (as often is the case in psychiatric research) that each time it is employed it has been administered in a reliable fashion. Rather, it behooves investigators of each new study to demonstrate empirically that reliability of administration once more has been attained (see Hersen & Barlow, 1976, Chapter 4). It is also of considerable interest to videotape such interviews and to rate on a retrospective basis verbal and nonverbal behaviors of the patient and to correlate these with Hamilton ratings. (This is being done in the laboratories of Rehm, Hersen, and Bellack.)

Third, Lewinsohn and Libet (1972) have demonstrated a significant correlation in moderately depressed individuals between level of mood and engaging in pleasant activities. However, despite the statistical significance of the correlations obtained, the absolute magnitudes are not overly impressive. Moreover, ratings of activities by subjects often are completed at the end of the day, not as they occur. Thus, the possibility for retrospective distortion is considerable. Also, in Lewinsohn's (1975) scheme, there is the implication that by engaging in a low rate of pleasurable activities, the depressed individual may become yet more depressed. This, of course, may be the case. But, since the studies reported by Lewinsohn and colleagues basically are correlational in nature, we do believe that the separate issues of correlation and causation may have been confounded. Correlation, as is well known, may, but does not necessarily, imply causation.

## Summary

To summarize, let us first reiterate the importance of making behavioral assessment in general more than an experimental endeavor of academic interest. Rather, it needs to be brought into the hands of the practicing clinicians. After all, they see most of the patients. Second, the important developments in the psychiatric classification of depression coupled with the innovations of behavioral assessment in the area would make for an ideal collaboration between psychiatric and behavioral researchers. A number of instances where such fruitful collaboration could take place have been indicated. Third, it was pointed out that there are some problems in the way both behavioral and nonbehavioral methods for assessing depression are being carried out. It is hoped that some of these comments may stimulate additional research in this still growing area of evaluation.

## References

Akiskal, H. S., Bitar, A. H., Puzantian, V. R., Rosenthal, T. L., & Walker, P. W. The nosological status of neurotic depression. *Archives of General Psychiatry,* 1978, *35,* 756–766.

Akiskal, H. S., & McKinney, W. T. Overview of recent research in depression. *Archives of General Psychiatry,* 1975, *32,* 285–305.

Andreasen, N. C., & Winokur, G. Secondary depression: Familial, clinical, and research perspectives. *American Journal of Psychiatry,* 1979, *136,* 62–66.

Bandura, A. *Principles of behavior modification.* New York: Holt, Rinehart, & Winston, 1969.

Beck, A. T., Ward, C. H., Mendelson, M., Mock, J., & Erbaugh, J. An inventory for measuring depression. *Archives of General Psychiatry* 1961, *4,* 561–571.

Beigel, A., & Murphy, D. L. Unipolar and bipolar affective illness. *Archives of General Psychiatry,* 1971, *24,* 215–220.

Bellack, A. S. Behavioral assessment of social skills. In A. S. Bellack & M. Hersen (Eds.), *Research and practice in social skills training.* New York: Plenum Press, 1980.

Bellack, A. S., & Hersen, M. Use of self-report inventories in behavioral assessment. In J. D. Cone & R. P. Hawkins (Eds.), *Behavioral assessment: New directions in clinical psychology.* New York: Brunner/Mazel, 1977.

Bellack, A. S., & Hersen, M. *Introduction to clinical psychology.* New York: Oxford University Press, 1980.

Bellack, A. S., Hersen, M., & Turner, S. M. Role-play tests for assessing social skills: Are they valid? *Behavior Therapy*, 1978, *9*, 448–461.

Bellack, A. S., Hersen, M., & Turner, S. M. Relationship of role playing and knowledge of appropriate behavior to assertion in the natural environment. *Journal of Consulting and Clinical Psychology*, 1979, *47*, 670–678.

Blanchard, E. B., & Hersen, M. Behavioral treatment of hysterical neurosis: Symptom substitution and symptom return reconsidered. *Psychiatry*, 1976, *39*, 118–129.

Bootzin, R. R., & Nicassio, P. M. Behavioral treatments in insomnia. In M. Hersen, R. M. Eisler, & P. M. Miller (Eds.), *Progress in behavior modification* (Vol. 6). New York: Academic Press, 1978.

Cautela, J. R., & Upper, D. The behavioral inventory battery: The use of self-report measures in behavioral analysis and therapy. In M. Hersen & A. S. Bellack (Eds.), *Behavioral assessment: A practical handbook.* New York: Pergamon Press, 1976.

Detre, T. P., & Jarecki, H. G. *Modern psychiatric treatment.* Philadelphia: J. B. Lippencott, 1971.

Eisler, R. M., Hersen, M., Miller, P. M., & Blanchard, E. B. Situational determinants of assertive behaviors. *Journal of Consulting and Clinical Psychology*, 1975, *43*, 330–340.

Eisler, R. M., Miller, P. M., & Hersen, M. Components of assertive behavior. *Journal of Clinical Psychology*, 1973, *29*, 295–299.

Eysenck, H. J. *The scientific study of personality.* London: Routledge & Kegan Paul, 1952.

Hamilton, M. A rating scale for depression. *Journal of Neurology, Neurosurgery, and Psychiatry*, 1960, *23*, 56–62.

Hauri, P., Chernik, D., Hawkins, D., & Mendels, J. Sleep of depressed patients in remission. *Archives of General Psychiatry*, 1974, *31*, 386–391.

Hersen, M. Self-assessment of fear. *Behavior Therapy*, 1973, *4*, 241–257.

Hersen, M. Historical perspectives in behavioral assessment. In M. Hersen & A. S. Bellack (Eds.), *Behavioral assessment: A practical handbook.* New York: Pergamon Press, 1976.

Hersen, M. Do behavior therapists use self-reports as the major criteria? *European Journal of Behavioural Analysis and Modification*, 1978, *2*, 328–334.

Hersen, M. Limitations and problems in the clinical application of behavioral techniques in psychiatric settings. *Behavior Therapy*, 1979, *10*, 65–80. (a)

Hersen, M. Modification of skill deficits in psychiatric patients. In A. S. Bellack & M. Hersen (Eds.), *Research and practice in social skills training.* New York: Plenum Press, 1979. (b)

Hersen, M., & Barlow, D. H. *Single case experimental designs.* New York: Pergamon Press, 1976.

Hersen, M., & Bellack, A. S. (Eds.), *Behavioral assessment: A practical handbook.* New York: Pergamon Press, 1976.

Hersen, M., & Bellack, A. S. Assessment of social skills. In A. R. Ciminero, K. S. Calhoun, & H. E. Adams (Eds.), *Handbook of behavioral assessment.* New York: John Wiley and Sons, 1977. (a)

Hersen, M., & Bellack, A. S. Behavior modification: Sophisticated or naive? *Behavior Modification*, 1977, *1*, 3–6. (b)

Hersen, M., Bellack, A. S., & Turner, S. M. Assessment of assertiveness in female psychiatric patients: Motor and autonomic measures. *Journal of Behavior Therapy and Experimental Psychiatry*, 1978, *9*, 11–16.

Hersen, M., Bellack, A. S., Turner, S. M., Williams, M., Harper, K., & Watts, J. G. Psychometric properties of the Wolpe–Lazarus Assertiveness Scale. *Behaviour Research and Therapy*, 1979, *17*, 63–69.

Hersen, M., Eisler, R. M., Alford, G. S., & Agras, W. S. Effects of token economy on neurotic depression: An experimental analysis. *Behavior Therapy*, 1973, *4*, 392–397.

Hersen, M., Miller, P. M., & Eisler, R. M. Interaction between alcoholics and their wives: A descriptive analysis of verbal and nonverbal behavior. *Quarterly Journal of Studies on Alcohol*, 1973, *34*, 516–520.

Kanfer, F. H., & Phillips, J. S. *Learning foundations of behavior therapy.* New York: John Wiley & Sons, 1970.

Kanfer, F. H., & Saslow, G. Behavioral diagnosis. In C. M. Franks (Ed.), *Behavior therapy: Appraisal and status.* New York: McGraw Hill, 1969.

Katz, M., & Lyerly, S. Methods of measuring adjustment and social behavior in the community: I. Rationale, description, discriminative validity and scale development. *Psychological Reports,* 1963, *13,* 503–535.

Kazdin, A. E. Assessing the clinical or applied importance of behavior change through social validation. *Behavior Modification,* 1977, *1,* 427–452.

Klerman, G. L., DiMascio, A., Weissman, M., Prusoff, B., & Paykel, E. S. Treatment of depression by drugs and psychotherapy. *American Journal of Psychiatry,* 1974, *131,* 186–191.

Kupfer, D. J., Foster, F. G., Detre, T. P., & Himmelhoch, J. M. Sleep EEG and motor activity as indicators in affective states. *Neuropsychobiology,* 1975, *1,* 296–303.

Kupfer, D. J., Pickar, D., Himmelhoch, J. M., & Detre, T. P. Are there two types of unipolar depression? *Archives of General Psychiatry,* 1975, *32,* 866–871.

Lewinsohn, P. M. Clinical and theoretical aspects of depression. In K. S. Calhoun, H. E. Adams, & K. M. Mitchell (Eds.), *Innovative treatment methods of psychopathology.* New York: John Wiley & Sons, 1974.

Lewinsohn, P. M. The behavioral study and treatment of depression. In M. Hersen, R. M. Eisler, & P. M. Miller (Eds.), *Progress in behavior modification* (Vol. 1). New York: Academic Press, 1975.

Lewinsohn, P. M., & Libet, J. Pleasant events, activity schedules, and depression. *Journal of Abnormal Psychology,* 1972, *79,* 291–295.

Lewinsohn, P. M., & Shaffer, M. Use of home observations as an integral part of the treatment of depression: Preliminary report and case studies. *Journal of Consulting and Clinical Psychology,* 1971, *37,* 87–94.

Libet, J. M., & Lewinsohn, P. M. Concept of social skill with special reference to the behavior of depressed persons. *Journal of Consulting and Clinical Psychology,* 1973, *40,* 304–312.

Mendels, J., & Hawkins, D. R. Sleep and depression: A follow-up study. *Archives of General Psychiatry,* 1967, *16,* 536–542.

Rehm, L. P. Assessment of depression. In M. Hersen & A. S. Bellack (Eds.), *Behavioral assessment: A practical handbook.* New York: Pergamon Press, 1976.

Rehm, L. P. The assessment of depression in therapy outcome research: A review of instruments and recommendations for an assessment battery. A report to the Psychotherapy and Behavioral Intervention Section, Clinical Research Branch, National Institute of Mental Health, November 1978. (a)

Rehm, L. P. Mood, pleasant events, and unpleasant events: Two pilot studies. *Journal of Consulting and Clinical Psychology,* 1970, *46,* 854–859. (b)

Rehm, L. P., & Kornblith, S. J. Behavior therapy for depression: A review of recent developments. In M. Hersen, R. M. Eisler, & P. M. Miller (Eds.), *Progress in behavior modification* (Vol. 7). New York: Academic Press, 1979.

Rosekind, M. R., Thomas, A. B., Coates, T. J., & Thoresen, C. E. Brief communication: Telephone transmission of all-night polysomnographic data from subjects' homes. *Journal of Nervous and Mental Disease,* 1978, *166,* 438–441.

Rush, A. J., & Beck, A. T. Adults with affective disorders. In M. Hersen & A. S. Bellack (Eds.), *Behavior therapy in the psychiatric setting.* Baltimore: Williams & Wilkins, 1978.

Swan, G. E., & MacDonald, M. L. Behavior therapy in practice: A national survey of behavior therapists. *Behavior Therapy,* 1978, *9,* 799–807.

Thomson, K. C., & Hendri, H. C. Environmental stress in primary depressive illness. *Archives of General Psychiatry,* 1972, *26,* 130–132.

Van Hesselt, V. B., Hersen, M., Bellack, A. S., Rosenblum, N. D., & Lamparski, D. Tripartite assessment of the effects of systematic desensitization in a multiphobic child: An experimental analysis. *Journal of Behavior Therapy and Experimental Psychiatry,* 1979, *10,* 51–56.

Wells, K. C., Hersen, M., Bellack, A. S., & Himmelhoch, J. M. Social skills learning for unipolar (nonpsychotic) depression: A clinical investigation. *American Journal of Psychiatry,* 1979, *136,* 1331–1332.

Williams, J. G., Barlow, D. H., & Agras, W. S. Behavioral measurement of severe depression. *Archives of General Psychiatry,* 1972, *27,* 330–333.

Winokur, G. Unipolar depression. *Archives of General Psychiatry*, 1979, *36*, 47–52.

Winokur, G., Behar, D., VanValkenberg, C., & Lowry, M. Is a familial definition of depression both feasible and valid? *Journal of Nervous and Mental Disease*, 1978, *166*, 764–768.

Winokur, G., Cadoret R., Dorzak, J., & Baker, M. Depressive disease: A genetic study. *Archives of General Psychiatry*, 1971, *24*, 135–144.

Wolpe, J. Transcript of initial interview in a case of depression. *Journal of Behavior Therapy and Experimental Psychiatry*, 1970, *1*, 71–78.

Wolpe, J., & Lazarus, A. A. *Behavior therapy techniques*. New York: Pergamon Press, 1966.

# 14

## Outcome Evaluation Strategies[1]

ALAN E. KAZDIN

Research on depression has reached a particularly interesting stage, even though systematic work has begun only recently. Major developments have emerged providing theoretical accounts of the basis of depressive states (e.g., Beck, 1967; Ferster, 1973; Lewinsohn, 1974; Rehm, 1977; Seligman, 1974). The developments have derived both from clinical observation of the characteristics of depressive patients as well as from infrahuman laboratory research suggesting antecedents that might account for these characteristics. On the basis of both theoretical and clinical developments on the nature of depression, several different therapeutic approaches have emerged. These developments are particularly noteworthy because considerations of etiology and treatment, at least at the level of psychological variables, are actively pursued and intertwined.

Both the theoretical basis of depression and its treatment have been examined directly or by implication in the outcome research. Specific treatments have been proposed and evaluated not merely to discover effective treatments but to address issues about the determinants of depression as well. Hence, many treatment studies have used outcome results as the basis for inferring theoretical postulates about the causes and correlates of depression.

Although research that reflects on both the theories of depression and the effective treatments is a major characteristic of this area of investigation, it is important to examine the issues somewhat separately. The outcome research in many ways is at a critical period of development. Several treatments appear to be effective, many comparisons of alternative treatments have been completed, and questions about the next steps for research have yet to be explicitly formulated.

[1] Completion of this chapter was facilitated by grant MH 31047 from the National Institute of Mental Health.

317

The purpose of the present chapter is to examine the different outcome questions that need to be evaluated for the treatment of depression. The alternative questions can be illustrated by diverse treatment design strategies. The chapter presents alternative design strategies for therapy evaluation, examines the priority that these strategies might be accorded, and critically evaluates the extent to which the outcome literature has addressed fundamental questions about alternative treatments. By outlining alternative strategies and the types of questions they address, the deficits in the outcome research should become apparent. In developing the different treatment strategies, the purpose is not to review the literature nor to evaluate the methodological problems of individual studies. Select studies are examined to highlight the need for research that focuses on unresolved questions in the literature.

## Characteristics of Outcome Research in Depression

The outcome research in depression can be characterized in several ways. A few of the characteristics that seem particularly salient are illustrated merely to provide the context for presentation of alternative evaluation strategies. Examination of selected characteristics illustrates the need for a wider range of treatment evaluation strategies in future research.

### Diffuseness of Focus

The diffuseness of focus refers to the wide range of treatment techniques that have been studied, the types of depression included in the research, and the range of outcome measures used. Perhaps the main issue is the many different treatments that have been proposed and applied. At this point, it might well appear from a review of the literature that many different procedures produce change in depression, including variations of cognitive therapy, behavior therapy, self-control training, relaxation, flooding, desensitization, role playing, modeling, and feedback (Rehm & Kornblith, 1979). It is especially interesting that, at this early stage of development, so many different techniques appear to produce change. Possibly, depression is not as difficult to treat as once thought, or truly important breakthroughs have been made. As likely, various characteristics of the methods of outcome research, enumerated throughout this chapter, have contributed to the present pattern of results.

At the outset, it is important merely to note that multiple approaches currently are applied and appear to produce therapeutic change. Accomplishments in the breadth of treatment approaches have been compensated by a relative paucity of research that carefully examines a particular technique and the parameters that contribute to its efficacy. More pointed questions about individual treatments are needed in place of, or as a supplement to, the proliferation of new treatments. The purpose is not to stifle creativity nor to delimit technique development. However, a firmer empirical base for understanding existing techniques is needed.

## Comparative Studies

The diffuseness of outcome research in the treatment of depression has led to the apparent and immediate need for comparative research. Such research often emerges early in the development of a technique, as is evident in many examples from contemporary psychotherapy research (e.g., Ellis, 1957; Lazarus, 1961; Paul, 1966). When a new technique emerges or several different techniques seem to be available, comparative research seems to take on a very high priority. Such research is of obvious importance and has a unique role in evaluating treatment. However, it often is resorted to prematurely, at least in my opinion. Indeed, it is unfortunate in some ways that a new technique can find its way so quickly into comparative studies when so little is known about it.

In depression outcome research, a relatively high proportion of the available studies are comparative in nature, contrasting two or more competing treatment techniques. The expectations may be too high for the conclusions that can be drawn. The initial techniques that are compared often are not well understood. Dimensions that maximize changes for the individual techniques included in comparative studies are not well known, and the type of depression or clients to which the techniques are more appropriately applied, the duration of treatment, and other conditions are not understood. The variations of treatment utilized in early comparative research may not be those that would have been utilized had the technique been developed more systematically with other types of outcome strategies.

Another issue is that comparative outcome research often raises design problems that are somewhat greater than other evaluation strategies (Kazdin, 1980). Treatments may vary in their required duration, the amount of therapist–client contact, the appropriateness of particular measurement modalities, and so on. Hence, comparative studies with conceptually and procedurally distinct treatments often are more difficult to evaluate than are other types of outcome research.

Despite the generally agreed upon importance of comparative research, it is useful to raise questions about the priority that this particular strategy is accorded in the current outcome research on depression. Relatively little is known about major treatment contenders, including cognitive therapy and behavior therapy, and the comparative studies do not shed light on whether these individual treatments operate in many of the ways proposed on conceptual grounds. Also, some of the problems of comparative research have greatly limited the conclusions that can be drawn about the treatments that are compared. For example, treatments occasionally have led to differential attrition (e.g., Rush, Beck, Kovacs, & Hollon, 1977). When attrition, as a dependent measure, reflects significant differences among alternative treatments, conclusions reached for any of the other measures are highly questionable.

## Type of Depression

In current outcome research, there has been a tendency to neglect different types of depression. To be sure, the gamut of depressive types has been included in treatment (Rehm & Kornblith, 1979). Yet, the outcome literature for depression generally is viewed in relation to a uniform problem rather than specific types of depression. Emerging evidence suggests that many different, albeit possibly related, disorders are included and might warrant separate examination. For example, unipolar and bipolar depression may differ in their etiological bases, as genetic and biochemical evidence suggests (Cadoret & Tanna, 1977; Gershon, Dunner, & Goodwin, 1971). Differential responsiveness of these types of depression to chemotherapy also has been suggested (Morris & Beck, 1974). Responsiveness to alternative treatments (e.g., various chemotherapies) may be related to the nature of the depression along other dimensions (e.g., recurrent and episodic, whether suicidal ideation is present) (see Becker & Schuckit, 1978; Kupfer, Pickar, Himmelhoch, & Detre, 1975). The nature and etiological bases may greatly influence the success of alternative psychological treatments, a prospect that has yet to be adequately addressed in the outcome research. Preliminary evidence suggests that alternative treatments (e.g., cognitive therapy) may differ in efficacy across patients varying in chronicity (Rush, Hollon, Beck, & Kovacs, 1978), but a systematic evaluation of chronicity, let alone other subject variables, has yet to appear.

In referring to the type of depression, one might object on conceptual and empirical grounds to traditional diagnostic categories. However, the concern about evaluating types of depression can be expressed without referring to these categories. Depressive patients might be evaluated according to the number and type of specific symptoms they evince (e.g., Spitzer, Endicott, & Robins, 1975). Alternatively, several dimensions might be invoked to provide a profile along cognitive, behavioral, affective, and environmental variables. Such a profile plus a finer analysis of the presenting problems of the depressed patient may suggest which treatments are more or less appropriate.

Depression often is spoken of as the "common cold" of mental health. This analogy is used to characterize the pervasiveness of depression in its many forms. Yet, the analogy might be pushed a little further. There are many different bases for the symptoms attributed to the common cold. The lack of breakthroughs stems in part from not delineating the different bases for similar symptoms. On the other hand, when breakthroughs in identifying some of the bases (e.g., identification of a particular bacterium or virus) have been made, advances in treatment have more readily followed.

In the absence of clear etiological determinants of the manifold forms of depression, it still may be valuable to examine treatments in relation to specific forms of depression or specific patient profiles. Preliminary evidence already suggests that different treatments for depression may alter different aspects of the disorder (Rehm, Fuchs, Roth, Kornblith, & Romano, 1979). Further work is needed to determine the relevant dimensions to be altered for particular patients and the extent to which treatments achieve these specific effects.

## Severity of Depression

Independently of the type of depression, severity of depression within subtype warrants examination. Depression research seems not to have profited from the lesson of behavioral outcome research in such other areas as the treatment of anxiety and avoidance behavior. Treatments focusing upon anxiety have been researched primarily in the context of college student populations whose fears are subclinical. Objections to research on college students with fears of small animals or test and speech anxiety have been voiced repeatedly (e.g., Bernstein & Paul, 1971; Hersen, 1979; Kazdin, 1978). Although much of the work in depression has encompassed patient populations, a large portion has evaluated techniques with relatively mild depression among college students enrolled in introductory psychology courses (e.g., Hammen & Glass, 1975; Shipley & Fazio, 1973). It is quite possible that some of the favorable results achieved with select techniques are a function of studying mildly depressed college students.

For example, research has suggested that self-monitoring of behavior alters one's mood (Hammen & Glass, 1975). These results suggest that self-monitoring, a component in different treatments for depression, may be an effective treatment in its own right. Such a possibility should not be ruled out. However, an already extensive literature is available showing that self-monitoring in other areas is a very weak treatment and produces transient effects (Kazdin, 1974; Nelson, 1977). Possibly, self-monitoring has appeared effective as a treatment in part because of the lack of severity of depressive behavior to which it has been applied. The external validity of treatment techniques shown to be effective with college student populations warrants attention. Rather than simply extending techniques to patient populations, research that examines severity of depression as a separate variable would be very valuable. Such research can better assess whether severity of depression is a relevant factor that mediates treatment efficacy.

## General Comments

The diffuseness of focus, the relatively great attention devoted to comparative outcome studies, and the lack of attention paid to the type and severity of depression as they may interact with treatment do not exhaust the characteristics of treatment research in depression. A few characteristics of the research are illustrated here to highlight the need for research on a broader range of outcome questions. The specific questions that can be asked about alternative treatments are not difficult to enumerate. However, it is useful to examine the different design strategies for depression research, the questions they address, and the relative attention or neglect that each strategy has received.

## Treatment Evaluation Strategies

As in any area of outcome research, a number of questions can be raised regarding the treatment of depression. These different questions are associated with specific evaluation strategies (see Kazdin, 1980). The different design strategies and the questions they address are important to delineate, because the treatment literature for depression is quite uneven in the development for a given technique and across different techniques.

### Treatment Package Strategy

The treatment package strategy refers to evaluating the effects of a given treatment as that treatment is normally conducted or advocated by its proponents. The term *package* is used to denote that the treatment may include multiple components. The components included in this treatment may be distinguished conceptually and even operationally. The treatment package strategy does not address the role of the separate components but only raises the general question of whether a particular treatment produces change. Put simply, "Does the treatment package with all of its components work?" To answer this question, treatment is administered in its entirety, with all components. In the basic study of a package strategy, treatment need only be compared to a no-treatment or waiting-list control group.

Treatment package research has been used relatively frequently in outcome research on depression. Typically, a particular treatment with many different components is compared with no treatment or a range of treatments that might be applied in routine outpatient (e.g., office consultation, supportive therapy, occasional medication) or inpatient care (e.g., ward milieu). For example, McLean, Ogston, and Grauer (1973) compared a behavioral approach involving training in social learning principles, feedback from spouses for negativistic social interaction, and behavioral contracts with a control condition involving several different treatments (office consultation, drugs) that patients received when they returned to their original treatment referral source. In measures of self-report and verbal behavior, the behavioral package led to greater reductions in depression at posttreatment and at a 3-month follow-up.

Treatment package research characterizes the strategies used in intrasubject replications designs where single-treatment interventions are compared with baseline (no-treatment) conditions. For example, use of reinforcement contingencies for a variety of behaviors, occasionally combined with extinction of depressive behavior, have constituted multifaceted treatment packages (e.g., Hanaway & Barlow, 1975; Hersen, Eisler, Alford, & Agras, 1973; Liberman & Raskin, 1971).

CONSIDERATIONS IN USING THE TREATMENT PACKAGE STRATEGY

This strategy is usually the first approach employed to evaluate a therapy technique. The technique may have developed from a problem-oriented approach in which a complex multifaceted treatment may be used to achieve the necessary changes. All sorts of ingredients may comprise the package, including some components that are unnecessary and perhaps even ineffective. Yet, at the early stage of research, ancillary ingredients are not of particular concern. Only after the main question is resolved—that is, does this treatment package alter the problem?—is a finer-grained analysis warranted.

The priority of treatment package research also stems, in part, from a concern for experimental efficiency. If the entire treatment package with all of its distinguishable components changes behavior, then the researcher can scrutinize particular components more analytically. Presumably, the package is the most effective variation of treatment. If the package does not produce behavior change, it probably makes little sense to delve further into the technique. Essentially, exploring the effects of the treatment package serves as a screening device for an investigator to assess whether further analytic research on the technique is warranted.

Of course, it is not necessarily the case that the failure of the overall package to produce change is grounds for dismissing the technique altogether. Therapists may not have been adequately trained to implement the technique correctly. Alternatively, specific components of the package may act antagonistically in altering depression so that components in a given treatment might, when combined, reduce the efficacy of therapy, a prospect made tenable by findings in other areas of outcome research (e.g., Meichenbaum, Gilmore, & Fedoravicius, 1971).

The importance of package research in the treatment of depression is obvious. The package strategy gives the highest priority to effecting therapeutic change, which may justify complex multifaceted treatments. Hence, the strategy usually is the initial one used in developing effective treatments.

## Dismantling Treatment Strategy

The dismantling treatment strategy refers to analyzing the components of a given treatment (Lang, 1969). Once a treatment package has been shown to work, research may begin to analyze the precise influence of specific components. The purpose of dismantling treatment research is to understand the basis for therapeutic change produced by the overall package. To dismantle a given technique, individual treatment components are eliminated or isolated from treatment. Comparisons usually are made between groups that receive the treatment package and those that receive the package minus the specific components. Essentially, different components of treatment are viewed as separate independent variables and withheld for some subjects, presented to others, or presented in varying degrees among subjects. Also, the separate and combined effects of different components can be evaluated. Differences among groups, depending upon the specific design, can suggest whether certain components are necessary and/or sufficient to produce behavior change and whether specific components produce additive or interactive effects.

The results of a dismantling strategy usually go beyond the implications of conducting treatment and bear upon theoretical notions that served as a basis for the derivation or explanation of the technique. By dismantling the treatment package, an investigator can comment upon whether the ingredients thought to be crucial for therapeutic change in fact are. Thus, dismantling research often has important theoretical implications and may produce results that call for revision of the theory underlying the total treatment package.

Many complex packages exist for the treatment of depression, and examples of programmatic dismantling research are difficult to find. The general approach of dismantling research can be illustrated in part by individual studies that look at small components of larger treatment packages. For example, cognitive therapy includes many different components, such as discussions with clients about connections between cognitions, affect, and behavior; self-monitoring of negative thoughts; examination of the basis (evidence) for distorted cognitions; substitution of reality-oriented interpretations; and homework assignments (Rush et al., 1977). A dismantling strategy would look carefully at the role of these individual components to determine necessary and sufficient conditions for therapeutic change. Research of this sort has yet to be completed.

An interesting study was reported by Coleman (1975), who required depressed college females to read positive self-statements to "talk themselves into the idea" of a more elated mood. The intervention increased elation in depressed subjects. The finding is interesting in part because it suggests the possible therapeutic effects of one ingredient or component of cognitive therapy. Additional research simultaneously evaluating the components of the larger package, more characteristic of the dismantling strategy, would certainly be warranted.

CONSIDERATIONS IN USING THE DISMANTLING
TREATMENT STRATEGY

The dismantling strategy requires that the treatment package consist of well-specified ingredients and that these ingredients be limited to some reasonable number. Theoretical notions as to the nature of the ingredients and their relative importance are also very helpful. Without a theoretical framework in which to view treatment, it is easy to trivialize the components. Actually, an indefinite number of components within any given therapy technique can be distinguished, some of which might be theoretically important (e.g., monitoring depressive thoughts within the treatment session) and others of which might not be (e.g., ratio of client to therapist verbalizations). The priority of components for research is determined by the theoretical basis for the technique that specifies the mechanism(s) of therapeutic change and, hence, the necessary conditions for behavior change.

Dismantling research may show that a particular theory is not plausible in accounting for the results of a given technique. In this case, the components of the technique might be reanalyzed along different dimensions to assess the plausibility of another theory. There may be no specific components that are basic; rather components may be defined by the theoretical interpretation of the technique.

Dismantling research may be particularly important in depression research. Many different treatments appear to have common ingredients. For example, cognitive, behavioral, and self-control treatments of depression often include such ingredients as engaging in specific homework assignments, self-monitoring behavior, and identifying immediate precursors to mood states (e.g., Fuchs & Rehm, 1977; Lewinsohn, Biglan, & Zeiss, 1975; Rush et al., 1977; Shaw, 1977; Taylor & Marshall, 1977). It is essential to evaluate the contribution of these and other specific components of individual treatments to determine their roles in therapeutic change. As yet, little can be said about the necessary or sufficient conditions for individual treatments among the major treatment contenders. Immediate candidates for dismantling research are individual treatments evaluated with and without their common components.

In addition to evaluating the common elements among alternative techniques, dismantling research is needed to study the various components of an individual treatment package. Many of the packages that have shown promising results are complex and multifaceted. For example, in one program, treatment included role playing, instructions, feedback, modeling, reinforcement, and homework assignments (Wells, Hersen, Bellack, & Himmelhoch, 1977). In another program, treatment included identification of coping skills and problematic cognitions and use of positive self-statements and high-probability behaviors (Schmickley, 1976). In these and many other treatments, the necessary and sufficient conditions to achieve therapeutic change warrant scrutiny.

Dismantling research for a given treatment of depression is likely to require several investigations. The reason for this pertains to the complexity of the packages and the need to examine components carefully. A single attempt to look at package components and their combinations is not likely to provide informative results unless a very large number of subjects is available for each of the many groups that can be derived. Unlike treatment package research, which might obtain relatively large differences between a treatment and a control (no-treatment) group, dismantling research is likely to produce relatively small differences. Hence, adequate statistical power requires a commensurately larger sample size within groups to detect differences among groups exposed to subtle variations in treatment components. With weak power, the predictable result is no differences among groups receiving treatments involving different components.

For example, a recent dismantling study evaluated components of self-control therapy (Rehm, Kornblith, O'Hara, Lamparski, Romano, & Volkin, 1978). Four different treatments, involving either the full self-control package (self-monitoring, self-evaluation, and self-reinforcement) or combinations of the subcomponents, were compared. The results indicated that both treatments generally were superior to no treatment but were not different from each other. These results might be expected in advance, because the overall number of subjects who completed treatment ($N = 45$), when divided among the five groups, yields a test with weak power. The lack of statistical power as a general problem in clinical research has been argued convincingly (Cohen, 1962). However, the problem becomes especially acute in research such as dismantling research, which can be predicted at the outset to find small differences among conditions.

## Constructive Treatment Strategy

The constructive treatment strategy refers to developing a treatment package by adding components to enhance therapy and is, essentially, the opposite of the dismantling strategy. With the constructive strategy, the investigator usually begins with a basic treatment component that is relatively narrow or circumscribed in focus. Research is conducted that adds various ingredients to the basic treatment to determine what enhances outcome. As research continues, effective components are retained and a larger treatment package is constructed. The addition of techniques to the package may not necessarily be led by theoretical considerations. Indeed, this strategy characteristically establishes components empirically, to show that specific ingredients, when added to treatment, enhance outcome. Essentially, the constructive treatment approach addresses the question, "What can be added to this treatment to make it more effective?" Phrased in this way, the question is never definitively answered. Research can continue to develop a given technique by adding components.

The constructive strategy has been used infrequently in depression research. An example that approaches the constructive strategy was illustrated by Shipley and Fazio (1973, Experiment 2), who examined whether positive expectancies for improvement enhanced a behavioral treatment designed to increase opportunities for reinforcement among depressed college students. Treatment was evaluated alone and in conjunction with inducements to expect positive therapeutic changes. Supportive therapy also was evaluated alone and in conjunction with positive expectancies. The behavioral treatment conditions led to improvement on scores on the depression scale of the Minnesota Multiphasic

Personality Inventory, an effect that was not enhanced by positive expectations. This investigation evaluated the addition of a particular component, positive expectancies, that did not enhance the overall treatment technique.

The constructive approach need not make merely procedural additions to treatment. Sometimes entirely different and conceptually unrelated treatments might be combined. The question asked still addresses whether adding new components to an existing intervention makes a difference. However, comparisons across different treatments may also enter into the research. (Comparative research is addressed as a separate strategy later.) For example, Taylor and Marshall (1977) evaluated the effects of cognitive and behavior therapy in treating mild to moderately depressed college students. Treatments consisted of cognitive therapy, behavior therapy, and a combination of these therapies. Although results for all treatment groups were superior to those for the waiting-list control group, results for the combined treatment group were superior to those for the others at posttreatment and 5-week follow-up assessment. This study can be fit into alternative design strategies, but the combining of different techniques into a single condition nicely illustrates the approach of the constructive treatment evaluation strategy.

CONSIDERATIONS IN USING THE CONSTRUCTIVE
TREATMENT STRATEGY

The advantage of the constructive treatment approach is that it empirically establishes a treatment package. Components that are shown to enhance treatment are added to the basic procedure. As this process continues, the package increases in strength. The empirical development of a treatment package is especially refreshing in clinical work, where treatments proliferate to no end and have no established body of empirically validated information.

The constructive treatment approach gives high priority to outcome. Understanding the mechanisms of treatment gives way to outcome. Indeed, the constructive strategy can proceed empirically so that the components are added to treatment without understanding how they operate or interact with other components. However, the ability of the constructive treatment approach to proceed without theory may be the main disadvantage of this approach. Adding components to treatment may not shed light on the mechanisms of change. Ideally, components would be added to treatment on the basis of theoretical considerations. Alternatively, as components are demonstrated to enhance treatment, they may at that point be placed into a theoretical framework.

## Parametric Treatment Strategy

The parametric treatment strategy refers to varying specific aspects of treatment to determine how to maximize therapeutic change. This strategy resembles the constructive treatment strategy insofar as the purpose is to examine dimensions that can be used to enhance treatment effects. However, the constructive approach usually evaluates the effects of adding or combining qualitatively distinct interventions to an existing treatment. Indeed, different treatment packages might be combined in a constructive treatment investigation. In contrast, the parametric strategy usually varies one or more dimensions within the existing treatment package. New treatments are not added.

In parametric research, the variation often is made along quantitative dimensions by providing more or less of a given portion of treatment. For example, parametric investigations might focus on such variables as the amount of treatment and the number, spacing, and duration of individual sessions. With parametric variations, each of the groups studied might receive the same general treatment and differ only in quantitative dimensions of variables ordinarily associated with that treatment.

Parametric treatment research often emerges when treatment package research is fairly well developed. For that reason, perhaps, relatively little parametric outcome research is available in the area of depression. One case application that illustrates the type of manipulations utilized by the parametric evaluation strategy was reported by Vasta (1976). A depressed college student was treated by trying to elicit positive self-evaluative responses. In an initial treatment phase, the client read a list of personal assets each morning, a procedure that did not increase the rate of spontaneous positive self-statements. A change in the procedure consisted of having the client read statements of personal assets hourly; this did appear to increase spontaneous positive self-statements. Of course, the design of this report, the confound of sequence effects with treatment conditions, and the absence of data on adherence showing that treatments were distinct preclude conclusions about the particular manipulation. Yet, the focus is one clearly needed in depression research. In the usual parametric study, a between-group design would be used in which different groups receive variations of treatment based upon parametric manipulation of one or more variables.

CONSIDERATIONS IN USING THE PARAMETRIC
TREATMENT STRATEGY

The parametric evaluation strategy is useful in many of the same ways as is the constructive evaluation strategy. The evaluation of specific treatment parameters can help build an effective treatment strategy. In addition to maximizing treatment outcome, the parametric approach can reveal important information about the theoretical basis of the technique and the mechanisms responsible for change. In this sense, the parametric approach also embraces some of the features of the dismantling strategy. Rather than taking components away from the treatment, the parametric strategy varies the amount of each component of treatment. In the process of varying specific dimensions, information might result that supports or is incompatible with the mechanism(s) assumed to account for change.

*Comparative Treatment Strategy*

Comparative treatment research refers to a comparison of different treatments and is widely familiar to researchers in the area of outcome evaluation. Essentially, two or more different treatment packages are compared. Comparative research asks the question, "Which treatment is better (or best) among those available for a particular problem?" The question of comparative research usually holds wide interest because of the theoretical battles over the bases of alternative techniques and practical clinical demands for improved treatment. Indeed, the enthusiasm over comparative research, in my opinion, has impeded many areas of outcome research and could well do so at this stage of outcome research in the area of depression.

Both the dismantling and constructive strategies might be viewed as comparative research, because comparisons are made among various treatments. Yet, in the dismantling and constructive approaches, different versions of a given treatment package are evaluated either to analyze or to develop a single treatment. In comparative research, two or more different treatments are compared and usually reflect different conceptual and technical approaches toward the target problem.

Comparative research has been used in outcome studies in depression. For example, investigations have encompassed comparisons of cognitive and behavior therapy (Shaw, 1977; Taylor & Marshall, 1977), cognitive therapy versus chemotherapy (Rush et al., 1977), behavior therapy versus chemotherapy (McLean & Hakstian, 1978), self-control versus social skills training (Rehm et al., 1979), and flooding versus supportive therapy (Hannie & Adams, 1974). The diffuseness of the manifold comparisons precludes clear statements at this point because of the many different measures, types of clients, durations of follow-up evaluation, and so on.

CONSIDERATIONS IN USING THE COMPARATIVE
TREATMENT STRATEGY

The comparative approach has obvious value, because it can establish which among available treatments should be applied to treat depression or whether it makes any difference to select one technique over another. Despite the seeming simplicity of comparing different treatments, comparative research often has special problems. In comparative research, it is particularly important to ensure that each of the techniques is fairly represented in the investigation. Invariably, an investigator who has selected this strategy has a predilection for one of the treatments that is being compared. The other treatment(s) included in the study may not achieve the same degree of authenticity necessary to make the results very credible.

In some cases, demands of experimentation may interfere with representing the treatments in the way that they might be used in actual treatment. For example, in an early desensitization study with speech-anxious college students, traditional insight-oriented therapy was compared with desensitization (Paul, 1966). To keep the duration of therapy constant, both treatments were held to five therapy sessions. Such a brief duration is not likely to provide a very adequate test of insight therapy, since treatment normally is viewed as more protracted. In such a comparative study, the interests in controlling treatment duration may conflict with the need to represent alternative treatments as they are likely to be conducted in practice.

Another issue that can be raised about the utility of comparative research is the matter of which treatment is better. This question may not be as useful in guiding research as it may first appear. The question greatly oversimplifies the complexity of clinical disorders and their treatment. The issue is not which treatment is better in any general sense but which treatment is better in altering a particular problem, as measured by a particular set of outcome measures. The complexity of outcome assessment alone is likely to preclude any simplistic answers to the global comparative questions, because many different measures are likely to lead to different conclusions about treatment (see Kazdin & Wilson, 1978). Different therapy techniques do not always set out to accomplish the same tasks, and the effects achieved may well depend upon the nature of the outcome measures that are selected.

Comparative research in depression has been restricted to a very narrow range of outcome measures related primarily to therapeutic changes immediately after treatment. Conclusions that are reached are hardly definitive, even omitting methodological issues that might be raised in individual studies, because the analyses have been relatively restricted. Average change at the end of treatment is only one type of measure and perhaps not the most crucial to reaching momentous conclusions about a particular set of treatments. Data on the durability and breadth of changes and the proportion of clients who achieve clinically significant changes are all potentially relevant and not necessarily positively correlated measures. Variables related to efficiency, cost, and adherence to treatment as well as those related to client satisfaction with treatment also are relevant.

## Client and Therapist Variation Strategy

The discussion of evaluation strategies to this point has implied that specific techniques have certain effects in a relatively straightforward fashion. No mention has been made of the clients and therapists who are involved in treatment and the influence their attributes and behaviors may have on therapeutic outcome. The client and therapist variation strategy examines these influences in two different ways. First, clients and therapists can be selected for specific attributes that serve as subject variables. Second, behavior of the clients or, more likely, of the therapists can be manipulated experimentally.

In the subject variable strategy, depressed clients may be selected on the basis of the severity or type of depression or for their differences in age, gender, socioeconomic standing, marital status, education, suggestibility, and so on.

Similarly, therapists might be selected on the basis of such characteristics as experience, empathy, warmth, or specific variables more clearly related to the dimensions considered important in treating depression. Alternatively, variables that emerge out of a particular client–therapist dyad can be categorized as a relationship variable and studied in relation to outcome (e.g., Parloff, 1961). The question addressed by client, therapist, or client–therapist combinations is whether certain matches in some way relate to outcome. The main question is whether treatment is more or less effective with certain kinds of participants or when administered by certain kinds of therapists. The client and therapist variation strategy may embrace direct manipulation of independent variables rather than merely subject or therapist selection. Characteristics of the therapist (e.g., warmth, empathy) may be manipulated directly by having therapists behave differently among clients (e.g., Morris & Suckerman, 1974).

The client–therapist variation strategy has been used infrequently in depression research, even though evidence, mentioned earlier, suggests that treatments may be differentially effective depending upon the type of depression. Occasionally, different criteria for selecting clients has been proposed as one of the reasons for discrepant results in depression research. For example, Lewinsohn (1975) noted that the failure of the Hammen and Glass (1975) study to support his finding that increased engagement in pleasant activities reduces depression may have been due in part to the different selection criteria used in the two studies. Such points require additional analytic research to evaluate simultaneously treatments with alternative types of subjects, as defined by alternative screening measures. To date, research of this sort has not been pursued systematically.

CONSIDERATIONS IN USING THE CLIENT AND THERAPIST
VARIATION STRATEGY

The selection of clients and therapists according to specific dimensions increases the precision of the treatment outcome evaluation. It is unlikely that a simple question such as which treatment produces greater change or which components enhance treatment will be the most productive. To these questions need to be added stipulations about characteristics of the clients as well as of the individuals who deliver treatment. The study of variables with which treatment effects are associated begins to define the boundary conditions associated with a given technique and the areas where different techniques produce different advantages. Essentially, the client and therapist variation strategy allows more refined questions to be asked about a given technique and its merits relative to other techniques. Hence, this strategy adds considerably to other strategies already mentioned.

## Internal Structure or Process Strategy

The above strategies refer to what traditionally has been known as outcome research and address the general question about the effects of therapy at the end of treatment. Process research has usually been distinguished from out-come research. It addresses questions that pertain to the transactions between the therapist and client and the type of interactions and their interim effects on client and therapist behavior. Process research often evaluates what client and therapist changes occur during treatment, how these changes arise, the rela-tionship between client and therapist behavior, what constitutes a "good" therapy hour, what factors in treatment contribute to client and therapist evalua-tions of treatment sessions, and the progression of client change over the course of treatment (e.g., Rubinstein & Parloff, 1962; Shlein, 1968; Strupp & Luborsky, 1962).

As usually discussed, process and outcome research are dichotomized. Process research is viewed as the study of activity within the therapy session while treatment still is in process. Outcome research evaluates the final effects of treatment when treatment has been terminated. The distinction can be maintained in certain types of research, because much process research ex-amines the effects of different variables within the treatment session only. Yet, insofar as client changes during treatment sessions are desirable, the effects of specific variables on client behaviors during treatment is one measure of the beneficial effects of treatment and, hence, is a relevant interim outcome mea-sure.

In depression research, relatively little attention has been devoted to internal processes during treatment. There may be reason to deemphasize process research at this stage of the field, because a clearer picture is needed about effective treatments. Yet, process research may be relevant for discovering effective treatments and for revealing the psychological processes involved in depression and its amelioration.

## Progression of Research

The treatment evaluation strategies discussed in this chapter address differ-ent but complementary questions. The strategy that is relied upon most heavily within a given area of treatment such as depression may depend upon the state of the evidence. Preliminary research for a particular technique is likely to adopt the package or constructive approach. After a technique is shown to be effec-tive, parametric or dismantling work is more likely to result. Also, client–therapist variation and internal structure strategies are warranted after prelimi-nary work attests to the efficacy of the technique. Along with this, investigators are increasingly likely to compare a newly established package with alternative techniques that claim or in fact have their own evidence for efficacy. In the area of depression, a prime candidate to include in comparative research is drug treatment because of its predominance.

Since there tends to be an evolution of the type of research strategy that is warranted, it is important to keep in mind the alternative strategies. Emphasis of one strategy over another can lead to uneven development. For example, comparative research outcome has received relatively great attention in most areas where treatments are developing. Comparative research is a dramatic way to develop visibility of a given technique long before the technique has been carefully established in package evaluation research. If the technique can be shown to surpass an existing technique, a flurry of enthusiasm is generated and attention seems to be greater than would be achieved with package research.

Yet, favorable results obtained in one or a few comparative studies are often distracting, in the sense that they may direct attention from more basic work for the techniques involved. It is quite possible that further comparisons would not yield very dramatic results. The techniques included may not be well understood, and the conditions that maximize their efficacy are bypassed in research. For example, it is of great interest to show that cognitive therapy may be superior to drug treatment (Rush et al., 1977). However, in addition to having potential methodological problems that might weaken the conclusions that are drawn, such a comparison might overlook larger issues. Evidence for cognitive therapy has only begun to accumulate. Rather than comparing the technique with other techniques, it is important to understand what aspects of cognitive therapy contribute to its efficacy. Parametric manipulations, dismantling research, and client and therapist variation strategies would contribute greatly to the development of that technique. When much of this research is completed, it would be very important to evaluate the relative efficacy of this technique with others.

It is important not to derogate the obvious importance of comparative research. However, without prior research on characteristics of the technique, conclusions that are reached may be of relatively little value. For example, if a newly developed technique is shown to be less effective than an alternative, it might be prematurely rejected. Yet, development of the technique in its own right might have yielded a much more effective product. Alternatively, if a newly developed technique is shown to be more effective than an alternative, it is important not to accept the degree of superiority as fixed. A much more potent version of the more effective technique might be available, as developed from analytic research on that technique.

Finally, superiority of one technique over another rarely reveals the components of the more effective treatment that accounted for change. It may well be that the superior technique is more effective for reasons that the investigator considers ancillary to treatment. Additional work to understand the basis for therapeutic change is important as well.

## Summary

Several characteristics of outcome research in depression can be identified that may prompt new directions or at least changes in emphasis in the coming years. At this early stage, research has tended to be diffuse in focus, generating a wide range of techniques rather than systematically and programmatically examining the characteristics, impact, and dimensions of individual techniques. Comparative studies have emerged, addressing the obvious questions about the relative effectiveness of major treatment options. At a preliminary stage of outcome research, comparative questions might be better deferred until additional information is available about the individual techniques. Along with technique research, additional attention is warranted regarding the type and severity of depression, the specific symptom pattern, and other characteristics of depressed patients and clients as they relate to treatment.

The present chapter highlighted several different strategies, including the treatment package, dismantling, constructive, parametric, comparative, client–therapist variation, and internal structure or process strategies. Each of these strategies address somewhat different but interrelated outcome questions regarding the treatment of depression. To date, research has given particular emphasis to evaluations of a single-treatment technique (treatment package research) and to comparisons of treatments stemming from different conceptual positions (comparative research). Both types of research occupy an important place in scientifically establishing alternative treatments. However, considerably greater attention is needed for those treatment evaluation strategies that will reveal the basis for the effects of a treatment package, the variables that contribute to its efficacy, and the conditions of administration that yield maximum results.

# References

Beck, A. T. Depression: Clinical, experimental and theoretical aspects. New York: Harper, 1967.

Becker J., & Schuckit, M. A. The comparative efficacy of cognitive therapy and pharmacotherapy in the treatment of depressions. Cognitive Therapy and Research, 1978, 2, 193–197.

Bernstein, D. A., & Paul, G. L. Some comments on therapy analogue research with small animal "phobias." Journal of Behavior Therapy and Experimental Psychiatry, 1971, 2, 225–237.

Cadoret, R. J., & Tanna, V. L. Genetics of affective disorders. In G. Usdin (Ed.), Depression: Clinical, biological and psychological perspectives. New York: Brunner/Mazel, 1977.

Cohen, J. The statistical power of abnormal–social psychological research: A review. Journal of Abnormal and Social Psychology, 1962, 65, 145–153.

Coleman, R. E. Manipulation of self-esteem as a determinant of mood of elated and depressed women. Journal of Abnormal Psychology, 1975, 84, 693–700.

Ellis, A. Outcome of employing three techniques of psychotherapy. Journal of Clinical Psychology, 1957, 13, 344–350.

Ferster, C. B. A functional analysis of depression. American Psychologist, 1973, 28, 857–870.

Fuchs, C. Z., & Rehm, L. P. A self-control behavior therapy program for depression. Journal of Consulting and Clinical Psychology, 1977, 45, 206–215.

Gershon, E., Dunner, D., & Goodwin, F. Toward a biology of affective disorders. Archives of General Psychiatry, 1971, 25, 1–15.

Hammen, C. L., & Glass, D. R. Depression, activity and evaluation of reinforcement. Journal of Abnormal Psychology, 1975, 84, 718–721.

Hanaway, T. P., & Barlow, D. H. Prolonged depressive behaviors in a recently blinded deaf mute: Behavioral treatment. *Journal of Behavior Therapy and Experimental Psychiatry,* 1975, *6,* 43–48.

Hannie, T. J., Jr., & Adams, H. E. Modification of agitated depression by flooding: A preliminary study. *Journal of Behavior Therapy and Experimental Psychiatry,* 1974, *5,* 161–166.

Hersen, M. Limitations and problems in the clinical application of behavioral techniques in psychiatric settings. *Behavior Therapy,* 1979, *10,* 65–80.

Hersen, M., Eisler, R. M., Alford, G. S., & Agras, W. S. Effects of token economy on neurotic depression: An experimental analysis. *Behavior Therapy,* 1973, *4,* 392–397.

Kazdin, A. E. Self-monitoring and behavior change. In M. J. Mahoney & C. E. Thoresen (Eds.), *Self-control: Power to the person.* Monterey, California: Brooks/Cole, 1974.

Kazdin, A. E. Evaluating the generality of findings in analogue therapy research. *Journal of Consulting and Clinical Psychology,* 1978, *46,* 673–686.

Kazdin, A. E. *Research design in clinical psychology.* New York: Harper & Row, 1980.

Kazdin, A. E., & Wilson, G. T. Criteria for evaluating psychotherapy. *Archives of General Psychiatry,* 1978, *35,* 407–416.

Kupfer, D. J., Pickar, D., Himmelhoch, J. M., & Detre, T. P. Are there two types of unipolar depression? *Archives of General Psychiatry,* 1975, *32,* 866–871.

Lang, P. J. The mechanics of desensitization and the laboratory study of fear. In C. M. Franks (Ed.), *Behavior therapy: Appraisal and status.* New York: McGraw-Hill, 1969.

Lazarus, A. A. Group therapy of phobic disorders by systematic desensitization. *Journal of Abnormal and Social Psychology,* 1961, *63,* 504–510.

Lewinsohn, P. M. A behavioral approach to depression. In R. M. Friedman & M. N. Katz (Eds.), *The psychology of depression: Contemporary theory and research.* New York: Wiley, 1974.

Lewinsohn, P. M. The behavioral study and treatment of depression. In M. Hersen, R. M. Eisler, & P. M. Miller (Eds.), *Progress in behavior modification* (Vol. 1). New York: Academic Press, 1975.

Lewinsohn, P. M., Biglan, A., & Zeiss, A. M. Behavioral treatment of depression. Paper presented at the meeting of the Association for Advancement of Behavior Therapy, San Francisco, 1975.

Liberman, R. P., & Raskin, D. E. Depression: A behavioral formulation. *Archives of General Psychiatry,* 1971, *24,* 515–523.

McLean, P. D., & Hakstian, A. Clinical depression: Comparative efficacy of outpatient treatment. Paper presented at meeting of the Society for Psychotherapy Research, Toronto, Ontario, June 1978.

McLean, P. D., Ogston, K., & Grauer, L. A behavioral approach to the treatment of depression. *Journal of Behavioral Therapy and Experimental Psychiatry,* 1973, *4,* 323–330.

Meichenbaum, D. H., Gilmore, J. B., & Fedoravicius, A. Group insight versus group desensitization in treating speech anxiety. *Journal of Consulting and Clinical Psychology,* 1971, *36,* 410–421.

Morris, J. B., & Beck, A. T. The efficacy of antidepressant drugs. A review of research (1958–1972). *Archives of General Psychiatry,* 1974, *30,* 667–674.

Morris, R. J., & Suckerman, K. R. Therapist warmth as a factor in automated desensitization. *Journal of Consulting and Clinical Psychology,* 1974, *43,* 244–250.

Nelson, R. O. Assessment and therapeutic functions of self-monitoring. In M. Hersen, R. M. Eisler, & P. M. Miller (Eds.), *Progress in behavior modification* (Vol. 5). New York: Academic Press, 1977.

Parloff, M. D. Therapist–patient relationships and outcome of psychotherapy. *Journal of Consulting Psychology,* 1961, *25,* 29–38.

Paul, G. L. *Insight versus desensitization in psychotherapy: An experiment in anxiety reduction.* Stanford: Stanford University Press, 1966.

Rehm, L. P. A self-control model of depression. *Behavior Therapy,* 1977, *8,* 787–804.

Rehm, L. P., Fuchs, C. Z., Roth, D. M., Kornblith, S. J., & Romano, J. A comparison of self-control and social skill treatments of depression. *Behavior Therapy,* 1979, *10,* 429–442.

Rehm, L. P., & Kornblith, S. J. Behavior therapy for depression: A review of recent developments. In M. Hersen, R. M. Eisler, & P. M. Miller (Eds.), *Progress in behavior modification* (Vol. 7). New York: Academic Press, 1979.

Rehm, L. P., Kornblith, S. J., O'Hara, M. W., Lamparski, D. M., Romano, J. M., & Volkin, J. I. An evaluation of major elements in a self-control therapy program for depression. Paper presented at meeting of the Association for Advancement of Behavior Therapy, Chicago, November 1978.

Rubinstein, E. A., & Parloff, M. B. *Research in psychotherapy* (Vol. 1). Washington, D. C.: American Psychological Association, 1962.

Rush, A. J., Beck, A. T., Kovacs, M., & Hollon, S. Comparative efficacy of cognitive therapy and pharmacotherapy in the treatment of depressed outpatients. *Cognitive Therapy and Research,* 1977, *1,* 17–38.

Rush, A. J., Hollon, S. D., Beck, A. T., & Kovacs, M. Depression: Must pharmacotherapy fail for cognitive therapy to succeed? *Cognitive Therapy and Research,* 1978, *2,* 199–206.

Schmickley, V. G. A self-managed program for overcoming debilitating depression. Paper presented at the meeting of the American Personnel and Guidance Association, Chicago, April 1976.

Seligman, M. E. P. Depression and learned helplessness. In R. J. Friedman M. M. Katz (Eds.), *The psychology of depression: Contemporary theory and research.* New York: Wiley, 1974.

Shaw, B. F. Comparison of cognitive therapy and behavior therapy in the treatment of depression. *Journal of Consulting and Clinical Psychology,* 1977, *45,* 543–551.

Shipley, C. R., & Fazio, A. F. Pilot study of a treatment for psychological depression. *Journal of Abnormal Psychology,* 1973, *82,* 372–376.

Shlien, J. M. (Ed.), *Research in psychotherapy* (Vol. 3). Washington, D. C.: American Psychological Association, 1968.

Spitzer, R. L., Endicott, J., & Robins, E. Research diagnostic criteria. *Psychopharmacology Bulletin,* 1975, *11,* 22–25.

Strupp, H. H., & Luborsky, L. (Eds.), *Research in psychotherapy* (Vol. 2). Washington, D. C.: American Psychological Association, 1962.

Taylor, F. G., & Marshall, W. L. Experimental analysis of a cognitive–behavioral therapy for depression. *Cognitive Therapy and Research,* 1977, *1,* 59–72.

Vasta, R. Coverant control of self-evaluations through temporal cueing. *Journal of Behavior Therapy and Experimental Psychiatry,* 1976, *7,* 35–38.

Wells, K. C., Hersen, M., Bellack, A. S., & Himmelhoch, J. Social skills training for unipolar depressive females. Paper presented at the meeting of the Association for Advancement of Behavior Therapy, Atlanta, December 1977.

# 15

## Ritual and Reality: Some Clinical Implications of Experimental Designs

MARJORIE H. KLEIN
ALAN S. GURMAN

All psychotherapy involves ritual. This statement is as valid for behavioral treatment as it is for psychoanalysis. Some long-time observers of the therapy scene (Frank, 1961) place major emphasis on persuasion, suggestion, and engagement of the patient in healing ritual to explain the power of psychotherapy to induce change in the patient's behavior and belief systems. Others, such as Bergin and Strupp (1972), distinguish specific techniques from nonspecific factors and hold that both are necessary components for therapeutic effectiveness. Moving along the continuum from global healing to specific curative act, we find most of the behavior therapies, which aspire to define and perfect techniques to the point where their effectiveness stands alone, apart from the "noise" created by expectancies, therapist style and other nontechnical factors. Where we as researchers and theorists stand on this continuum is also a matter of our choice of theory, and probably of our personal predilection and tolerance for experiencing ambiguity. This stance, however, is *our* choice. Where our patients are, and what the clinical realities are, may be a very different matter.

Throughout this chapter, we will argue that while the perspectives of theorist, researcher, clinician, and patient may lead to very different perceptions of the clinical experience, some inevitable clinical realities are involved in the problem-solving enterprise known as psychotherapy. These different perspectives, of course, are useful for different purposes. The focus of the theorist and the experimental researcher on specific variables allows them to construct a situation in which technical operations can be refined and tested experimentally. The contrasting perspectives of the helpless, despairing, depressed patient and the

337

therapist willing to adapt a range of strategies to his or her personal style are more representative of the context in which the theoretical and experimental developments in behavior therapy for depression must ultimately be tested.

The primary purpose of behavior therapy research in depression is to develop effective treatment techniques by applying principles derived, broadly, from social learning theory and, more recently, from cognitive theory. The explicit or implicit intent of this research is to maximize the potency of technical operations available to the therapist and to minimize the necessity of the nonspecific factors. Our purpose in commenting here on this research in the area of depression is to consider whether, to what extent, and under what circumstances this goal of specificity is ever possible, given the constraints and complications of the clinical situation. Our discussion will be organized into major categories that conform to the various design strategies used in this area. They closely follow the cycle of therapy technique development and refinement described by Bergin and Strupp (1972). We do not intend to suggest methodological refinements or adjustments to the various steps in this process—discovery, analogue study, treatment packaging, comparative study, and clinical dissemination. Rather, we intend to remark on some of the practical and conceptual problems that arise when each strategy is used in the clinical setting or when the results of empirical research in nonclinical settings are generalized more widely.

Problems in clinical research fall into at least two classes, according to their origin in either the clinical process or the research process. The clinical process, whether in a pure clinical or in a research setting, has its own set of rituals and demand characteristics; the research process has others. Often these two processes are in conflict: The rigors of research design can constrain or even warp the clinical process, and this in turn may create clinical complications. More often, clinical needs can intrude upon research designs. This tension is apparent in each of the strategies we discuss in this chapter and imposes limits on the theoretical and clinical utility of the results from each.

## Design Strategy I: The $N = 1$ Context of Discovery

While the history of single-case experimental studies is not limited to their appearance in the behavior therapy literature (cf. Chassan, 1967; Davidson & Costello, 1969; Shapiro, 1957), such experimental studies have been especially significant in the behavioral realm and, in the view of some (e.g., Yates, 1970), provide *the* defining characteristic of behavioral treatment. Because single-case studies have played such a prominent role in the development of behavioral treatments for depression (Rehm & Kornblith, 1979) and in their dissemination to the mental health field at large, we will focus in this section on three fundamental questions about such designs that have direct bearing on clinical practice. Comprehensive discussion of the methodological nuances and subtleties of single-case experimental studies can be found elsewhere (e.g., Hersen & Barlow, 1976).

### When Is Minitreatment Enough?

While single-case experimental studies can be used to assess the power of treatment packages, their typical use in the literature on the behavioral treatment of depression involves either the analysis via "dismantling" of a treatment method already found to be effective or, even more commonly, the "construction" of an effective method via the combination of specific interventions. The ideal empirical goal, of course, is to produce maximally positive clinical impact with the minimal treatment, akin, in some ways, to the medical principle of "least severe intervention." Rehm and Kornblith (1979) seem to have come close to this observation in noting that all behavioral treatments for depression "identify a core symptom or behavior and assume that modification of this core behavior will lead to improvement in a wider spectrum of behaviors identified as depression [p. 41]." We call this "common implicit assumption" (Rehm & Kornblith, 1979, p. 41) among the behavior therapies the minitreatment principle. By way of contrast, then, maxitreatments would be roughly equivalent to complex treatment packages.

We assume that minitreatments are likely to be thought effective for depression as a function of the theoretical view of the nature of what constitutes the "core" of depression. These implicit views, at least as suggested by the research literature, range from narrow definitions, such as decreased speech rate (e.g., Robinson & Lewinsohn, 1973) or restricted speech content (Johansson, Lewinsohn, & Flippo, 1969), to definitions invoking broader clusters of behavioral deficit or excess, such as those found in cognitive behavior therapy (Beck, Rush, Shaw & Emery, 1979). Thus, if within a given behavioral perspective depression is nothing more than the (public) topography of a very limited range of symptomatic elements, single-case experimental studies are quite efficient and practical in terms of demonstrating the efficacy of the treatment method (e.g., verbal conditioning). When, however, treatment models (e.g., cognitive behavior therapy) assume that depression is multidimensional (e.g., cognitive, affective, behavioral) and multileveled, then interventions must be aimed at, and change must occur on, multiple criteria in order for treatment to be deemed effective.

When the latter conditions obtain, a within-subject constructive research design may place a good deal of personal strain on the therapist. For example, a cognitive behavior therapist may be asked, for experimental purposes, to withhold using graded task assignments, and very likely a number of other interventions thought to be essential to the package, until a predetermined point in time. At that point, task assignment becomes "allowed" by the (multiple baseline) design; at a still later point, another intervention is allowed, and so on. The problem in this situation is that the therapist may feel him- or herself to be more a professional function than a (technically skilled) caring person. If nothing else, such an experience may have the undesirable effect of dampening the therapist's enthusiasm for the treatment method.

## What Contingencies Maintain the Therapist's Behavior?

There are other potential sources of personal strain on the therapist in the context of single-case experimental studies, in addition to the one mentioned in the preceding section. Two illustrations will serve to make our point. First, the use of reversal designs, even when applicable, may test the therapist's loyalties severely. In clinical practice, the therapist's first loyalty is to the patient. In controlled research, it is to the design protocol. Reversal designs, which profoundly challenge the clinician to define his or her loyalties in ways that may meet with disapproval from (e.g., nonbehavioral) colleagues.

Second, single-case experimental studies require daily monitoring of the relevant target behaviors (Hersen & Barlow, 1976; Kazdin & Wilson, 1978). While even in controlled environments (e.g., an inpatient psychiatric ward) this is a demanding task, it is usually overwhelming in outpatient settings. (E.g., who is to do the monitoring? Severely depressed patients are unlikely candidates.) What are the therapist's alternatives? In most cases, the only "alternative" is a double-bind: therapists are damned if they do continuous assessment by the extraordinary demands of the task and damned if they don't do continuous assessment, since the variability and unreliability of the data thus gathered defeat the entire raison d'être of single-case experimental studies.

## Do All Things Come to Those Who Wait?

A related issue involves the contingencies that govern a patient's willingness to be a single-case experimental subject. Since, as Kazdin and Wilson (1978) note, "most treatments are not that powerful when applied separately, because clinical disorders are maintained by several interacting variables [p. 170]," must we not wonder about the characteristics (hence, generalizability of findings) of a suffering patient who agrees that the therapist will apply only one technique at a time and/or that only one target behavior or symptom will be treated at a time? Such patients, we surmise, must be enormously compliant (in the skill deficit sense), dependent, or desperate. If this is so, then, a patient's very willingness to be the subject of a single-case experimental study, especially of the constructive variety, seems to define him or her as belonging to an unrepresentative subsample of clinically depressed patients.

We agree completely with Kazdin and Wilson's (1978) assessment that very few clinicians can meet the rigorous demands of most single-case experimental investigations. To that, we would add that very few patients are likely to pass this burdensome test as well. As Kazdin and Wilson (1978) note (and we would underline with particular regard for treatment of depressed patients), "In short, single-case experimental studies, conducted properly according to strict methodological and ethical requirements, will almost always be done as research qua research [p. 171]."

## Design Strategy II: Analogue Research

The second general design strategy in the cumulative, synergistic process of therapeutic technique development is the analogue approach. Psychotherapy studies are said to be of the analogue variety when they only approximate or, more accurately, fail to approximate naturalistic clinical situations. They maximize internal validity, through experimental control of sources of variance that may affect treatment outcome, at the expense of external validity and generalizability of findings. In order to potentiate experimental treatment variables, analogue studies usually require homogeneity with respect to subject–client characteristics (e.g., target problem, age, gender), to therapist contribution, and most particularly, to the precision, uniformity, and regularity with which treatment procedures are carried out. Because they usually use nonclinical volunteer subjects, with neophyte therapists (often functioning more as technicians), analogue studies have practical advantages, which include the greater availability of willing subjects, the increased chances of completing treatment trials in short periods of time, and the opportunity for the researcher to withhold treatment entirely or to withhold selected treatment components with minimal ethical concern (Kazdin, 1978; Kazdin & Wilson, 1978; O'Leary & Borkovec, 1978).

There is consensus among researchers that analogue studies may contribute to general knowledge about the mechanisms and processes of behavioral change. Yet, there seems to be about as little agreement on the external validity of their findings as there is about most fundamental issues in psychotherapy research and practice. But the difference in articulate and pointed opinion is not, as one might expect, merely between the champions of psychodynamic theories (e.g., Luborsky, Singer, & Luborsky, 1975) and those of behavioral (e.g., Bandura, 1978) perspectives. Indeed, even within the field of behavior therapy, it is easy to discern both highly positively valenced (e.g., Bandura, 1978; Kazdin, 1978; Kazdin & Wilson, 1978) and highly negatively valenced (e.g., Marks, 1978; Mathews, 1978; Rehm & Kornblith, 1979; Royce, 1978) attitudes toward analogue studies. It is interesting and worthy of note that, even within the behavioral fold, defenders of the analogue approach tend to come from academic psychology, whereas detractors tend to be affiliated with psychiatric, medical, or other clinical settings. For example, Marks (1978) adopts the view that "analogue and clinical experiments belong to different universes of discourse which only come together at a few points [p. 494]." At the other extreme, Kazdin and Wilson (1978), whose position is similar to that of Bandura (1978), has taken the provocative position that "all psychotherapy and behavior therapy research is analogue research insofar as it constructs a situation in which the phenomenon of interest can be studied [p. 161]" and, therefore, "it is not only fruitless, but also counterproductive to speak of 'analogue' versus 'nonanalogue' or 'clinical' research [p. 162]." That is, conducting research is not typical of clinical situations. This perspective is clearly not true in all cases, however. Indeed, according to at least one prevailing model of behavior therapy, each patient is viewed as the subject of an $N = 1$ experiment. Thus, this limiting yet common case seriously challenges the universality of Kazdin's position.

Here, we will briefly consider some of the clinical realities impinging on analogue studies that render such research on the treatment of depression of limited generalizability to the clinical situation. Kazdin (Chapter 14, this volume; Kazdin, 1978; Kazdin & Wilson, 1978) has offered the most incisive and scholarly discussion of this issue to date. His argument may be summarized in this way: Of the many dimensions along which a given study may vary from the clinical situation, each must be considered in its own right in terms of (a) its (dis-)similarity to the clinical situation and (b) the extent to which the dimension in question relates to treatment efficacy. Thus, "the importance of a given dimension to the generality of the results needs to be evaluated directly. Research is needed that investigates the influence of departures from the clinical situation along various dimensions [Kazdin & Wilson, 1978, p. 163]." While adoption of the familiar refrain "It's an empirical question" is quite defensible, it is in itself insufficient to the problem at hand. Thus, Kazdin (1978) himself has argued that "the issue is how to decide the generality of results of a study that, in some way, only resembles the clinical situation [p. 682]." But the "how" has not yet been addressed directly. Retreating to an empirical determination of the relevance of the (dis-)similarity of a given dimension to the clinical situation is likely to falter on two grounds. First, the expenditure of time, money, and investigative energy on such questions is probably too draining to be accomplished. Second, and much more importantly, the question cannot be answered in the terms in which it has been posed. That is, to view single treatment dimensions out of their usual context is to distort the meaning of those dimensions beyond clinical recognition. Such an analysis of treatment-relevant dimensions one at a time (or even concurrently in small numbers) constitutes the essence of what is called "constructive treatment research" (Kazdin, Chapter 14, this volume; Kazdin & Wilson, 1978). It will be argued and elaborated herein that the analogue approach may render research findings of seriously limited utility toward the goal of improving clinical treatment efficacy because the contextual meaning of a given dimension is lost when it is isolated experimentally. Note that this can work two ways. An isolated (i.e., dismantled) variable may be rendered ineffective by being taken out of its context. In some cases, however, the reverse may occur; a variable may be highlighted so that its effectiveness is exaggerated. We suspect the latter is more often the case, if the rate of weak or inconsistent findings in clinical replications of analogue studies is any indication. Attempts to construct a clinical context for single dimensions by logical integration or summation of results across studies are impossible and can be achieved only metaphorically because these results are independent events. Furthermore, even when components shown to enhance outcome are added to basic (i.e., initial) procedures in a subsequent study, a flawed logic is operating, in that it is impossible to construct a contextual meaning of a given bit of behavior (e.g., treatment technique) that approximates the clinical situation by simply combining it with additional bits of behavior. The context of a behavior, or of a behavioral sequence, is more than the mere sum of its component parts. *Once removed from context, a given "bit" of behavior cannot simply be recontextualized since its next occurrence arises in an entirely new context.*

Analogue research on behavior therapy for depression fails to consider two clinical contexts in which single treatment-relevant dimensions exist: symptom context and treatment relationship context.

## *Symptom Context I: Intraorganismic*

Intraorganismic contextual variables generally refer to the configuration and severity of target problems. The severity of depressive target symptoms may be assessed clinically by their phenomenological impact (i.e., degree of felt suffering) or by the amount of their intrusion on interpersonal, vocational, recreational, or cognitive activities. But use of similar criteria for target problem severity in nonclinical populations (even to the extent that the subjects experience serious disruption of their affective state in everyday life) is not sufficient to insure external validity, unless the total symptom array is covered. The appearance conveyed by many published reports on behavior therapy for depression notwithstanding, it seems to be the infrequent depressed patient in clinical practice who presents with a monosymptomatic, or unidimensional, depression. Indeed, such a clinical picture is probably best thought of, not as a depression at all, but rather as a highly circumscribed behavioral excess or deficit. Moreover, the usual coexistence of multiple problems in a depressed patient, some of which may not be related to the depression as either cause or effect, renders an experimental focus on depressive targets quite arbitrary. While focal treatment techniques may be consecutively and successfully added together to construct an increasingly efficacious treatment package, no experimental design is powerful enough to construct real patients. Analogue attempts to do so are like stitching together one organ system from each of a number of intact humans until the requisite number of systems have been accumulated and then arguing that the organism thereby constructed (literally) is no different from other human organisms that have not been pieced together. It is an interesting paradox that in analogue studies, the most likely research context in which to find constructive research strategies used, the gestalt of the patient's symptomatology is systematically dismantled. While it is questionable whether treatment techniques themselves can be believably dismantled (see section on treatment relationships), it is certain that, whether it pleases researchers or not, patients cannot be dismantled. In fact, it can be argued that all that can be genuinely dismantled in psychotherapy research is the researcher's cognitive representation of the phenomenon of investigative interest! Indeed, the contextual embeddedness of a target symptom may be the most important distinction between the clinical patient and the nonclinical volunteer or recruit.

Even more important, as Marks (1978) has noted in a related context, and concurrent with our experience: "In some patients their presenting psychopathology is the least of their difficulties. A (phobia or obsession) can simply be a respectable admission ticket for treatment of some other problem [p. 494]." Since analogue treatment studies by their very nature prescribe, and therefore restrict, the range of interventions available to the therapist, goals that emerge in the course of therapy, which were not stated by or perhaps not even known by the patient at the outset of treatment but which may become much more salient than initial depressive target behaviors, will have no way of finding their way into the assessment of treatment outcome. The absence of an assessment of such emergent goals (Gurman & Klein, 1980; Gurman & Kniskern, 1981) in analogue studies produces findings with little meaningful generalizability to the clinical situation. This obstacle to external validity appears profound, since, in our experience, a therapeutic focus on emergent goals very frequently characterizes a great deal, if not most, of clinical psychotherapy and clinical behavior therapy.

Thus, we are not very persuaded by Rehm and Kornblith's (1979) conclusion that "basic similarities between solicited populations and client outpatients seem to have been pretty well established [p. 35]," since their sole basis for this significant conclusion is the comparability of target symptom severity between the two populations.

### Symptom Context II: Ecological

By the ecological context of depressive symptoms, or target behaviors, we refer primarily to the everyday interpersonal context in which the behaviors occur, particularly in the sphere of such intimate relationships as marriage and the family. This point is similar to Mathews's (1978) reference to "the presence of adverse social environments [p. 390]" and to Marks's (1978) reference to the "disruptive social relationships [p. 494]" of clinical subjects that may confound treatment programs in fear reduction research, but it is not identical to their descriptors. While the notion may be foreign to most behavior therapists, even behavioral marriage therapists (e.g., Jacobson & Margolin, 1979), it is widely believed among marital and family therapists that an individual's symptomatology, including depressive symptomatology, may be quite functional for the maintenance of homeostasis in the marriage or family system. This view is quite different from that of a behaviorist, who would emphasize the consequences of the depressed patient's symptoms for his or her intimate relationships and the consequences of the behavior of intimate persons for the depressed person's behavior. In many nonbehavioral views, depressive behavior not only has consequences for intimate relationships but also may serve to define and equilibrate those relationships. In a related vein, Paykel, Myers, Dienelt, Klerman, Lindenthal, & Pepper (1969) found that marital difficulty is the most commonly reported life event for women in the 6 months prior to the onset of depression. The behavioral position is somewhat the more optimistic, for it assumes that once individuals know the consequences of their behavior they will fully and rationally choose positive behavior; the "functionalist" view allows for pathology to persist, reflecting resistance or at least a tendency toward consistency.

Since almost half of the existing outpatient studies of the behavioral treatment of depression with patient samples of 10 or more have used college student subjects (see Rehm & Kornblith, 1979), the danger of generalizing the ecological symptom context of such privileged and protected, and single, subjects to usual clinical situations is severe: Women are at greater risk for depression than men, at the rate of two to one (Weissman & Klerman, 1977), and marital difficulties are the most frequent problem presented by depressed women seeking psychotherapy (Paykel et al., 1969). Indeed, given the perspective that depressive symptoms may be functional for intimate relationships, it follows that roughly 50% of the existing outpatient behavioral treatment studies of depression lack external ecological validity. Thus, even when college students are self-referred patients for such research projects, the social factors motivating their depression are likely to be weak compared to noncollege samples. When college student subjects are recruited for research purposes, the ecological meaning and function of depressive symptoms is even less likely to resemble the usual clinical context of these symptoms.

## Treatment Relationship Context

The two major dimensions on which recruited subjects and clinical patients can be contrasted, and which serve, in large measure, to influence the treatment relationship context of depressive symptoms, are the manner of subject recruitment and the subjects' motivation for treatment. These dimensions are interrelated.

Kazdin (1978) has identified two forms of subject recruitment for the experimental investigation of treatment: (a) "captive" subjects are "mildly coaxed" (p. 679) into participation, often with reinforcements that do not obtain in the clinical situation (e.g., partial course credit for college students); and (b) subjects are solicited by media advertisements (and may be paid for their participation or at least receive free treatment). Despite these procedural differences, and the possibility that the latter recruitment method may uncover subjects who are more motivated for treatment, both have one crucial motivational commonality. That is, subjects who are recruited for study, by whatever means, come to help us, whereas clinical patients come for us to help them (Gurman, 1978). What is at issue here, and what is crucial in limiting the generalizability of studies using any recruited subjects who come to us outside usual referral sources, is the subject's definition of self in relation to the therapist–experimenter. Indeed, it can be argued that it is this definition of self in relation to the therapist that forms the core of the interpersonal relationship between patient–subject and therapist. To the extent to which the efficacy of any behavioral treatment of depression is a function of factors that transcend technological considerations, those non-equivalent patient–subject self-definitions entirely change the implicit, but powerful, interpersonal meaning of the relationship between subject–patient and therapist. Indeed, the definition and presentation of self in interpersonal transaction forms the basis of much nonbehavioral psychotherapy (e.g., Sullivan) and itself becomes the central treatment issue. Thus, from this perspective, subjects obtained by either of Kazdin's (1978) two methods are fundamentally not comparable to clinical subjects.

Moreover, the definition of self relates in important ways to the realm of patient–subject motivation for treatment. Kazdin (1978; Kazdin & Wilson, 1978), echoing the view of Bandura (1978), has offered the curious argument that "the *less* resemblance of the study to the clinical situation for a given dimension, the *more* difficult it would be to change behavior [Kazdin, 1978, p. 683, emphasis added]." In the context of patient–subject treatment motivation, the rationale, would be that "clients (who seek help) may be likely to comply with therapeutic instructions and perhaps even accept the treatment rationale relatively uncritically [Kazdin, 1978, p. 683]," and might be "more likely to continue in therapy and adhere diligently to therapeutic prescriptions [Kazdin & Wilson, 1978, p. 163]" than the less severely impaired subject recruited for research. This unusual reversal offered by Kazdin seems to hinge on the assumption that greater pain predicts greater help-seeking dependency, which, in turn, predicts enhanced compliance with treatment. While this sort of dependency may facilitate therapeutic change, the argument stems from a rather incomplete analysis of the actual forces motivating most patients who seek help. As most psychotherapists know, yet relatively few behavior therapists have acknowledged publicly (cf. Goldfried & Davison, 1976), most patients have internally paradoxical and conflicting feelings about being in psychotherapy, that is, about changing their behavior (or feelings, attitudes, etc.). While more elaborate psychodynamic explanations of this observation could be offered, it will suffice here to suggest that the overriding force working against such straightforward treatment compliance is the patient's desire (whether conscious or unconscious) to present an integrated sense of self, even a sense of self that includes his or her symptoms, dysfunctions, and suffering. This view is based in part, of course, on the premise that many psychiatric symptoms represent a compromise solution to internal conflict and that such a compromise is required in order to maintain a sense of self-consistency, even in the throes of emotional pain.

Thus, the curious turnabout offered by Kazdin (1978; Kazdin & Wilson, 1978) fails to acknowledge the everyday fact of, and basis for, resistance to therapeutic change. Indeed, much of the work of psychotherapy, and even of most behavior therapy, centers on overcoming a patient's internal resistance to change. It seems reasonable to us, and in direct contradiction to Kazdin's position, that non-help-seeking subjects are less likely, as a rule, to be internally ambivalent about changing their behavior or cognitions. If this is in fact true, then it follows that the usual argument that nonclinical subjects are more likely to comply with behavior change efforts would, in fact, obtain, and, in our view, render such subjects' motivation for treatment quite dissimilar from that of help-seeking patients, and in a manner that has tremendous influence on the efficacy of treatment.

We would like to add a thought on the remarkable dissimilarity between clinical and nonclinical studies in terms of one other factor defining the patient–therapist relationship. In clinical practice, the therapist's primary responsibility and loyalty is to the patient. To whom is the therapist loyal in a nonclinical study? We suspect that, at least implicitly, he or she is more loyal to the research protocol than to the subject. Indeed, there is an explicit primary loyalty to the research design that is required by experimental designs, since to be loyal to one's patient would often require the therapist to abandon the preordained "script." We think it is self-evident, then, that this matter of varying therapist loyalties significantly reduces the generalizability of the treatment relationship context of nonclinical studies to usual clinical conditions.

Finally, it is interesting to note that nowhere in the five tables summarizing the results of 49 studies of behavioral treatments for depression in the exhaustive review by Rehm and Kornblith (1979) is the therapist–patient relationship even mentioned. The absence of such references strikes us as a clear instance of what one of us (Gurman & Kniskern, 1978) has labeled "technolatry," that is, the worship of therapeutic technology at the expense of the interpersonal context in which that technology is offered.

## Design Strategy III: Comparative Study

There has been a clear trend in behavior therapy research for distinct techniques, after a period of independent clinical trial, to be combined in treatment programs, or packages, for further research and clinical use. Essentially, there are two domains in which such studies may occur. First, there are comparisons that derive from experimental manipulation of components within a given treatment package, that is, *internal* comparative study. Second, there are comparisons with conditions of treatment other than those represented by the package in question, or *external* comparative study. In this section, we will consider the clinical value and meaning of selected, commonly used research approaches within each of these domains and will conclude with discussions of the choice of outcome criteria in comparative treatment research and some of the forces influencing the effects of comparative research on the everyday clinical practice of psychotherapy and behavior therapy.

## Internal Comparative Study

There are three main subclasses of experimental manipulation within internal comparative studies: (a) technique variation; (b) structural variation, such as the location (e.g., home versus office) or duration of treatment; and (c) participant variation. A fourth subclass, labeled by Kazdin (Chapter 14, this volume; Kazdin & Wilson, 1978) as parametric variation, focuses on varying specific aspects of technical components (e.g., length of patient exposure to anxiety-arousing stimuli in the behavioral treatment of agoraphobia). We view parametric variations as special instances of technique variations. That is, whether an individual treatment technique is completely eliminated from a clinical trial (i.e., treatment is "dismantled") or applied in varying degrees (e.g., varying the length of the exposure component), these variations exist along the same continuum of the relative presence–absence of a treatment component.

Here, we will focus on technique variation, since this dimension seems to us to raise the most significant interpretive clinical dilemmas.

### TECHNIQUE VARIATION

Technique variation is a more inclusive, and as will be seen, less loaded, synonym for what is typically referred to as "dismantling." Dismantling is a strategy in which selected treatment (read: technical) elements are eliminated from treatment, so that outcome comparisons can be made between the delivery of the original package and the package-minus-element $X$, or minus $X$ and $Y$, etc. The impact on clinical practice of dismantling effective treatment packages may hinge especially on two characteristics of the original package, that is, its complexity and its integrativeness. By complexity, we refer simply to the number of technical elements viewed as central to the treatment package; hence, the greater the number of clearly specified elements, the greater the package's complexity. We certainly cannot formulate any mathematical rule by which to determine or predict the clinical impact of dismantling packages with different numbers of relevant components. On the other hand, illustrations of these conditions may be instructive. For example, systematic desensitization is probably the most dismantled treatment strategy available. Dismantling of desensitization has had to contend with only three technical components: (a) training in relaxation; (b) hierarchy construction; and (c) exposure. Thus, in effect, even in this case of limited dismantling, only three dismantled components, and only three pairs of dismantled components, need to be tested (a plus b, a plus c, b plus c, and a, b, and c alone). On the other hand, imagine a scenario involving the dismantling of cognitive behavior therapy. If the technical components of graded task assignment, self-monitoring, use of the Premack principle, identification of cognitive and affective linkages, recognition of negative beliefs, examination of the evidence for and against distorted cognitions, substitution of alternative interpretations, all of which are important technical package elements, were to be systematically varied, one would ultimately have to test the efficacy of well over 100 combinations of essential cognitive therapy techniques. While one could easily map the relevant combinations requiring outcome evaluation, it is unlikely that even the most dedicated of research teams would live long enough to be able to do all the relevant comparative studies. Thus, we agree with Kazdin and Wilson's (1978) statement that, in planning dismantling research, "these [technical] elements be limited to some reasonable number [p. 144]." But, what is reasonable? The dismantling of desensitization's three important technical components, which has led to significant changes in clinical practice, has required the efforts of hundreds of investigators over more than a decade. By extrapolation, the systematic dismantling of cognitive behavior therapy might be accomplished, by a conservative estimate, around the year 2145!

On this basis, we may formulate the following principle about the dismantleability of treatment packages: The more complex the treatment package, the less likely it is ever to be thoroughly dismantled. Conversely, the more limited the number of technical elements in a treatment package, the greater the probability of successful dismantling. If the premise holds that the more limited the number of technical elements, the more restricted the range of clinical applicability of those elements (e.g., desensitization is applicable to fewer clinical conditions than is cognitive behavior therapy), then a corollary of the above principle may be suggested: The greater the dismantleability of a treatment package, the less need for dismantling the package in the first place!

The second issue impinging on the clinical implications of the dismantling strategy involves the degree of integration of central package elements. This integration occurs on two levels: conceptual–logical and personal. By conceptual or logical integration, we mean the degree to which identifiable treatment elements necessarily occur in a given sequence in order for those elements to produce positive outcomes and additive treatment effects. For example, eliminating the step of labeling cognitive–affective–behavioral links in cognitive behavior therapy renders the use of a patient's examination of the evidence supporting his or her cognitions, or of the substitution of alternative cognitions, clinically (i.e., phenomenologically) meaningless. By way of contrast, teaching a patient how to relax per se may never be meaningless, since relaxation may be used for purposes other than systematic desensitization. Thus, another principle: The experiential credibility limits of a dismantled treatment package are determined by the degree to which single treatment elements have the power to be used therapeutically in isolation from one another. This principle is a variation of Kazdin and Wilson's (1978) view that "different components of treatment can be viewed as separate independent variables [p. 143]." But what is to be noted is that, at times, individual components cannot be used clinically as if they were independent variables. Our assessment is that Kazdin and Wilson's view is a useful guideline only for treatments involving a very small number of elements presumed to be central in yielding positive treatment gains.

These constraints operate even more powerfully in participant variation designs where therapists are expected to vary their behavior across clients according to some more general dimensions. Kazdin and Wilson (1978) offer the example of the experimental manipulation of therapist empathy or warmth. That such styles of relating cannot be manipulated without entirely destroying the essence of the variable in question (i.e., choosing to be empathic is ingenuine and, therefore, not empathic) reduces the suggestion, and this possible experimental manipulation, to clinical absurdity. More generally, any experimental manipulation that requires therapists to refrain from behaving in ways that they, as individuals, believe facilitate the progress of treatment produces a clinical experience that has no counterpart in clinical practice. It is interesting to note that the dictionary definition of the verb *dismantle* is "to make unuseable for its original purpose." As suggested earlier, it is as difficult to "dismantle" a therapist as it is to "construct" a patient.

In summary, once treatment programs are coherently packaged, it would seem to be very difficult to remove elements meaningfully one by one. When one technique is removed, the question of what has taken its place remains: Is there something else in the same general theoretical spirit and thus equally effective? The alternative of leaving holes and gaps that disturb the continuity and distort the general thrust of a treatment program is equally problematic. Therapist variables may be especially important in this regard; once a therapist is well trained in a given package, it may be as difficult to dismantle the therapist as it is to dismantle the patient's problems.

PERSONAL INTEGRATION, NONSPECIFICS AND METAMESSAGES

A related design problem for research with treatment packages flows from the central role of "nonspecifics." Taylor and Marshall (1977) state this succinctly with respect to both behavioral and cognitive treatment: "The methods of treatment described here are relatively simple; the difficult task is to induce the cooperation of the subject, develop rapport, and, in particular, to delineate the situations in which depression occurs so that the message can be applied to the individual case [p. 66]." (Compare this position with Kazdin's [1978] view, discussed earlier, of the high degree of compliance among clinical research subjects.) We are certainly inclined to agree with this assessment of the situation and are compelled to note that the list of factors presented (more or less as an afterthought in the description of the treatment package) conforms very closely to the potent nonspecifics that have been described by Bergin and Strupp (1972); Goldstein, Heller, and Sechrest (1966); and others. The importance of these factors, we suspect, make it nearly impossible to "unpack" elements of a program for specific testing. The skill, resourcefulness, creativity, and enthusiasm that are communicated along with specific techniques may heavily influence the outcome and seriously confound research designs dependent on technique variation.

The degree to which a given therapist has mastered both the general principles and the specific treatment operations, together with his or her interest and motivation in performing the treatment, may considerably affect the therapist's ability to orchestrate the specifics. Even the most explicitly defined treatment techniques seem to be most effectively applied when they have become well integrated into the therapist's unique personal style, analogous to the properly timed and technically well-executed gross motor behaviors required to drive an automobile that are second nature to most experienced drivers. (Indeed, if a great deal of attention were focused on such gross movements during this activity, it would undoubtedly interfere with smooth, effective performance.) What is involved is the distinction between therapeutic strategies and therapeutic techniques (Goldfried, 1979). Techniques refer to highly specified actions (e.g., assigning homework), while strategies refer to plans basic to classes of actions (e.g., to expose depressed patient to information that contradicts his or her negative self-image). In our view, experienced therapists rely a great deal more on the use of flexible strategies of intervention than on isolated techniques. To the extent that the treatment effectiveness of highly experienced clinicians is an area of important concern, and we think it should be, dismantling strategies may be quite difficult to implement with these therapists, for whom focusing attention on single technical elements may require them to work in ways that feel "unnatural." To the extent that behavioral treatment packages also allow the therapist flexibility in the specific target symptoms chosen and in the contextual or relationship background for the therapeutic work, there is even more room for variance due to familiar therapist variables.

Participation in research protocols may exert another class of unwanted and untoward influences on a therapist's delivery of the treatment. Variations in the therapist's enthusiasm and willingness to participate in research and the extent to which the highly programmed activities are viewed as either tedious, inconvenient, or clinically counterproductive may greatly affect the way in which a package is presented on an individual basis. Unless our experience with practicing clinicians is atypical, we find that the more rigid and structured the treatment instructions, the more draining it is for the therapist. On one hand, there is a danger of boredom following the initial enthusiasm for mastering the technique; on the other hand, there are unanticipated events that lead therapists to abandon packages. No matter how in charge the therapist may wish to be, and how much control he or she may wish to exercise over clinical matters, it is nonetheless true that patients, their families, and stressful life events do not always perform on schedule or in the preferred order. Here particularly, therapist variables may intrude more into research designs than is wished; for example, relatively inexperienced therapists may have a lower threshold than seasoned therapists for patient backsliding and may not feel competent to cope with competing pressures exerted by research design on one hand and patient demands on the other. In contrast, experienced therapists who are able to "save" treatment protocols in the face of emergencies and fluctuations in patient motivation may introduce unwanted flexibility or personal style into the way in which treatment procedures are implemented on a day-to-day, moment-to-moment basis. Many of the design and interpretive problems, of course, may be easily cleared up if research designs involving treatment packages can accurately assess these variables, for example, via implementation checks on therapeutic interventions. To date, however, this has not been generally true of research in the behavior therapy area. Thus, while most designs require very good record keeping with respect to patient behavior, parallel observation and assessment of therapist behavior with respect to both the specifics and the nonspecifics of treatment are less common.

The picture is further complicated if we consider the powerful metamessages that may be transmitted along with the specific technical operations in packages that are therapeutic in their own right. There is considerable clinical and even some research evidence to suggest that the very acts of problem definition, specificity of focus, and progress monitoring may have considerable beneficial impact (e.g., Hart, 1978). Even the explicit rationales of the behavioral treatments, with expectancies for relatively quick and tangible results as well as their concerns with patient control, may be perfect antidotes for the hopelessness of depression. The integral role played by monitoring and feedback deserves special mention in this regard. All behavioral programs are very result oriented. Goals are generally defined so that quick benefits are realizable and made immediately clear to the patient. Therapists, because they are usually involved in data collection, may also receive more detailed and specific feedback about intermedidate stages of treatment efficacy and thus have more opportunity to modify and improve their delivery than would be forthcoming in clinical trials. This is certainly the case compared to the clinical practice of nonbehavioral methods. We suspect that the contrast between research and clinical applications of behavior therapy is sharper than many academicians would care to admit. It is also possible that the data collection has a particularly synergistic effect on behavior modification procedures because it is so consistent with their spirit and focus.

CLINICAL PROBLEMS

When we move from a consideration of problems with treatment packaging from a research standpoint to clinical applications, other issues arise. The role of such nonspecifics as assessment, persuasion, and rapport (already mentioned as research problems) become even more important when we turn to clinical implementation. In a word, therapists may have considerably less power over their paying clinical customers than researchers have over volunteer subjects (even with equated clinical problem levels) who have been screened for willingness and who have the added mystique of making a contribution to research, plus the assurance provided by consent procedures that the "real" therapy can be implemented after their short-term research participation is over. While, of course, clinical patients are subject to different motivations and different pressures, some of which may be equally powerful for their adherence to all kinds of "mysterious" rituals, it is our sense that the balance of power is considerably different in the clinic than in the laboratory. While this may not be a problem for the clinical application of the results of research, as we will discuss later, it raises considerable problems for clinical trials of treatment packages carried out as part of research projects.

## External Comparative Study

External comparative study focuses on the relative efficacy of a given treatment package and either other treatment packages or the absence of formal treatment.

### THE COMPARATIVE–COMPETITIVE STUDY

In order for two active treatments to be compared usefully, each should have already amassed a good deal of evidence for its efficacy in the treatment of the clinical disorder of interest. That is, why bother to compare Method X to Method Y in the treatment of Z if either X or Y (or worse, both) is not yet known to be effective? A somewhat less optimal, but in our view acceptable, condition for comparing two active treatment methods also exists. The prerequisite would be that when either or both has not been tested for efficacy in the treatment of a given disorder, but when there is evidence of the method's effectiveness for other common clinical problems and when important parameters of the clinical disorder now in question bear some logical relationship to major parameters of the successfully treated disorder, comparative study is then also justified.

In general, however, we believe that comparative treatment studies are largely motivated by nonempirical considerations and usually have at least as much to do with proselytizing and political concerns as with ultimate concerns for the delivery of clinical service to patients. In general, we think it will also be most profitable for the field at large, in terms of the impact of research on practice, for advocates of different treatment methods to get their own empirical houses in order before trying to do statistical blockbusting of unfamiliar neighborhoods.

### COMPARING TREATMENT WITH NO TREATMENT

The minimal accountability test of any treatment method, of course, involves the relative efficacy of its application to the efficacy of its absence. That is, comparative study, dismantling study, participant variation study, etc. are empty gestures if the method has not been shown to be more helpful than no treatment. By "no treatment," we refer to the gamut of control procedures that are used in psychotherapy research (e.g., no formal treatment, waiting list, attention-placebo) and that share the commonalities of withholding the active treatment under study and of (attempted) nonprovision of experiences that are likely to produce positive psychological changes.

Two major limitations of any control procedure may be identified. First, there is no such thing as a "true" control group. It is no secret (Bergin & Lambert, 1978) that supposedly "untreated" patients often get themselves "treated," either by the local bartender, a close friend, or even another professional therapist (outside the research protocol, of course). There is little reason to suspect that this is not also the case for depressed patients. The willingness of some researchers to believe that untreated depressed patients remain untreated is closely linked to what may be called the "Depressed Patient Remittability Myth." In our clinical and empirical work, we find little evidence that depressions of the degree that bring patients to seek professional help are self-limiting and short lived. Indeed, the great majority of depressed patients in our research program have suffered from either chronic depressions or intermittent and recurrent depressive episodes. In the end, then, what we really have in many, if not most, supposedly controlled outcome studies are, in the usual terminology, comparative studies. The only problem, and it is a significant one, is that under such naturalistic life conditions, we do not know with what our formal treatment has been unintentionally compared.

A second matter in the use of untreated control groups is that, while researchers usually do their best to match treated and untreated patients according to variables either known or suspected to be relevant to outcome, clinical naiveté may prevail. Even if the depressed patient does not seek help elsewhere while in our untreated condition, do we really believe that people who are willing to wait for our research design to offer treatment (i.e., waiting-list control) or who accept various pseudotreatments (e.g., attention-placebo) in place of "the real thing" represent the same clinical phenomena as those treated patients with whom they are matched on such mundane variables as age, sex, socioeconomic status, etc.? The issue here is a variation on the common theme of treatment compliance, that is, no-treatment compliance. What kind of depressed patient is likely to submit to being told that treatment will not be available for x number of weeks or to believe even the most credible of placebo treatments? In the former case, we would suspect either questionable motivation for treatment or such serious symptomatic impairment (not touched by our assessment methods) that alternative help is not sought, while in the latter, we would suspect a lack of psychological mindedness of a magnitude that we think is likely to characterize very few people who seek help.

Moreover, the usual matching of depressed patients in treatment and no-treatment conditions almost always fails to consider what we referred to earlier (see the section on analogue research) as the ecological context of depression. We would argue that regardless of the number or range of dimensions on which no-treatment subjects are matched with treated subjects, if the intimate (e.g., marital) interpersonal context of the depression is not assessed, the match thereby achieved is not very likely to realize its purpose. The point here is, more concretely, that while depressions certainly have intrapersonal parameters, they occur between and among people, and to match depressed patients solely on intraorganismic variables is clinical folly. Fortunately, there is an alternative control procedure for the behavioral researcher of the treatment of depression that allows control patients to remain essentially untreated—formally, that is— yet minimizes the ethical dilemmas inherent in controlled treatment research. This control procedure, known as "treatment on demand," was developed in the Boston–New Haven collaborative studies of the psychotherapy of depression and is discussed elsewhere (DiMascio & Klerman, 1977; Gurman & Kniskern, 1981).

OUTCOME CRITERIA IN THE COMPARATIVE STUDY

We agree fully with both Kazdin's (Chapter 14, this volume; Kazdin & Wilson, 1978) and Garfield's (1977) recommendations that outcome assessment in psychotherapy research needs to go well beyond usual symptomatic, phenomenological, personality, and social skill dimensions. Various client-related criteria (importance of the goals achieved, proportion of improved patients, breadth and durability of changes) and efficiency and cost-related criteria (e.g., treatment duration, manner of treatment administration, costs of professional training and disseminability, direct patient costs) also need to be considered in the intricate matrix of factors influencing judgments of therapeutic efficacy.

In addition, all that glitters is not gold, and some of what in psychotherapy remits is remiss. There is a serious need, in the study of behavioral treatment of depression, to examine the impact of treatment on people other than the patients themselves. The impact of symptom removal is a crucial area for further study, especially in the treatment of depression, particularly of depressed women (Gurman & Klein, 1980; Klein, 1976). First, given the high degree of co-occurrence in women of depression and of severe marital problems (e.g., Paykel et al., 1969), the impact of symptom removal will have unpredictable, yet important, consequences for the marital relationship. In some cases, this impact may be entirely positive; yet in (we suspect, many) others, it may be potentially disruptive of the relationship. This negative secondary effect of apparent positive effects may occur in either of two common circumstances:

1. When the depression has been long standing, the marital interaction patterns may have been noticeably altered by depressive symptomatology; for example, formerly depressed patients (of either gender) and their spouses may have accumulated depression-based modes of relating that are now quite dysfunctional in the absence of depression.
2. When a spouse's depression has been functional for the relationship (e.g., leads to caring and attention that was not forthcoming before the depressive episode) or for the other spouse (e.g., the appearance of depression in one spouse may mask, or simply delay, the appearance of depression in

the second spouse), "effective" symptom removal may lead to marital chaos.

In addition, regardless of her marital status, "effective" symptom removal may just as well signal a woman's submission to repressive social stereotypes. Thus, Klein (1976) has noted that "pain in response to a bad situation is adaptive, not pathological. . . . The depression, and later the anger, of the woman trapped in an unsatisfying role [e.g., marital] . . . may be healthy steps in recognizing and doing something about a dehumanizing situation [p. 90]."

On the other side of the outcome ledger, a woman's newly developed social skills (e.g., assertiveness or increased self-confidence) may also lead to major challenges to previous role relationships in her marriage. If behavioral treatment research fails to incorporate the kinds of ecological assessments suggested here, it will be contextually quite arid. Most generally, nonattendance to these sorts of ecological contexts of apparent positive gains in the behavioral treatment of depression may lead to either overestimations of outcome (e.g., the patient improves, but the marriage falters), or to underestimations of outcome (e.g., symptom removal and social skill enhancement rejuvenate a tired relationship), if outcome is defined, as we think it should be, by dimensions that transcend typical narrowly defined—that is, intraorganismic—criteria.

## A Proposed Design Strategy IV:
## A Process-Outcome Approach

In view of the limits to what can be learned from the sequence of design strategies just reviewed, we would like to propose an additional step, which we believe can carry us further toward the ultimate goal of integrating the results of research into clinical practice. We begin with the premise that we have gone as far as we can with results from nonclinical settings or with relatively weak results based on significant, but often minor, differences between outcome in relatively complex and similar treatment programs, using global outcome criteria. At this point, we think it is necessary to return to a more microscopic level of inquiry in order to disentangle the contributions of specific techniques and nonspecific effects. This seems particularly true for the field of behavior therapy for depression, where there now exist many well-defined therapy techniques whose effectiveness has been documented, at least when appropriately articulated, into treatment programs. It seems to us that the next logical step in psychotherapy research is to identify both the general principles and the specific technical operations in such a way that they can be tested both within and outside of their primary or original therapeutic contexts.

The question we propose to address is that of the impact of a specific technical operation relative to the more general, or nonspecific, effects of the theoretical and therapeutic context in which it is carried out. This assumes that the impact of a particular operation reflects (*a*) the specific operation; (*b*) the operation of the theoretical principle on which it is based; (*c*) the operation of other more general psychological change principles that are not the exclusive province of the parent orientation; and (*d*) whatever other potent nonspecifics are in effect. This view assumes that treatment theories do not always enumerate all of the operative principles and that principles may readily cross theoretical boundaries. The notion of learned helplessness (Seligman, 1975) provides one example of a model reflecting principles specific to some behavioral therapy programs as well as a general psychological principle that may be tapped by apparently divergent theoretical schools. This means that some technical operations may be potent wherever they occur, even when done outside of their main theoretical setting. A focus on assertiveness enhancement may be as powerful in dynamic–expressive therapy as in therapy with a more behavioral orientation. This may also mean that seemingly different technical operations may be similar in principle and can be substituted for one another. Assertiveness training and confrontation of helpless ideation may be viable alternatives for dealing with aspects of depression. This perspective implies that specific techniques can be found and described as they occur, even in therapies other than the one emphasizing the particular technique's salience and necessity. Thus, in the effort to identify powerful techniques for the treatment of depression, one can raise the researchable question of the relative effectiveness or influence of specific technical operations within a "parent (originating) therapy" context versus its impact in other therapeutic contexts. The question of the frequency, apart from the effectiveness, of "borrowed" or "alien" technical operations in naturalistically occurring therapy is itself interesting. This assumes an hierarchy of generalizability, ranging from the extreme of a technique embedded in its parent context (social skills training by Hersen or Lewinsohn) through the intermediate stage of the technique as practiced by newly trained therapists in other settings with similar orientations (social skills training by cognitive therapists) to the more remote case where the technique is carried out in an entirely different therapeutic context (social skills training as one phase or part of dynamic therapy). We make this distinction with the understanding that to be most effective and useful, a technique should be both "transportable" or "transplantable" and generalizable. The design required by this proposal would involve a comparative outcome study in clinical settings, with experienced therapists and real patients, with a major process study built in, so that analyses other than the traditional factorial–ANOVA combination may be used. Such an approach might add a great deal to our understanding of the specific mechanisms of psychological change (in the treatment of depression), a major concern of Bergin and Strupp (1972) in their withdrawal of support for the potential clinical utility of findings generated by large-scale collaborative research efforts, which all too often have failed to shed much (if any) light on such change-inducing mechanisms.

A large-scale collaborative effort is essential for the multilevel process-outcome strategy that we propose. The two-step or multilevel design allows, in our opinion, for the fullest possible use of the data. The major obstacle in the past to the pooling of data from single-setting studies has been their lack of common procedures, patient samples, or measures sufficient for any really meaningful combined or more focused data analyses. This means that only the most general or the strongest trends survive and that other patterns characterizing specific subgroups, etc. are minimized or appear in the literature only as interesting footnotes.

The basic thrust of our proposal is that the relative effectiveness of the therapy orientations and operations be compared both in their original parent settings and as learned or applied in other settings. There are two stages to this approach:

1. An experimental and quasi-experimental design that compares the overall effectiveness of orientations or therapies as wholes in either the parent setting or as learned in secondary settings. The basic issue here is the comparison of the impact of a treatment as a whole in different settings (e.g., cognitive therapy in Philadelphia versus as learned and practiced in Wisconsin).

2. A naturalistic, corelational process-outcome analysis of these same data. At this second stage, we are more directly concerned with specific technical elements of the various orientations as they occur in practice, regardless of what the technique as a whole is labeled. This reflects our assumption that, to be most effective, a technique must be demonstrated to have impact independent of either its parent setting or its main theoretical context (with different expectations, charismatic factors, nonspecifics, etc.).

How can this strategy be implemented? The familiar factorial design is most appropriate for the first stage of the research. Here, outcomes for patients receiving different therapies (as wholes) are compared, with such important factors as setting, therapist experience, severity of depression considered (i.e., controlled experimental design with random assignment of patients to different groups). Other variables that might also be important are to be looked at as factors in subsequent data analysis (quasi-experimental design phase).

The second stage of analysis of the same body of data involves a shift in perspective away from the controlled-factorial-hypothesis-testing approach to a naturalistic process study, wherein the effect of all the variables across settings is the concern. What are needed for this process study or, more correctly, process-outcome study are the following:

1. Definition of some of the key elements or technical operations of each therapy modality is necessary. This might be guided by the results of the factorial design in the first stage or a priori from the recommendations or concerns of the parent theorists.

2. A process of defining the technical operations to everyone's satisfaction

has to be developed. It would be necessary to define these operations in measurable ways (perhaps some combination of self-report and rating of tapes or sequences of tapes). It would also be necessary to demonstrate the reliability and validity of any of these procedures before defining technical operations. The next step would be to apply the scale or procedure to the data or to portions of the interview data from all cases, regardless of setting.

3. All of the technical operation variables so defined could then be subjected to multivariate correlational analyses that would consider the relative contribution of each technical variable to the overall pattern of outcome or to specific (target) outcomes. It would also be possible to identify combinations or sequences of techniques that are more predictive of outcome than any one technique alone. Discriminant analysis, multiple regression analysis, or techniques such as path analysis that consider temporal sequences (initial patient variables—techniques—patient outcome) would be appropriate for such questions. It would also be important to include measures for some of the usual nonspecific relationship factors in order to test or further understand the conditions necessary for the most effective use of the specific technical ingredients of the different therapy orientations under study.

For example, cognitive therapists might propose that one important operation in this treatment worth studying is the therapist's systematic challenging or confronting the patient's hopelessness cognitions (expressed as hopelessness verbalizations). To measure or define this technical procedure, one might develop two rating scales: one for patient verbal content and the other for therapist confrontation–challenge. The next step would be to rate all tapes or a subset of tapes across the entire array of therapy cases in the experimental design (cognitive, behavioral, and expressive). After these analyses, we might find that hopelessness confrontation is always predictive of positive outcome or that it correlates with outcome most strongly when certain other operations, such as assertiveness training and hostility catharsis, are also present. If measures of some of the usual nonspecifics were added as well, we could also test the general relational limits for these more specific effects.

Likely candidates for comparative study within the behavioral domain relevant to depression would be cognitive behavioral therapies, social skills training, and self-control programs. Outside the behavioral domain, we would recommend time-limited expressive dynamic therapy, as described by Malan (1976) and Mann (1973), and interpersonal therapy as set down by the New Haven–Boston Collaborative Depression Project (Weissman & Paykel, 1974). All of these approaches are aimed, with differing degrees of specificity and emphasis, at some central components of neurotic depression (e.g., depressed affect and vegetative symptoms, cognitions of hopelessness–helplessness). The major difference is one of therapeutic strategy and/or technical specificity, based on somewhat different etiological and/or symptom maintenance assumptions.

A strong case can be made for the use of multiple outcome measurement strategies in a study of this sort. It is useful to distinguish between the short-range, specific, immediate effects of techniques and the long-range, general outcomes (which may reflect the cumulative effect of several techniques). Turning to our example, we might consider the distinction between mediating and ultimate goals in deciding what specific target behaviors to use for assessing a given operation. For instance, in hopelessness confrontation, we might find (based on theoretical models or experience) the immediate impact to be to increase the patient's anger toward the therapist and the long-range impact to be to decrease reported hopelessness–helplessness in conversations with others outside the therapy setting or to increase nonangry assertiveness. This distinction would have the potential to provide clues to the processes of change that are instigated by the therapeutic techniques and to lead to greater technical specificity and refinement. Another way that these data might be used would be to identify necessary ingredients of a technical operation. An example would be to compare hopelessness confrontation with other operations directed at the same target behavior, such as hopelessness-support or hopelessness-ignore behavior on the part of the therapist, that theoretically would be expected to have very different impacts. This would clarify whether it was the focus on hopelessness, the confrontation alone, or the particular combination of the two that contributes to the potency of the treatment technique.

## Clinical Dissemination

Clinical practice is the ultimate proving ground for research results. All of the findings imaginable are for naught if either the techniques lose effectiveness upon wider application or practicing therapists are unmotivated to use them. The problems of generalization, well known to the behavioral therapist, become more acute and difficult as clinical applications widen. Factors that lead a therapist-to-be to seek a specific training experience and to use the results may be very different from those that lead the practicing therapist to modify or refine techniques within his or her dominant orientation, to try a novel method from a different orientation once or twice (or for limited classes of problems), or, far more rarely, to change methods all together in midcareer. The common determinants, at each level of generality, rest more within the therapist's person than with the research credentials of the method. That is to say, therapists are complex, not always predictable, and not always responsive to research results. Beyond the desire for increased effectiveness that may make therapists responsive to "big effects," we suspect that such motives as boredom, curiosity, frustration, and competitiveness lead a therapist to try new moves. Whether a technique once tried is adapted, incorporated, distorted, or abandoned may depend on a host of factors never considered in our carefully designed strategies: Beyond effectiveness, therapists' needs for cognitive consistency, theoretical identity, their personal enjoyment of or comfort with a technique, or the response of patients and colleagues may ultimately determine acceptance. In any case, the implication is that researchers must do more than demonstrate effective techniques to change patient behavior; we must change therapist behavior as well! This means we must look within therapists for targets for change and concern ourselves with the contingencies that affect their behavior. One way to concretize this suggestion would be for us to establish clearer linkages between specific techniques and therapists' decision-making and problem-solving strategies and to identify those points in the therapeutic process where therapists are open to innovation. One example might be to study therapeutic impasses and to develop and evaluate methods in this context. (Bergin and Strupp suggested this approach in 1972.)

Efforts at clinical dissemination of research are also severely hampered by fundamental differences in style and outlook between clinician and researcher. Clinicians, being immediately on the spot, are more likely to notice and to be impressed by immediate and dramatic results. Researchers, functioning at greater distance, are in a better position to discern more complex trends and to construct patterns for cumulative results. This leads researchers to a concern with fine details that most practicing clinicians would find obsessive. This same attitude also leads researchers to chip away relentlessly at whatever conceptual or empirical ground they gain, that is, to dismantle each finding in pursuit of higher truth.

This digression is relevant to any consideration of naturalistic clinical research. A most crucial difference between research and clinical practice rests with the greater complexity, variety, and importance of therapist variables in the latter. The same complex motivational and situational forces that lead a therapist to practice a given technique will inevitably color the operation and may indeed transform the technique into something quite foreign to its origin. Some techniques may be improved in this way, but we suspect that weakening or attenuation of effectiveness is more frequent. This may be particularly true if therapists succumb to the temptation to overgeneralize their successes by trying innovations on broader and broader patient populations (Klein, Dittmann, Parloff, & Gill, 1969).

The effect of this situation on naturalistic research is to make it essential to identify (rather than control) as many sources of variance as we can. Aside from the strain imposed on patients and therapists who often are called upon to provide much of the data, this makes our research more complex. In the case of positive findings for a given technique, it is necessary ( a) to consider important contextual factors involved in any specific process-outcome links; and (b) to uncover and/or control spurious or confounded process-outcome connections. In the case of weak or negative results, it is necessary to show how a technique has been weakened or transformed in operation so as to no longer constitute a valid test.

In the last analysis, we may simply have to accept the fact that clinicians and

Shapiro, M. B. Experimental method in the psychological description of the individual psychiatric patient. *International Journal of Social Psychiatry,* 1957, *3,* 89–102.

Taylor, F. G., & Marshall, W. L. Experimental analysis of a cognitive–behavioral therapy for depression. *Cognitive Therapy and Research,* 1977, *1,* 59–72.

Weissman, M. M., & Klerman, G. L. Sex differences and the epidemiology of depression. *Archives of General Psychiatry,* 1977, *34,* 98–111.

Weissman, M. M., & Paykel, E. S. *The depressed woman: A study of social relationships.* Chicago: University of Chicago Press, 1974.

Yates, A. B. *Behavior therapy.* New York: Wiley, 1970.

# 16

## Future Directions

LYNN P. REHM

Behavior therapists have produced a great deal of research on the treatment of depression in a relatively short time span. The intent of this book has been to summarize these developments from a variety of methodological and theoretical perspectives. The task remaining is to attempt to describe and to recommend directions that future research should take. This task is made easier by the critical assessments of the state of the art made by the authors of this book.[1] A number of conclusions and general themes of criticism can be drawn together at this point. As to the status of behavior therapy for depression, three major points stand out.

First, there is promising evidence for the efficacy of behavior therapies for depression. Research to date seems to indicate that at least a subset of behavior therapies have demonstrated efficacy in ameliorating depression. Reviewers cited, in particular, Beck's cognitive behavior therapy, Rehm's self-control therapy, and McLean's behavior therapy program. Lewinsohn's modular approach and social skill training might be added to this list. It is also clear, however, that there are a number of very serious limitations to this conclusion. Most studies demonstrating clear effects have been done primarily by the originator of the technique. There are relatively few replications, especially by independent investigators. In most of these studies, the $N$s are small, interventions are brief, and follow-ups are limited. Often the techniques themselves are not well specified, and the effects of nonspecifics cannot always be ruled out. Control conditions may not have been given sufficient chance to show an effect on their own terms.

---

[1] In addition to these chapters, the papers, discussion, and specific recommendations made by the authors and other participants of the NIMH conference, Research Recommendations for the Behavioral Treatment of Depression, Pittsburgh, April 1979, constitute a wealth of material on which I have drawn heavily in constructing this chapter.

BEHAVIOR THERAPY FOR DEPRESSION

The populations studied are often unclear. While the problem of the definition of depression is relevant to all depression research, behavior therapy studies in particular have been poor in specifying the population being studied. Specificity with regard to subtype and possible subtype interactions with treatments have not been given attention. Subclinical populations have often been used. Outcome measures are inconsistent and lack comparability. Comparisons with drug treatment are particularly lacking (cf. Blaney, Chapter 1; Hollon, Chapter 2; Craighead, Chapter 3).

Second, the effective ingredients of behavior therapy programs for depression are essentially unknown. A good deal of the behavior therapy research in depression has investigated the effectiveness of complex therapy packages. These complex packages appear to be more effective than single techniques. This is especially so for packages that include both behavioral and cognitive interventions. It may be that packages more effectively cover multiple problems of individual clients; they may cover the particular problems of a higher percentage of subjects; or they may be more heavily loaded with so-called nonspecific effects. Relatively little work has been done to isolate effective ingredients systematically. Studies that dismantle or disassemble complex packages are only beginning to be done. Comparisons between packages are inconsistent in their findings, subject to biases, and lacking in comparability and generally shed little light on the issue.

Third, the majority of research on behavior therapy for depression has been done in relative isolation. Three kinds of isolation can be identified.

1. Research programs have been isolated from one another. This is probably an expected result of a rapidly growing field where publication lag and other factors mean that the same problems are being addressed in different labs without knowledge of how they are being handled elsewhere. Most of the studies lack direct comparability. It is difficult to compare studies in terms of populations used, treatment parameters, time parameters, outcome measures, length of follow-up, etc. As already mentioned, there is also a lack of independent replication.

2. Much of the behavior therapy work on depression is isolated from other important current research on depression. Behavioral research has often assumed a continuity between normal and clinical depressions with little attention to the possibility of important discontinuities. Little attention has been given to recent work on subtyping. For example, the unipolar–bipolar distinction has not been made in classifying subjects. Also, such dimensions as severity, chronicity, age, course, and number and duration of episodes have not been taken into account. Work in the biological area has not been incorporated, including the potential influence of genetics, sleep research, or biochemical assessment. Sociological and epidemiological research has not been sufficiently incorporated either. Issues of family interactions of depressed indi-

viduals, life events, treatment history, and stress reactions have only occasionally been investigated in the behavioral literature.

3. The behavior therapy work in depression has been relatively isolated from research involving somatic interventions. The research on pharmacological interventions in depression may be instructive to behavioral researchers in terms of handling design and assessment issues specific to depression. For example, wash-out periods and initial predrug periods of placebo in drug trials allow for the assessment of a stable baseline of depression apart from momentary stresses or other influences. Assessment formats and schedules in drug trials have been geared to the instability of depression and to the expected course of response, that is, periodic monitoring within treatment. The assessment of response to subclinical drug doses has been explored as a means of prediction of the success of a full course of treatment. Examination of differences between responders and nonresponders to a particular drug has contributed to predictive subtyping. Parallels have not been developed in the behavior therapy depression literature. There is a notable lack of collaboration in the literature between biological and behavioral investigators.

## Recommendations for the Future

Given these observations on the status of the field, a number of recommendations can be made. These can best be summarized under a series of headings as follows.

### Population Definition

Behavior therapy intervention research is needed for all types of abnormal depression. Most research has used one of two general populations. The first is college students who have scored above a certain criterion on a depression scale. While depression in college students should not be dismissed as an insignificant problem, proof of this fact lies with the investigator. If the argument is to be made that there is a valid continuity between these mild depressions and the moderate and severe depressions that cause people to seek out treatment, then it will be necessary to document the occurrence of symptoms that correspond to those in more serious manifestations. Do these mild depressions interfere in the daily lives of the subjects in terms of such issues as productivity, fatigability, sleep disturbance, eating disturbance, etc.? Are they of sufficient duration to warrant intensive interventions? The second population that has been studied can be loosely described as clinically depressed outpatients. Whether solicited volunteers, referrals from other agents, or self-referrals to clinics, these subjects can mostly be characterized as being in the neurotic (nonpsychotic) range of disturbance. The effects of various modes of entry into studies are generally unknown but are deserving of study. There may be important differences in motivation, history, attitude toward treatment and the disorder, and expectations about treatment efficacy.

Little research has been done to date on behavior therapy with psychiatric inpatients, Shaw's (Chapter 9) work being an exception to this rule.

A number of populations that have largely been ignored in the past can be suggested as important targets for future research. These include drug-resistant depressions; patients in postdrug therapy maintenance programs; recurrent depressions; severe depressions; childhood, adolescent, and aged depressions; and such high-risk populations as certain relatives of depressives.

The clearest recommendation is for greater care in delineating and describing populations in order to enhance comparability among studies. Many descriptive dimensions can be suggested. Demographics, incidence of various specific symptoms, course and history of the disorder, and family history are types of variables that would aid in establishing comparability between studies as well as provide the basis for post hoc investigations of outcome prediction. It would also be of value to assess factors related to the incidence of depression in the general population. For example, epidemiological studies suggest that continuing stresses related to marriage, family, job, etc. are associated with depression. Traumatic life events, especially those involving loss, have been found to precede the onset of many depressions.

The high frequency of polysymptomatic subjects suggests assessing additional dimensions of psychopathology. Anxiety in particular should be assessed, but perhaps obsessional tendencies and other dimensions of neurosis should be assessed as well. Explicit exclusion criteria are desirable.

A second major recommendation in this area is for more behavior analytic descriptions of subjects. That is, subjects should be assessed on dimensions specific to behavioral theories of depression and behavioral models of intervention. From the point of view of behavior therapy, traditional diagnoses only establish the comparability of a sample with samples used in other studies. They do not indicate specific behavioral or cognitive deficits that are in need of remediation. Social skill approaches should assess specific skill deficits demonstrably related to depression. Self-control approaches should assess self-control behavior related to depression. Cognitive deficits hypothesized to represent the core of depression should be evaluated independently of global depression measures. The social environment of depressed individuals may have to be assessed in order to measure constructs related to reinforcement schedules, marital dysfunction, etc. Such assessment is a natural and necessary precursor of attempts to match treatment to patient.

## Outcome Assessment

In behavior therapy research on depression, assessment in multiple modalities is clearly necessary. To assess the syndrome of depression, the various overt behavioral, verbal–cognitive, and somatic symptom modes should be assessed from the perspectives of patient, clinician, direct behavioral observation, and peer evaluation. It is hoped that developments in assessment of depression evolve in close coordination with treatment research. An optimal standard battery for assessment of treatment outcome can probably not be derived from presently existing instruments.

Some instruments exist that fit into single cells of an overall assessment plan, but for the most part, the area is plagued by instruments that are diffuse and unsystematic in their coverage of the range of dimensions, modalities, and perspectives. There is a need for the development of new instruments that would assess dimensions systematically across modes and perspectives of assessment. There is a particular need for systematic, validated behavioral observation measures. Behavior therapy and therapy research would be greatly assisted by the development of better behavioral assessment (cf. Craighead, Chapter 3). More sophisticated measures of cognitive deficits are also needed (cf. Hammen, Chapter 11). Assessment methods are needed to measure the specific cognitive deficits postulated by current theories of depression. For the present, researchers should attempt to incorporate into their assessments at least a minimum standard battery of assessments to enhance comparability between studies.

Dimensions of outcome assessment should include magnitude, generality, universality, stability, acceptability, and safety of effects as suggested by Hollon (Chapter 2). Assessment should be extended in duration. Multiple baseline assessments, ongoing therapy assessments, and extended monitoring at follow-up are desirable. It is particularly important in assessing outcome on depression to attend to the temporal characteristics of the disorder. Depression can be cyclic, episodic, and shifting in symptom pattern during its course. These facts present particular problems in instrument development and in assessing the stability of both disorder and outcome. The development of new assessment batteries or instruments should give due attention to the variety of complex validity and reliability problems inherent in depression. Such instruments, however, should also be usable in clinical practice and not just in well-funded research settings (cf. Hersen, Chapter 13).

A number of novel directions for assessment research appear to have potential value. Behavioral observation methodologies might be strengthened by looking at conditional probabilities of classes of patient behavior following certain classes of behavior by another person, as in Jacobson's work (Chapter 12). The importance of assessing the patient's ability to cope with life stresses should be emphasized. One suggestion is to assess the patient's response to laboratory "stressor probes" as potentially valid and predictive behavior samples. For example, the patient's response to failure or loss on a laboratory task might be related to real-life failure and loss experiences. Other suggestions include the use of client-generated criteria, evaluations of cost effectiveness, and evaluations of the ecological impact of interventions (e.g., the impact on the patient's family).

## Treatment Specifications

There is a general need for a taxonomy of interventions and for analyses and identification of the common and unique elements in therapy packages. Carefully written manuals with a standard format to maximize comparability with other manuals would go a long way toward this end. Other suggestions are for self-administered subject manuals and computer-assisted therapy programs. It is also important to identify and isolate the so-called nonspecific factors operating. Investigators should include independent checks in research studies to evaluate the adequacy of the implementation of the treatment manual. The verbal behavior in the therapist–client interaction also deserves analysis (cf. Ferster, Chapter 7). Observation and study of therapy sessions should be encouraged.

## Matching Subjects to Treatment

The behavioral research on therapy for depression needs to attend more to the psychotherapy ideal of matching subject to treatment, with the match perhaps also including therapist and time factors. There is a major need for behavioral analysis of subgroups of individuals more likely to respond to different techniques. One way to approach this problem is by post hoc analysis of the relationship between variables in heterogeneous populations and outcome (cf. McLean, Chapter 8). One could ask, "Who does best in treatment X?" or "Do treatments X and Y work most effectively for different sets of people?" Likely matching variables would include behavioral assessments of such constructs as self-control or social skill deficits, cognitive distortion, helplessness, etc., as well as more traditional diagnostic and personality factors, such as subtypes of depression, personality test scores, treatment response histories, family history, and demographic variables.

A second research strategy would be to evaluate matches between subject and therapy based on theoretical considerations. Subjects high and low on measures of helplessness, cognitive distortion, and social skill or self-control might be matched to treatments based on these models. Finer matchings between more specific deficits and components of complex therapy programs could be similarly pursued. For example, specific social skills found to be deficient would then be targeted for training. Other strategies might include matching on the basis of the patient's choice of the most compatible therapy or on the basis of the best response to a brief sample of different therapies.

Ultimately, this type of research might result in therapy programs that match specific deficits with a therapy program made up of corresponding components. A flowchart strategy was suggested by Liberman (Chapter 10), in which a subject would receive a sequence of different interventions based on assessment of need in logical order. That is, one would assess a person for deficit a and if it is present then assign the person to treatment A. Following treatment A, or if deficit a is not present, one would assess for deficit b, and so on. Perfect matching strategies may not be possible, and ways of tailoring general programs to individual cases should also be explored.

## Design Strategies

There is a need for large-scale validation studies. Such studies would have several advantages. First, they would simply insure more reliable and valid findings, especially if conducted on a collaborative basis across multiple sites. Secondly, they would allow the possibility of many analyses within the design, for instance, the identification of subgroups of patients for whom the treatment was particularly effective. Third, there is a need to demonstrate the effectiveness of behavior therapies in a manner that would allow a valid endorsement of a particular therapy program for general use in the nation's mental health system. While researchers may believe that attempts to do this would be premature until we can better identify the precise mechanisms that are essential to effective programs, it is desirable to disseminate the most effective therapies presently available.

A second recommendation is for theory-directed studies aimed at identifying the effective ingredients in treatment packages. Recommended designs are those that would systematically disassemble therapy programs by subtracting out hypothetically critical elements or construction designs that would systematically add them in (cf. Kazdin, Chapter 14). Factorial designs that compare all possible combinations of selected elements may also contribute, as may parametric studies that systematically vary such factors as frequency, length, and number of sessions.

The types of questions being asked should be expanded. Behavior therapy research should give attention to some of the factors that have been studied in traditional psychotherapy research. Subject and therapist personality variables and group versus individual versus family formats are examples of such factors. Greater attention should be given to the importance of the so-called nonspecific factors in therapy, such as relationship factors, patient motivation, patient perception of the problem, acceptance of the therapy rationale, etc. There is a need to evaluate some of the procedures often employed in behavioral research, such as the use of deposits (which are returned to subjects as they comply with various features of the therapy program), or the influence of different methods of recruitment of subjects for research.

Studies that make simple comparisons of two or more complex therapy packages probably add little to our understanding and improvement of therapy methods. There are two possible exceptions to this conclusion. Comparison designs that look for differential outcome for different measures or for different sets of patients may be contributory. Second, more comparisons of behavior therapy with drug conditions are needed (cf. Hollon, Chapter 2). These studies would be most valuable when they include evaluations of the interaction between the therapies, differential outcome profiles, and different patterns of long-term effects in follow-up studies. For example, it might be expected that drug conditions would produce quicker response on neurovegetative signs whereas behavior therapies might have stronger and more lasting effects on social adjustment and coping skills.

In addition to outcome designs, there is a need for attention to process issues (cf. Klein & Gurman, Chapter 15). Observational studies of the interaction between therapist and patient may aid in establishing mechanisms of change. Such studies might involve empirical validation that procedures in therapy manuals are being followed or evaluations of therapist skill in verbal shaping processes in interviews. Designs should be evolved that allow combinations of traditional designs, such as process with outcome or single-subject within group designs.

### Prevention and Development

Therapy research depends heavily on, and interacts with, research on prevention and development of depression. Depression therapy research would be enhanced by research studying unaided recovery from depression, the natural course of depression, and coping strategies in normals who are able to avoid depression. New ideas for therapy strategies could emerge from this work. The assessment of preexisting deficits in individuals who later become depressed would be important to the development of interventions for high-risk populations. There was a sense that prophylactic treatment is a real possibility in the area of depression, because contemporary psychological theories postulate deficits in cognitive and behavioral skills that are teachable in cost-efficient ways.

### Theory Development

Finally, continued theory development in the behavioral approaches to depression is desirable (cf. Chapters 4–7). While many models have proliferated in recent years, it will be important in the future for models to handle a wider variety of data as they accumulate from different fields of depression research. Psychological theories should be able to interface with developments in the biological sciences on the genetics, biochemistry, and physiology of depression; they should be able to interface with sociological and epidemiological evidence on stress factors and environmental influences on depression; and they need to take into account an expanding array of data on the psychological–behavioral correlates of depression. The need for cross-fertilization between disciplines is clearly indicated.

## Conclusions

As a research area, behavior therapy for depression is likely to continue to be very active. Depression is a major mental health problem, and methods to treat the disorder should continue to be a high priority. Treatment research may gain added importance because of certain political pressures in the United States and elsewhere. As the costs of psychiatric treatment increase, and as more and more public and private third-party agents are paying for it, greater pressure will be exerted on the field to demonstrate the unequivocal effectiveness of psychosocial interventions for depression and other disorders. Cost-effectiveness calculations will become increasingly important factors in deter-mining which procedures are reimbursed and therefore which procedures are practiced. Given their successes to date, behavior therapies for depression should be among those treatments that are prime candidates for large-scale validation and dissemination into the mental health care system.

Another factor that will continue to motivate a high level of research activity around behavior therapy for depression is innovation in behavioral models of depression. Behavioral depression research has become very popular in recent years, partly because so many creative and testable behavioral models of the disorder have been proposed. Data generated from these studies has been the impetus for revision of theory (cf. Seligman, Chapter 5; Kanfer & Hagerman, Chapter 6) and for the generation of new models (Biglan & Dow, Chapter 4). Many theory-generated questions remain, and continued research interest appears assured.

Surely, future research on behavior therapies for depression will be plagued by many of the problems and deficiencies identified in this book. We can be hopeful about future directions, however, because there is evidence of trends toward improved quality of research. Comparability of studies is becoming possible because of the greater care recently shown in specification of popula-tions, treatment, and outcome.

There does appear to be a growing accumulation of data that is adding to our understanding of depression and its treatment. Reviews and critiques can sometimes contribute to this process by providing direction and coordination to research efforts. It is hoped that this volume may do so.

# Author Index

# Subject Index